ANGLO-FRENCH
NAVAL RIVALRY
1840–1870

Anglo-French Naval Rivalry 1840–1870

C. I. HAMILTON

CLARENDON PRESS · OXFORD

1993

Oxford University Press, Walton Street, Oxford OX2 6DP

Oxford   New York   Toronto
Delhi   Bombay   Calcutta   Madras   Karachi
Kuala Lumpur   Singapore   Hong Kong   Tokyo
Nairobi   Dar es Salaam   Cape Town
Melbourne   Auckland   Madrid
and associated companies in
Berlin   Ibadan

Oxford is a trade mark of Oxford University Press

Published in the United States
by Oxford University Press Inc., New York

British Library Cataloguing in Publication Data
Data available

Library of Congress Cataloging in Publication Data
Hamilton, C. I.
Anglo-French naval rivalry, 1840–1870 / C. I. Hamilton.
p.   cm.
Includes bibliographical references and index.
1. Great Britain—History, Naval—19th century.   2. Great Britain—
Foreign relations—1837–1901.   3. Great Britain—Foreign relations—
France.   4. France—Foreign relations—Great Britain.   5. France—
History, Naval—19th century.   6. France—Foreign
relations—1815–1870.   I. Title.
DA88.H36   1993   359'.00941'09034—dc20   93–21761
ISBN 0–19–820261–X

1 3 5 7 9 10 8 6 4 2

Typeset by Graphicraft Typesetters Ltd., Hong Kong

Printed in Great Britain
on acid-free paper by
Bookcraft Ltd., Midsomer Norton, Bath

To the memory of

C. O. Hamilton

Preface

I owe a great debt to the staffs of all the libraries and archives I have worked in during the research for the present volume. However, by sheer weight of books and manuscripts demanded, I must mention in particular those working in the Cambridge University Library, the Public Record Office, the National Maritime Museum, the Archives nationales, and the *Service historique de la Marine* at Vincennes. In regard to the latter, I wish to remember the late M. Joël Audouy, my first guide to what is an exquisite library and a precious collection of naval material.

To the *Service historique* I am much obliged for permission to see not just their archives but also the naval material at the Archives nationales.

Certain private individuals were good enough to give me permission to consult their ancestors' private papers, where the access was restricted. Mme Anne Gruner Schlumberger allowed me to see relevant papers of the Guizot collection; M. le comte de Paris permitted me to see the Maison de France papers at the Archives nationales; and, in Britain, the late Sir Fergus Graham, Bt., was gracious enough to allow me to consult the unfilmed portions of Sir James Graham's papers at Netherby Hall before the collection was transferred to the Carlisle Record Office.

I gladly acknowledge the permission of the following to quote from certain collections: for the Minto Papers in the National Library of Scotland, the Trustees of that Library; for the Napier, Palmerston, and Martin Papers, the British Library; for the papers of J. W. D. Dundas and Henry Codrington, the Trustees of the National Maritime Museum; for the Seymour of Berry Pomeroy Papers, the Devon Record Office; for the Palmerston Papers in their care, the Trustees of the Broadlands Archives; for the Grey Papers, the Department of Palaeography and Diplomatic at the University of Durham; and the Public Record Office for various items from ADM 1, ADM 3, and ADM 83. Sir Charles Graham, Bt., and the Earl of Clarendon were also kind enough to allow me to quote from their ancestors' papers.

My obligations to individual scholars are even more varied than to keepers of archives, but first, four names have to be mentioned. I have to thank Correlli Barnett, whose chapter on Jellicoe in *The Swordbearers* (London, 1963) proved to be stimulating to the point of incandescence, rekindling a childhood interest in naval history, and thus suggesting an initial direction for historical research. That research did not lead me to reject all his conclusions, but to confirm the essential truth in them. The second name is that of C. J. Bartlett, whose standard work, *Great Britain and Seapower, 1815–1863*, led my interests towards the early and mid-Victorian navy, and whose later generous guidance was crucial to my researches and to the construction of the present work. Thirdly, the late Stephen Roskill was a kind mentor to me, as to many other aspiring naval historians. Fourthly, to Sir Harry Hinsley, first my research supervisor, and later an esteemed colleague, I owe much of what I am as a scholar and practising historian.

Colleagues and friends at Cambridge, Durham, and the University of the Witwatersrand played their own important role along with my students, and, perhaps above all, army officers at Madingley Hall and in Cyprus aiming at the Staff Course, in shaping the interpretations in this volume, whether passively or actively. Very much on the active side rank numerous conversations with Hew Strachan, often as part of the early days of the Cambridge War Studies Seminar; furthermore, his published works have been invaluable, giving a solid foundation of Victorian military history on which to rely, and allowing me more time to spin out my purely naval skein. I owe particular thanks to the Cambridge research community in Paris in the shape of Robert Tombs, John Keiger, and Albert Vaiciulenas: their help and hospitality during my time in the city, turned what could have been a fearsome experience into one mostly of charm and interest, and with a proper weighting of the subtext of research. However, it was a Cambridge English historian, Mark Goldie, who was responsible for introducing me to a romantic link with my research topic by taking me into perhaps the most salubrious of breakers' yards, the combination room at Gonville and Caius College where the panelling was made from the timbers taken from the great screw ship of the line, the *Duke of Wellington*.

I owe a great deal to the generosity of St John's College, Cambridge, which made possible much of the research for this volume, including my visits to Paris.

Robert Tombs, along with Charles Burnett, Graham Neame, and Michael Bratchel deserve commendation for ploughing through earlier versions of my manuscript: they, along with the copy editor of the Oxford University Press, saved me from an embarrassing number of solecisms, historical and otherwise.

Furthermore, I cannot omit mentioning A. W. H. Pearsall, who first introduced me to the manuscript collections of the National Maritime Museum, and in the years since then has generously allowed me to draw not just on his wide knowledge of manuscript sources but also on his encyclopaedic acquaintanceship with naval history.

Finally, in this list of thanks to individuals, must be mentioned Kevin Walsh, who gave me a marvellous cantrip for converting PC files from one program to another, thus saving a great deal of work, quite apart from my sanity. Then there is Larrie Rourke, who finally managed to give me the incentive necessary to complete and submit my manuscript to Oxford University Press. And Wolfgang and Friedrich played their part, at times by not being there.

I must also acknowledge a fundamental debt to the published works of scholars. One is the classic by J. P. Baxter, *The Introduction of the Ironclad Warship*, a marvellous example of the comparative approach in naval history, and still a standard text, despite having appeared in 1933. For long after that, little was printed on the British and French navies of the mid-nineteenth century, but in more recent years the dearth has been broken, at least for the British navy. Brian Lavery has told us much about the development of the sailing ship of the line; but, given the period and the interests of the present book, more pertinent to me have been writings by D. K. Brown, the late G. S. Graham, A. D. Lambert, M. S. Partridge, and N. A. M. Rodger. Though I have not always agreed with the conclusions, their works have stimulated, informed, and at the very least saved me from a good number of errors and misapprehensions.

Unfortunately for me, three pertinent books appeared, or in one case came to my attention, after the submission of the manuscript. They are: Lawrence Sondhaus, *The Habsburg Empire and the Sea: Austrian Naval Policy, 1797–1866*, (Purdue University Press, 1989); Donald L. Canney, *The Old Steam Navy: Frigates, Sloops, and Gunboats, 1815–1885*, (Naval Institute Press, Annapolis, 1990); and

A. D. Lambert, *The Last Sailing Battlefleet: Maintaining Naval Mastery 1815–1850*, (Conway Maritime Press, London, 1991).

I should have liked to draw upon these, especially the first and the last; though I must add that they would not have altered the main lines of my argument. Rather, that argument could have been developed. For instance the Lambert volume, admittedly in the context of the 'Symondites', emphasizes the potential role in naval battle of a fast squadron of battleships. Sondhaus illustrates, with regard to the race between Austrian and Italian ironclad fleets, some elements also found in the larger-scale race between the British and French, above all the ability of an energetic administrator to take advantage of a period of technological change when he has influence with the head of state. But some interesting differences are suggested, too, that reflect not just the particular nature of the states involved but also the significance of the historical longevity of a national rivalry.

My final comment is the usual and vital one: acknowledgment does not imply complicity. For good or ill, the author accepts the responsibility for faults or errors in what he has written.

C. I. HAMILTON

History Department,
University of the Witwatersrand.

Contents

Glossary and Usage

Bâtiment à vapeur: a fast warship; the designer having given the priority to steam power rather than sail. Thus *vaisseau à vapeur*, fast battleship; *frégate à vapeur*, fast frigate. See also next entry.

Bâtiment mixte: a sailing warship with auxiliary steam power. Thus *vaisseau mixte*, sail/steam battleship; *frégate mixte*, sail/steam frigate.

Block: traditionally an old sailing warship, reduced to being a permanently moored floating battery for harbour defence. The steam blocks of the 1840s and 1850s, on the other hand, were screw line battleships (somewhat slow *vaisseaux mixtes*).

Corvette cuirassée or *cuirassé de station*: an ironclad for cruising in distant stations.

Currency: at this time one pound sterling equalled 25 French francs.

Employé: a clerk. See also *fonctionnaire*.

England and the English: used in the text from the French point of view to mean Britain and the British.

Fonctionnaire: a clerk higher in grade than an *employé*, but the difference in function is difficult to specify. In Balzac's *Les Employés*, Bixiou argues that the frontier is simply a salary of 20,000 francs.

Grand corps: The body of French executive naval officers. After 1840 essentially made up those who had passed though the *Borda*, or perhaps the *École polytechnique*.

Hélice affolée: a screw that was disconnected from the shaft when the vessel proceeded under sail alone, and revolved freely in the run of water. The alternative, common in the British service, was a disconnected screw that was drawn up out of the water via a well.

horsepower: where given, nominal horsepower is meant which is a figure based on the dimension and speed of the piston, rather the power available from the steam (the indicated horsepower). By the middle of the century, the nhp and ihp of an engine were drawing significantly apart. See D. K. Brown, *Before the Ironclad* (London, 1990), 188.

The Ordinary: the warship reserve.

Pound weight: the French pound was slightly heavier than the British one. The French 30-pounder threw a slightly heavier ball than the British 32-pounder, these being the standard solid-shot weapons on the sail and screw liners of the two fleets.

La Royale: the French Navy, under any régime.

Royal Navy and RN: only used in the text to mean the British Navy. See *La Royale*.

Rue Royale: the road on which the Ministry of Marine is sited in Paris; hence a name for the Ministry itself.

tonnage: unless otherwise specified, displacement tonnage is given. Builder's Old Measure, often used by the Royal Navy in the mid-nineteenth century, occasionally mentioned in the present text, is an old form of measurement, and yields a figure roughly two thirds that of displacement tonnage. For instance, the *Victoria* was 4,127 tons BOM, and 6,930 tons displacement; *Warrior* was 6,109 tons BOM, but 9,137 tons displacement.

I

Introduction

A Frenchman speaking around 1815 of *une ennemie puissante et perfide* or, even more obviously, *une nation de boutiquiers*, was clearly referring to only one state. And who can doubt who was being marked out when an Englishman of the same period spoke of 'an ancient rival, envious and unscrupulous', or 'an immoral and fickle people'? After a long war, the two nations had much reason to think ill of each other, and the coming of peace did not entirely soften acerbities. British responsibility for the return to their original owners of some of the loot gathered by the French government during hostilities laid the foundation for the new and flourishing myth of *hypocrisie anglaise*. And the old British belief in the lightness and loose living of the folk across the Channel was soon to be reinforced by the 'scrofulous French novels' that Victorian society so liked to shock itself with.[1]

The war had not only generated dislike and thus rivalry between the two powers on a general level: the unequalled series of victories for the Royal Navy had given a new and vicious twist to the long-established Anglo-French naval rivalry, helping to mint some fresh stereotyped phrases relating to that rivalry and confirm old ones. Once again, there is no ambiguity. A Briton referring to 'the nation that lives only to revenge Trafalgar' obviously meant France. (The Spanish were either forgotten, or dismissed as being too despicable to worry about.) And a Frenchman could easily turn similar phrases, such as *le tyran de la mer*, or (more poetically—the author was Chateaubriand), *le séducteur des vagues*, or (factual rather than slanderous), *une ennemie audacieuse, maître de la mer*. And if nothing else seemed quite adequate, he could fall back on a particularly resonant historical parallel—Carthage and Rome. The words *Delenda est Carthago* on the title page of a French work on naval matters are as good as a précis of the contents.

---

[1] François Crouzet, 'Problèmes de la communication franco-britannique aux XIXe et XXe siècles', *Revue historique*, 254 (July–Sept. 1975), 105–34.

Not that naval rivalry looked likely to be a swelling theme in Anglo-French relations soon after the Treaties of Vienna. Britain, victorious, was turning inward to demobilize and to repress dissent. France, defeated, also turned inward, afflicted with Restoration myopia. The French navy suffered from purges and an infusion of returning royalist officers. The army suffered similarly, but it was the navy that provided what became seen as the supreme proof of the incompetence of the *rentrants*, the loss in 1816 of the *Méduse*, commanded by Duroys de Chaumareys, a shipwreck transmuted into a powerful icon of romanticism and revolution by Géricault. The French navy could ill afford such infamy at this time; most Frenchmen saw the need for a strong army, but the attitude to the navy was usually indifference or even hostility. Why, some asked, should France support a force which, even after the victorious allies had confiscated thirty-one battleships and twelve frigates, still amounted to forty sound battleships, built and building, with many smaller vessels? Neither commerce nor the colonies required such a generous shield. Not until 1824 did French maritime commerce regain its pre-revolutionary level; and the French colonies remaining after 1815 were only a few specks on the world map. In the Restoration Chamber of Deputies many of the agrarian right and liberal left thought that the navy was too large and expensive. They put their faith in the army. As one deputy of the right said in 1821: 'l'existence de la marine compromet la défense des côtes . . . des défaites sur mer devant décourager les habitants et l'armée.'[2]

But by 1821 the navy was beginning to recover in reputation and readiness. Already in 1817 there had been a large—even an over-large—purge of *rentrants*, and from December 1818, for three years, the Minister of Marine was baron Portal, the man later popularly credited with the naval revival. He, as an ex-*armateur* and *directeur des colonies* at the Ministry of Marine, wished to develop the navy, and was able to draw support from the country's slowly recovering colonial and commercial interests. It was he who presented the Chamber with the Hobson's choice of increasing the naval credits, or having the fleet dwindle away into powerlessness. The restorative work continued under his successors, notably Chabrol (1824–8). They gave an accent to exploration and hydrography that Portal

---

[2] Joannès Tramond, *Manuel d'histoire maritime de la France* (Paris, 1916), 897.

had been reluctant to countenance. And, supporting their efforts to revive the navy—though not on the grounds of furthering scientific enquiry—were some of their ministerial colleagues, particularly Villèle (chief minister 1821–8), who himself had been a naval officer before the Revolution. For even if the country at large did not appreciate the utility of a navy, the executive did, and the reviving fleet found itself increasingly involved in French foreign policy, gaining glory for itself as well as reputation for the nation, and slowly educating the electorate about naval power.

Already in 1819, albeit in co-operation with a British squadron, a battleship and a frigate had been sent off to encourage the rulers of Algiers, Tunis, and Tripoli to check the slave-trade. In 1823 there had been a far greater opportunity for action, thanks to the invasion of Spain by the French army. The navy gave valuable support, most notably by blockading Cadiz and then capturing the fort at its entrance. In 1828 there was a fine case of successful naval suasion, when Rear-Admiral Roussin's squadron persuaded the Brazilian government to change its mode of blockade of the Plate estuary.[3] The previous year there had been a far more spectacular and famous exercise of naval power—Navarino—when the combined Anglo-Franco-Russian squadrons, somewhat to their surprise, had found themselves in battle with the Turko-Egyptian fleet, sinking it and thus ensuring Greek independence.

Nevertheless, the French naval revival had not gone very far. By 1827 the total number of officers and men in warships in commission was some 17,000, an increase since 1820 of nearly 7,000, but still only half the British level. Admittedly, the Admiralty had begun to show some signs of concern, worrying over a squadron despatched to South America in 1820, and being distinctly suspicious about the motives behind the several French voyages of exploration in the Pacific during the 1820s. However, the British fixation on the French navy as yet lay ahead. During the first half of this decade, the Admiralty considered the US navy as the most likely enemy. The American fleet was relatively small, but it was potent and growing. The large US frigates had proved a very successful type during the war of 1812–15, and to follow these a number of very powerful line-of-battleships had been laid down,

---

[3] Jacques Aman, 'Un blocus pacifique en 1828: L'amiral Roussin au Brésil', *Revue maritime*, 222 (June 1938), 767–91.

although their construction proceeded in some cases with extreme slowness. There was also a possible cause of serious quarrel between the two governments, the dispute over Oregon. However, this question was settled in 1827 — at least for a time — and relations gradually improved, the prospect of war receding.

Even now the British had a more serious naval rival than France. However quickly the ships rotted, however lubberly the aristocrat-officers and serf-seamen, the Tsar's fleet at least had impressive numbers, and was kept largely mobilized when ice left its ports. Fearful old admirals in their London clubs were only too susceptible to visions of a sudden descent by the Russian Baltic fleet upon an unready Britain. The early 1830s saw the peak of British concern over the Russian fleet, and the Russian threat was the most potent lever of any for getting larger naval credits from the House of Commons.

The concern was especially great because of a clear clash of interests with Russia over Turkey. To the British government the Sultan's territory was an essential barrier against Russian southern aggrandisement. But in 1833 the Russians gained a diplomatic triumph, for by the treaty of Unkiar Skelessi in that year the Sultan agreed not only to close the Dardanelles against the warships of other nations if Russia went to war, but gave Russia the right to support him against his enemies — a virtual *carte blanche* to interfere in Turkey's internal and external affairs.

The threat was clear enough to bring the British and French governments together to protect their Mediterranean interests. The basis for an entente had already been laid in 1831–2, when Palmerston, then Foreign Secretary, had worked with the new regime under Louis-Philippe to settle the Belgian crisis. There was also a community of interests in Iberia, as is shown by the signing of the Quadruple Alliance in 1834 between France, Britain, Spain, and Portugal. But, now as later, it was the threat from another great power that brought the two powers together most closely. Nevertheless, even the Russian menace did not bind Paris and London together securely. Certainly, in 1835 and 1836 the Admiralty believed that the greatest naval threat to Britain came from the Tsar, and in the latter year the Commons unanimously voted 5,000 extra seamen; yet both in 1836 and 1837 there were British naval demonstrations off the Tunisian coast that were implicitly aimed at France, to remind her that there was another Mediterranean naval

power. Even at its warmest, the entente only sublimated more
hostile feelings, never quite superseded them. For in the Mediterranean, despite some common goals, British and French interests were fundamentally contradictory, and this was to lead to the
rivalry between the two powers moving into an overt phase, where
each side—and each navy—saw the other as its most serious and
dangerous enemy.

British maritime involvement in the Mediterranean was long
standing, going back to the piratical English *bertoni* of the sixteenth
century and the campaigns of Admiral Blake during the Commonwealth. After 1815 the involvement became greater than before.
There were new possessions. Britain had long had Gibraltar, but
now there was Malta, on one of the crucial passages between the
eastern and western halves of the sea. She had also gained the
Ionian Isles, though they proved troublesome to rule, and were
ceded to Greece in 1864.

If her new territories helped bind Britain to the Mediterranean,
so too did a series of important international problems. The first
was the war for Greek independence (1821–31), which raised
serious questions for Whitehall, not least because of the strong
philhellene sentiment of many in and out of government. The
Greeks finally won their independence, but the Eastern Mediterranean continued to cause serious concern to diplomatists. The root
cause of the area's instability yet remained: the decline of Turkish
power. With the enfeeblement of the Sultan's hold on his empire
—even after the Tsar had been persuaded to accept a revision of
Unkiar Skelessi—and with the continuing aggressiveness of Russia
towards Turkey, the scene was set for an Eastern question of ever
greater intricacy and danger, periodically erupting into open crisis.

The British government also found itself involved from time to
time in other parts of the Mediterranean, keeping the fleet in almost
continual motion. There were, for instance, constant calls for naval
support from the British consuls in the various ports; they seem
never to have felt entirely secure unless there was one of their
nation's cruisers stationed in sight. On occasion, there were serious
diplomatic squalls, when diplomacy called for nothing less than the
appearance of a squadron of battleships, for example during the
unification of Italy in the middle of the century.

Nevertheless, the protection of Turkish territories was Whitehall's
greatest continuing Mediterranean concern during the nineteenth

century. This was primarily due to the growing importance of the
routes to India that passed through the Mediterranean even before
the completion of the Suez Canal in 1869. India was becoming an
ever more precious possession of the British, both because of its
military power and because it was an enormous market for
Lancashire cotton goods. Until 1869 there was no alternative to the
long, slow, and vulnerable Cape route for the great bulk of Anglo-
Indian trade, but with railways and steam despatch vessels it had
become clear that speedy communications between what were the
two centres of the British Empire could be organized via the
Mediterranean. The best route was settled on and developed only
gradually. By 1837 it was at last recognized that the overland route
via Mesopotamia could not be relied on (though certain promoters
attempted to revive it later). But by using the much shorter route
via Suez a great deal was achieved. Already in 1836 the future line
was being sketched out: regular steam services existed between
Southampton and Malta, and trials were then being made of a
monthly steam service from Suez to India. All that was needed was
an extension of the Malta service to Egypt, and the establishment
of a trustworthy land link from the Mediterranean to the Red Sea.
In 1820 it often took two months for mail or passengers to reach
Constantinople from London, but by 1850 Calcutta could be
reached in the same time — a gain of more than a month over the
fastest vessel taking the Cape route. As soon as it was articulated,
this great new east–west nexus became seen as an essential lifeline of
empire, to be shielded against any great power that attempted to
come close.[4]

Russia was a power that did seem to threaten that lifeline, and
Turkey was seen in Whitehall as the buffer to keep the threat at
a safe distance. But, of course, France had as much, if not more
disruptive potential as Russia, and this was becoming clear to the
Admiralty by the end of the 1830s. In her case there was no buffer:
both in the Atlantic and Mediterranean she fronted directly on to
British lines of communication, and especially in the Mediterranean
her interests were coming into friction with British ones.

Barred from interference in Central and Eastern Europe by
defeat and the Treaties of Vienna, France was constrained to look
elsewhere to gain prestige and replenish her stock of *amour propre*.

[4] H. L. Hoskins, *British Routes to India* (London, 1928).

In 1823 Louis XVIII's government was able to intervene in Spain, an opportunity that was taken with great pleasure; and afterwards France continued to take a close interest in Iberia. But attempts to interfere in territories to her north and east had less success and continuity, above all when frontier rectifications were proposed; they awakened too many uncomfortable memories for the other powers. In the early 1830s, for example, during the Belgian crisis, the Orleanist government had to be convinced—chiefly, on this occasion, by Palmerston—that there was no question of France absorbing Belgium as a price for supporting that country's secession from the Netherlands. This was not the first such rebuff; and an earlier one had already encouraged the French government to explore alternative means of expansion. Back in 1829 the French chief minister had proposed a deal to the Russians: in exchange for recognition of large Russian gains at Turkish expense, France was to be compensated on her northern border. The suggestion was rejected, naturally enough; and, as was also natural, the French government was spurred to look elsewhere, and found an opportunity in the Mediterranean. In 1830 France seized control of Algiers.

The occupation was not at first ostensibly permanent. The *coup* was said to be a response to an insult by the Bey of Algiers, and in effect similar to the British naval bombardment of his city in 1816. In fact, right from the beginning the occupation was intended to last. The action had obvious implications for British use of the Mediterranean sea links. France's ability to seize Algiers did not say too much about the strength of her navy at that time; the fleet that took the army to North Africa was hastily gathered and manned, and was more of a convoy of transports than an effective war-fleet. But the mere fact of a French presence in Algiers meant that there was a powerful incentive to continue the French naval renaissance with greater seriousness. In arguments in the Chamber of Deputies over naval credits, the government could henceforward point to an excellent reason for France having a powerful navy—the need to protect and maintain communications with North Africa. Unfortunately, this need contradicted the British need to protect and maintain their own east–west link.

The danger was that each power would want to achieve maritime hegemony in the Mediterranean, the better to safeguard its own use of the lines of maritime communication and, if necessary, to deny them to the other power. It was not as if reasons were lacking for this approach, even ignoring the special demands made by Algiers and India. History had its own part to play, reminding each power of its traditional interests in the area, encouraging those who argued for exclusive control. We have already noted that England had long been engaged in this sea. And France had been involved even longer. Egypt had been an area of French interest since Louis IX in the thirteenth century. The mention of Egypt reminds us also that very recent history had kept the Mediterranean well to the fore in British and French minds, which was bound to help shape later policy-making in Paris and London. Napoleon's victory over the Mamelukes, Nelson's destruction of a French fleet at the Battle of the Nile, Sidney Smith's brilliant contribution to the defence of St-Jean d'Acre, the occupation of Egypt by General Abercromby's army; these and various other Mediterranean events during the Great War (as the Victorians dubbed the Revolutionary and Napoleonic Wars), gave — according to one's national point of view — numerous spurs either to emulation or revenge.

Perhaps it should be remembered also that the Mediterranean occupied a particularly important place in the affections of educated Europeans, and more so in the nineteenth century than ever before. Neo-classicism had already prompted a fascination with the Greek and Roman heritage, but in Romanticism there was an even larger concentration on Mediterranean subjects. The Mediterranean became part of the immense zone of the imagination and expectations that, at least for Victor Hugo, stretched from Spain to China—the Orient.[5]

Not only the imagination was engaged, but also the intellect. Scientific investigations were pursued under cover of the Napoleonic and then British invasions of Egypt, achieving their most brilliant fruit in the discovery of the Rosetta Stone and the decipherments of J.-F. Champollion. With peace it was diplomacy rather than armed force that sheltered further research and exploration: most blatantly in the cases of Botta and Rawlinson who took advantage of their diplomatic postings to study the old civilizations of Mesopotamia.[6] Where imagination and science

[5] 1829 preface to *Les Orientales: Œuvres poétiques*, ed. P. Albouy (Paris, 1964), i. 580.

[6] C. W. Ceram (K. W. Marek), *Gods, Graves and Scholars: The Story of Archaeology* (London, 1979), chs. 18, 20.

went, policy went as well, inextricably intertwined. This happened
perhaps most obviously in Greece. It was only in the imagination
that the many bandits fighting for independence appeared as
modern versions of Pericles or Lycurgus; thus the sympathies of
the French and British with the Greek national cause, and the aid
they afforded it, were in part based on misconceptions: but the aid
was real enough. Similarly, British forecasts of the prospects for
strengthening and reviving Turkey, or French hopes of prosperity
and developments in Algeria, were themselves built on poor
evidence and romantic notions, but this did not alter the policies
pursued.

There was, therefore, more than one reason for Britain and
France to attempt to develop their influence in the Mediterranean.
Moreover, there was more than one instrument. Commerce, loans
to governments, loans to private companies, and even religion
could be and were of importance as elements in diplomacy. Military
force also has to be considered in this context, albeit less in the case
of Britain than of France with her large armies both in Algeria and
the metropolitan country. However, ultimately it was naval force
(combined, of course, with diplomacy) that was the most effective
means of exercising influence in the Mediterranean. The movement
of armies depended predominantly on sea transport. Even more
obviously, those vital French and British sea links depended on
naval power. The implicit clash between British and French
Mediterranean policies, therefore, could be very largely realized in
terms of naval rivalry.

This rivalry became a juggernaut, frequently dominating Anglo-
French relations, and for a long time it appeared unstoppable. As
with almost all such intense rivalries, it did not develop slowly,
but was set in motion by a great impulse, a sudden crisis. This
happened in 1839–40. By that time, the French navy had recovered
well from the early Restoration naval malaise. The Orleanists had
continued the work begun under the last Bourbons, the navy had
become far more powerful; furthermore, thanks to *coups* such as the
forcing of the entrance to the Tagus (supposedly impregnable) by
a squadron under Roussin in 1831, it was more accepted and
applauded by the electorate. For some years it suffered from the
weakness that no squadron of evolution was regularly sent to sea to
practise fleet manœuvres. But this changed in 1839, when
Lalande was appointed to the Mediterranean, and he began—first

with three battleships, later with more — not only to create a battle-worthy fleet but also to reforge a naval tradition.

This new squadron posed particular dangers for the Royal Navy. Both powers, one must stress, kept in the Mediterranean the most powerful portions of their fleets in commission. Their respective interests led them to do so, but there was also a home-dockyard factor, though it operated in different ways upon the two navies. The French Mediterranean squadron could be kept so strong because it was never far from Toulon, France's premier naval arsenal. The British squadron, on the other hand, was distant from its home yards, but this had its own benefits, the Admiralty prefer-ring to keep warships well away from what were renowned centres for crimps, drink, and venereal disease. However, the causes of this concentration are secondary to its possible consequences. It was clear that any serious clash between the two forces in this one sea could have even more serious repercussions than the severing of links with Algeria or India, above all for Britain. If, for instance, the British Mediterranean squadron were destroyed at little cost to the enemy, then the Admiralty would have few immediately dispos-able reserves to prevent the enemy from sailing to the Channel, perhaps to mount an invasion of Britain. Given time, thanks to the enormous superiority of British maritime resources, especially of warships preserved in the Ordinary, any losses could be far more than made up. But time, it was seen, was not necessarily going to be available. Thus it was felt in Whitehall that Britain's global mari-time power depended to a very large extent on the balance of naval forces in commission in the Mediterranean.

Lalande's creation of an effective battlefleet was therefore hardly welcomed by the Admiralty, especially since its British opposite number was not obviously more capable. There were three problems. First, post-war retrenchments had meant there had not been any regular British squadrons of evolution. The Royal Navy had battleships, but not a battlefleet. Secondly, thanks to a very poor manning system, the Admiralty had enormous difficulties in quickly adding to the fleet in commission. The French had a superior system of manning, and Whitehall feared that at least in the short term Lalande's fleet could gain a clear numerical superior-ity over its rival during the early stages of a conflict. Thirdly, there were weaknesses in the British warships. As victor in 1815, the Royal Navy had found itself with a large fleet, but one that was becoming obsolescent. The French fleet, by contrast, had lost many ships during the war, and lost yet more with the peace as a form of indemnity; but it retained some very powerful craft, including many of the latest design still on the building slips. By 1839 most of the British battleships in the Mediterranean were inferior in weight of broadside to their possible opponents. There was the one advantage that the British force had more steamers in attendance than did Lalande's, but steam was as yet an unknown quantity in naval warfare. All in all, therefore, the Admiralty was not over-confident of victory should a crisis with France turn to war.

And crisis there was. The second half of the 1830s had seen the withering away of the earlier entente, and in British eyes Russia had been replaced by France as the most probable enemy. There had been some quarrels over affairs in Iberia (Whitehall thought France was being too friendly towards the Carlist rebels in Spain) but a definite split came through internal upsets in an area of obvious sensitivity to the two powers—the Turkish Empire. France supported Mehemet Ali, the Pasha of Egypt, whose power was greatly increased in April 1839 when his forces defeated the army of his nominal suzerain, the Sultan. Whitehall, however, continued to support the latter, wanting to check his over-mighty subject, and, if possible, to reduce French influence in Egypt and thus safeguard the increasingly important Suez land link. The French government, directed by Thiers, remained determined, showing this chiefly by further building up Lalande's fleet, until it amounted to nineteen powerful battleships, virtually equal to the British fleet in numbers, and stronger in gunpower. Thus Lalande and his officers were confident, and eager for a little revenge. The temper of the government at home was similarly exalted. In November a great gesture was made when some battleships under construction were renamed: the *Bucentaure* became the *Wagram*, the *Diomède* the *Tilsitt*, the *Éole* the *Eylau*, the *Ajax* the *Austerlitz*, the *Achille* the *Breslaw*, and the *Alexandre* the *Donauwerth*. The navy was tapping the core of Napoleonic military glory, a prelude to the grand flourish of the following year when the frigate *Belle Poule* brought the Emperor's body back to France from St Helena. With such signs of determination, with a superior naval force available, and the quarrel concerning an important Mediterranean question (one involving a protégé of France), it must have seemed either that the French would win their point, or that there would be war.

In the event, neither happened. Palmerston showed what even for him was remarkable confidence and strength of will. He came to an agreement with Russia and Austria, isolating France, and sent the fleet to deal with Mehemet Ali. Thiers was faced down, though he remained bellicose outwardly, and was removed from office by Louis-Philippe, who realized perfectly well that even if the French fleet won the first battle, it had very few reserves of men or *matériel*, and could not sustain a long war. Guizot came to power; and, after being kept waiting by Palmerston for a time, France was graciously allowed to join with the other great powers in settling the Egyptian question. Mehemet Ali, already defeated—largely by the Royal Navy—had to remain content with what the powers offered him. France, it appeared, had been humiliated, despite her fleet.

The humiliation was keenly felt in Paris, but this was not allowed to reflect upon the fleet: quite the reverse. It was strongly argued in the Chamber of Deputies that the navy had to be further developed so that it would be able to sustain a long-drawn-out war. At the same time, all the old stereotypes about England and English arrogance were recharged. One of these was that England owed her vast territories and her commercial and financial power to a strong navy. Another was that the English respected only force. A stronger French navy, therefore, would serve several purposes. It would not only help protect France from injury, preserve the link with Algeria, and impress the Mediterranean nations with French power; it would also enable France to enjoy the benefits so far gained only by England, and force that same England to treat France with all the respect due to her.

In other words, the 1839–40 crisis gave a strong impetus to French naval expansion. Whitehall, in its turn, could not idly accept this expansion, but in response had to improve the British fleet, especially given the weaknesses that the crisis had brought to light. As is predictable, this British expansion prompted the French government to even greater naval efforts of its own, and so *ad infinitum*. By 1840 a secure groundwork had been laid for a self-sustaining Anglo-French naval rivalry and naval race. It is this rivalry, this race, that is the subject of the following pages.

In stressing how crucial the two navies were to each other during the mid-nineteenth century, one does not imply that other navies were of no importance. During the ebb and flow of international tensions, France and Britain were each occasionally forced to pay close attention to the fleet of another power that might suddenly become a hostile one. An example is the acute British concern with the US fleet in 1846, during renewed disagreement over Oregon. Moreover, the Ministry of Marine was always conscious of other fleets, since it believed that they might, at need, be brought in on the French side in a grand alliance against 'le tyran de la mer'. Naturally, the Admiralty was also sensitive about this possibility, particularly fearing a war with both France and the USA at the same time. There were occasional official memoranda during the period arguing that the Royal Navy ought to maintain a three-power standard, and be ready to meet Russia at sea, as well as France and America.[7]

However, France remained the prime naval threat to Britain, and vice versa. As the years rolled on from the early 1840s into the following decade, the various policy memoranda tend more and more to reflect this. Technical innovation undoubtedly had a great responsibility for this focusing. Once the race between the two powers got under way, they began to well outdistance the navies of the other powers technologically. It was thus reasonable for other forces to be regarded as largely peripheral. By the time of the Crimean War, the Russian navy, though still the third naval force in the world and certainly impressive in numbers, was almost an obsolete irrelevance in comparison to the two fleets that—somewhat oddly—found themselves in alliance after many years of common hostility.

Technology not only helped to shape the degree of exclusivity of the rivalry, but had other effects as well; creating many problems for the naval planners, but also offering them opportunities of a kind not truly available previously. We cannot limit ourselves to the Mediterranean: for though the period of intense Anglo-French rivalry began in that sea, and often reverted there, it had to spread beyond — above all to the Channel, which at times became the greatest area of friction, thanks to the increasing capabilities of the steamer and the fears these aroused of naval attacks close to the centres of power of the two nations. We shall have to look beyond

---

[7] Memorandum by Lord Minto, 9 Sept. 1841, ADM 3 265; Memorandum by W. F. Martin, 15 Mar. 1858, Martin Papers, BM Add. MS 41410, fos. 50–124; paper by Lord Halifax, 16 Dec. 1870, Gladstone Papers, BM Add. MS 44185, fos. 111–14. Generally on British naval policy and diplomacy, see the standard work by C. J. Bartlett, *Great Britain and Sea Power 1815–1853* (OUP, 1967).

Europe as well. Already in the 1840s London and Paris were disagreeing about territories in the Pacific. Indeed, there seem to have been few enough places on the globe where British and French commercial, colonial, or religious interests could not clash; and thanks to the flexibility of naval power, the two rivals were able to support these interests with naval force virtually wherever there was enough water to float a warship. Naval strategy will have to be considered at some point and, by extension, naval tactics. Questions concerning the officers and seamen, including the recruiting and training systems that lay behind them, must be addressed, so that we can come to some conclusions about the relative effectiveness of the two navies and the truth underlying the fierce rhetoric of rivalry, as far as one can discern it. We shall also need to make a comparison of the dockyard facilities on the two sides. Also relevant is the 'mechanism' of the rivalry, including an explanation of how the 'self-sustaining naval race' we have so far been describing ever managed to lose momentum, became less overt. Furthermore, in the course of the discussion a question will be raised that is the King Charles's Head of this study: why was it that, albeit after a hesitant beginning, the French navy proved to be the superior in terms of technological innovation, the introduction of major warship types? This question will ultimately lead to what should always figure in any account of a naval rivalry, a comparison of the opposing naval administrations.

Having tried to explain the origin of the rivalry, we shall turn in the following two chapters to discuss the various developments in naval *matériel* that occurred between 1840 and 1870, including an account of the diplomatic upsets—even wars—that gave an added impetus to naval innovation and growth. These two chapters will lay the foundation for the succeeding ones, setting out a basic chronology for the years of the rivalry, and explicitly or implicitly raising the topics that will be considered later.

2

Anglo-French Diplomacy and the Transition from Sail to Screw

I

The two fleets that so nearly clashed with one another in 1839–40 were composed predominantly of wooden, unarmoured sailing-vessels. Such craft had long been the backbone of naval power, but from 1815 were being improved at a greater pace than ever before. Each new vessel of a given rate was larger than its predecessor, carrying more or heavier guns (and often both). Furthermore, naval architects were continually refining their art. There were occasional embarrassments, such as the discovery by the French that the great new four-decker *Valmy* (launched in 1847) had insufficient stability, and needed extra timber worked in around the waterline (a *soufflage*). In Britain there was argument about the warships designed after the system of William Symonds, Surveyor of the Navy from 1832 to 1847: his vessels were fast, but had relatively limited stowage space and uneasy motions under sail. Nevertheless, by the 1840s, within the limits of the technology and materials of the time, the sailing-warship was reaching its peak of perfection. As two senior members of the Surveyor's Department wrote to their new chief in 1848, perhaps with a little exaggeration: 'the experience of late years has brought the best form of [sailing] Ships within a comparatively narrow compass, so that educated Naval Architects generally differ but little from each other.'[1]

The large-scale introduction of steam upset any comfortable assurance about warship design. Already in the crisis of 1839–40 the great utility of steam-powered warships had been demonstrated; not of course in battle between the two fleets but in operations undertaken by the British, under their Mediterranean Commander-in-Chief Sir Robert Stopford, against Egyptian land forces. First

[1] Submission of 1 Aug. 1848, ADM 83 51.

there were landings, where paddle-steamers were of great use. Secondly, there was the bombardment of the fortress of St-Jean d'Acre. Steam-power enabled Stopford to have his battleships towed into the best positions for the attack. Furthermore, by transferring his flag to a steamer Stopford was better able to view and direct the operation.

The British success not only spurred the French sense of naval rivalry, but helped give it a specific technological direction. One of the main fruits of the new determination in France to improve the navy was a large programme of paddle-vessel construction. For some time the French had been satisfied with less powerful steamers than the British ones. In 1837–8 the Royal Navy had set a new standard with the launching of the *Gorgon* and *Cyclops*, vessels of over 1,100 tons BOM and 320 hp, much more powerful than the contemporary French *Véloce* class of only 220 hp. At last, in January 1840 the *Infernal* was laid down at Rochefort, eventually fitted with 400 hp engines.[2] Later in the year six powerful steam-frigates of 450–650 hp were begun, followed during the next two years—amongst many smaller steamers—by fourteen fast armed despatch vessels of 450 hp. This construction effort was to give an edge to the renewed Anglo-French diplomatic friction after 1842, and to concentrate the attention of the naval authorities and pamphleteers on the Channel. This attention, in turn, was to have a powerful effect, encouraging the British government to take an important new step in naval construction.

However, let us look first at the renewed diplomatic tension between the two powers. In 1841 relations took a definite step for the better when Sir Robert Peel's government came to power. Palmerston thus went out of office, and with him went the bluster that had so offended other European statesmen about his style of foreign policy. Lord Aberdeen was the new foreign secretary, and he showed himself willing to come to an understanding with the French government. Thanks largely to his good personal relations with Guizot, his opposite number, an entente once again grew. But good personal relations at the top level could not wholly arrest the inertial force of Anglo-French rivalry. There were many interests

---

[2] E. A. M. Laing, 'The Introduction of Paddle Frigates into the Royal Navy', *Mariner's Mirror*, 66 (1980), 331–43. M.-C.-M.-R Testu de Balincourt and P. Le Conte, 'La Marine française d'hier: V. Navires à roues', *Revue maritime*, 154 (Oct. 1932), 472–512. D. K. Brown, *Before the Ironclad: Development of Ship Design, Propulsion and Armament in the Royal Navy, 1815–60* (London, 1990), ch. 6.

that could clash, and it was only too easy to arouse old antipathies. The new entente was soon troubled.

The upsets began in the Pacific. The Admiralty had been concerned during the 1820s about active French exploration in that ocean. At that time, French interests there were primarily scientific; but soon commercial and then political affairs began to intrude. Whitehall kept fearing that the French intended to found a new empire; in fact, neither Guizot nor Louis-Philippe was attracted by the cost of supporting distant colonies, nor wished to offend Peel's ministry. But the two were drawn in despite themselves, first by religious imperialism in the Pacific (attempts by Protestant missionaries to exclude Catholic priests, and vice versa), and also by the difficulty of controlling the actions of French naval officers at a distance of 12,000 miles. Some of the latter took an active part in local quarrels, whether over religion, trade, or whatever, and acted as they thought their orders allowed and, a dangerous point, as their concept of national honour demanded. In theory, their actions could always be disavowed once news had reached Paris, but in reality this was sometimes very difficult. As Guizot discovered, popular opinion was at times only too eager to involve itself in diplomacy. Once it did so, the government might find itself constrained to accept a rash action by a distant agent, with possibly grave effects on relations with Britain.

That was virtually what happened over Tahiti. In August 1842 the commander of the French Pacific squadron, Dupetit-Thouars, made the island into a French protectorate. Whitehall was displeased; even more so in February 1844 when news arrived that the admiral, (going beyond his instructions), had deposed the Tahitian queen and annexed her territory. This put Guizot in a very unpleasant position. He valued the entente, and knew that Whitehall was already doubtful enough about his policy aims thanks to proposals made in 1842–3 for a Franco-Belgian customs union, inevitably seen in London as a disguise for traditional French designs on the Low Countries.[3] He and his master thus steeled themselves, and disavowed the annexation. Yet this did not quieten British public opinion, and it enraged opinion in Paris: the newspapers on both sides of the Channel became increasingly strident and bellicose.

[3] Alfred de Ridder, *Les Projets d'union douanière franco-belge et les puissances européennes (1836–43)* (Brussels, 1932), chs. 3–4.

The affair then worsened. Soon after the disavowal, the prince de Joinville—sailor son of Louis-Philippe—published an over-exciting article. This was the notorious *Note sur l'état des forces navales de la France*. It was also quickly published in Britain, and had great influence in both countries, though rather for what it was supposed to say than for the actual argument, being another of those works that are more spoken of than quoted, and more quoted than read and understood. The Prince had suggested how France could hope for large benefits from steam in a war with her old rival; paddle-warships, he thought, could fasten on England's fat maritime trade, and they could mount powerful raids against the English coast, since in the new conditions the Channel would no longer be the sure defence of old. All this, the author said, would be in the future, since at the time he wrote, despite the recent construction efforts, the French steam fleet seemed to him notably inferior to the British one. But the article was still the stuff of which war scares are made. For one thing, in Britain at least, the authorship implied that the article expressed the views of the French government. (Actually it embarrassed both Guizot and the King; and the fuss soon made Joinville himself wish that he had never published the piece.) Moreover, it excited opinion on both sides of the Channel, giving more substance to the belligerency already generated over Tahiti.

The essential problem was the volatility of public sentiment. The national membranes had been inflamed, and it was easy to irritate them again. More trouble came in July, on the return to Britain of Mr Pritchard, a bumptious Protestant missionary who had been consul in Tahiti. He claimed that he had been badly treated and even imprisoned by Dupetit-Thouars during the annexation. Then came a crisis in an obviously sensitive zone—North Africa. The French government wished to chastise the Moroccans for sending troops into Algerian territory. An army under Marshal Bugeaud was sent to the frontier of Morocco, and a naval squadron ordered to her coast. The first reaction in Whitehall was that a new Algeria was in the making, and suspicions were only heightened by the announcement that the prince de Joinville was to command the naval force. Guizot and the King well realized that the appointment would give offence in London, but knew the Prince to be a capable officer and wished to prove to him that they had forgiven him his article. They did their best to soothe British opinion in the matter:

for example, the Prince was urged to use supply facilities at Gibraltar and thus appeal to British naval *amour propre*.[4] They also firmly promised that the French forces would soon retire. And so they did—but not without victory: in August Joinville's vessels bombarded the fortifications of Tangier and took the island of Mogador (present day Essaouira), and Bugeaud defeated the Moroccan army at the battle of Isly. Thus, despite the later withdrawal, the entente was damaged: the French had more cause for an aggressive pride, and the British suffered from jealousy tinged with fear.

The entente did not fully break down until the summer of 1846 when Guizot arranged a marriage between the royal houses of France and Spain: this action was strongly resented in Whitehall since it seemed to cement French influence in Iberia, and was contrary to a previous agreement between the entente governments. But Guizot probably thought he had little to lose by this stage; Palmerston was now back in office, and he had long shown that he thought of the French alliance as an arrangement primarily to benefit his own country. Yet even before Palmerston's return, the entente had been a broken-backed affair. The troubles over Tahiti and Morocco had convinced most of Peel's cabinet that Guizot was untrustworthy, if only because behind him, and the probably pacific but ageing Louis-Philippe, was a fresh and remarkably military set of royal princes (Joinville had several brothers), and a bellicose and anglophobic public opinion.

Bad relations with France fuelled disquiet in Britain over the growing French fleet. It was not France's sailing fleet that gave the most concern, nor yet her paddle-warships as *warships*. The newspaper-reading public, including many naval officers, was frightened by the potential of the steamer as transport vessel, quickly ferrying large numbers of French troops across the Channel, nimbly avoiding the sailing-warships in defence. Two Britons in particular were responsible during the 1840s for popularizing fears of steam invasion. One of these was the Duke of Wellington; a man whose achievements gave him his own place in the Victorian constitution. In a famous letter of 9 January 1847, soon leaked to the press, he wrote that large bodies of infantry could be thrown ashore on any

---

[4] Louis-Philippe to Joinville of 17 July 1844, Joinville Papers, 300 AP III 111. Roger Bullen, *Palmerston, Guizot and the Collapse of the Entente Cordiale* (London, 1974), chs. 2 and 5.

part of the South Coast except before Dover Castle: these men could then capture a harbour, land their cavalry, artillery, and supplies, and march straight on London. To oppose a possible striking force of 40,000 men, Wellington thought only 5,000 of Britain's scattered army could be gathered in time.[5]

The letter attracted a large and apprehensive readership. But the fears it expressed were already part of the currency of debate: Wellington merely reinvigorated an argument that had somewhat abated over the previous year. Joinville himself had suggested 'steam descents' on the South Coast in his 1844 article, and in 1845 the idea had been taken up by Palmerston in his usual forceful way. He was the other great popularist of steam invasion, and was responsible for that emotive term 'a steam bridge'. As he put it in a Commons' speech of July 1845, 'the Channel is no longer a barrier. Steam navigation has rendered that which was before impassable by a military force nothing more than a river passable by a steam bridge.' He believed that the French had enough steamers (public and private) to be able to throw 30,000 men across the Channel before the British fleet could be alerted. Even if the fleet were to be warned, he asked, what could it do? The main reliance of the defence would have to be on the navy's steam-warships, since only they shared the steam-transport's alleged immunity to the effects of wind and tide. Certainly, the British had more steamers, but they tended to be dispersed: the Admiralty sent many to help police the empire and to check the West African slave-trade. The French, on the other hand, kept their forces more concentrated in home waters. As a result, Palmerston feared, France could gain a local superiority in the Channel for an invasion.[6]

Palmerston's private letters confirm his fears for British security, and show more of his reasoning. In a note of 24 December 1846 to Sir Charles Wood (a future First Lord of the Admiralty), he wrote:

I think we are all too apt from old impressions, which were true enough of old but which have been rendered erroneous by the application of Steam to Ships, to consider that our wooden walls are a complete defence against invasion. My firm conviction, and it is as strong as of my own existence, is that we can no longer depend upon our ships as a complete security. That in the first period of war we could not put a sufficient number to sea, to

[5] A full copy of the Duke's letter is in the Panmure Papers, GD 45 8 23.
[6] *Hansard*, Ser. 3, vol. lxxxii, cols. 1223–8, speech of 30 July 1845.

have command of the sea; and that even if we had what is called a decided
Superiority at Sea we could not be secure against invasion.[7]

Such attitudes were to lead him to call for greater expenditure on
the purely military defence of the UK. The letter also hints at a
problem that was not brought out in the 'steam bridge' speech, but
which was in the minds of many British politicians before and after
1845. France had a well-organized and well-established seamen
reserve system. Britain, however, had no system of mobilizing
seamen to man the navy for war, apart from the press-gang. Many
Britons feared that if war came this would prove impracticable in a
country grown used to liberty: as Cobden melodramatically put
it in 1849, the gangs might be sent out again, but they would be
shot![8] And even if the gangs did produce seamen, they were still a
far more crude, wasteful, and slow system than the French had
available. So another twist was given to the fears of steam attack.
Not only would the steamer 'always get through', and the French
have a local superiority of steamers, but the French would have
their steamers manned and prepared for war first.

Palmerston, of course, was in opposition when he made his
'steam bridge' speech. Sir Robert Peel replied on behalf of the
government, speaking comfortingly, if a trifle vaguely, about the
country's vast latent powers. Yet we know that by now the cabinet
was suspicious of French intentions; and Peel himself, whilst
prepared to combat invasion nerves in public, took good care to
prepare the national defences. As he told Wellington:

Whatever may be the real state of our defences, I presume even the
strictest regard for truth does not compel a Minister of the Crown publicly
to proclaim that his country is in a most defenceless state . . . if we are in a
defenceless state, it is one thing publicly to confess it, and another to take
practical measures for the improvement of our condition and the increase
of our means of resistance.[9]

The practical measures he spoke of were to be primarily naval.
One of them had been long spoken of—harbours of refuge along
the South Coast. These were to act as shelters for merchantmen
caught in storms, but also as shelters against man as well as
weather, and points of concentration for steamers guarding Channel trade routes and the coastline. Both the British and French

---

[7] Broadlands Papers, GC WO 186 1–4.   [8] *Hansard*, Ser. 3, vol. ciii, col. 939.
[9] C. S. Parker, *The Life of Sir Robert Peel* (3 vols., London, 1899), iii. 207–8.

Channel coasts were poorly provided with ports accessible in all tides. The problem was thoroughly investigated in Britain in the early 1840s. One commission reported to the Admiralty on the harbours of the south-east coast, a Commons' select committee reported on shipwrecks, and another commission reported on harbours of refuge. These investigations, and the apparent threat from France, led in 1845 to the decision to build large fortified breakwaters at Dover and Portland, and a smaller one at Harwich, with the aim of creating protected centres of naval operations. Later, it was decided to build refuges in the Channel Islands, though this work was to be bedevilled by constant changes of plan. With improvements to other ports, and with the development of coastal communications thanks to a growing network of railways and telegraph lines, so information and troops could be sent from port to port, a great defensive chain was built up. Naturally, it took some time for such massive works to be completed. For instance, the 800 ft. long pier at Dover was not finished until 1854.[10] Thus the national defence demanded other action, as well. Legislation for a militia was drawn up under Peel, though its implementation was delayed. More effective and speedy was the action taken to improve the fleet, and with interesting results.

Peel put great weight on the fleet. He realized it was financially impossible to build enough fortifications to defend the empire: in any case, fortresses could not protect maritime trade. Naval forces, though, could keep control of the narrow seas and offer some protection to the colonies and to trade, especially if the country took advantage of recent developments in naval construction. For, as Peel realized, steam need not be to the advantage of the French alone: by adopting *screw*-propulsion in new warships the country's defensive power would be greatly increased. Thus it was that work commenced on what was to be the world's first screw-fleet.

Why did the government not continue to favour paddle-vessels? The type had long had its sponsors, chief among them General Henri Paixhans. In his book *Nouvelle force maritime* (1822), he

[10] Harbour Commission, PP (1840), xxviii. 383–401. Select Committee on Shipwrecks, PP (1843), ix. 1–689. Harbours of Refuge Commission, PP (1845), xvi. 1–268. See also PP (1847), lxi. 65–102, and PP (1851), lii. 415–42. M. S. Partridge, *Military Planning for the Defense of the United Kingdom 1814–1870* (New York, 1989), 35–8, 95–9. On French Channel harbours, see the report of the meeting of the *Conseil d'amirauté* of 7 Mar. 1856, AN BB8 886 (*marine*), 47–55.

argued that paddle-steamers were the warships of the future. He thought that if they were armed with shell-guns they could destroy even battleships. Shell-guns had been used occasionally at sea before he wrote, and—thanks largely to careless handling by poorly trained men—had usually led to disaster. But, if properly used, they were very powerful weapons. In trials Paixhans demonstrated their enormous effectiveness: they could tear great gaps in wooden scantlings, or set the whole target ship on fire. The pyrotechnics were persuasive, and encouraged navies to introduce shell guns on all rates of warships.

His advocacy of the paddle-steamer itself was less effective, for there were important objections against it. First, it was not the stuff of which global naval power was made. Sailing-warships were capable of remaining at sea for two or three months without putting in for supplies, and thus had an enormous range. Steamers were far more limited. Even by the 1840s, when they had been greatly improved from the ones Paixhans first wrote about, paddle-vessels remained coal greedy and could keep up steam for only a few days. And there was always the possibility of mechanical break-down. Fortunately, the paddlers' engines and low-pressure boilers had a certain crude ruggedness; generous lubrication and emergency blacksmithing answered most problems. But a serious break-down could be crippling, all the more so when ships were distant from a dockyard. Efforts were made to give paddlers more freedom of action by fitting heavy masts and rigging, but the paddles and paddle-boxes meant that the ships were heavy sailers. Even with the paddles dismantled, under sail these vessels could not hope to keep station with traditional warships. All in all, therefore, in wishing to supersede the sailing-warship, Paixhans was trying to replace craft that had a strategic capacity with others whose significance was primarily tactical.

It is not even as if his chosen instruments were as powerful tactic-ally as he suggested. Here lay the second serious objection to the paddler. Certainly, shell-cannon were remarkably potent, at least in comparison with the cannon firing the traditional solid-shot pro-jectile. But first the target had to be hit. This was not a simple task, even for solid shot. Ordnance was still smooth-bore, and fire soon became inaccurate as the range lengthened. At 3,000 yards, as was shown by a trial in 1846, all the expertise of the Royal Navy's gunnery ship *Excellent* was insufficient to produce one hit on a battleship-sized target during a whole day's shooting with solid shot.[11]

This inaccuracy was one of the reasons for warships mounting large broadside batteries: the more guns one had firing, the better the chance of a hit. Paddle-steamers, of course, could not mount large batteries: their paddle-boxes got in the way. But they could still be potent adversaries with their few guns, Paixhans would have argued, since the smashing effect of a shell was so great that even a few such projectiles reaching the target would ensure victory. However, that argument ignores one unfortunate feature of the shell-fire of the time. Shells, being lighter than solid shot, could be propelled only just over half as far by the smooth-bore cannon of the day. At 1,300 yards the optimum range for the British thirty-two pounder was some 500 yards greater than that of the eight-inch shell-gun.[12] Thus, to bring her shell-guns into range, a steamer might have to brave the opponent's solid-shot batteries for several hundred yards. Success was not assured even when the steamer was in shell range, since so too was her enemy; for from the 1830s sailing-warships were also equipped with at least some shell weapons. During the following decade a proportion of 10 per cent shell to shot weapons was not uncommon in British and French warship batteries, and one should note that by the end of the 1840s special shells were being produced to be fired from the standard solid-shot cannon.[13] In the next decade the proportion of shell-guns rose as production caught up with requirements, reaching over 50 per cent in some battleships. All this would have meant a fearsome body of fire, solid shot as well as explosive, opposing the paddle-vessel that attacked a powerful sailing-warship. The only real chance of success would have been for the steamer to catch her opponent becalmed, and then approach on a 'blind angle'—ahead or astern—where the armament was weakest. Even here, the attack could be perilous; the supposed victim might be able to swing herself around to bring her battery to bear on the attacker. Furthermore naval designers, aware of the danger, took

[11] Note of 22 Sept. 1855, Cap.H.324, ADM 1 5658.
[12] D. F. Macmillan, 'The Development of British Naval Gunnery, 1815–53', unpub. doctoral thesis (London, 1967), 230.
[13] Sir Howard Douglas, *A Treatise on Naval Gunnery* (5th. edn., London, 1860), 252. Macmillan, 'British Naval Gunnery', 301. Meeting of the *Conseil des travaux*, 5 Feb. 1851, V BB8 1128. 161–70.

greater care in the 1840s to try to cope with it. For instance, the Admiralty ordered heavy pivot guns fitted to forecastles. The French, having no equivalent to the superb British sixty-eight pounder often fitted as a pivot (their own fifty pounder was much inferior), tended to augment the number and power of the forecastle guns.[14]

The paddle-steamer had yet one more disadvantage. Its paddle-boxes were particularly vulnerable to enemy fire, and so too was the machinery—some of which always had to be above the water-line to drive the paddle-shaft. With this, and the restricted range and inadequate fire-power, the paddler was not seen as a true warship. By the 1840s the majority of naval opinion, British and French, regarded the type as useful only as scouts, despatch vessels, and tugs—though very useful within these limits. The only oppon-ents it was thought fit to attack were merchantmen or other paddle-warships.

With *screw*-propulsion, on the other hand, the steamer could be a true warship. Without paddle-boxes or paddles and with the machinery lodged below the waterline, the screw-warship was far less vulnerable to enemy fire. Moreover, a full broadside could be fitted; the transition, when cruising, from sail to steam was comparatively simple; and the characteristics of the screw-vessel when under sail could be little different from those of a pure sailing-vessel.

These advantages were not entirely obvious in the mid-1840s; at the time the British decision to proceed with a screw-fleet was a bold one. The screw was not then a wholly proven device. Only in the late 1830s had working screw-vessels begun to be built, includ-ing one designed by John Ericsson, the famous Swedish engineer. His vessel performed for the Board of Admiralty in 1837, but failed to impress—thanks, apparently, to the antipathy of the Surveyor. But the screw could not long be ignored. In Britain one of its most active proponents was Francis 'Screw' Smith. A vessel of his, the *Archimedes*, was ready for trials in spring 1839, and not only con-vinced Brunel that his own *Great Britain* should be propelled by screw rather than paddles, but also suggested to the Admiralty that the screw might have real merit. The Board approved some small screw-vessels over the following few years, though it was only

[14] Meetings of the *Conseil des travaux* of 4 Apr. 1849, V BB8 1124. 281–8; 5 Feb. and 10 May 1851, V BB8 1128. 108–70, 470–8; 8 May 1852, V BB8 1130. 295–6.

in 1842 that work commenced in Britain on a screw-warship, the *Rattler*, which began trials in October 1843.

Whatever the delays had been, the Royal Navy was not behind its competitors at this time. The French navy also completed a screw in 1843, the famous despatch vessel *Napoléon*, later renamed the *Corse* when her even more famous namesake was completed. The US navy had been the first actually to order a screw-warship —the *Princeton*. She was the best of the three. Like the other two she had a wooden hull—for long the only material thought proper —so she had no superiority there. But she was better armed than the *Napoléon*, and—unlike the *Rattler*, which was powered by an adapted paddle-engine—had all her machinery below the waterline. However, the *Princeton* began trials only in February 1844.[15]

It was the *Rattler*'s trials that were most important in convincing the Admiralty, and Peel and the rest of the cabinet, that screw-warships were entirely feasible. It was not yet accepted that screw-propulsion was superior to paddle (and this remained true even after the famous tug-of-war test in April 1845 between the *Rattler* and the *Alecto* paddle-vessel). But the advantages of having true steam-warships, and the need to have a counter to the apparent French threat, seem to have been decisive, and in 1844–5 the Royal Navy went ahead with a large screw-fleet, paddle-vessel construction greatly declining.

Essentially two types of screw resulted from the construction programme. The first was the screw-cruiser, designed to patrol the sea lanes in the way that the sailing-frigates and sloops had done. The second was a more radical type—one that had the temerity to touch on the sail of the line itself. This was a type that originally was designed for harbour defence and, appropriately enough, had been proposed by a mixed services commission on harbours of refuge and home fortifications. This body had been set up in August 1842 at the suggestion of the Master of the Ordnance. By 1844 it had changed its personnel completely, and was headed by Sir Thomas Hastings, captain of the *Excellent*. Besides him were two army officers, one an artilleryman, the other an engineer. Their

---

[15] E. C. Smith, *A Short History of Naval and Marine Engineering* (CUP, 1938), ch. 5. Frank M. Bennett, *The Steam Navy of the United States: A History of the Growth of the Steam Vessel of War in the US Navy, and of the Naval Engineer Corps* (Pittsburgh, Penn. 1896), 62–4. Spencer C. Tucker, 'US Navy Steam Sloop *Princeton*', *American Neptune*, 69/2 (1989), 96–113.

report, forwarded to Peel in November 1844, set out a plan for the conversion of some battleships and frigates into screw-steamers. The vessels were to act as mobile harbour batteries for the defence of the Thames and the South Coast, and were to be constantly at readiness, in case of a French *coup de main* in the early stages of a war before the navy could be fully mobilized.[16]

In the event, in August 1845 four battleships—the *Blenheim, Hogue, Ajax,* and *Edinburgh*—were authorized for conversion to steam. The type was not entirely novel. During the War of 1812–15 the US Navy had built the *Demologos*, from the design of Robert Fulton. She was a powerful vessel for the time, with a heavy armament and a paddle-wheel operating between her twin hulls. But she was a moveable battery, not a seagoing battleship.[17] The four British conversions were enormous improvements. They were called 'blockships', somewhat inaccurately, since the term had previously applied to unseaworthy vessels, moored to defend a harbour. Perhaps the word expressed much of the original intention for the *Blenheim* and her sisters, but they eventually showed themselves to be far more capable than first thought.

Their steam-engines gave them great tactical power, but they could carry coal for only three to four days continuous steaming. Fortunately, they retained a great deal of the original design. Admittedly, the storage capacity had been slashed to make room for the steam machinery and coal bunkers, thus cutting endurance under sail. The amount of canvas was also somewhat reduced, but the blockships remained reasonably handy under sail alone, and still had a certain strategic capacity, meaning that they were eventually able to undertake duties far wider than those envisaged originally. It finally became clear that the blockships were not so much steam-batteries as the first of the new type of capital ship—the screw line-of-battleship or, as they were often called, screw-liners.[18]

But this discovery came some years after the original decision to convert. Technical difficulties ensured that the first of the four to go to sea—the *Blenheim*—showed her true qualities only in 1848.

---

[16] Parker, *Peel*, iii. 211. Norman Gash, *Sir Robert Peel* (London, 1972), 524. Hastings' Commission Report, 'Coast Defence' vol., ADM 1 5543. Haddington (First Lord) to Peel, 18 June 1845, Peel Papers, Add. MS 40458, fos. 76–9.

[17] *Jane's Fighting Ships, 1914* (London, 1914), 465 ff.

[18] Peel to Haddington, 25 June and 11 Aug. 1845, Peel Papers, Add. MS 40458, fos. 92–3, 159. Corry to Peel, 8 Sept. 1845, Add. MS 40573, fos. 352–7. PP (1847–8), xxi. pt. 1, p. 263.

The original intention was that the blockships should be ready by May 1846, and then to fulfil a specific and narrow task, to act as the last line of naval defence of the South Coast. As Peel saw it, with the blockships fortifying the harbours, and the screw-cruisers sweeping the Channel, Britain would be safe from all but minor predatory attacks.[19]

The technical problems met by the blockships were part of a larger difficulty, typical of technological innovation. The screw-cruisers met similar problems. The best forms for the hull and screw were long debated, and there were many trials, often crudely empirical. Another question concerned the proper horsepower for a given tonnage; that is, what relative value one should give to steam as against sail. High coal consumption and poor mechanical reliability made it impossible to rely only on steam-power. For most of a cruise, a screw-vessel had to depend on her canvas, which led in turn to another question, concerning the best way of dealing with the screw when it was not needed. One answer—adopted by some French designers—was simply to disconnect the screw from its shaft, and let it revolve as it willed (the *hélice affolée*). But the favourite solution in Britain was to equip warships with screw-wells and screws that could be raised from the water. The idea was simple, but posed even more questions of its own, notably concerning the solidity of the vessel aft. This was typical: each solution appeared to lead only to new problems. British naval architects faced a vast task in attempting to design the first screw-warfleet. Yet it was one they thought had to be dealt with quickly, to defend a vulnerable country. Foreign powers did not have quite the same reasons for haste.

Meanwhile, the Royal Navy did gain a definite lead in screw-propulsion. The Admiralty had reacted boldly, though not too boldly (with the exception of some orders for iron-hulled screws that, time suggested, were perhaps not fully effective warships[20]). The ruling idea had been to retain as much as possible of the endurance of the sailing fleet, at least with regard to the screw-cruisers. As the Board realized, these vessels had to defend not just the Channel but also the country's far-flung colonies and exten-sive maritime communications and trade links. Thus it had been believed that in fitting the screw one should as far as possible leave intact those sailing-vessel characteristics that gave strategic 'reach'

[19] Peel to Haddington, 24 Aug. 1845, Peel Papers, Add. MS 40458, fos. 169–70.
[20] Brown, *Before the Ironclad*, 82–98.

—spread of canvas and storage space for victuals and water. The screw-cruisers might have to be detached on distant service, or need the capacity to endure lengthy blockade operations off the French coast: their design consequently showed a balance that favoured endurance rather than steam-power.

One sees the kind of vessels produced, and the Admiralty attitude towards steam at this time, in one report of 1847 and the Board comments on it. The report came from Commander Moorman, captain of the *Rattler*. He was very proud of his ship, and thought her excellent under canvas alone, but was more interested in her performance under steam. He reported that she was more effective than a paddle-vessel in steaming against a head-wind, but argued she was underpowered since she was faster under sail and steam combined than under steam alone. This was heresy, and one of the Naval Lords noted that the *Rattler* should not have been forced against a head-wind, even as an experiment, since that strained the machinery and consumed much fuel. As to the vessel having too little power, the reply was that the ship's superior qualities under sail and steam showed one should *not* increase the horsepower. The Board much preferred seeing a delay in a war-ship's passage due to the boilers not being fired, than have her arrive at a battle only to be crippled by lack of coal.[21]

At this point, nothing better than *bâtiments mixtes* were wanted in the screw programme, as against *bâtiments à vapeur*, where steam-power was more important than sail. It appears that the Admiralty had not so much appreciated the potential of steam, as attempted to make use of its then state of development to answer a specific French threat. However, more boldness was to come, thanks to the way the British construction effort spurred the French to treat steam-power with greater seriousness. This eventually took the form of a conscious attempt not merely to counter the rival's preparations, but to overleap them technologically, thus giving a new twist to Anglo-French naval rivalry.

II

The Ministry of Marine was not immediately prompted to radical steps. The fine sailing fleet that had been built up during the Syrian

[21] Moorman's report of 30 Aug. 1847; comments 28 Sept.; ADM 95 20.

crisis was for long seen as the ideal of naval power, and French naval officers showed the same kind of conservative attitudes one finds amongst their opposite numbers in Britain. For example, the captain of the paddle-vessel *Phénix* was treated little better than Captain Moorman had been. At a meeting of the *Conseil des travaux* in 1850 there was praise for the steamer captains who used their canvas when they could. But the captain of the *Phénix* did not impress. He had replied to some criticism of his coal-burning habits by saying that he acted with economy in view, hoping to arrive at ports in time to benefit from the tide. The council commented acidly that one could get the same profit from delaying under sail as from racing under steam.[22]

Yet even well before this meeting, powerful influences were at work on the French navy that were to make steam—and the costs of steam—appear less unpalatable.

One of these was the great British defence effort from 1844. As is common in military and naval rivalry, defensive measures by one side were seen as primarily offensive by the other. The whole system of steamers and harbours of refuge, backed by a network of telegraph and railway lines, was seen in Whitehall as a shield rather than a sword. To some French observers this was simple hypocrisy. Charles Dupin, a naval engineer and an acknowledged expert on England, spoke of 'la création de nouveaux ports d'aggression, ou, si l'on veut, de défense et de refuge . . .'; and described the projected and existing ports as forming a great chain, a means of concentrating troops and ships and despatching them to the French coast in seven hours at the most. In February 1845 a M. Gervaize, then a *sous-ingénieur* in the French navy, having just visited England for ten weeks, sent an elaborate description of the new ports to the prince de Joinville. Gervaize also saw a chain, adding that it was admirably suited to the requirements of the powerfully armed and fast but short-ranged steamers of the Royal Navy. (He was speaking only of the paddlers.) His conception of the role of the British steam fleet in war was scarcely different from that of Dupin's: 'Colonnes mobiles toujours prêtes à protéger son commerce, à inquiéter nos côtes, se reliant toutes les unes aux autres et pouvant au premier signal se porter avec rapidité sur un même point.'[23]

---

[22] Meeting of the *Conseil des travaux*, 7 Aug. 1850, V BB8 1127, 123–7.

[23] *Annales maritimes et coloniales*, non-official pt., 91 (Paris, 1845), pt. II, pp. 622–39.

We have to consider also the galvanizing effect on French naval planning of the series of diplomatic crises mentioned in Section I. Also important is one affair not noted so far, since it had far greater impact in France than in Britain, possessing direct significance for French naval development. The question at issue was the reciprocal right of search allowed to French and British warships respecting suspected slavers sailing under the two countries' flags. This right had been first agreed in the conventions of 1831 and 1833; and in 1841 a similar convention was drawn up between five powers, including Britain and France. Unfortunately, only two months before the signing, an RN warship had been maladroit in the way it seized a French merchantman, the *Marabout*, making the whole question of interference with the French flag at sea a very sensitive one. Similar seizures in the 1830s had generated only local incidents but, probably thanks to the wounding of French maritime pride in 1839–40, the *Marabout* case caused a furore in Paris. Many Frenchmen appear to have regarded this case as more evidence of a systematic persecution by the old tyrant of the sea. Their anger was further fuelled by an agreement on the slave-trade between Washington and London in August 1842, which did not include the right of search, thus suggesting that it was not necessary. Moreover, there were reports that filtered through to Europe later that year, showing that slaves freed by RN patrols were being sent as workers to British colonies, ensuring the latter's labour supply at the same time as checking the supply to the colonies of other nations. In the face of all this evidence, Anglophobia was the only rational prejudice: the Chamber could not bring itself to ratify the 1841 convention, and Guizot had to patch up a compromise, without the right of search, in 1845.[24]

Another set of factors to be considered is internal in nature, not external. The 1840s were an awkward and generally embarrassing time for the Orleanist naval administration. There was a whole series of mishaps and disasters during the 1840s which sapped the French navy's morale. The periodic riots of the naval cadets at Brest were almost comic interludes, easily overshadowed by such incidents as the discovery in 1845 of a seething mass of administrative

[24] Lawrence C. Jennings, 'France, Great Britain, and the Repression of the Slave Trade, 1841–1845', *French Historical Studies*, 10/1 (1977), 101–25. André-Jean Tudesq, *Les Grands Notables en France (1840–1849): étude historique d'une psychologie sociale* (2 vols., Paris, 1964), ii, book II, ch. 4.

corruption at the arsenal of Rochefort, and the great fire at Toulon in August which destroyed millions of francs worth of buildings and naval stores.

If the administration appeared to be defective, so too did the *matériel*. The steamers often broke down, and there were serious doubts about their seaworthiness and that of the small sailing-warships. During 1845–6 no fewer than ten royal ships were lost at sea, five steam and five sail. The former tended to get stranded on rocks and shoals; the latter had a penchant for sinking un-expectedly, sometimes without the poor excuse of bad weather. Other powers had similar problems, notably with their small, fast sailing-vessels, in whose construction much had been sacrificed for speed, and which were badly over-rigged. The US navy, for instance, built five especially speedy brigs in the 1840s, the *Somers*, *Bainbridge*, *Truxton*, *Lawrence*, and *Perry*, two of which capsized in squalls (and there was an embarrassing mutiny on a third, encour-aged by the cramped conditions).[25] Even so, the French navy had an unenviable record of sinkings during this decade.

The prince de Joinville must also be mentioned in this catalogue of woe. We have noted the effects his 1844 pamphlet had on British opinion, but the work also encouraged dissatisfaction in France with the French navy. He suggested a bright future, but also stressed that at the time of writing the French paddle fleet was notably inferior to the British one. Moreover, he raised the fear in some circles in France that the British would steal the Prince's petard and take advantage of their existing steam superiority to blow up the French coastline. Charles Baudin, by now *préfet mari-time* at Toulon, and one of the country's most respected admirals, was but one of those who anticipated an English attack at almost any moment, and criticized the Prince (who had served under him) for giving good ideas to the enemy. Baudin could equally well have quoted now the words of Fontenelle that he once threw at the head of another young officer who had had some bright ideas on naval warfare, and who wanted to publish them: 'Si j'avais la main pleine de vérités, je ne l'ouvrirais pas.'[26]

Joinville was also involved in an incident that reflected badly on the French navy's preparedness for war. In April 1846 he arrived at

[25] S. E. Morison, *'Old Bruin', Commodore Matthew C. Perry* (OUP, 1968), 144.
[26] Private letters of 22 Dec. 1841 and 1 Sept. 1844, letter book 1841–4, Baudin Papers, AN GG2 15 (*marine*).

Brest by land, hoping to proceed to Le Havre by steamer. He had not been expected, but rather naturally anticipated that France's second military port would have a vessel available. But there were no steamers at all. The Prince was just about to leave by land when the war steamer *Canada* came into port: unfortunately this did not save the day and the navy's reputation, because there was not enough coal in the great arsenal's steamer stores to fuel the ship for even twenty-four hours. The depots of the victualling service had to be scoured so that Joinville could get to sea. The incident caused much political fury.[27]

One ought not to paint the picture in too uniformly sombre a tone. There were the occasional naval glories. In the otherwise black year of 1839 a squadron under Charles Baudin bombarded and captured the Mexican fortress of St-Juan d'Ulloa. In 1845 there was the forcing of the Argentinian batteries on the River Parana at Obligado by an Anglo-French force. Much of the acclaim went to Captain Tréhouart, the senior French officer, who led the main attack with great dash, and whose white hair, standing out in the fight, earned him the title of *el pelo blanco*. And there were those other French *coups* near this time, the bombardment of Tangier's fortifications and the taking of Mogador by Joinville's squadron.

Contemporaries, though, tended to look on the pessimistic side. The Chamber of Deputies in particular was prone to be gloomy about the navy. One tendency was to believe that vast sums were lost through inefficiency and even corruption. The Deputies were influenced by their generally bad opinion of the state administration. The Teste–Cubières affair of 1847, resulting from the crooked financial manœuvres of two ministers, was only the best known of a series of cases that seemed to show that something was rotten in the regime as a whole. In this context, naval scandals could appear very sinister—above all the corruption uncovered at Rochefort. It was not understood that the discovery was a sign of administrative health, for the peculations had been discovered by agents of the *Contrôle* (audit), re-established as a separate section in June 1844 and ending the attempt made in 1835 to fuse inspection and administration. Rochefort was evidence that the organization of the Ministry of Marine was moving in the right direction. But few gave

---

[27] Yves Le Gallo, *Brest et sa bourgeoisie sous la monarchie de juillet* (2 vols., Paris, 1968), i. 154–8.

weight to the means of discovery: the corruption itself was too fascinating and suggestive.[28]

There was also a basic misunderstanding about the costs of naval change. Neither in France nor in Britain did the parliaments understand why naval credits could go up and up and the number of warships in commission decline. They could not comprehend the expense brought by the increasing size of warships and the coming of steam. One finds even Sir Robert Peel asking somewhat incredulously in 1844 why, when the navy absorbed more money and men than ever before in peacetime, there were fewer available ships of the line.

Steam was particularly expensive. The annual upkeep of a twenty-six gun sailing-corvette such as HMS *Cleopatra* was only £13,404, but it cost no less than £30,145 to maintain a large paddle-steamer of sixteen guns like the *Penelope*—including over £6,000 for coals.[29] One of the few ways to compensate for the added costs, without depriving the fleets of the now vital power of steam, was severely to limit the number of large sailing-warships in commission—though the foreign offices hardly welcomed this when they looked around in a crisis for a battlefleet.

Another expense of a steam navy was the necessary development of appropriate facilities in the dockyards. The French navy's needs were greatest here, due to the fact that the nation's private industry could not supply heavy castings, machinery, and boilers to the standards of British private manufacturers. The state had to compensate. During the 1840s, some eleven million francs were spent on establishing steam factories at Cherbourg, Brest, Lorient, and Rochefort; and there were preliminary studies for a great facility at Castigneau, alongside the existing arsenal at Toulon. Furthermore, there was a great state factory at Indret, an island in the Loire. The quality of its products became high; but the establishment was costly, two and a half million francs being spent in the 1840s alone on new plant and machinery there.[30] However,

[28] C. Châtelain, 'Le Contrôle de l'administration de la marine devant l'opinion publique et devant le parlement', *Revue maritime et coloniale*, 156–9 (1903), 660 f.

[29] Sir George Seymour, 'Notes on Naval Policy as a member of the Board of Admiralty, 1841–1844', Seymour Papers, CR 114 A 409. 334–5.

[30] J. Cros, *Considérations sur le matériel de notre flotte: améliorations à introduire dans le régime de nos arsenaux* (Paris, 1850), 48. J. A. Babron and J. Turgan, 'Les Établissements impériaux de la marine française: Indret', *Revue maritime et coloniale*, 23 (1868), 123–43; 24 (1868), pp. 494–526.

the Chamber remained generally unconvinced that great sums should be spent on state manufactures. As in Britain at the time, government enterprise was thought to be synonymous with extravagance. The state was urged to rely on private enterprise. The *Enquête parlementaire sur la Marine*, set up in 1849, proposed strongly that Indret should be shut, and the work continued in the private sector. The Chamber, before and after the 1848 revolution, did not want precious naval credits 'locked up' in support facilities: they wanted a larger warfleet. Perhaps they could not be expected to realize that their country was slowly building up the means necessary for the construction of a large and technologically advanced steam fleet.

The willingness of many in the Chamber to believe the worst of the naval administration was, up to 1847 at least, in part due to a matter of personal sympathy. Parliaments' understanding of naval affairs often seems to be more influenced by their opinion of the naval representatives in their midst than by strictly professional matters; and, unfortunately for the French navy, the Minister of Marine between 1843 and 1847 was Vice-Admiral de Mackau, one of the long line of *ministres-amiraux* who ruled *la Royale* during most of the period 1800–70. Military or naval men, brought up as they are in hierarchical and closely ordered organizations, are usually clumsy and ill at ease in democratic assemblies, but Mackau was more clumsy than most. He all too often infuriated when he should have soothed, even when dealing with the King, and irritated the deputies by blatantly regarding their opinions on the navy as both inexpert and amateurish. Therefore he could appear both maladroit and insufferable. Just one example is his reply when asked why so many steamers had run aground: the reason he gave was the very perfection of French naval design, arguing that commanding officers were led by over-confidence into taking unjustified risks. The deputies' response was not constructive: angry men are not partial to ingenious paradoxes.[31] As so often with Mackau, there was an element of truth in what he said, but it was presented in so curious a way, and so carelessly and superciliously, that it satisfied few, and encouraged a dark view of the naval administration.

[31] Debate of 8 May 1847, Le Gallo, *Brest et sa bourgeoisie*, i. 148–9.

However, it is perhaps not of great importance that poor under-standing, or undue significance being attached to secondary matters, led to too sombre a view being taken of the state of the French navy. Whether well or inadequately based, dissatisfaction ultimately had the same effect—to encourage greater naval pre-paredness and greater boldness in French naval policy. Notably, despite doubts about the naval administration, the Chamber was generous with credits—surely a sign of the seriousness with which the rivalry with England was taken. In one of his extended histor-ical speeches, Thiers contrasted the positions of the Ministers of War and of Marine: the former regularly had his budgets cut, but the latter sometimes had extra funds thrust at him. This happened in 1843, Thiers commenting: 'Voilà comme on le traite! On a exigé, malgré ses refus, que trois millions fussent ajoutés à son budget!'[32]

By 1846 the Chamber was showing itself willing to vote a very large sum to be used for naval construction over several years. This provided the resources that would make possible a radical step in French naval policy.

The grant came through the famous Law of Ninety-Three Millions, providing thirteen million francs a year to be spent on new naval construction for seven years, over and above the normal budget. It was intended that the money would make it possible to realize the royal ordinance of February 1837, which had ex-tended the establishment of the fleet, but not made provision for the added cost. Mackau had originally asked for 93,100,000 francs, and a Chamber commission had suggested reducing the total to 73,000,000. But the Chamber as a whole restored al-most all the total requested and, what is more striking, voted it unanimously.

The new law encouraged technological innovation in two ways. First, obviously enough, it made the necessary funds available. But the initial use of the enlarged budget was hesitant, and this was important in convincing at least some naval authorities that enough was enough; that the time had come for bold action. They had become frustrated at the decision of the Ministry in 1846–7 to con-centrate funds on well-proved types and not on screws. Admittedly, the first French screw experiments had often been discouraging.

[32] *Annales du parlement français* (Paris, 1846), viii. 573–5, 592, 620.

The despatch vessel *Napoléon* (or *Corse*, as she will be known hereafter), was a success; but she did not have a significant armament. The first true French screw-warship was the *Pomone*, a converted sailing-frigate. She was sent to sea as a *frégate mixte* in August 1846, but her steering was found to be so faulty that she had to return to her builders, and did not go to sea again until May 1848. Then there was the *Chaptal*, the first French screw-warship built as such from the keel up. She was launched in 1845 and went on her first trials two years later. There were some breakdowns during those trials, and the vessel became notorious when she crossed the Atlantic in 1848, suffering from excessive vibration and the fracture of her propeller shaft. But whatever the teething troubles of French screws, it still seems curious how heavily the construction programmes of 1845–7 were weighted in favour of sailing-, and paddle-vessels. The concept set out in the Law of Ninety-Three Millions was of a principally sailing fleet, with only 100 steamers as against 226 sailing-warships. In the event, rather more steamers were begun than the law prescribed. But these were almost all paddle-vessels. Taking the period 1845 to 1847, and thus including some construction approved when the budget was more stringent, no fewer than twenty-five paddle-vessels of assorted tonnages were laid down, and over twenty sailing-vessels, the latter including five frigates of forty-two to fifty-six guns laid down as late as 1847. The screw hardly figured at all. By 1844 work was in progress on five; all but the *Pomone* were small iron-hulled vessels of but two to four guns. Only six more were begun over the following three years: five of these were iron, thus leaving only one 'real' warship, the *Roland* of eight guns. The proportions in the Ministry's construction programme clearly appear wrong, and more so than can be explained by a prudent desire to see how the costly British screw experiments were progressing before committing themselves too far.[33]

One could argue that the new construction grants had to be spent, or they might well have been lost; so proven—if obsolescent —types continued to be approved. But this is hindsight. At the

[33] I have argued elsewhere that one reason for the continuing French attachment to the paddle warship was the way that the prince de Joinville's 1844 pamphlet popularized certain naval questions, and helped freeze the terms of debate on fleet development: 'The Diplomatic and Naval Effects of the prince de Joinville's *Note sur l'état des forces navales de la France* of 1844', *Historical Journal*, 32/3 (1989), 675–87.

time, the Ministry was satisfied with its programme, and was not
fully aware of the significance of the latest British construction. It
was not until late 1847 that true concern grew in the Ministry over
the rival's new fleet. The change seems to have come with the
delivery of a report of 21 September from M. Moll, a respected
naval engineer. He had just been across the Channel, and had been
astounded at the progress made. He reported that no fewer than
thirty-nine screw-warships were on the stocks or completed, comprising a wide range of types. The largest type was the blockship,
and there were also many cruising vessels, from the *Amphion* and
Arrogant (*frégates mixtes*, like the *Pomone*), down to smaller and
faster frigates and sloops. Finally, there was a group of screw gun-
vessels which carried only a few cannon.[34]

Moll's report was not an entirely accurate account of the fleet
that the Royal Navy was to have. He included some vessels soon to
be cancelled, and also four frigates with iron hulls, the *Simoom*,
Vulcan, *Megaera*, and *Greenock*: doubts about their battle worthiness
were to lead to the last being sold, and the rest being down-rated
to transports with weaker engines replacing the powerful ones
originally designated. Moll could scarcely be blamed for failing to
foresee such developments, but he was to blame in the way he
tended to over-simplify the fleet he saw in preparation, trying to
fit all the vessels into only five categories. He implied that the
Admiralty had proceeded according to a consistent construction
plan. Actually, the screw-fleet had been created in a piecemeal
fashion. This was made clear in another report by a French engineer, M. Forquenot, some two years later. His visit to Britain had
shown him that there was no comprehensive plan: the English, he
said with some truth, had built one experimental ship after the
other, proceeding by chance.[35] Ultimately, however, Forquenot's
point was immaterial. Even if it was a fleet of samples, the British
screw-fleet remained a great and unequalled naval force. The Ministry of Marine came to accept how far in advance the Admiralty had
progressed. It proved to be the last straw for the French when
added to the years of diplomatic disappointment and humiliation,
and the frequent accusations about the incompetence and corruption of the naval administration.

---

[34] AN BB8 876 (*marine*), 165–9.
[35] *Note sur l'état actuel du matériel de la marine anglaise* (31 Mar. 1849), Mackau
Papers, 156 AP 1 36, dossier 6.

III

It is in the nature of nineteenth-century naval archives that they rarely provide one with expositions of general policy. Sometimes this is due simply to the destruction of crucial papers, occasionally thanks to damp rot, more usually to over-zealous weeding. We have, for example, no adequate minutes for the meetings of the Board of Admiralty in our period. But when accounts of planning meetings do survive, one often finds only a mass of technical detail, since that was all that was discussed. In other cases, it appears that the very process of noting the important debating statements, and their arrangement into a harmonious and copperplate whole, has leached away much of general and human significance. For instance, the secretaries responsible for the minutes tended to gloss over or ignore the professional reminiscence, even anecdotage, that enlivened many meetings of naval committees and boards in Paris and London. But, more important, the minutes usually do not report the broad reasoning behind proposed measures. Certain expectations might not have needed to be mentioned in a meeting since they were, at the time, obvious to all; and if they had been uttered the secretary might well have felt that such truths did not require noting.

Occasionally the historian is more fortunate, and in the minutes of two sessions of the *Conseil d'amirauté*, on 2 and 6 November 1847, he finds material that appears to retain some of the flavour of the meetings and much of the broad argument. This material also helps support what was said in the previous section about the consequences of the French naval frustrations of the 1840s.

The main speaker was baron Tupinier, a very senior and highly regarded naval engineer, and a veteran of the Ministry of Marine: he had been *directeur des ports et arsenaux* between 1824 and 1842 (Tramond and Reussner go so far as to call him the real minister of those years[36]). He was reporting on a new plan; one which, he argued, gave France a great opportunity. Since the coming of steam, he said, the French navy had been scarcely able to keep its place, and had merely followed behind as the Royal Navy forged

---

[36] Joannès Tramond and André Reussner, *Eléments d'histoire maritime et coloniale contemporaine (1815–1914)* (Paris, 1947), 20–1.

ahead. The English, he accepted, had enormous advantages; besides the royal dockyards they possessed large private shipyards and engineering works, and also had the world's largest mercantile navy—all excellent foundations for a steam war navy. France was much less well-endowed. Thanks to this fact, French steam-vessels so far had been only the results of imitation, although often very good in themselves, and equal or superior to the originals. 'Mais faut-il', he went on, 'que toujours notre marine reste à la traine et qu'elle se borne à suivre de loin les progrès que les marines rivales doivent à l'esprit entreprenant du commerce de leur pays?' This was the kernel of the discussion as he saw it; for with a new plan at hand, one of a steam-battleship, a *vaisseau à vapeur*, a type that no state as yet possessed, France could finally take the lead: 'Cette gloire a certainement son mérite et pour l'obtenir on peut s'imposer des sacrifices avec d'autant plus de résolution qu'ils seraient largement compensés si l'entreprise était couronnée de succès.' The English, he admitted, could soon overtake France in the construction of the new type of warship once they had heard about it, for their financial and industrial resources were so much larger. But at least they would be following the French for once, and that would be a great deal.

For all the persuasiveness of the Baron's arguments, the unusual expense and ambitious nature of the proposed new ship meant that there was bound to be some opposition in the council. The *sous-secrétaire d'état*, M. Jubelin, a naval administrator only a few years junior to Tupinier, was obviously perturbed: he intervened during the discussion to suggest, in an eloquent bureaucratic way, that there would be inconveniences in building and experimenting on too great a scale. But Tupinier had a yet more serious opponent, his fellow Baron and veteran, and almost as noted a naval engineer, the savant, politician, and industrious writer, Charles Dupin. He had long been an observer of industrial and naval Britain, and in 1820 had published nine volumes entitled *Force militaire de la Grande Bretagne*.

Dupin resented the strength that he saw over the Channel and, as is often the way in rivalry, regarded what he disliked as something of a model. He thought the best policy for France was what Tupinier took so much objection to — imitation. As the council had only recently been reminded by M. Moll, the old rival was continuing to build up its *bâtiments mixtes*; to Dupin, therefore, the proposed *vaisseau à vapeur* was very unwise, and he urged his colleagues not to approve it. He wanted vessels with more than the two months' provisions allowed in the plan, and with engines of half the size—about equal to those fitted in the blockships. In other words, he wanted a battleship with a wide radius of action under sail, and only auxiliary steam-power. Dupin and Tupinier were far apart, and their meeting in council must have been an interesting sight: the rather staid and reactionary authority looking across the table at what was very probably the irritating sight of a slightly older, and scarcely less experienced man, who was agreeing with the navy's young and dangerous innovators. The two were unlikely to influence each other's opinions, and after one stage in the argument, when Dupin had ranged himself firmly on one side and Tupinier had been joined on the other by M. Boucher, the then *directeur des ports et arsenaux*, it is difficult not to find a touch of sarcasm in the secretary's comment in the minutes, 'Chacun des honorables membres persiste dans son première opinion.'[37]

Although the fight was tough, in the end the council approved the new plan. However, this alone did not necessarily decide the matter. Unlike the Board of Admiralty, the *Conseil d'amirauté* was simply an advisory body. The Minister of Marine was responsible for all decisions. The *Conseil d'amirauté* was not even the only advisory body on construction policy. There was also the *Conseil des travaux*—which, the previous May, had been distinctly chilly towards the *vaisseau à vapeur*. But powerful forces were at work behind the scenes. The prince de Joinville had earlier become interested, and tried to get the Ministry to act boldly. He had intervened in May 1847 when Mackau had resigned and Guizot—with whom the Prince had long been friendly—took over as interim minister. The Prince urged him to take advantage of his temporary powers, so that the navy could rise 'au dessus des vieux préjugés et des craintes de la responsabilité'. Mackau, he wrote, would have appointed a commission that would have modified the plan, so discouraging the designer and wasting time. But through

[37] Meetings of 2 and 8 Nov. 1847, AN BB8 876 (*marine*), 150–77, 193–9. If Dupin had mixed feelings about England, some Britons were sure about their opinion of him. During the 1830s George Villiers, later Lord Clarendon, called him 'that prince of jackasses', and Dr John Bowring wrote that he was 'vain, shallow and spiteful', B. M. Ratcliffe, 'Great Britain and Tariff Reform in France, 1831–6', *Trade and Transport: Essays in Economic History in Honour of T. S. Willan* (Manchester University Press, 1977).

the stroke of Guizot's pen the ship could be laid down at Toulon, the engines begun at Indret, and the vessel completed within the year.

Guizot was enthusiastic. He replied: 'Une belle idée à appliquer, un jeune ingénieur distingué à encourager et V[otre] A[ltesse] R[oyale] à seconder, j'accepte volontiers cette responsabilité là.' The project, he said, would be sent off to the *Conseil des travaux* at once, examined that day, approved in principle, and the orders sent out the following day so that the ship could be begun without delay. The Prince had judged his man correctly, but the actual events fell short of what was promised. For one thing, it was now that the *Conseil des travaux* chilled the plan, raising doubts about the size and nature of the proposed engines, suggesting the plans be returned to the designer for revision. Guizot did not have much time to impose his fiat, but was soon replaced by the duc de Montebello, the permanent appointee, who, though he was to prove a supporter of the project, was not the enthusiastic convert that Guizot had been. Whatever chance there had been for building the ship in a year vanished. But Joinville did not remain idle, and the men in the Ministry—like Boucher—who agreed with him were presumably active in lobbying their colleagues, some of whom perhaps only needed a breathing space to accustom themselves to the battleship of the future. By the time the *Conseil des travaux* again discussed the scheme, on 14 July, the tone was much warmer. It accepted then that work should go ahead, albeit only as an experiment. Then, in November, came Tupinier's victory in the other council. The final act came when Montebello, who had participated in the November meetings of the *Conseil d'amirauté*, accepted the recommendations, and the vessel was laid down on 7 February 1848.[38]

A delay of even three weeks more, and the laying down would have been upset by the revolution that swept Louis-Philippe out and the Second Republic in. As it was, the construction was delayed by the drying up of construction funds, due to the emergency. The revolution also encouraged labour troubles: as late as 1851 strikes and absenteeism at Indret seriously impeded work on the engines, ensuring that the ship could not be got ready for sea until the following year.[39] And the vessel was hindered,

[38] Joinville to Guizot, May 1847, and the reply of 26 May, Guizot Papers, 42 AP 190, letters 4 and 4 *bis*. Correspondence relative to the *Napoléon*, 1847 and 1848, V 7DD1 143.   [39] Report of 6 Dec. 1852, V 7DD1 143.

paradoxically, by the revolution not bringing sufficient change, not sweeping away more of the conservative administrators at the Ministry. Before and after 1848 the *Conseil des travaux* pressed for a geared engine to be fitted, not the lighter and cheaper direct-acting machine preferred by the designer. There was also a dispute over the method of fitting the screw. The council wanted a screw-well to be fitted, as in the British *bâtiments mixtes*. The designer much preferred an *hélice affolée*. The latter, he said, offered little obstruction to the flow of the water. Moreover, he believed a well seriously weakened the stern, and sneered (at least in private) at the English system and its *boutique de l'arrière*. He won this fight, at least on the prototype *vaisseau à vapeur*, but had to submit over the geared engines. At the cost of further annoying delay, he had to revise his plans to save the extra weight that the gearing demanded.

The delays, and the continuing arguments, ought not to disguise the way that, in the years after her laying down, the new ship was becoming more acceptable in naval and governmental circles. The radicals in the Second Republic saw reflected in the ship their own revolutionary attitudes, as is suggested by the names suggested for her in April 1848 — *Vengeur*, *Redoutable*, *Républicain*, and the stirring one that for a time was actually chosen, the *Vingt-Quatre Février*. But all Frenchmen interested in naval affairs were capable of appreciating her qualities, not just those on the left. For the design was brilliant, the product of the best naval architect of his day, Dupuy de Lôme. He was still only thirty in 1847, a *sous-ingénieur* at Toulon, and had a long and distinguished career in front of him. His ship, of course, was the *Napoléon*, the name finally chosen for the launching on 16 May 1850, replacing one that seemed too unsettling and evocative of tumult to the staid men now running the Second Republic. The new name was also appropriate, given that Louis-Napoleon Bonaparte was now President and soon to be Emperor. (Naturally, neither the old nor the new name appeared wholly appropriate to the by now exiled prince de Joinville, whom Dupuy de Lôme thought of as his ship's godfather. Fortunately, the Prince was more amused than annoyed by the various christenings of his *gros filleul*.)[40]

[40] Dupuy de Lôme to the prince de Joinville, 20 Sept. 1849, Joinville Papers, 300 AP III 114, dossier 1.

Much of the appeal of the new vessel lay in its great steam-power. This was no mere coastal battery, but a ninety-gun line-of-battleship whose prime motive power was steam. The sail area was large, but was still somewhat less than normal, being only slightly greater than that of an eighty-gun sail of the line. Her engines, though, were of 900 hp, and in a *mémoire* submitted to the Ministry of Marine in April 1847, Dupuy de Lôme predicted that a speed of at least ten knots could be expected under steam. In fact, he expected more, and rightly so; on trials the vessel perhaps attained over thirteen knots. But he had kept his estimate low, in case he aroused too much incredulity.

The obvious disadvantage in the design was that, due to the powerful engines, there was not space for more than two months' supply of water and provisions. Nor could coal for more than ten days' steaming be stowed. But, in return—and while the coal lasted —there was a superior steam speed. Even ten knots was more than most screw-warships at this time could hope to attain under steam alone, and was nearly twice what the blockships were normally capable of. This was a precious asset, and appeared to make certain operations feasible. As Dupuy de Lôme suggested in his *mémoire*, a number of *vaisseaux à vapeur* could wage a potent *guerre de course* against the English, being able to catch even fast mail steamers.[41] Also, they would put England's numerical superiority in warships at a discount: for example, any blockade formed by *vaisseaux mixtes* could be penetrated by a few faster vessels. And once on the high seas, a fast squadron could choose its own time and opportunity to fight. Furthermore—and a very important point to the Ministry of Marine, which, with the exception of 1858–60, was also the colonial ministry during our period—fast battleships could ensure constant communications in a war between France and Algeria. As one flag officer said during the 8 November meeting of the *Conseil d'amirauté*, 'Coûte que coûte . . . il faut que nous assurer des communications promptes et que rien ne puisse empêcher avec nos possessions d'Afrique, si la guerre venait à éclater.'

The new design also promised one more thing. Dupuy de Lôme argued that the fast battleship would give the army a great new amphibious capability. At last the British Isles might be assaulted. Up to now, he said, steam descents on a hostile coast had been

[41] 1847, V 7DD1 143.

possible, but very dangerous to the attacker: a steam transport fleet could not be protected properly, since existing battleships could not keep up with it. Now all was changed: the *vaisseau à vapeur* could match any steam fleet in speed, and hold its own against any enemy vessel. As he might have gone on to argue: with his ships the 'steam bridge' became a reality.

The project indeed appeared to be *multum in parvo*. One of its strongest attractions was that in itself it promised the attainment of the majority of French naval policy aims. With the restricted room for supplies, and the great reliance on steam-power, the *Napoléon* was clearly designed primarily for operations within European waters, close to the facilities that were so rare in the world beyond. But this was not much of a disadvantage in French terms. There were always some far-reaching French aims, such as the protection of deep-sea shipping, or of the colonies, or—most far-reaching of all—the safeguarding of French prestige and the ensuring of what was called the 'freedom of the seas'. And the great fleet encounters of the eighteenth century in the Indian Ocean and North American waters were never entirely forgotten; hence the plans that were occasionally made in the Ministry for despatching battlefleets to distant stations. Nevertheless, as far as one can judge from the records of the time, often reading between the lines, the prime policy aims—which essentially meant the ones to be realized in case of a war with England—were almost entirely limited in scope to European waters. It was usually assumed that the battlefleets would be deployed only there. These prime aims were largely those that Dupuy de Lôme argued could be attained through his *vaisseaux à vapeur*. His *mémoire* omitted to mention only one obvious French naval requirement, the defence of the French coast and of French coastal shipping; only there was his design not well suited.

No wonder he had his supporters. But also, no wonder there were doubters, if for only one reason—the expense. The prototype was estimated to cost over four million francs, a million more than a first-rate ship of the line. Those with faith, such as Tupinier, had wanted several of the type to be laid down at once, so that a definite lead could be built up. But that was too rash to be adopted. The final decision about sister ships had to await the prototype trials. This meant, in theory, that the Admiralty might hear about the experiment, lay down several fast battleships of its own, and take all the glory—as well as retaining British naval mastery. This did not happen. French naval policy-makers could accept with comparative ease a vessel that was fast though relatively restricted in range. But, as the duc de Montebello realized, such a type was not equally attractive to a power with global interests. The Admiralty, with those interests in mind, had already decided to introduce the *bâtiment mixte*, and was bound to be out of sympathy with the new design. Indeed, even the Ministry of Marine might not have accepted it had the humiliations of the 1840s not given an extra stimulus. The 1840s, of course, had not been humiliating for the Royal Navy: rather the reverse. For whatever reason, the Admiralty was so out of sympathy with Dupuy de Lôme's design that its first reaction to it was incomprehension. A conscious attempt in France to keep the design secret meant it was not until 1850 that Sir Baldwin Walker—Symond's replacement as Surveyor—received the details, and he concluded that the vessel had to be a mistake. As we shall see in the following section, it proved difficult enough in the years after 1847 for the Admiralty to move closer to the *vaisseau mixte*, let alone the *vaisseau à vapeur*.

IV

It might well appear to us an obvious step for the Admiralty to combine the experience of converting sailing-battleships into steam-batteries with that of building screw cruisers, to produce screw-battleships of medium steam-power and as great a range as feasible. But the British battlefleet was not to be changed so easily. It was the last bastion of the pure sailing-warship, with the exception of the four blockships as yet unspoiled by noisy engines and belching, smutty funnels. There were aesthetic objections to change. And, crucially, there was a deep reluctance to take the chance of damaging what was seen as the prime support of British sea power. What could be tried on cruisers was yet too experimental for the line-of-battle. Even as advanced an officer as Captain Spencer Robinson—a future Controller of the Navy—said in 1847 that the sail of the line were Britain's strength:

they carry overwhelming batteries, large complements, vast resources of all kinds; and are independent for many months of any supplies but those which their great capacity enables them to carry within themselves.[42]

[42] Spencer Robinson, *Observations on the Steam Ships of the Royal Navy* (London, 1847), 10–11.

It appeared that even a small sacrifice in stowage, to make room for a steam-engine and coals, might prejudice British sea power.

There was another important mark against steam-battleships, one hardly mentioned during the debates in France on the *Napoléon*, but common in British naval circles. This was the fear that steam-engines made screw-warships too vulnerable to enemy fire, even if not as much so as paddlers were. The machinery could be fitted below the waterline, but splinters or shot might still penetrate to it, with possibly appalling effect. Moreover, the mere shock of firing her own guns, it was anticipated by some, might damage the mechanisms below. Even a victorious battle could well mean extensive and difficult repair work, and this might be impossible if the fleet were far from the home dockyards. Sir Baldwin Walker argued in early 1848 that a battleship would be destroyed by being given screw machinery. He thought the country's lead in numbers of sail of the line was not sufficiently secure to make even some experimental conversions desirable. He and many other officers accepted that the battlefleet might well need the aid of steam, but thought primarily in terms of having a paddle-vessel assigned to each liner, to act as a tug if needed, or even to be lashed alongside its charge.

This does not mean that the Admiralty was quite deaf to progress. Indeed, for some time the Admiralty had been in the forefront of change. The advice of the Hastings Commission would hardly have been accepted so smoothly in 1845 had there not been important innovators within the naval administration. One must point first to the formidable Sir George Cockburn, First Naval Lord 1841–6. Unfortunately, there is little direct evidence of his enthusiasm for steam, but we know he so dominated the Board during Peel's ministry that we have to assume that he favoured striking innovation, despite occasional anecdotes that suggest a reactionary side. He was doubtless deeply conservative in social terms, but not, one would suggest, in his attitudes towards *matériel*. Another innovative naval officer at the Admiralty, this time one whose favour to screws is well documented, was Captain Alexander Ellice. He came after Cockburn, being appointed Controller of Steam Machinery in December 1846: not only did he press for screw cruisers, but was particularly eager to see the screw extended to the battlefleet. Then there was the very important civilian element on the Board. Perhaps with the exception of Cockburn, the civilians often showed themselves more willing than the Naval

Lords to introduce screw propulsion. One has to mention Sidney Herbert, First Secretary, September 1841 to February 1845, and H. T. Lowry Corry, Civil Lord whilst Herbert was Secretary, and his successor from 1845 to 1846. Admittedly the most important civilians on the Board, the First Lords, were generally less enthusiastic, with perhaps the exception of Lord Auckland, who held the office from 1846 until his early death at the beginning of 1849.

There was at least one steam Erewhonian at the Admiralty, in clear opposition to any radical tendency: that was Sir William Symonds. He retired in 1847, but a survey of evidence given before a Parliamentary Select Committee early the following year might well suggest that he left behind him some important colleagues almost as conservative as he was. It was now, for instance, that Walker spoke of the screw 'destroying' the sail of the line. John Edye, Walker's Chief Assistant and Draughtsman, inherited from Symonds, agreed with his new chief. His testimony included the somewhat startling suggestion that, thanks to their need for a well at the stern, ships fitted with the screw were more vulnerable to shot and shell than were paddle-vessels. This streak of pessimism continued on up to the Board. Lord John Hay, the Naval Lord responsible for the Surveyor's Department, also showed himself dubious about many aspects of the screw.[43]

Significantly, all three were to prove less resistant to change than their evidence suggests. Edye, for instance, had already designed a screw liner in 1846–7, and was to continue to serve under the new technological dispensation until retiring in late 1857. The three of them might have been reluctant to abandon the kind of battleship they had known all their professional lives, but they must be allowed credit for being willing to be convinced that even the battlefleet had to move with the times.

Their attitude was probably the predominant one at the Admiralty by late 1847 to early 1848, now that Cockburn, Herbert, and Corry had all gone. In the circumstances of the time, this was prudent; there was no threat that necessitated hasty action. The British had built up a great lead in *matériel*, qualitative as well as quantitative, and could afford to wait for further evidence from trials. Designs

[43] Evidence taken before the Select Committee on the Navy, Army, and Ordnance Estimates, PP (1847–8), xxi, pt. 1, pp. 267–9, 272, 275, 301. See also Brown, *Before the Ironclad*, ch. 11.

were developed on paper, if not always on the slipways. Detailed planning continued in 1847 for a screw-liner to be laid down at Devonport: this was Edye's design, and was eventually to be christened, appropriately enough, the *James Watt*. Talks also went on about completing as a steamer a battleship that had been laid down only recently, the *Agamemnon*. There was little sense of haste. For instance, the *Agamemnon*'s conversion plans were completed on 15 December 1847, but then were passed on to the Committee of Reference (a short-lived body, the nearest equivalent in the Admiralty to the *Conseil des travaux*), which argued over them at its leisure for some time.

With the beginning of the new year came the February Revolution and the overthrow of the Orleanist Monarchy. Initially, the spectre was raised of a renewal of the wars with the first French Republic, but the pacific words of the new ministers in Paris, and the economic and political troubles that came to beset the country, soon made it clear that for some time the naval threat from France would be largely reduced. The Royal Navy thus lost one reason for laying down expensive new vessels, which was just as well given that Britain, too, came to suffer from economic depression. Nevertheless, early 1848 did see the Admiralty taking something of a step forward, at least conceptually. Oddly enough, it was the principle of economy that acted as a spur. The Board had become worried about what could be done with the engines originally intended for the *Simoom*, *Vulcan*, and *Megaera*. They were very powerful, varying from 556 to 780 hp. They were far too valuable to be wasted; yet, as Walker glumly accepted, could be used only by completing some screw-battleships. Their existence was responsible for something of a false dawn for the British screw-battlefleet in early 1848, when plans were drawn up to convert the sail of the line *Nile* and *London* to the screw, and the March survey of construction work for the coming year showed the *James Watt* as ordered to be built at Devonport.[44] But the Admiralty was none too eager to proceed, as one can guess from the rather graceless way Lord John Hay admitted in April that 'the reason for thinking of . . . [these conversions] is, that we found those three larger engines, and we have no other way of disposing of them'.[45] Given this attitude, it is not surprising that conversion work did not begin immediately, or that the *James*

---

[44] ADM 83 49.   [45] PP (1847–8), xxi, pt. 1, p. 264.

Watt was rescheduled to be laid down at some unspecified future time at Pembroke, leaving a Devonport dock free for the construction of a ninety-gun sail of the line. Sailing-vessels, indeed, still thrived: there were long discussions in mid-1848 about the design of some new sailing-frigates of fifty to sixty guns. But there was at least a Board caveat to the Surveyor, of July 1848, which instructed him to bear in mind the possibility of conversion to the screw when drawing up the plans of new sailing-vessels. Nothing more positive could be done than this, the Board thought, until there was more evidence about large screw vessels.[46]

By mid- to late 1848 the evidence needed was at last becoming available. HMS *Blenheim* had been finally completed in the spring, and soon proceeded for trials. In the summer, in company with the new *frégate mixte* the *Amphion*, she joined a squadron under Sir Charles Napier, winning golden tributes. The blockship showed she could manœuvre under canvas alone, albeit somewhat sluggishly, but it was when the screw was lowered that the ship's merits became obvious. As Sir Charles reported to the Admiralty on 2 September, 'the effect was instantaneous, and quite wonderful, she crawled up on our weather beam in no time'. As many officers now realized, vessels like her could easily change the course of a naval battle, bringing aid to a threatened point, whatever the direction of the wind, or concentrating forces where the enemy was weak. Captain Henry Ducie Chads, late of the *Excellent* (he had succeeded Hastings), and serving under Napier during the *Blenheim* trials, wrote that henceforward no fleet could be considered properly appointed unless it had one or two steam-liners; adding— rather obscurely—that the sixty-gun *Blenheim* was equal to an eighty-four gun sail of the line. By February 1849, in the words of Captain Ellice, 'the question of placing a Steam Power in Ships of the Line, is materially altered since 1847—it can no longer be received as a hazardous experiment, or one of doubtful results'.[47]

By 1849 Ellice's own position was weakening somewhat. Originally, he had been seen by the Board as a counterweight to Symonds, but with the latter gone, and Walker establishing his

---

[46] Board to Surveyor, 13 July 1848, ADM 83 50. Surveyor to Board, 1 Aug., ADM 83 51.

[47] Napier to Board, 2 Sept. 1848, Napier Papers, Add. MS 40046. 133–6. Ellice to Surveyor, 12 Feb. 1849, ADM 83 54.

authority, it appeared increasingly anomalous that there should be a steam department independent of the one supposedly responsible for warship design, the Surveyor's. The point was finally reached in February 1850 when the latter absorbed the former, and Ellice was moved to become Comptroller General of Coastguards. But too much had happened by 1848–9 for any weakening in one man's authority to check the screw. Inertia can have positive effects, as well as negative, and the blockships and screw cruisers of the mid-1840s created an inertial pressure for change that was difficult to resist. The *Blenheim* trials helped inspire the later British screw-battleships. The screw cruisers added their own force, yielding more evidence about the effectiveness of screw propulsion: they also had a particular contribution to make. Some officers had been very concerned about the possibility of the paddle-steamer pumping shells into the 'blind' areas of a becalmed sail of the line; but the screw steamer offered a far greater threat. She could manœuvre as freely as a paddler, but could mount a potent broadside armament. A battleship immobile before such an opponent might not find sufficient protection in a pivot gun, it was suggested. The solution of detaching a paddle-vessel for each sail of the line was a cumbersome one; how much better, it came to be accepted, to fit the battleship with its own engine, even a small one.

The evidence of the screw trials, the anticipation of the possible shape of future naval engagements, and—as Captain Ellice so often reminded the Surveyor—the presence of the three surplus engines, all contrived to give British construction policy a direction by late 1848, but not yet a timetable: only French construction policy could give that. No British screw-battleships were approved in 1848. But the following year was very different. At its beginning it was realized in Whitehall that despite all the problems brought by the revolution, France had begun more than one screw-liner. That was all that was needed. In the construction plan approved by the Board on 5 February, three screw-liners were approved: the *James Watt* was finally to be laid down at Pembroke, the partially built *Agamemnon* and *Sans Pareil*—whose construction as sail of the line had been suspended the previous April and October respectively— were to be converted to the screw. This number was soon added to. A submission of Captain Ellice on 12 February shows that by then the French navy was supposed to be building, or about to build, no fewer than six screw-liners. The Board's response was swift: on 16 February Ellice was asked to forward sketches for the conversion of the *Nile* and *London*.[48]

Progress was still somewhat erratic. There was a great deal of changing of minds, and the various construction proposals juggled with hulls and engines and dockyards. For instance, an order for the commencement of the *Agamemnon* was given on 3 July 1849, but the design was frequently altered. Back in June she had been earmarked to take the 780 hp spare engines; but then Ellice pressed for her to have ones of 400 hp. It was not until March 1850 that her design was fixed in its essentials: drawings originally specified for the *James Watt* were now adapted for her, and the engines were to be of 600 hp. Fortunately, as the Admiralty well knew, the French screw programme was meeting delays of its own, and the British could afford to proceed so slowly, trying to find by experiment the proper dimensions and forms for speed, and the best balance between horsepower, coal supply, and victuals and water.[49]

If there was still some confusion, there had been a certain progression from the ideas of 1848, and it was increasingly accepted that screw-liners could be much more than mobile coastal-batteries. More evidence from trials was coming in, and while it was little different from that available in 1848, perhaps conviction came by force of accumulation. The trials of the Lisbon squadron under William Fanshawe Martin were of particular importance. Martin commanded a blockship (the *Hogue*), two screw-frigates, two sail of the line, two sailing-frigates, and the great 800 hp paddle-frigate *Terrible*. It appears to have been generally accepted only after these trials that the screw was superior to the paddle in steaming, and that it offered significant advantages in towing. More important, the trials definitely showed that screw and sail could be combined in one vessel to produce either economy or speed. According to Martin, they showed also that a vessel under canvas and steam could still be manœuvred by the screw. As he wrote: 'the fact that the screw cannot be overrun by any velocity the ship may acquire

<hr/>

[48] Surveyor's plan of work, 1849/50, ADM 83 54. Board to Surveyor, 18 May 1849, ADM 83 56. PP (1861), xxvi. 428. Surveyor's recommendation of 30 Oct. 1849, ADM 92 14, p. 86.
[49] Board to Surveyor, 3 July 1849, and order of 20 June on verso, ADM 83 57. Surveyor to Board, 19 Oct. 1852, Walker Papers, WWL 1.

by canvass [*sic*], forms a very important element when considering the relative value of the screw and the paddle.'[50]

A certain reluctance remained to 'spoiling' the sail of the line with steam-engines. As late as 1851 one of the chief intentions of Admiralty policy was to build up a reserve of fifty sail of the line. But the screw programme only got larger, thanks chiefly to what was seen as a growing French construction menace. There was even another naval scare. One shock to tremulous Britons was a genuine combined operation by the French army and navy in April 1849. A military force was ordered to cross to Italy to support the Pope against revolutionaries and, only ten days after the order was telegraphed to Toulon, 7,561 men, 344 horses, two batteries of field artillery, one siege battery, and victuals for twenty days were disembarked at Civitavecchia, after a crossing of a hundred leagues. The implications for a Channel crossing really did not need emphasizing.

These fears were later enhanced thanks to a pamphlet by an engineer in the army of the Swiss Confederation, baron Maurice. He published a detailed plan describing how France could invade England, and the work was translated and published in London in 1852. By then, of course, further encouragement to anticipations of invasion had come in the *coup d'état* of December 1851 that renewed and enhanced the powers of the French President. Since that President was a Bonaparte, the *coup* had particular resonance for the British public, reawakening memories of the Great War and the threatening camp at Boulogne.[51]

In the circumstances, the Admiralty and the British public kept a particularly keen eye on the growing French fleet, to ensure that a numerical superiority was retained. By October 1852 the Royal Navy had a considerable steam battlefleet in the making, even ignoring the blockships. The *Sans Pareil* had been launched in March 1851, and the *Agamemnon* in May 1852. The *James Watt* had been left somewhat behind, and did not go into the water until April 1853. Well before then, in September 1852, another screw-battle-ship had been launched, for some time the largest screw-liner of all.

---

[50] Report, with Martin's marginal comments, Martin Papers, Add. MS 41432, fos. 78–96.

[51] P. E. Maurice, *De la défense nationale en Angleterre* (Paris, 1851). See also Sir Francis Head, *The Defenceless State of Great Britain* (London, 1851), and Richard Cobden, *The Three Panics: An Historical Episode* (London, 1862).

This was the *Duke of Wellington*, of 131 guns, lengthened on the slipway by over 30 feet so that she could accommodate the largest surplus engines of all, of 780 hp. She displaced no less than 5,829 tons (3,771 tons Builders Old Measure). Added to the above, there were four other steam-battleships under construction, either conversions from existing vessels or designed for the screw virtually from the keel up.

This was not enough. In November and December 1852 the Surveyor instituted a large new programme, in order to overmatch new French moves. Eight more conversions were then approved, joined in the following May to July by one more conversion plus two screw-liners laid down as such. A definite numerical lead had been opened up by this stage, with nineteen British screw-battleships built or building (plus the blockships) as against the fourteen that the French were believed to have in preparation. Below the battlefleet, the British lead in screw vessels was even greater, as one would expect. In early 1853 the Royal Navy could boast of eleven screws of fifty to twenty-four guns, built or building, against only two French. And there were twenty-three more of under twenty guns, in contrast to ten French (including the *Corse* but, as in the British case, excluding all iron-hulled vessels). Britannia still appeared to be very safe.[52]

Or was she? The numbers made happy reading, but ought the Admiralty to have taken the *vaisseau mixte* as the model? There were enthusiasts for the type. To Captain Halsted it

engrafts . . . the powers of the Present day, upon the honoured practices of the Past. We have thus in our power a System, which violates the integrity of no Principle, and gives offence to no honourable prejudice; but which harmonises with the entire course of naval education;—Naval discipline; —and Naval feeling.[53]

The above should be compared with what Xavier Raymond wrote in the *Revue des deux mondes*:

L'hélice, en débarrassant le navire à vapeur de ses tambours, permet de lui rendre les formes des anciens navires à voiles: c'est ce que l'amirauté semble considérer presque exclusivement dans ses combinaisons nouvelles. Refaire de l'ancien, cela lui paraît admirable, et le nouvel instrument

[52] Surveyor to Admiralty, 19 and 30 Oct., 2 and 19 Nov., and reports of 25 Sept. and 22 Nov. 1852, Walker Papers, WWL 1.
[53] E. P. Halsted, *The Screw Fleet of the Navy* (London, 1850), 143–4.

deviendra un simple auxiliaire de la voile. L'amirauté prépare en consé-
quence toute une flotte de vaisseaux du genre qu'on a appellée mixte; elle
parait ne rien voir au delà, ni se douter que l'hélice puisse être employée à
un autre titre.[54]

To understand the wisdom, or otherwise, of the Admiralty
policy of building *vaisseaux mixtes*, it is helpful to look a little more
closely at the vessels that were built. It then becomes clear that
there were two types. The first was a vessel especially designed to
accommodate the screw, engines, and coal. Either she had been laid
down as a steamer from the first; or, though originally built, or
partially built, as a pure sailing-vessel, she had been taken in hand
again and lengthened amidships, and perhaps also at the stern,
allowing for the fitting of the new equipment and stores without
unduly diminishing the storage space for victuals and water.
Whether new or converted, it was only this type, to use Halsted's
words, that engrafted steam-power on to the endurance of the old
battleships. Take the example of the *Agamemnon*. She had engines
of 600 hp and a maximum speed under steam alone of over eleven
knots. She carried 485 tons of coal, sufficient for six and a half days'
steaming. She was also fully-rigged, and carried water for three
months' consumption and provisions for over four.

But compare her with an example of the other type of screw-
battleship, the *Royal George*. She was a cheap conversion to the
screw, engines and coal being squeezed into the existing hull by
reducing storage space and ballast. The latter was cut by two-
thirds, water stowage by nearly three-quarters, and provisions by
nearly a half. As a result, engines of 500 hp and coal for five days'
steaming could be fitted in, and a steam speed of nine knots was
attained. Endurance had been cut: water was not so much of a
problem as it might seem because while there were coals the
engines could distil water for drinking; but there were now victuals
for only eighty-four days. Moreover, the vessel's seagoing qualities
had suffered. The loss of ballast and the fitting of engines shifted
the centre of gravity upwards, resulting in 'crankness' under sail.[55]

[54] Raymond's series of articles, which began in the *Revue des deux mondes* in 1861,
are collected together in his *Les Marines de la France et de l'Angleterre, 1815–1863*
(Paris, 1863); see pp. 120–1.
[55] 'CRANK ... the quality of a ship, which for want of a sufficient quantity
of *ballast* or cargo, is rendered incapable of carrying sail without being exposed to
the danger of oversetting.' William Falconer, *A Universal Dictionary of the Marine*
(London, 1780), 89.

The problem was never fully solved, though the ship was often taken in hand, first to reduce the rigging, then to take off the poop and, finally, a whole deck, eventually reducing a 120-gun ship to one of 90 guns. Her crew cannot have found her a pleasant ship in which to serve. Ventilation was inadequate, for instance, and during the summer campaign in the Black Sea in 1855 the temperature in the stokehold reached 150 °F. As her first captain often complained, the ship was just too full: he described her in a letter to the First Naval Lord as 'prepared for Machinery but Certainly not for officers and men to live in, nor in her fitments as a man of war'. The stokers, at least, would have agreed wholeheartedly with him.[56]

The *Royal George* is a somewhat extreme example; she was a relatively old vessel, as conversions went, originally built in 1827, and her timbers had been fitted on an obsolete model. But she was not unusual as a steam-battleship in regard to her limited endurance or 'strategic reach'. Out of the nineteen British screw-battleships in hand in June 1853, no fewer than eight were cheap conversions, little better than the blockships. There was also the *Sans Pareil*, built specifically for the screw, but on so mean a scale as to have little more endurance than the ordinary conversions.[57]

There were obvious advantages to the kind of conversion attempted on the *Royal George*: cheapness, speed of construction, and little need for additional building timber (always a scarce commodity). Yet what use were such vessels to the Royal Navy, given what one might call the 'colonial imperative'? One answer is that despite a consciousness of the importance of the colonies and the trade routes, and thus of the need of at least some warships with a strategic capacity, imperial defence was in large part a matter for European waters. The fact that there were as yet no great navies outside Europe (the US fleet was only a partial exception), coupled with the commanding geographical position of the British Isles with respect to the Continent, gave the Admiralty the ability to concentrate most of the fleet at home and yet exercise a global sea power. As long as the battlefleets of the Continental powers were covered, the Royal Navy had very much of a free hand in the seas beyond Europe. And, of the Continental powers, the really important one was France. Any challenge made by her navy in home

[56] Codrington to Hyde Parker, 7 Feb. 1854, Codrington Papers, COD 109 2.
[57] For the balance within the entire British screw-battlefleet, see A. Lambert, *Battleships in Transition: The Creation of the Steam Battlefleet, 1815–60* (London, 1984).

waters had to be met, whatever form it took; once it was met, the British Empire of rule and influence remained secure from all but minor shocks from naval attack.[58]

This leads to another question. How could the *Royal George* type hope to counter vessels like the *Napoléon*? Could even an *Agamemnon* have coped with a *Napoléon*? To the latter question the answer is perhaps 'yes', at least according to D. K. Brown in a recent book. He argues that the British vessel's engines, whilst nominally less powerful, actually delivered more power to the screw, and that the *Napoléon's* trials were poorly conducted and misleading, giving overestimates of her speed.[59] If true, it would suggest that Dupuy de Lôme was right to favour direct-acting engines—the type in the *Agamemnon*—as against the heavy and wasteful geared ones insisted on by the *Conseil des travaux*. But would it free Admiralty shipbuilding policy from the accusations of Raymond? Even the best British screw-liners had been designed as *mixtes*. They had an obvious rationale, with the endurance to match any steam force that the French might deploy in foreign waters. That endurance had a European significance as well, since it would be vital were it again necessary to blockade French ports, blockade being perhaps the most exhausting and demanding of all operations. But how could the British expect to maintain tight blockades with their steam battlefleet, containing some good *mixtes*, admittedly, but also many slower vessels with reduced endurance, when faced with a force of improved *Napoléons*? Furthermore, what were the possibilities for maritime warfare generally in European waters between the British fleet on the one hand, and on the other a force that was smaller, and limited in endurance, but homogeneous, and able to fight or flee as circumstances dictated? Dupuy de Lôme seemed to offer the French navy a policy that not only would take a lead for France, instead of letting her lag, but by tailoring the fleet closely to the country's strategic needs, promising—if not ultimate

---

[58] See G. S. Graham, *The Politics of Naval Supremacy: Studies in British Maritime Ascendancy* (CUP, 1965), 61–2, 110–11.

[59] Brown, *Before the Ironclad*, 129–30. A contrary position to Brown's is taken by René Estienne in a substantial article on Dupuy de Lôme and the *Napoléon*, in *Marine et technique au XIXe siècle: Actes du Colloque International* (Service historique de la marine and Institut d'histoire des conflits contemporains, Paris, 1989). Estienne makes the interesting point that there seems almost to have been a tradition in Britain of refusing to accept French figures for the speed of the first *vaisseau à vapeur*.

naval victory in a war with Britain—then at least opportunities lacking on previous occasions for striking shrewd and dangerous blows.

V

So far a sharp contrast has been suggested between British and French naval construction policy at the end of the 1840s. We have observed on the one side a predilection for short-term planning, empiricism, and traditional strategy; and on the other a greater boldness in gambler's luck, but at least tending to look towards the future rather than the past. However, the reality was more complex than this, French policy less laudable than Raymond, say, implied. The British *vaisseaux mixtes* had their proper opponents, for the French navy did not concentrate on the *vaisseau à vapeur*. Indeed, the construction policy of the Ministry of Marine was for a time even more diffused than the Admiralty's.

For the laying down of the future *Napoléon* did not end all French doubts in the design. One naval officer, the showy but still able Bouët-Willaumez, affirmed in 1853 that a few years before he had been one of the few to support the project, when several *notabilités maritimes* had gone so far as to say that the ship would never float. As construction proceeded, admittedly, many of the technical objections dropped away as it came to be appreciated how capably Dupuy de Lôme had dealt with the various problems. But one potent objection remained, illustrated by the words of one naval engineer whom the designer bumped into as his vessel was approaching completion: the man accepted that with the chosen method of construction the long hull would be solid enough in a seaway—the point over which he had been very dubious before—but he had a Parthian shot: 'on voit bien que vous ne la faites de votre poche.'[60] A bill of four million francs was clearly a great deal to swallow, and the Ministry, for one, was not prepared to do it more than once, at least not until the prototype had shown her prowess at sea.

However, the Ministry was prepared to sanction *mixtes* similar to those proving successful in the Royal Navy: that appeared a safe

---

[60] Letter of Bouët-Willaumez, Joinville Papers, 300 AP iii 113, dossier 1. Dupuy de Lôme to Joinville, 20 Sept. 1849; ibid., 114, dossier 1.

option. The 'fleet of samples' criticized by Forquenot remained a French model. Even Mackau, hesitant in so much, implied that France could do better. After his own tour of the British steam fleet, he argued in a report of March 1851 to the Minister of Marine that France did not have the resources to waste that Britain did: 'Pour nous il s'agit d'avoir un plan bien étudié, conçu en raison de nos resources et des opérations que nous nous proposons d'exécuter en temps de guerre.'[61] The Ministry at least learned something from the British experience, and avoided the same degree of wasteful experiment, but it did not yet choose between moderate or full steam-power.

The Ministry had been rather lazily considering plans for *vaisseaux mixtes* since 1846. Studies continued into 1847, but urgency came only after February 1848 when the prospect arose of England leading another grand coalition against revolutionary France. A hasty programme of conversion of some sail of the line into weakly powered blockships was then considered for coastal defence. Fortunately, it was not put into effect, and when the fear of war receded, attention concentrated on projects that would show some superiority to the *Blenheim* type. By 1849 it was decided to convert into *mixtes* two vessels that were virtually complete, though still on the stocks, the *Hector* (renamed *Charlemagne* on 2 August 1850), and the *Austerlitz*. Great care, and frequent revisions of designs, were involved in their transformation, as the designers strove to achieve the best compromise between sail, steam, and endurance, without great alteration to the hull. (In other words, they were close to the *Royal George* type, though better planned in detail.) Their number was swelled in April 1850 by the decision to convert the *Jean Bart* on the same general lines.

By building *mixtes* as well as a fast battleship, the French were not necessarily acting in a contradictory way. Of course, in some operations of war, the two types would have been incompatible: incorporating *mixtes* and *Napoléons* would have limited squadron speed, and restricted the options open to the Admiral. But both types could have contributed to satisfying French naval policy aims. If nothing else, in case of war with Britain, the *Charlemagne–Austerlitz* type could have helped defend the country's coastline and ports, acting as the blockships had been intended to act, a task for

[61] Mackau Papers, 156 AP 1 36, dossier 6, carton 108.

which the *Napoléon* would have been wasted. In such a war the conversions would certainly have been far more useful than they could have been as originally built. As with the *Royal George*, the conversion was a relatively cheap way of exploiting *matériel* that otherwise would have become quite obsolete: perhaps the only real danger lay in the way that this option drew some attention and resources away from the vision of Tupinier and Dupuy de Lôme.

That the French steam-battleship programme *was* too diffuse is proved only by the fact that yet another, and singularly useless type was being built by mid-1851, one we might call the *vaisseau minable*. This was the *Montebello*, and she was to remain the sole example of her type. She originated in trials to discover the smallest engine that could move a large battleship at a few knots. In July 1849 the 150 hp screw steamer *Pélican* managed to tow the 120-gun *Valmy* at some four to four and a half knots, and from this experiment came the essential part of a conversion plan that was supposed to bring the benefits of steam, yet leave endurance under sail virtually untouched. Engines of 150 hp were chosen (only a third of the power of any so far fitted in a screw-liner); work began to fit them into the *Montebello* in mid-1851, and was completed a year later. Also, proposals were made to build smaller sisters. In July 1850 the *Conseil des travaux* called for plans to be drawn up for seventy-four-gun, 80 hp battleships, and the project was still being considered in January 1852. It was believed that vessels like the *Montebello* could satisfy an important strategic need, being capable of lengthy operations on foreign stations; and the type was supported not only by men like Charles Dupin, but even by Dupuy de Lôme. But disillusionment soon came. Even before the *Montebello* had been sent to sea there were serious doubts about her utility.[62]

The doubts came from the trials of the *Charlemagne* in late 1851. This 450 hp screw displayed handiness under sail (she had a screw-well, one should note), and was surprisingly fast under steam alone, with spurts of up to nine and a half knots. As one may observe from discussions in the *Conseil d'amirauté* on 22 and 29 May 1852, it was now accepted in the Ministry that the future battlefleet would be a steam one, and that pairing a paddle-vessel with each sail of

[62] Evidence of C. Dupin, *Enquête parlementaire sur la situation et l'organisation des services de la marine militaire* (2 vols., Paris, 1851), i. 160–5. Dupuy de Lôme to Joinville, 10 Oct. 1851, Joinville Papers, 300 AP III 114, dossier 1. Meeting of the *Conseil des travaux* of 21 Jan. 1852, V BB8 1130. 30–6.

the line was not sufficient. The Council also pressed for the work of modernization to begin soon, and the Minister agreed: four, and later seven, sail of the line were marked for conversion into steamers.

Significantly, these seven battleships were to be powerful *mixtes* of 650 hp. The *Charlemagne* trials had suggested how unfortunate it might be for a slow and lumbering steamer like the *Montebello* to be intercepted by an enemy *mixte*. The *vaisseau minable* was now to be ignored. The Minister stated at the 22 May Council meeting that France intended to concentrate her steam battlefleet at home, where its speed and power would be most threatening to the enemy; henceforward, he said, only frigates and lesser warships would fight under the *tricolore* on distant seas if war came with England.[63]

The *Charlemagne* trials had at least one other important effect. If that ship could steam at nine knots, it was realized, then Dupuy de Lôme's estimate of ten knots for a vessel of twice the horsepower might be too conservative — which, of course, was intentional.

The trials only added to a reputation that was already growing by late 1851. At least some members of the *Assemblée nationale* saw in the fast battleship an answer to their many naval hopes. The difficulties of the French navy during the 1840s had led, in the Second Republic, to the setting up of an *Enquête parlementaire sur la Marine*, on which fifteen deputies sat, including flag officers, a lawyer, a doctor, and men with industrial and commercial interests. The ubiquitous Charles Dupin was also a member, but the inquiry did not reflect his attitude of mind. The imagination of most members was caught by the prospects of the *vaisseau à vapeur*, and there were strong suggestions that more should be laid down. The *coup d'état* of December 1851 swept away the inquiry as well as the *Assemblée nationale*, which meant no final report was ever made. Yet the inquiry still had influence. It had encouraged discussion about possible naval policies. Moreover, one of its members, Captain Charner, became *chef d'état major* and *chef du cabinet* to the man who was Minister of Marine from December 1851, Théodore Ducos.

Charner found that the Ministry shared the growing enthusiasm for the fast battleship. Dupuy de Lôme's patent ability to overcome construction problems brought the approval even of the *Conseil des*

---

[63] The 22 and 29 May meetings of the *Conseil d'amirauté* were secret ones, at which only some of the members (*membres titulaires*) and the secretary attended. AN BB8 853 (*marine*), pages unnumbered.

travaux. And in May 1852, even before the trials of the prototype, the *Conseil d'amirauté* proposed the laying down of two successors. Admittedly, no work was begun on them, perhaps because the new conversions absorbed all immediate resources, more likely due to the nearness of the prototype trials. The latter finally took place in the summer, and appeared triumphant, obviously marred only by the relatively poor response of the *Napoléon* when under sail alone in light breezes. The *Conseil d'amirauté* was almost entirely won over, and the success of the *Charlemagne* quite overshadowed. As Ducos told the Council, previous expectations about the fast battle-ship had been far too low.

There was a consequent change of emphasis in French construction policy, a further concentration. The future shape of virtually the whole fleet was affected. For instance, previously acceptable steam-frigate projects were now obviously inadequate. The thirty-four gun frigate design of 550 hp accepted the previous May seemed to the September *Conseil d'amirauté* as but a mouthful for enemy fast battleships. The Council now wanted great sixty-gun *frégates à vapeur* capable of operating in a fast steam fleet. And, naturally, the Council wanted more *Napoléons*.

The French were fortunate that, for the first time since the 1848 Revolution, ambitious plans could be realized. It was only in 1852, due to economies on inessentials, and to a more generous budget (made possible by a reviving economy, and the naval interests of Louis-Napoleon), that substantial funds were beginning to become available for new construction. The first expression of the surplus had been the conversion programme, but resources were now to be more concentrated on fast steamers. Some of the large and fast frigates wanted by the *Conseil d'amirauté* were approved—six eventually—and an impressive and unequalled fast battleship squadron was begun. In January 1853 the *Bretagne*, a first-rate sail of the line on which little work had yet been done, began her conversion into a fast battleship of 131 guns. She was to be even larger than the *Duke of Wellington*. Between March and September five fast second-rates, improved *Napoléons*, were laid down, followed by two more in the next year. Also in 1854 the task was begun of converting the *Eylau*, a virtually completed sailing-battleship, by considerably extending her amidships and fitting engines of 900 hp.

By 1853-4 the French navy was taking up a position in advance of the Royal Navy, pushing ahead with vessels that were good in themselves, homogeneous in the principles behind them, and which well-suited French naval policy aims. A challenge was being made which, in the nature of the game, the British were bound to resent. First, however, the Admiralty had to accept that they had been outdone. This began to happen, it appears, with the trials of the *Napoléon*. In July 1853, perhaps as a consequence, the British began a high-powered liner of their own, the *Conqueror* of 800 hp and 101 guns. But the Crimean War was the true revelation, beginning with an incident at the Dardanelles in October 1853 that brought embarrassment to the Royal Navy.

3

Anglo-French Diplomacy and the Transition from the Screw-Liner to the Ironclad, 1854 Onwards

I

The rival screw-fleets that we have seen being built against each other so energetically never did meet to fight. Rather, they never met to fight on opposing sides: instead, strange reversal, they went to war as allies against a common enemy. The causes of that war have been described often enough, and will not be dealt with here. Nor will the progress of the land war be looked at in any more than a passing way. Our concern is with the maritime war against Russia, and what it showed of the state of the naval art, and how it affected construction policy.

The one thing convincingly demonstrated by the maritime war was the crucial importance of steam-power. On the one hand the *bâtiment mixte* showed itself greatly superior to the sailing-warship. And the *bâtiment à vapeur* showed itself superior to both. Even before the war began there was an important incident. The time was October 1853, when tension between Turkey and Russia was reaching a height, and the British and French governments were increasingly concerned about a possible Russian amphibious assault against Constantinople. The allied fleets were already at the entrance of the Dardanelles, but it was realized that due to the predominant winds and currents, the allies might well not be able to reach Constantinople before the Sebastopol fleet could descend on the Bosphorus. It appeared wise for the allies to move their forces further north, and on 22 October the warships weighed anchor and tried to pass the straits, the sail of the line under tow. Both the allies met with disappointments. The *Charlemagne* took the *Valmy* in tow, but found the opposition too great, and had to slip the tow before she could pass the straits herself. Nor could the British *mixte*, the *Sans Pareil*, make progress, towing a collier. Of all the towing operations, only two seem to have succeeded. The *Gomer*, 650 hp, the most powerful paddle-frigate built for the French navy, managed to pass the straits with the *Iéna*, albeit very slowly. The *Napoléon* was more impressive. She took the French flagship the *Ville de Paris* with her and passed the straits with apparent ease. Left behind were most of the French warships and all the British. The allies had to await more favourable winds before they could get their fleets to the Bosphorus.[1]

The success of the *Napoléon* had a great effect on some observers. Xavier Raymond tells us that the British naval officers at the Dardanelles were humiliated by the relative failure of the *Sans Pareil*, hoping she lived up to her name and that the Royal Navy would never be burdened with another like her. Yet we know not all were unhappy. The British naval C.-in-C., J. W. D. Dundas, had never approved of the *Napoléon*, commenting acidly in 1852, when she joined the *escadre d'évolutions*, about her screw 'dangling at the stern' (he meant the *hélice affolée*), and adding that the vessel was 'very leaky from vibration — she is fast, but slow in getting around and is certainly a failure'. One may suspect he was not entirely displeased to be able to report on 27 November 1853 that she had sailed to Toulon for repairs to her overstrained machinery. For, despite the impressive show the previous month, the *Napoléon* had been severely strained by the tow of the *Ville de Paris*. Since first commissioning, the vessel had been bedevilled by mechanical problems, especially difficulties with the bilge and feed pumps, and the excessive vibration that Dundas had heard about, which came from the irregular movement of the slide-valves. The trip up the straits exacerbated all the old faults and created new ones: a main bearing overheated, and just before coming to the anchorage speed had had to be reduced, in order to avoid a total breakdown. It appears that humiliation had been as close to triumph on 22 October as madness is supposed to be to genius.[2]

---

[1] Dundas to Admiralty, 22, 27, and 31 Oct. 1853, Dundas Papers, DND 4. *Sans Pareil* logbook, ADM 53 4637. *Notice sur les travaux scientifiques de M. Dupuy de Lôme* (Paris, 1866), 26–7.

[2] Raymond, *Les Marines de la France et de l'Angleterre*, 113–14. Dundas to Sir Thomas Byam Martin, 2 Apr. 1852, Martin Papers, BM Add. MS 41370, fos. 190–3. Dundas to Admiralty, 27 Nov. 1853, Dundas Papers, DND 4. Hamelin to Ducos, 28 Oct. 1853, V 7DD1 143, 1853 folder.

The Ministry of Marine naturally tried to keep the mechanical failure secret: thus many never learned of the drama inside the *Napoléon*, and must have thought the *vaisseau à vapeur* entirely vindicated. Yet the implications ought to have been little different to the objective observer whether privy to the breakdown or not. The *Napoléon*, after all, was a prototype. The fast battleships laid down after her were to an improved design and could be expected to perform much better. In particular, as Dupuy de Lôme surely did not fail to point out to members of the *Conseil des travaux*, the later design included the kind of simple, light, and robust direct-acting engines originally intended for the prototype. Certainly both in London and in Paris, the Dardanelles incident promoted the idea of the fast battleships.

However, there was only one *vaisseau à vapeur* in commission at the beginning of the Crimean War, and only two by the end. The fleets that bore the burden of the conflict were composed of sailing warships, paddle-vessels, and *bâtiments mixtes*. This meant that the most obvious contrast was not between the full steamer and the auxiliary but between sail and steam.

The war quickly put the sailing warship at a discount. The Russians—who had few enough paddle-steamers, and no large screws—showed what they thought of the allied fleets by keeping their numerous sail of the line safe in harbour. The allies' prime task at sea, consequently, was not to fight battles but to ensure their continued use of sea communications, so their armies could be transported and maintained. Here the greatest enemy was the elements, to which sailing fleets were particularly vulnerable, as was demonstrated by several incidents.

The earliest of these was the cruise in the Black Sea by the allied battlefleets in January 1854 to protect Constantinople from the Russian fleet. The operation was diplomatically a delicate one, since Britain and France were not yet at war with Russia: their declaration was still three months away. The two admirals opposed the cruise, though on operational not diplomatic grounds. They argued that sailing-vessels were not fit to cruise in the Black Sea winter. Nevertheless, they were ordered to go, and the poor state of their ships on the return, under three weeks later, show the wisdom of the previous objections. Dundas wrote testily to the British ambassador at Constantinople (the man responsible for the cruise), that if Nicholas I could have chosen the time to send the allied battlefleet into the Black Sea, he too would have picked January.[3] But if the sailing-vessels had suffered, the steamers showed they were more hardy: a steam-force sent to escort some Turkish transports to Trebizond the following month coped well with the winter. The message was often reinforced as the war went on, notably during the great gale of 13–14 November, when many vessels were caught at anchor on exposed roadsteads: the ones with steam-engines mostly survived, keeping their screws turning to relieve the anchor cables, or steaming out to safety in the open sea; those without steam were in great peril, and many were wrecked.

With their enhanced ability to operate in poor weather and against wind and tide, the steam-warships took on the greatest burden of the maritime war in the Black Sea. Sailing-warships, notably the line-of-battleships, were relegated to secondary tasks. In late 1854 one finds even J. W. D. Dundas hoping rather wistfully that the *Napoléon* would soon be repaired (after yet another breakdown) and rejoin the combined fleet, adding that he 'never knew so well what value screws were, both in action and in bad weather'.[4]

There was another major theatre of war—the Baltic. Here the weather conditions were even less favourable to naval warfare, and here too the steam-warship proved itself. This theatre was something of a British preserve. The French government despatched a fleet, mostly of sailing-vessels, but the major naval force was always British, and most of that was steam. In 1854, out of forty-five RN warships sent to the Baltic, forty were steamers; in 1855 all the RN force was steam-powered (apart from some mortar 'floats'). Steam made it possible for the British to make their presence felt much earlier than had been the case in their incursions during the Napoleonic Wars. In 1854 the fleet entered the Gulf of Finland in May, two months before the fleet sent out in 1808 had been able to do, and a scouting force had preceded it in April. Perhaps, though, the best evidence of the capacity of the steamers in the war against Russia comes from the efforts made, in two seasons' campaigning, by a squadron of steam frigates under Captain Watson. His force hung on in the Gulf of Finland late into the campaigning year, despite snow, blizzards, and a westerly gale that turned the Gulf into one vast, jagged lee shore. The Russian ports were blockaded

---

[3] Dundas to Lord Stratford de Redcliffe, 22 Jan. 1854, Dundas Papers, DND 1.
[4] Dundas to Sir James Graham, 3 Dec., Netherby Papers, box iii, bundle 4 c.w.

until they were partly or completely frozen up. As Watson admitted, it was only strong steam-power that enabled his ships to remain so long.[5]

The Baltic campaigns also showed that it was possible to maintain large steam fleets at a distance from the home dockyards, where there were no British possessions or nearby allied power. Initially it had been thought in the Admiralty that coal would be a serious problem. One of the officers who had served in the Baltic during the Napoleonic Wars, Sir Thomas Byam Martin, believed that all the fleet would be able to do was to dash into the Baltic when the ice broke, on the chance of finding a daring Russian squadron that had put to sea, but that soon it would have to withdraw, with empty bunkers. Operations would then be limited to a blockade of Russian trade from the Naze of Norway, where the fleet would be close enough to Britain to be certain of regular coal supplies, and could retire at need for water and provisions to the Firth of Forth. In the event, Sweden and Denmark allowed some of their unfortified ports to be used as supply points, and since coal was never declared contraband, those two powers did not feel their neutrality was offended by the establishment of coal depots at Kiel and Faro Sound. And there were other depots—on Russian soil. The British fleet took over Nargen and Baro Sound, and British colliers brought and landed coal stocks. Fuel never became a difficulty: even the blockships sent to the Baltic, with their limited coal bunkers, do not seem to have run short of fuel. Indeed, the coal supply outran the demand: by the end of the 1854 campaign a surplus of 5,000 tons had been built up in the various Baltic depots.[6]

The war demonstrated that, in European waters at least, naval power could and even had to mean steam-power. Furthermore, the war made it clear that steam-power meant screw-power. Paddle-vessels were very apt for certain functions; with their relatively shallow draught they were invaluable for dashing around the shoal water off a coastline or up a river. But, of course, screw-vessels had important advantages over paddlers, especially their full broadside armaments. The latter were best displayed on 17 October 1854 when the allied fleets bombarded the seaward defences of Sebastopol. Two British screw-liners (*Agamemnon* and *Sans Pareil*)

[5] Napier Papers, BM Add. MS 40026, fos. 277–80.
[6] Napier to Andrew Buchanan (British envoy-extraordinary to the Court of Denmark), 15 Sept. 1854, Napier Papers, PRO 30.16.13, fo. 387.

were amongst the vessels that approached the enemy batteries most closely, and it was largely thanks to them that the allies drew some reputation from the naval bombardment. The two were able to draw to as short a range as the shoals made possible, where their fire was most effective, and also to tow away vessels that found themselves in difficulties from rocks or enemy fire.

Ultimately the war did not confirm the worth of the *bâtiment mixte*. Operational experience emphasized the importance of the size of engines. Increasingly, as the war progressed, the screws that were valued were those with the greater engine-power, confirming the lesson drawn at the Dardanelles in October 1853.

The war also had other lessons of importance. One of them concerned the 'steam bridge'. This had been spoken of often enough during the 1840s, and in 1849 there was the example of the French army crossing over to Civitavecchia. It was not until 1854, however, that a large army crossed the sea by steam-power in order to invade a country, despite the fact that the latter possessed a large fleet. The career of the allied armies once they had landed was not entirely happy; but the crossing itself was speedy and well organized and the disembarkation equally well managed. The expedition demonstrated that large-scale steam invasions could be successfully mounted, at least in certain circumstances.

There was also another important lesson: that it was very difficult for pure naval power, even if equipped with powerful steamers, to damage an essentially land power. War with Russia faced the allies with a crucial problem. Armies could be carried to the Crimea, and they could be supplied; the Russian ports in the Black, Baltic, and White Seas could be blockaded; but what else could the allied navies do to strike the enemy unless—as seemed increasingly unlikely as the war went on—the Russian fleets were sent out for slaughter? There were a few obvious tasks, such as looking out for the odd enemy warship or merchantman that had not found shelter, or organizing small expeditions ashore to destroy the Tsar's property, when it was not too far from the sea. And in 1855 the allies forced an entrance to the Sea of Azov, cutting Russian supply lines by water to Sebastopol. Furthermore, the previous year there had been a combined expedition to take the isolated fortress of Bomarsund on the Åland Islands. But there was nothing else of importance that could be done in terms of maritime warfare, unless either large new armies could be landed on Russian territory, or—far more practical—the allies created special naval instruments for attacks on Russian territory.

The need for such instruments was not clear in early 1854. Even many naval officers seem to have thought that the new screw-warships were capable of great deeds against coastal towns and fortifications. And poor, untutored British popular opinion was very sanguine. The large fleet sent to the Baltic under Sir Charles Napier left a Britain enjoying fond dreams of the fortresses of Kronstadt and Sweaborg crumbling into ruins and St Petersburg itself in flames. The 15 April editorial of the *Portsmouth Times and Naval Gazette* was hardly alone in its hyperbole that 'In the Baltic Fleet . . . there is sufficient power to batter down the most formidable obstacles, to shake their rocky ramparts about the skulking enemy.'

The use of such language shows an inability to understand that even screw-warships were not capable of levelling granite fortresses, or that the mere attempt would lead only to futile damage to the fleet. Fortunately, Sir Charles did not make the attempt.[8] The public was naturally disappointed by the end of the year's campaigning. Opinion in naval circles, on the other hand, was by then less sanguine than it had been. The bombardment of Sebastopol in October had demonstrated that granite fortifications might have their fire smothered for a while by naval batteries, but that they were very difficult to destroy and could cause heavy damage to the attacking battleships: the success of the *Agamemnon* and *Sans Pareil* had been only local in its effect. There had also been some interesting trials, two months before, against the walls of the captured Bomarsund. They showed that broadside warships armed with smooth-bores had to get within a few hundred yards of stone batteries in order to demolish them. The implications were serious. First, attacking vessels would have to suffer enemy fire for some time whilst they moved into position. Secondly, many maritime

---

[7] Maurice Berkeley to Sir Charles Wood, 1 Nov. 1855, Halifax Papers, BM Add. MS 49532, fos. 1–3.

[8] C. I. Hamilton, 'Sir James Graham, the Baltic Campaign, and War-Planning at the Admiralty in 1854', *Historical Journal*, 19 (1976), 89–112. For an extended treatment of the British maritime contribution to the Crimean War, see A. D. Lambert, *The Crimean War: British Grand Strategy, 1853–56* (Manchester University Press, 1990). On the British (and Finnish) effort in the Baltic, there is B. Greenhill and A. Giffard, *The British Assault on Finland 1854–1855: A Forgotten Naval War* (London, 1988).

fortresses were surrounded by shoal water that would prevent large warships from coming sufficiently close for their batteries to be of optimum effectiveness. The trials offered one more unpleasing piece of evidence. Bomarsund had been built cheaply, using granite-faced brick rubble. Kronstadt and Sweaborg, it was known, were far more substantial, with much solid granite. It seemed that the traditional kind of fleet, albeit endowed with steam-power, would have little chance of breaking down such walls before being burned to the waterline.

This conclusion led to the construction of three different types of specialized vessels. The first was a new class of blockship. Five sail of the line, the *Pembroke, Russell, Cornwallis, Hastings,* and *Hawke* were taken in hand over the winter of 1854–5 and fitted with engines of 200 hp. The idea behind them appears to have come from Napoleon III, who said it was better to risk old battleships worth half a million francs each against granite than to send a fleet worth perhaps fifty million to possible destruction. However, he had said that the vessels should be armour-plated; the Admiralty, though, did not have enough time to have this done for the 1855 campaign. This failure made the whole exercise a waste of time. However cheap the new blockships, they had to be manned, and each carried over 600 men. Seamen were too precious to be risked on foolhardy missions; it was immaterial the ships themselves were cannon-fodder. Unfortunately, they were good for little else than moveable batteries. Soon after their completion, two of them were surveyed by a naval engineer, and he thought they were slow under steam, with no power against a head-wind, without sufficient canvas to spare if their engines failed. All in all, they meant a loss of precious timber, labour, machinery, and nearly £100,000.[9]

There was a far better way of engaging maritime fortresses, and that was by using small screw-vessels equipped with long-range weapons. Experiments had been made with long-range shore bombardment before the war. Some powerful shell-guns had been strengthened at the breech and fired using specially weighted spherical shells at high angles of elevation. H. D. Chads, the

[9] Surveyor to Board, 28 Sept. 1854, ADM 1 5632; also 4 Dec., enclosing the Emperor's plan, dated 16 Nov., ADM 1 5633. Michael Seymour (Napier's Captain of the Fleet) to Graham, 27 Apr. 1854, Netherby Papers, box III, bundle 14 c.w. Rear-Admiral Baynes to R. S. Dundas, 7 July 1855, Melville Papers, GD 51.2.1088.2.

Captain of the gunnery ship *Excellent*, had directed the trials, and they had shown that ranges of 5,000 yards and over could be obtained—rather more than was possible with mortar-fire. Henceforward, Chads concluded, Cherbourg, St Malo, Le Havre, Boulogne, and Calais might all be bombarded beyond the range of the protecting batteries.[10] The enemy had changed by 1854, but the central idea remained the same, and as the war went on the Admiralty ordered the construction of more and more small screw-vessels to carry heavy shell-guns.

The guns were not the same type that Chads had experimented with. The first of the British screw gun-vessels, the *Arrow* class, carried an early form of rifled cannon, the Lancaster gun, which was capable of very long-range fire. But it was erratic, and its elongated shells were difficult to produce (and expensive—the first ones cost £12 each). Only a few of the later screws were fitted with Lancasters. The war encouraged industrialists both in Britain and France to design rifled cannon, some of which showed promise even before the war ended and were to have an effect on post-war naval construction policy. But they were not ready in time for the myriad smaller versions of the gun-vessels, the gunboats, that were ordered in 1854–5. Instead, the Admiralty fitted its cockleshells with standard smooth-bore ordnance, sixty-eight and thirty-two pounders. These did not have unusual range, and thus in attacking a Russian installation would necessarily have been in range of any protecting batteries. But the attacker had an advantage. Gunboats were small and elusive targets, whilst the enemy batteries, and the dockyards and arsenals behind them, could scarcely avoid being hit.

Not that the prime function of the small screws was to bombard. The Lancaster gun confused the issue for a time, since its elongated shell carried a heavy powder charge—up to 12 lb. Spherical cannon-shells, on the other hand, were much less powerful: the powder charge of the eight-inch shell, which could be fired from the sixty-eight pounder, was a mere 2 lb. 4 oz. Once the Lancaster system came under a cloud, as it had done by early 1855, it became clear that the best weapon for bombarding land targets was still the heavy mortar, of 10 and 12 inches. The shells could be fired at over 4,000 yards, and they carried a heavy explosive charge. Moreover, mortar shells had a far greater smashing effect than ordinary shells,

[10] Report of 1 July 1852, ADM 13 1, pp. 88 ff.

since they were fired at high elevation: the mortar shell climbed steeply, and fell almost vertically on to its target from a great height, penetrating deeply into the earth and exploding with all the force of a mine.[11] A few British mortar-vessels were laid down in 1854 and many more during the rest of the war. They were not steam-powered, merely what were called mortar 'floats',[12] but they were to give the British Baltic fleet a new striking power; though they depended greatly on the gun-vessels and gunboats, which had the vital function of moving the floats into firing position and then protecting them against any attack from enemy flotilla vessels. This combination was far superior to the previous sail and oar flotillas, which had depended on abundant nearby reserves of manpower, and were very ill fitted to face deep-sea conditions. The new force, of course, depended on coal, not muscle, and is worthy of the name of steam-flotilla. It was not a mere short-range, fair-weather fleet. Some of the gun-vessels proved excellent sea-boats. Even the gunboats were capable of long sea voyages (some went as far as China) once precautions were taken, such as removing the heavy ordnance before the passage and sending an escort. With the steam-flotilla, in short, the Royal Navy had a potent new means of 'projecting' force.[13]

In speaking of the new blockships and the steam-flotilla, we have somewhat disregarded the French navy. This is inevitable. The special construction was primarily for the Baltic, a war zone of particular naval significance, and of particular British interest. Unlike in the Black Sea, the allies did not have a large army there. Bomarsund was taken with a mere 10,000 troops, all French, and they did not return in 1855. Thus it was in the Baltic that the question was posed most starkly of what sea power could achieve against land power, ships against soldiers. The question was one that the British had often faced before, and they were the principal ones to face it on this occasion. French naval resources were strained by the Black Sea campaign, and the French squadrons sent to the Baltic were definitely second rate, mostly composed of sail of the line. Furthermore, it was only the British government that

[11] Sir Howard Douglas, *Naval Gunnery* (4th edn., London, 1855), 355.
[12] The only other British vessels armed with mortars were four 'mortar frigates', converted from four vessels which began, but never completed, conversion to screw-frigate blockships as part of the 1845 harbour and coast protection scheme.
[13] See A. Preston and John Major, *'Send a Gunboat': A Study of the Gunboat and its Role in British Policy, 1854–1904* (London, 1967).

thought it important to strike a great blow in the Baltic. White-hall believed a chance lay there to redeem Britain's less than impressive war-making in the Crimea. From the first wartime winter onwards increasing efforts were made, in the royal and private dockyards, to build the kind of vessels that could take the war to the main Russian maritime fortresses. Hence it was that the new blockships were converted, and hundreds of screw gun-vessels, gunboats and mortar floats were built. The French government, which had neither the same need nor the same construction capacity available, built no blockships at all and completed less than three dozen flotilla craft. However, the French did make one important contribution.

Before the war, it had been commonly believed that shells would be a devastating weapon, at least by naval officers: the Earl of Auckland, when First Lord, had been shocked to be told by his professional advisers that an eighty-four-gun sail of the line, costing perhaps £100,000 to build, could be destroyed by an enemy liner with three broadsides in as many minutes.[14] The opinion had been given very calmly: officers, one presumes, had become inured to the prospect of brief and fiery engagements; their training and habits militated against any rejection of an option simply because it was expensive in men and ships — as long as the fleet of the probable enemy was not too different from their own, and would have to pay the same kind of price in battle. But some kind of imaginative failure was also involved: the high cost of a modern naval battle could not be truly envisaged until one had occurred. Only a few officers wondered whether shell-guns might be countered in some way with armour. Then came the battle of Sinope, in November 1853, when a Turkish squadron was virtually annihilated by a Russian fleet employing shell-guns. The quest for an effective protection against shell-fire now became urgent, above all because Napoleon III himself became involved, and called for trials.

There had been trials of armour in the previous decade, but all had been negative. As we can now appreciate, they had not been well organized. Sometimes the armour tried was weak because it had been made of several sheets of thin iron bolted together; or the armour was stronger, comprising thick plates of homogeneous

---

[14] Sir John Briggs, *Naval Administrations 1827 to 1892: The Experience of 65 Years* (London, 1897), 84.

wrought iron, but was not given a backing to absorb the shocks and could be shattered by a few shots. However, after Sinope more effort and intelligence was employed in the search. At Vincennes it was discovered that four-inch thick wrought iron, well supported by timber, could resist a very heavy concentration of shot, and shrug off shell. Consequently, in June 1854 the Ministry of Marine authorized the construction of ten—later five—steam ironclad-batteries, vessels fit to take on the Russian fortresses without being destroyed.[15]

As part of the rather surprising degree of allied co-operation then current, the plans of the batteries were sent to London, and it was proposed that each country should build a certain number for Baltic operations in 1855. Details of the Vincennes trials were also sent, but the Admiralty wanted more proof, as one sees from the following letter sent to the Foreign Secretary (Lord Clarendon) by Sir James Graham, the First Lord:

I am anxious to meet the wish of the Emperor and to join in building Floating Batteries on the plan suggested by the French Engineers. But as the outlay will be large if this construction is adopted, and as I must be responsible to Parliament for the measure, I have thought it prudent to test the experiments of the effect of shot on iron of the proposed thickness . . . The plan rests mainly on the success of similar experiments tried at Vincennes . . . All our previous experiments have led us to the conclusion that Iron is not to be trusted under a heavy fire, as a material for shipbuilding: but in the French plan Iron is combined with wood, and is of a greater thickness than in any of our previous trials.[16]

The British tests confirmed those of the French: five batteries were laid down to meet the French programme, and the Admiralty authorized four more the following year (one of them to re-place one of the previous five accidentally destroyed by fire on the slipway).

They were like great flat-irons, of some 1,600 tons displacement, only partially rigged and with small engines of 150 hp, so could not be expected to be good sea-boats. According to the testimony of Lieutenant Dawkins, who served on the *Glatton*, their canvas was 'utterly useless'. Even with the furnaces lit, the batteries proved slow—four knots was the best speed—and difficult to steer. The

[15] J. P. Baxter, *The Introduction of the Ironclad Warship* (Harvard University Press, 1933), 69–73.   [16] 15 Sept. 1854, Graham Papers.

allies exchanged information about their unruly offspring, but found no solution. Even with large lee-boards, the vessels were not trustworthy at sea, and when some were despatched to fight the Russians they were towed by powerful steamers.[17]

Yet as fighting machines they had some great strengths. They were powerfully armed (the French were each armed with sixteen fifty-pounders); they had the protection of 4 inches (10 cm) of iron; and with a draught of only 9 feet (a third that of contemporary battleships), they could penetrate coastal shoals. Once in the right position they could show themselves off to excellent effect. None of the British batteries were completed in time to take part in the war, but three of the French ones, the *Lave*, *Tonnante*, and *Dévastation*, had an important role in the attack of September 1855 on the fort of Kinburn, situated on a small peninsula jutting north-west from the Crimea. They positioned themselves a mere 800 yards from the enemy guns, but suffered few casualties, and those resulted from the Russian shot that came in through the gun-ports. The armour itself was scarcely damaged: on later inspection only slight dents and rust marks were found where hits had been made. This was all most impressive, especially because the batteries' fire had been very effective. Other vessels had taken part in the operation, at a more discreet range admittedly, but Sir Edmund Lyons judged that the batteries alone could have brought down Kinburn's walls in only three hours. He wrote to the First Naval Lord that he could 'take it for granted the floating batteries have become elements in amphibious warfare, so the sooner you set about having as many good ones as the French the better it will be for you'.[18]

Kinburn, of course, was in the Black Sea. Why had the batteries not been sent to the Baltic, as indeed, had been originally intended? The answer appears to be that the allied Baltic commanders in 1855, R. S. Dundas and Charles Pénaud, preferred to do without them. Dundas was afraid that they might get isolated from the allied gunboats amongst the Russian shoals, be surrounded by the

[17] M.-C.-M.-R. Testu de Balincourt and P. Vincent-Bréchignac, 'La Marine française d'hier: Les cuirassés: I. Batteries flottantes', *Revue maritime*, 125 (May 1930), 582–3. G. A. Osbon, 'The First of the Ironclads', *Mariner's Mirror*, 50 (1964), 189–98. Journal of Lieutenant Richard Dawkins, 20 June 1855, Dawkins Papers, DAW 3. Letter to Isaac Watts from M. Guieysse at the Ministry of Marine, 5 June 1855, S9992, ADM 87 59.

[18] Captain S. Eardley-Wilmot, *Life of Admiral Lord Lyons* (London, 1898), 368–9. Lambert, *The Crimean War*, 257–9.

enemy flotilla, boarded, and captured. Dundas, as so often, was being pessimistic. But he and Pénaud agreed that batteries were not necessary in the Baltic war: far better, it was thought, to rely on the gunboats and mortar-vessels. The batteries, after all, were designed to batter down walls; to create breaches that could then be exploited by troops—as at Kinburn. But there was no allied army in the Baltic in 1855, nor any likelihood that there would be one. Therefore the allies were well advised to rely on naval weapons that could destroy the centres of enemy arsenals, not merely the walls.[19]

That gunboats and mortar-vessels could strike such a blow was amply demonstrated on 9–10 August 1855 when the allied navies bombarded Sweaborg. Only twenty-one mortar-vessels and seventeen screw-gunboats and gun-vessels were present, though useful added fire came from thirty small rocket-boats, and from four French ten-inch brass mortars landed on a rock 3,000 yards from the fortress. In comparison with what would become available when the Royal Navy's enormous wartime steam-flotilla programme had been completed, the means of attack at Sweaborg were limited; so limited, indeed, that Dundas had thought beforehand little impression could be made on the arsenal, feared heavy casualties from the Russian fire, and wanted to cancel the operation. Pénaud, on the contrary, had been far more sanguine, and managed to persuade his Scottish colleague to attack. The result was spectacular: most of the centre of Sweaborg was burned out, principally by mortar fire, and two gunboats with Lancasters managed to drop one or more of their heavy if unpredictable shells on to a three-decker battleship. Dundas confessed afterwards that the destruction had surprised him. The enemy had been able to do little in response. A Russian steam-flotilla did not emerge to attack, as Dundas had anticipated: one did not exist. Nor did Sweaborg's defending cannon cause many casualties: only one allied sailor was killed, and more were wounded by firing mishaps than through enemy action.[20]

[19] R. S. Dundas to Wood, 13 June 1855, Halifax Papers, BM Add. MS 49533, fos. 73–7. Wood to Dundas, 3 July, Melville Papers, GD 51.2.1088.2. Pénaud to Hamelin, 13 June, AN GG2 85 (marine).
[20] R. S. Dundas to Wood, 31 July and 14 Aug. 1855, Halifax Papers, ibid., fos. 122–6, 132–6. Pénaud to Hamelin, 24 July, and report of 20 Aug., AN GG2 42 (marine). See also W. Laird Clowes, The Royal Navy: A History (7 vols., London, 1897–1903), vi. 491–8. Lambert, The Crimean War, ch. 20.

Thus both the steam-flotillas and the ironclad-batteries had their own, separate triumphs; and each of them had important effects on post-war naval policy. The Crimean War at sea, primarily a coastal war, was distinctly peculiar in comparison with the kind of wars the British and French navies were accustomed to, where for the most part the great events had been engagements on the high seas. This peculiar war, and the new naval instruments it gave rise to, for some years closely shaped men's conceptions of future naval wars, even where the supposed opponents were Britain and France themselves. The steam-flotilla, it appeared to many, would take a very large part in warfare: Captain Henry Codrington, who fought in the Baltic, was not alone in his opinion that 'almost all war afloat will now be litoral [sic] warfare'.[21]

Such attitudes were not strong enough to lead to any general loss of faith in the battlefleet, which remained the central element of naval power. But, of course, the experience of the Crimean War did have important implications for the way the battlefleet would develop. Henceforward, as we have noted, for a vessel to be seen as fit to lie in the line-of-battle, she had to be equipped with a screw steam-engine, and preferably a powerful one. There were also the lessons of Sinope and Kinburn. These took some time to be absorbed, and once again the French took the lead. It was the Ministry of Marine, rather than the Admiralty, which first accepted that a battleship required armour as well as engines.

II

Peace was signed in March 1856, and relations between the British and French governments rapidly lost their warmth. Whitehall thought that the French Emperor was seeking a rapprochement with his Russian brother indecently quickly, and by the end of the year the Admiralty was taking care to ensure that the Royal Navy in the Black Sea was capable of meeting both the French and Russian squadrons there. The following year relations were less fraught. The differences were mostly settled.[22] A sign of

[21] Codrington to Rear-Admiral Peter Richards, 7 July 1855, Codrington Papers, COD. 109.2.

[22] Lynn M. Case, Édouard Thouvenel et la diplomatie du Second Empire (Paris, 1976), ch. 5. T. W. Riker, 'The Concert of Europe and Moldavia in 1857', English Historical Review, 42 (1927), 227–44.

composition was a joint attempt to put pressure on China to open herself more to western trade and influence. Furthermore, the French government showed itself disinterested, even generous: it helped settle a British dispute with Persia, and offered transit across France to British troops being sent to quell the Indian Mutiny. However, neither Whitehall nor the British public showed much gratitude: indeed, both powers, from governmental down to popular levels, remained suspicious of the other.

The naval rivalry was not immune, and by 1858 was entering a new and more intense phase. This phase lasted until the first two to three years of the following decade. It was a time when the naval construction race was at its most hectic, spurred on by and itself spurring on what was an unprecedented rate of technological improvements in gunnery, engines, armour-plate, and hull construction.

However, as before, diplomatic disagreements were the foundation of poor relations. Turkey still remained a problem. In some ways the heritage of the Crimean War ensured continuing Anglo-French co-operation; the two powers being concerned to ensure that the balance tipped in Turkey's favour by the Crimean War was not disturbed. Yet sharing an interest in preserving Turkey as a bastion against Russia did not mean automatic cordiality, as one sees from the behaviour of the British and French representatives at Constantinople. The city was made for confrontation, intrigue, and personality politics; at times the two ambassadors were in a state of undeclared war. The battle extended to the two governments. First because each thought it worthwhile on general principles to have the pre-eminent voice in the Turkish capital, and secondly because, for seven years from 1859, with little rest, each side tried to persuade the Sultan to favour its policy over the project to build the Suez Canal. Whitehall was opposed, believing that it was not a feasible scheme (because of the supposed differences in level between the Mediterranean and the Red Sea) and—often at the same time—thinking that it was feasible and, once built, would fall under French influence and pose a threat to British links with India.[23]

The French government had tended to favour the project from 1856, though began to support it fully only in 1859. France had long been interested both in Egypt and a canal: measurements had

_____

[23] H. L. Hoskins, *British Routes to India* (London, 1928), ch. 14.

been taken of water levels—unfortunately with some gross errors — after Napoleon defeated the Mamelukes and occupied the country. Moreover, the canal promoter in the 1850s was himself a Frenchman, Ferdinand de Lesseps, and thousands of his countrymen had purchased shares in his company. British influence prevented the Sultan from approving the canal until 1866. But the Egyptian viceroy was virtually a sovereign prince, and French influence at Cairo was very strong. In 1859 the first cutting began, despite the Sultan, and proceeded as quickly as finances allowed. By 1865 the first small steamer had scraped its way from sea to sea, and in 1869 came the grand formal opening.

The French interest in Egypt and the canal was seen in Whitehall as but part of an attempt to gain influence both in the Mediterranean and on the routes to the Far East. In 1858 French warships began operations in Indo-China that were to lead, by 1861, to the seizure of large territories around Saigon, and rights of overlordship in Cambodia. To support the new conquests, regular lines of communication had to be set up, and the *Messageries impériales* began a service from Suez to Bombay and Saigon in competition with the P. and O. line. With the taking of Obock, opposite Aden, a useful port of supply and refreshment became available on the route (1862). However, the French Far East empire had as yet more pretensions than substance: it was involvement in the lands bordering the Mediterranean that most excited Whitehall.

In this connection, apart from Egypt, there was the Lebanon. In 1861–2 the French intervened with military as well as naval force, because of massacres of Maronite Christians by Druses which the Turkish authorities were for a time unable or unwilling to prevent. Difficulty came with Britain because, while the Maronites were traditionally regarded as under French protection, the British felt possessive about the Druses. The question thus became one of the relations between the clients of great powers. There was also a particular reason for British sensitivity. Whitehall, remembering Algeria only too well, was very much afraid that Paris wanted to create a Lebanese colony, not at all believing protestations to the contrary.[24]

This was all very reminiscent of 1844 and the French intervention in Morocco, not only in the nature of the British suspicions

[24] Marcel Émerit, 'La Crise syrienne et l'expansion économique française en 1860', *Revue historique*, 207 (1952), 211–32.

but also the degree of mistrust and the extent to which Anglo-French relations had soured from an earlier *entente*. One dissimilarity was that in 1844 the nadir was yet to come. In 1860−1 that point had already been reached, thanks to another Mediterranean problem—the unification of Italy.

The French war against Austria, on behalf of Piedmont, offended both friends and enemies of Italy in Britain. The Italophiles believed that the cause was just, but were jealous that it should be France that upheld it so vigorously. Of course, once Napoleon III fell short of achieving full Italian unification, by agreeing an armistice with the Austrian Emperor, then the Italophiles easily moved to a condemnation of France for deviousness and inconsistency. On the other hand, those (such as the Queen) who favoured Austria saw the French war as disturbing to the European balance, and as one more step in a plan of Napoleon's to revenge his family on each of the victors of 1815 in turn: Russia had been defeated, it was said, Austria was now under attack, and Prussia and England were next. Whatever his attitude to Italy, therefore, the Briton tended to condemn France in 1859−60, particularly because she appeared to be achieving a dominance in the Italian peninsula that would further bolster her Mediterranean position. That French policy was directed southwards, and that it was unscrupulous, seemed to be only too well demonstrated by Napoleon's manœuvring in early 1860 to get Piedmont to cede Savoy and Nice to France as payment for services rendered.[25]

The various international crises over Italy naturally had naval implications, encouraging both Britain and France to maintain large Mediterranean squadrons, not only in case of war between themselves, but also because naval demonstrations in the Italian ports were regarded by both powers as essential supports to their diplomacy. This degree of preparedness in itself sharpened rivalry, but the Italian question had managed to encourage that rivalry well before France and Austria went to war in 1859, in the shape of a full-blown naval scare.

1858 had begun quietly enough for Anglo-French relations; but on 14 January the Italian nationalist Orsini and his fellows tried to blow up Napoleon III who, they thought, had not been doing enough for the Italian cause. Britain had been Orsini's base, and

[25] Denis Mack Smith, *Victor Emanuel, Cavour, and the Risorgimento* (OUP, 1971), 158 ff.

Birmingham his bomb factory, and there was much anger in France—particularly among some army colonels—over England's excessive hospitality.[26] Palmerston was Prime Minister, and tried to be conciliatory. He did not remind the French that their Emperor had once found Britain a congenial political base, and he attempted to make it more difficult for foreign revolutionaries to use the country as a base for assassination. The Conspiracy to Murder Bill was drawn up, the intention being to make it a felony to plot in Britain to murder someone abroad, but Palmerston, of all people, was accused of truckling to the French. Some Liberal MPs revolted against the government, were joined by the Conservatives, and the Bill was defeated on 19 February on its second reading, to the fury of loyal Frenchmen. Lord Derby then became Prime Minister, and found himself presiding over a developing unpleasantness with France. As a concomitant to the diplomatic crisis, there was a naval scare, natural in any Anglo-French crisis at this time, but exacerbated by the angry colonels, who were allowed to publish petitions in the official newspaper *Le Moniteur*, asking to be allowed to cross to London to drive the revolutionaries out of their lairs.

As before, friction with France led to the British looking to their home defences. They found the situation normal—there were few naval forces in the Channel and it seemed unlikely, thanks to the inadequate seaman-reserve system, that the warships preserved in the Ordinary could be manned as quickly as the French reserve fleet could be. Furthermore, and this was novel and very disturbing, it was appreciated that even if the full battlefleet were commissioned, it would not be much or at all superior to the rival's. As Sir Baldwin Walker informed the Board in March, and as became widely known, both navies had thirty screw-battleships built, excluding the nine British blockships. And if the then rate of construction were continued, it appeared that by 1859 the French would have forty and the British only thirty-six. Moreover, Walker added, the French steam-line-of-battle was faster, and almost as heavily armed. The existing French battleships had engines with a combined hp of 19,810, and mounted 2,752 guns; the British hp total was only 15,650, though they could bring 2,796 guns into action.[27]

---

[26] Letters of 19 and 29 Jan. 1858 from the comte de Persigny, French ambassador in London, to the comte de Walewski, Minister of Foreign Affairs, Quai d'Orsay, Correspondence politique: Angleterre, vol. 704, fos. 41, 98–101.

[27] Surveyor to Board, 24 Mar. and 13 Nov. 1858, ADM 1 5705.

To combat public unease, Derby's First Lord—Sir John Pakington —announced in April that in an emergency no fewer than twenty screw-battleships could be manned and stationed in the Channel in one month. This estimate exaggerated slightly the number of vessels available. More seriously, it assumed there would be no difficulty over getting the seamen. Admittedly, the men were clearly available for nine of the twenty: these were the *blockships*. The previous year they had been allocated as coastguard ships, along with some screw-gunboats. Each blockship had gone to one of the nine coastguard districts, and could be manned by the local coastguards at need. They could be relied on, therefore; but the Admiralty would have had great trouble in manning any more battleships, as is well shown by the attempts made to complete the crews of some warships early in 1858. Something of a national scandal grew up about these ships, especially the new *vaisseau à vapeur*, the *Renown*. She was commissioned on 21 November 1857, but by 5 December she had only 170 seamen, and not until March was the ship able to put to sea: even then, with 633 men, she was still over thirty short of complement.[28] The coincidence with the Orsini crisis was unfortunate, and the manning problem redoubled the naval scare.

By the summer, having spent much money bringing ships forward from the Ordinary and giving bounties to volunteer seamen, the Admiralty had managed to gather a Channel squadron. But popular fears of a French invasion did not ebb away. As in 1844–5, troubles came in battalions, including one of especial significance to Channel watchers. Since the previous century, a great new port had been in the making at Cherbourg. As the nineteenth century wore on, more and more facilities were brought into use; new basins, new docks, new fortifications. At last, in 1858, the enormous mole protecting the harbour was completed, and in August a splendid ceremony was organized to open the naval arsenal formally. The Queen and Prince Albert were invited, and given a sumptuous entertainment, including a feast aboard the *Bretagne*, which had come round from the Mediterranean to Cherbourg for the occasion with the rest of the *escadre des évolutions*. Yet neither the Queen, nor the public left at home, found much to celebrate. Never before had France had a great arsenal and excellent harbour directly facing the Channel and the South Coast of

---

[28] PP (1857–8), xxxix. 341–50.

England. Capable of outfitting, sheltering, and despatching a great invasion fleet, Cherbourg seemed like a knife pointing directly at Britain's jugular.

The evidence that seemed to be building up from 1858 of the aggressiveness of France's foreign policy and the expanding capabilities of her navy had one immediate British response, a serious effort to develop the seagoing fleet and to ensure a numerical superiority, above all in screw-battleships. As in 1852, the Surveyor geared up himself and the dockyards for a spurt in construction and conversion. Sir Baldwin calculated that by the end of 1860 the French navy would have fifty screw-liners. To counter this force, he believed the Royal Navy needed eighty (excluding the blockships). He wanted a fleet of twenty battleships to be available for the Mediterranean, the same number in the North Sea, and thirty more in the Channel. The remaining ten were to be under repair or acting as reliefs. His plan is of interest as demonstrating the desire, under the new conditions of steam-warfare, to keep a very large proportion of the fleet in home waters in the event of war.

There was also a lesson for peacetime deployment. From 1858 onwards, more often than not the Royal Navy maintained a Channel Fleet; something it had not been accustomed to do in peacetime. This fleet never approached thirty battleships, of course; that was a wartime level. Moreover, as Walker realized, it was a level that could not be achieved even in war for some time. In the short term, he admitted, the best to be hoped for was simple numerical superiority over the French. In an ordinary year, the royal dockyards were capable of launching three battleships plus three frigates and six sloops. With large infusions of money and 4,000 more dockyard workers, the Surveyor argued in November 1858, in two years there could be as many as nine new battleships ready for sea, plus eight sail of the line converted to the screw. The result would be a battlefleet of fifty-six vessels (again excluding the blockships). If not the ideal size, this would at least be larger than the French equivalent.[29]

The Admiralty pressed forward as fast as it could with the expansion of the screw-fleet. The constraint was not money: the Commons proved very generous when confronted with the vision of French troops in London. The real limit was the shortage of

[29] As n. 27 above. Pakington to Lord Derby, 23 Nov. 1858, Pakington Papers, 3835, parcel 11 (iii).

trained shipwrights and the supply of seasoned wood, of which the latter was the most critical. Normally the yards consumed 25,000 loads a year, but the new programme meant an extra 8,000 a year— only 2,000 under the total that could be got by exhausting all available sources in Britain, Italy, Africa, Cuba, the East Indies, and elsewhere.[30] Oddly enough, the shortage was to prove fortunate. It encouraged a turn to a substitute; a superior one as it happened. More important for the present argument, it meant the Admiralty could not further increase the screw-programme and waste even more money.

It was not that there was much wrong with Walker's proposed battleships, as examples of their type. The screw conversions were as powerful as could be reasonably expected; and, thanks to the Crimean experience, from 1855 onwards all new British battleships were *bâtiments à vapeur*, as were many of the small vessels. No fewer than thirteen battleships were laid down between February 1858 and October 1860, all of them fast second-rates, like the *Napoléon*. The British had certainly surpassed the construction plan approved by Ducos in 1853–4. Unfortunately, already by 1858 the French navy had again taken a new course, and the Admiralty was building a large but obsolete fleet.

III

For the French navy, too, had been taught by the Crimean War. One thing learned, as with the Royal Navy, had been the crucial importance of steam and of the screw engine. What Admiral Hamelin (Ducos's successor) said in 1857 may be applied to both navies:

If war had not broken out in 1854, one would perhaps still be discussing today the utility of a sailing navy compared to a steam navy . . . the hostilities were hardly declared when already the opinion of a few became the opinion of a majority.[31]

Albeit of *mixtes*, the wartime British Baltic screw-fleet was a powerful example to French officers. In October 1854, Robiou de

[30] Report of the Storekeeper-General, folder 29 July 1858, ADM 1 5698, pt. 2.
[31] F. W. Wallin, 'The French Navy during the Second Empire: A Study of the Effects of Technological Development on French Governmental Policy', unpub. Ph.D. thesis (Berkeley, California, 1953), 73.

Lavrignais, whilst acting (temporarily) as *directeur du matériel*, backed his arguments in favour of increased screw construction by citing the appeal made by the French Baltic C.-in-C. of 1854, Vice-Admiral Parseval-Deschênes. The admiral had been convinced of the importance of steam by the daily spectacle of the superiority of the British squadron over his own mostly sailing-squadron; and he asked that all or at least most of his battleships be converted to steam over the winter of 1854–5.

Robiou de Lavrignais took Parseval's appeal as a basis of a plan of his own for the entire battlefleet. He accepted that more *vaisseaux mixtes* should be built, but not simply as a war-emergency measure. He thought that a fleet needed both fast battleships and ones of moderate speed. A fleet only of *Napoléons*, he thought, would be too expensive. It would consume too much coal, and the cost of maintenance would be high: the movement in a seaway of the long hulls would lead to great wear on the engines and screw-shafts. Furthermore, *mixtes* had better nautical qualities under sail alone. Consequently, the battlefleet should consist of both types. The proportion he wanted was one fast to two *mixtes*, since one *Napoléon* could easily tow two vessels of its own rate. In a properly composed fleet, if it became necessary to proceed under steam, each fast vessel could take two *mixtes* in tow, with the economy that only a third of the fleet had to burn coal. He thus proposed the immediate conversion of six sail of the line into *mixtes*, with sixteen others to follow; and three sail of the line to be transformed into *vaisseaux à vapeur*. The end result was to be a total French battlefleet of thirty-three *mixtes* and fourteen fast battleships.[32]

The plan was regressive, sacrificing the important principle of quality, the main point of superiority that the French fleet could have over its rival. Ducos approved the initial conversions suggested (six *mixtes* and three fast), but the whole plan—a truly English compromise, apart from its rigour—was not adopted.

In 1855 a *Commission supérieure centrale* was appointed, under the presidency of Parseval-Deschênes, to consider the future shape of the fleet. Robiou de Lavrignais was one of the members, but the commission's report sketched out a fleet very different from his. To begin with, the scheme dealt with the entire fleet, not just its battleships. One of the recommendations was for a transport fleet

---

[32] Submission of 19 Oct. 1854, AN GG2 41 (*marine*).

capable of carrying 40,000 troops, their equipment, and horses. Moreover, the commission fixed firmly on quality as the best way to counter enemy numerical superiority. According to Dupuy de Lôme, though not a member himself, the commission had been convinced by the war of 'l'incontestable supériorité des navires à vapeur sur les navires à voiles et des vaisseaux à vapeur rapides sur les vaisseaux à petite vitesse'. The commission was even prepared to sacrifice some of the battleship's military qualities to its speed under steam—a significant concession for officers in a fighting navy to make. Henceforward, it was said, the state's principal naval arm should be a fast fleet, composed of twenty-five battleships of ninety guns, fifteen of seventy (a new type), with twenty forty-gun frigates, thirty corvettes and sixty sloops of the first and second classes.[33]

The scheme was subjected to one radical change. Sinope, the armour trials at Vincennes, and the combat at Kinburn suggested to the Emperor that the 1855 commission might have been too conservative. Another commission was appointed in November 1856 to study the future of the fleet. This time Dupuy de Lôme was one of the members, and he persuaded his colleagues to adapt the conclusions of the 1855 commission by making it possible, if it seemed necessary, to build not screw-liners but screw ironclad-frigates. He very possibly used the arguments he was to employ in a work of 1866, a description of his scientific work printed to support his candidature for the *Académie*.[34] He wrote there that iron armour was a means to equal the Royal Navy: invulnerability, coupled with great speed, meant that one did not need to fear superior numbers. And since armoured raiders could not be destroyed, the nation with the most to fear from naval war, he added pointedly, was the one with the greatest sea-borne trade. Armour, in short, further satisfied the tactical and strategic principles that lay behind the *vaisseau à vapeur*.

Dupuy's bold attitude was supported by trials at Lorient of rifled guns. Tests against wooden targets showed that such weapons posed an especially serious threat to the screw-liner. Once equipped with accurate long-range shell-guns, it was realized, small vessels could confidently hope to destroy unarmoured battleships: rifled

---

[33] Ibid. Report dated 11 Aug. 1855. See also the meeting of the *Conseil d'amirauté* on 14 Jan. 1854, V BB8 1134. 29–38.

[34] *Notice sur les travaux scientifiques de M. Dupuy de Lôme*, 32–3.

guns seemed to vindicate Paixhan's 1822 book. As a result of the
gunnery tests, the first section of the *Conseil des travaux* proposed on
13 January 1857 that all work on screw-battleships be stopped.[35]
The advice was not taken: the task of producing a steam fleet had
gained an inertia of its own: all liners under construction were
completed, albeit with great slowness in some cases, and until 1858
more sail of the line were taken in hand for conversion into screws.
But the French were fortunate: since March 1855, partly because of
pressure of work in the dockyards and partly because of doubt over
the most suitable design, no new screw-liners had been laid down.
The break in construction probably aided the Ministry of Marine to
think more open-mindedly about the shape of the future battlefleet;
and it also meant that, after the change to the ironclad, the French
were not encumbered with the weight of new but obsolete ships
that burdened the Admiralty.

It seems to have been the Emperor who made the final decision
that the ironclad would replace the screw-liner. There was of
course some support in the Ministry of Marine. But Hamelin, the
Minister, though a worthy officer, perhaps would have preferred to
continue with the fast battleship: he certainly lacked the drive and
receptivity to new ideas of his predecessor, Ducos, or his successor,
Chasseloup-Laubat. It was the Emperor who decided that the new
directeur du matériel should be Dupuy de Lôme, appointing him in
January 1857, at the same time promoting him to *directeur des construc-
tions navales*, the second highest rank for a French naval engineer.
Dupuy was now responsible to the Minister for the design, construction, and repair of the warfleet. During 1857 he matured his
plans and with Napoleon's support was able to begin an armoured
construction programme. Three ironclads were ordered in March
1858 (including the famous *Gloire*), yet another in September, and
two more the following June. Even more ambitious plans were
made in 1860, after the *Gloire* had proved herself in her trials of
August–September. Plans were drawn up for ten more ironclads,
which Hamelin approved on 16 November. By the end of 1860,
therefore, the date Sir Baldwin Walker had set for the Royal Navy
to gain a decisive lead in screw-battleships, the French navy had
struck out boldly on a quite new path. The Admiralty won its own
race, realizing too late that there was no competitor.[36]

[35] V BB8 1140. 25.   [36] Baxter, *Introduction of the Ironclad Warship*, ch. 6.

The complex story of the acceptance by the British navy, government, and parliament that the screw-liner had been made obsolete has already been well told by J. P. Baxter. Only its main elements need to be presented here. The first is the initial reluctance of the Admiralty to see the demise of the screw-liner. The first reaction of the Naval Lords to the news of the first French ironclads is reflected in the comment by the then First Naval Lord, W. F. Martin, that now one had to lay down even more screw-liners. Perhaps the main doubt about the screw-liner at this time concerned not its vulnerability to fire but the weakness of its armament. In the late 1850s the US navy began to complete seven large screw-frigates. They were very powerfully armed. The *Merrimack*, for instance, carried two ten-inch guns, four nine-inch, and fourteen eight-inch. The *Niagara*, even larger, had an enormous battery of fourteen eleven-inch cannon. In reply, the Surveyor's Department designed some formidable frigates of its own; they carried a ten-inch and sixty-eight pounder armament and also had powerful engines and high speed, a great advance over the US originals, which were poor steamers. All this meant a large displacement: the new frigates were virtually the same size as first-rate screw-battleships; moreover, their heavy, long-range armament was in certain ways superior to anything else afloat. Some senior British naval officers were more concerned by the need to re-establish the position of the battleships *vis-à-vis* the frigate than by the threat of the ironclad. Thus in late 1858 the Board of Admiralty spent time considering the plans for a new 100-gun screw-liner, over half the armament of which was to consist of ten-inch and sixty-eight pounders.[37]

However, trials organized at Portsmouth, which demonstrated once more the great resistance to shot and shell of thick, well-backed wrought or rolled iron, and—as always the major influence—the fact that the French had already acted, meant that the Admiralty was constrained to build some ironclads. In May 1859, a year after the *Gloire* was laid down, work began on the first British seagoing ironclad, HMS *Warrior*, followed five months later by a sister ship, the *Black Prince*, a most suitable name, considering her armour and black paint, albeit demonstrating the usual lack of attention to French susceptibilities.

[37] ADM 116 1 and 2, p. 20. ADM 1 5698, pt. 2, 29 July 1858. Letter of Sir Baldwin Walker, 13 Oct. 1857, Walker Papers, WWL 1. The battleship design is dated 11 Dec. 1858.

This did not at all mean the final victory of the ironclad over the screw-liner. As yet the new type was seen by the Surveyor as merely a supplement to the fleet. He made this clear in a submission to the Board of November 1859. Ironclads, he said,

must be regarded as an addition to our force as a balance to those of France, and not as calculated to supersede any existing class of ship;— indeed, no prudent man would at present consider it safe to risk, upon the performance of ships of this novel character, the naval supremacy of Great Britain.[38]

Some within and without the Admiralty did have a rather higher opinion of the ironclad, and their views were supported by the successful trials of the *Gloire* in August and September 1860. But there was no connection between those trials and the suspension, in October, of work on the seven newest British screw-liners. By that date it had become clear that a lead had been built up in unarmoured battleships. Thanks to French concentration on armoured vessels, the Royal Navy now had nearly twenty more screw-liners afloat, fifty-three against thirty-five, again excluding the blockships. It was therefore quite safe for efforts to be devoted to ironclads, so that a lead could be built up in them also.

Only by the spring of 1861 was British opinion swinging clearly in favour of the ironclad. It was now accepted even by a doughty opponent to the type, the gunnery expert Sir Howard Douglas, that ironclads could be opposed only by other ironclads. As he admitted in what was almost a death-bed recantation, 'so long as our neighbours—the French—persist in building iron-cased ships, we *must* do likewise . . .'.[39] But this view did not imply that the screw-liner was obsolete. Palmerston, again Prime Minister, was strongly in agreement here, and he battled with the Chancellor of the Exchequer to get funds for screw-liners as well as armourclads, for he believed that each type had its proper sphere of action, with screw-liners likely to remain supreme on colonial stations. The British ironclads had iron hulls, which easily became fouled. Iron hulls could not be sheathed in copper to inhibit marine growths, since no way had yet been found to control the galvanic action between copper and iron under water, an action that eroded the

[38] Baxter, *Introduction of the Ironclad Warship*, 127. Walker's belief in the screw-liner, and doubt about the ironclad, is confirmed in a letter of Admiral Sir George Grey of 9 Apr. 1859, Grey Papers.

[39] *Trans. of the Royal Institute of Naval Architects*, 2 (1861), 2–7.

iron. On home stations, there were the facilities for regular docking, so iron vessels could have their hulls regularly scraped; beyond
Europe such facilities as yet scarcely existed. Palmerston described
the consequences in a letter of December 1860 to the Duke of
Somerset, the First Lord:

The Iron plated Ships would never be general cruizers for distant
Stations—They must be chiefly for Home or for Stationary Service for
Defence of Coasts and Harbours or for attacking Forts or invading
squadrons.[40]

Thus the cessation of work on the seven latest screw-liners was
intended to be only temporary. The temporary, though, was soon
to become permanent. More British ironclads were laid down, all as
yet in private yards; two were begun in December 1859, two more
in March and February 1861. But the French had got a fine head
start; stronger action was needed. By now, too, there was a new
Surveyor—or Controller, as that officer had been rechristened in
1860. In February 1861 Sir Baldwin Walker resigned, after years of
overwork, and was given the Cape command in part to allow him
to convalesce in a decent climate. His successor was Rear-Admiral
Spencer Robinson. Walker had warmed to the ironclad after 1859,
but there is no denying that the new man was a more forward-
looking officer. He was quoted in the last chapter as being somewhat regressive about the sail of the line, but this was perhaps
exceptional for him. As far back as 1843 he had predicted that
young officers would see ships without rigging in their own life-
times. He came to the Admiralty in time to take advantage of the
growing opinion in favour of the ironclad and the patent need to
catch up with France. In May 1861 he was even able to get approval
for his proposal that, in order to have another British ironclad
quickly at sea, one of the screw-liners abandoned on the stocks the
previous year, the *Royal Oak*, should be taken in hand for armour-
cladding. This example was soon followed as more news arrived of
the progress of the French construction programme. A few days
after the conversion of the *Royal Oak* was approved, four sisters
were added to the list, and eventually all of the seven screw-liners
frozen on the slipways were to be launched as ironclads.

[40] Letter of 15 Dec. 1860, Palmerston Papers, BM Add. MS 48541, fos. 30–1. See
also Palmerston to Gladstone of 29 Nov. 1859 and 25 Feb. 1861, Philip Guedalla
(ed.), *The Palmerston Papers: Palmerston and Gladstone* (London, 1928), 114, 160.

One might take the decision to convert as the effective end of the screw-liner in the Royal Navy: the type served afloat in the seagoing fleets for several more years yet, but the latest generation of screws had been sacrificed to the ironclad and no new examples were laid down. Furthermore, the converted vessels proved well suited to service on distant stations. Their wooden hulls could be sheathed in copper, and thus were not as subject to fouling as iron ones. They were able to take over the screw-liner's last strategic role.

Of course, in 1861 the significance of the conversions was unclear. Massive appropriations continued to be made for timber for the royal dockyards, with at least one eye on future unarmoured battleship construction. In May 1861 the Commons approved expenditure on wood of £949,371, nearly three times as much as the average annual expenditure on wood over the previous decade. There was some opposition: William Lindsay, MP, himself a ship-owner, suggested that given recent changes one could safely reduce the grant by £300,000, but his amendment was defeated. Even in 1862 there was a large timber grant—some £600,000.[41] Only in this year was it finally widely accepted that the screw-liner was obsolete. In April, two months after the timber estimate was approved, there occurred the battle of Hampton Roads. First the Confederate iron-clad *Virginia* sank two wooden frigates, and then went on to fight a stand-off battle with the Federal ironclad *Monitor*. After this engagement it was patently obvious that all battleships had to be armoured. The British Parliament and press realized that the country's screw-liner fleet was obsolete and that recent shipbuilding policy had been purblind and wasteful.

IV

In one way, though, the Royal Navy was not remiss, indeed was considerably advanced. The British ironclads mostly had iron hulls, the French ones mostly had wooden. Iron construction offered many advantages. To begin with, it avoided the basic incompatib-ility between steam machinery and wooden hulls that affected even the best-designed steamer. Both fire and water conspired against

[41] *Hansard*, Ser. 3, vol. clxiii (23 May 1861), col. 52; vol. clxv (24 Feb. 1862), col. 663.

the union: fire was always a threat, given the closeness of furnaces and flues to the timbers, and water—in the shape of condensation from the boilers and engines—worked away slowly to encourage wood-rot. Furthermore, wood and iron had their own strengths and weaknesses, responding very differently to stresses; the natural flexing of the timber hull in a seaway put enormous strains on the metal of the machinery, particularly severe in the case of the long screw-shaft. An iron hull was virtually a necessary complement to iron machinery.

It had other benefits as well. Iron's relative lightness for a given strength, the way it could be knit together more solidly than wood, and the fact that industry could produce far larger beams than nature was capable of, meant that bigger and sturdier vessels with longer, finer lines, could be built than had ever been feasible with wood. With iron, there could be sufficient displacement and stability for ample storage space, powerful steam-engines, a battery carried well above the waterline, and heavy rigging. It also made effective watertight compartments feasible. It is instructive to compare the first British and French ironclads, the iron *Warrior* and the wooden *Gloire*. Not all the differences, of course, were due to the construction material chosen; each vessel reflected the national naval strategy. Hence the *Gloire*, primarily designed for short-range operations, was given reduced rigging; and the closeness of her battery to the waterline suggests that the Mediterranean, with seas less robust than the Atlantic, was her preferred station. Nevertheless, the fact that she was built from wood also had crucial effects, forcing a degree of design compromise that Dupuy de Lôme fretted under. In the *Warrior*, on the other hand, iron gave her designers much more freedom. She was over half as large again than the *Gloire* (9,137 tons displacement as against 5,630), more heavily rigged, carried her guns higher out of the water, and was graced with fine lines and powerful engines that made possible fourteen knots under steam alone—over one and a half knots more than the rival could manage. There is one more point: iron construction was also very durable; many British ironclads of the 1860s had extremely long lives. Obsolescence and the breaker's yard got them before decay did, and—as is famously the case with the *Warrior*—if the breakers were cheated, then the vessel could easily survive for a final and potentially lengthy stage in its career afloat, as museum and national monument.

We appear to be presented with a paradox. The naval administration that we have been praising was retrograde over iron construction, whilst the otherwise reluctant innovator was not. At least
it is easy to explain the first. Dupuy de Lôme realized perfectly well
that iron was preferable to wood; but he was hamstrung by the
paucity of iron-working facilities in the French dockyards, and the
backwardness of French industry. Of all the ironclads ordered
under the programmes of 1858–60, it was found possible to build
only two with iron hulls.

It is much less easy to explain the new-found eagerness of the
Admiralty to innovate; particularly because a decade earlier—
like the Ministry of Marine—the Admiralty had thought it had
scorched itself by being too precipitate about iron. Quite apart
from the *Simoom* and the three other large iron screw-frigates,
during the 1840s the Royal Navy commissioned some fifteen iron
warships, almost all paddlers, plus various ancillary craft. The
French navy began twenty iron paddle-warships between 1843 and
1847; furthermore, with the exception of the *Corse*, *Pomone*, and
Roland, all their screw vessels begun before 1848 were iron-hulled.

But the more of these vessels that were completed, the more they
were regretted. For iron did have some drawbacks. Iron hulls easily
became fouled and then there was the possibility of a ship's iron
hull influencing the compass. It was not until the mid-century that
the means of protection were clearly understood. In a fog an iron
ship, steering by dead reckoning, might find herself on top of some
totally unexpected rocks. Even more serious for the iron warship,
there was the threat of gunfire. Tests in Britain and in France
demonstrated that shot and shell could tear enormous holes in iron
hull-plates, in the process throwing up lethal showers of iron
splinters.[42] Such tests convinced the authorities that iron vessels
were not warships; hence the Admiralty's decision to reclassify the
Simoom and her sisters as transports and to use only wood for
warship hulls.

By the late 1850s, opinion had changed somewhat. The discovery
of effective armour was one reason. After all, if the hull were
protected by armour, then there would be no question of the kind
of multiplication of shrapnel effect that one had seen in the tests
against iron hull-plates. However, one must still be struck by the

[42] Baxter, *Introduction of the Ironclad Warship*, 37–8. Sir Howard Douglas, *Naval Gunnery* (3rd. edn., London, 1851), 167–70, 617–29.

Admiralty's courage in 1859, especially because the *Warrior* and her iron successors were not wholly armoured: since large areas of hull-plate remained open to enemy fire, the shrapnel effect was still very possible, even if one admits that the quality of iron hull-plate available in the late 1850s was far superior to that subjected to trials a decade before. What had appeared to be militarily unacceptable was so no longer.

One undoubted reason was the greater realization—thanks to Sinope—that wooden construction itself had serious disadvantages. The shell suggested not only iron armour but also iron scantlings: projectiles might shatter iron, but at least they could not burn it. Might one also argue that, as had happened to the Ministry of Marine in the 1840s, the humiliation of being outpaced by the rival spurred the Admiralty to take a radical solution? There may be some truth in this. We can certainly agree that by 1859 the Admiralty had become more conscious of the importance of innovation in design. At least they were now open-minded enough to see that the potential effects of enemy fire on the unarmoured portions of an iron-hulled ironclad were more than compensated for by the advantages of iron construction. Rather one should say that the constructors were now more open-minded. Perhaps the Crimean War had an effect here, in the way the war-emergency programme forced the Surveyor's Department to co-operate with private ship-builders. Lessons were then taught that must have lasted into peacetime. In particular, one must wonder whether there were lasting links created between one famous private builder—John Scott Russell, famous as the man who built and was bankrupted by Brunel's *Great Eastern*—and the constructors in the Admiralty. Russell's was one influence among many on the Surveyor and his staff, and its degree remains obscure; one would very much like to know, for instance, about the relationship between Russell and the Admiralty's chief constructor, Isaac Watts, the man who put his name to the *Warrior* design. It is interesting that that vessel followed many of the principles enunciated previously by Russell himself. At least the private sector ought to be allowed some part in the inspiration of the design of the Royal Navy's brave new ironclad fleet.[43]

[43] G. S. Emmerson, *John Scott Russell: A Great Victorian Engineer and Naval Architect* (London, 1977), 160–4. H. Lyon, 'The Relations between the Admiralty and British Industry in the Development of Warships', in B. Ranft (ed.), *Technical Change and British Naval Policy, 1860–1939* (London, 1977), 37–64.

Certainly, at least by the very end of the 1850s the Admiralty constructors had become serious advocates of the iron-hulled ironclad. This one sees from the comments made in 1860 on plans requested from the dockyard master shipwrights for plans of coastal-defence ironclads. Suggestive of the degree of relative conservatism of those shipwrights, only one of the plans specified an iron hull (from the Deptford master shipwright). Watts and his assistants Loyd and Large noted that iron hulls were far superior for armoured vessels.[44]

The constructors were one thing, the executive officers on the Board were another. As far as one can judge, given the paucity of Board minutes during all our period, they seem to have been more struck by the disadvantages of iron than by the opportunities it offered. They do not seem to have been greatly moved even by the chance, with iron, of satisfying some traditional British naval requirements far better than had been possible even with wood. One does not mean here the 'imperial imperative': in 1859–60 scarcely anyone contemplated stationing iron-hulled battleships beyond European waters: maintenance would have been far too difficult. Rather one means British European requirements. Even at home the Royal Navy needed vessels of great endurance and sea-keeping qualities, to defy Atlantic and Channel storms while sweeping the seaways for weeks on end or maintaining lengthy blockades. The Warrior class was well suited to such tasks—but the full realization of the class's capabilities appears to have come only after the actual sea trials: it does not seem to have played a crucial role in the Naval Lords' acceptance of iron hulls. Perhaps Dr Lambert is right that the size and speed of the *Warrior* was due to her being originally envisaged not as a battleship, but as a kind of super frigate, part of a fast squadron, ready to pounce on any enemy point of weakness in battle.[45] Given that, her iron construction appears more understandable, something experimental that senior officers saw as acceptable for a specialist craft if not for the battlefleet itself.

However, it was perhaps not a coincidence that she was ordered during Derby's second Ministry, when Corry had returned to the Admiralty as First Secretary. In the absence of the Board minutes we cannot be sure of his role, but it appears at least likely that the

[44] S7953, ADM 87 77; S7490, ADM 87 74.
[45] A. Lambert, *Warrior: Restoring the World's First Ironclad* (London, 1988), 18.

return of the man who in the 1840s had helped sponsor not just the screw but also iron-hulled warships, had some responsibility for the Admiralty's bravery in May 1859.

Admittedly, by the time the *Black Prince* and two smaller ironclads were laid down late in the year, the Tories were again out of office, and yet iron hulls were still specified. It was surely important that the precedent had been set; as always, 'C'est le premier pas qui coûte'; but one must not ignore another factor, quite possibly fundamental to the first British ironclad programme: the need to have recourse to the private yards. The royal yards were crammed with work, notably with the screw-battleships that still appeared vital; only the private sector could produce the ironclads to counter the latest French programme. This in itself meant iron construction. As had been shown by the wooden gunboats built by private builders during the war, wooden construction outside the dockyards meant less than first-class workmanship, and the use of much unseasoned wood. The private yards could not afford to maintain large stocks of timber, unlike their government counterparts, and the latter could not afford to let their own stocks be drained by others. Iron, fortunately, needed no seasoning, and the quality of iron shipbuilding in the private yards was generally high. Thus came the first British iron-hulled ironclads, essentially *faute de mieux* at least in the eyes of the Naval Lords, as is suggested by the idea emanating from them in 1860 that if the *Warrior* and *Black Prince* did show themselves to be useless as warships, they could always have their armour stripped off and be used as transports— an eerie echo of the fate of the *Simoom* and her sisters.

However reluctantly, the Admiralty authorized an iron-hulled ironclad squadron. It might well appear, therefore, that a pattern was set of French wood against British iron. Yet the appearance is deceptive. Not only did the French build iron-hulled battleships when the capacity existed, but the British built some wooden-hulled ones. Some of these were the conversions from the screw-liners on the stocks, the *Royal Oak* and her sisters, a sensible way of utilizing material that otherwise would have been quite obsolete. However, two others—the *Lord Clyde* and the *Lord Warden*— were built from scratch, following a strong appeal in 1863 from Robinson arguing first that a new class of ironclads should be built to counter French construction, and second that this class should have wooden hulls. One reason for this apparently retrograde step was that he had been impressed by the converted screw-liners, thinking that with their complete armour belts they were perhaps better able to meet the French battleships than the iron-hulled, partially protected ironclads. He specifically saw the new vessels as improved Royal Oaks. Also, the experience of building even iron vessels in the private yards had not been entirely happy, with serious cost and time overruns; not in retrospect surprising given the novelty of the vessels, but worrying at the time. The Navy wished to return to the degree of supervision and control of warship construction they identified with their own yards, which in 1863 implied wooden construction.[46] Of course, it would have been best to convert the dockyards to build in iron; but this could be done only slowly. Chatham was the guinea-pig; in 1861 one of the later improved Warriors was ordered to be built there.

At least Robinson's proposal to build as many as five 'improved Royal Oaks' was not approved; even so, the British ironclad battlefleet had a variegated look. For instance, four successors to the *Black Prince*, the *Defence*, *Resistance*, *Hector*, and *Valiant*, might have had iron hulls, but in other ways they were very different, being smaller, slower, and less heavily armed. Their main justification seems simply to have been cheapness. They were more handy than the *Warrior*, but hardly the better suited thereby to form a line-of-battle with her. Individually, at least the *Defence* and *Resistance* were not even equivalent to the *Gloire*, and show that, out of economy, the Admiralty was willing to sacrifice squadron homogeneity. Here was a great contrast with France, where the Ministry of Marine was greatly impressed by the importance of building battleships designed to operate together as a fleet, a principle that underlay the programmes of 1858 to 1860.

V

To carry the story of the development of British and French naval *matériel* right up to the end of our period would be to study increasing variety in warship types. The main reason for this variety was a quicker pace of technological innovation, which made it possible for each new battleship to be greatly superior to its

---

[46] Controller to Board, 11 Feb. 1863, ADM 1 5840; 25 May 1863, ADM 1 5841.

predecessor of only the previous year. In consequence, one observes the emergence of fleets of samples.

Nevertheless, one can discern essentially three types of battleship of the line.[47] First, there was the central-battery vessel, where the heaviest guns were concentrated amidships, behind the heaviest armour, in a kind of citadel, rather than being dispersed along the broadside behind a thin belt of iron. Secondly, there was the rigged turret-vessel, like the *Monarch* and the unfortunate *Captain*, laid down in 1866–7. Thirdly, there was the unrigged version, the first examples being the *Devastation*, *Thunderer*, and *Dreadnought*, of 1869–70.

Below these first-class battleships, however, were others, perhaps not always fit to lie in the line-of-battle, but still armoured. Some were plainly experimental, destined to lack offspring. But, to generalize again, one may discern three essential types of importance in the remainder: the first is the ram, the second the colonial ironclad or *cuirassé de station*, and the third is the turret coastal-defence vessel.

In surveying all the various types, and in general the shape of the two fleets in the mid- to late 1860s, several points have to be made. One is the exceptional attention paid to the ram. The imperviousness of armour to shot had turned naval minds to alternative ship-killers, and—perhaps due to a classical education—many officers looked to the precedent of galley warfare. Some of the first ironclads were equipped with vicious spurs, and later versions were also given enhanced forward fire the better to support ram attacks. But, some asked, why build large ironclads? Smaller rams could be just as deadly, it was argued. In October 1861 came support for this idea, when the Confederate 'tinclad' turtle-decked ram *Manassas* managed to hit the USS *Richmond*. The attacker was not very formidable, and did not sink her opponent, but suggested what could be

---

[47] See Oscar Parkes, *British Battleships* (London, 1970), 24, 30. The details that follow of RN ironclads are taken largely from Parkes, Baxter's *Introduction of the Ironclad Warship*, Gardiner's *Conway's All the World's Fighting Ships 1860–1905* (London, 1979), and the well-known 'Black Battlefleet' articles by Admiral Ballard that began in *Mariner's Mirror* in 1930 (most easily consulted in G. A. Ballard, *The Black Battlefleet*, ed. and abbr. G. A. Osbon and N. A. M. Rodger (London, 1980)). Baxter and Conway are useful also for French ironclads, but the main source is R. Testu de Balincourt and P. Vincent-Bréchignac, 'La Marine française d'hier: Les cuirassés', *Revue maritime*, 125 (May 1930), 577–95; 135 (Mar. 1931), 289–317; 138 (June 1931), 775–91; 143 (Nov. 1931), 615–46; 150 (June 1932), 759–61.

done.[48] By the end of 1863 the British and French navies were each building a small ironclad-ram, the *Pallas* and the *Taureau* respectively. They were very different in design, but both demonstrated an overweening faith in the power of the spur. The *Taureau* in particular, an improved *Manassas*, was wildly overestimated as a weapon of war. In the mind of Chasseloup-Laubat, who sanctioned her, she was to be a powerful instrument both for coastal protection and for fleet actions, and in general 'le plus terrible instrument de guerre imaginable'.[49] But her trials were very disappointing, above all in regard to her stability. Given also her meagre coal supply, it became clear that her only feasible task was harbour protection, and there was some regret that four larger but similar vessels had been approved a year before the prototype trials. Even French innovators, it appears, could go terribly awry! Not that the ram was thus entirely overshadowed. The Battle of Lissa of 1866, when the Austrian flagship *Ferdinand Max* rammed and sank the large Italian ironclad the *Re d'Italia*, reinvigorated the ram enthusiasts. It was not until the 1870s, with improvements in gunnery, and with the development of paravane torpedoes to dissuade ramming, that serious doubts began to be cast on ramming tactics in fleet engagements.[50]

Another point raised by the *matériel* of the 1860s is that one finds the palm for innovation in warship types is no longer with France. Looking at all the world navies, it is difficult to forget the effusion of inventiveness brought by the Civil War to the Federal and Confederate navies in the first part of the decade. But even in the European context France ceased being the technological leader. The Admiralty had learned a lesson; more than that, the naval administrative infrastructures had been geared to accept and sustain change. The Royal Navy was now more willing to be the first to introduce novelty. Another contributory factor was the strong private sector in Britain. This meant that there was a relatively large pool of inventiveness to be drawn upon by naval architects there. But one must also accept that the French were less eager than before to adopt new measures, at least bold ones. It might

[48] W. N. Still, *Iron Afloat: The Story of the Confederate Armourclads* (Vanderbilt University Press, Nashville, Tenn., 1971).

[49] Chasseloup-Laubat to Bouët-Willaumez, 9 Nov. 1863, and his 'Note sur l'organisation de la flotte', 2 July, Chasseloup-Laubat Papers, iv. 303, v. 36–40.

[50] Theodore Ropp, *The Development of a Modern Navy: French Naval Policy 1871–1904* (pub. version, Annapolis, Md., 1987), 113–14.

appear superficially that the Ministry of Marine in this decade was attempting to maintain squadron homogeneity at the expense of innovation in successive ships. It would be more accurate to emphasize the burden of completing the great construction programme of 1860. There were some resources available for experiment. The seven battleships laid down supplementing the original programme represented no fewer than four different classes, but the French were now more intent on consolidation than innovation.

There was at least the similarity between the two sides that both accepted innovation was desirable, and that it would continue to be so. This in itself was important, a significant change from the 1840s. It was also indicative of a general Anglo-French naval consensus. The 1860s saw a surprisingly similar approach in the two countries to certain aspects of naval policy, even including ideas of what constituted a properly balanced fleet.

In this last respect one sees an obvious consequence of France's success in building herself up as a rival. In the 1840s she had been a serious contender in European waters. That remained twenty years later, but now she was also a potent global rival. In the 1860s her construction of frigates and lesser cruising vessels, the essential workhorses of a global naval power, was little inferior in number to British construction. She had also been the prime mover in the introduction to colonial waters of her greatest innovation, the ironclad, in the shape of the *cuirassé de station*.

It is worth considering this type, if only because it demonstrates that there were limits to Anglo-French naval convergence. Chasseloup-Laubat had a precise understanding of the definition. Such a vessel, he believed, needed to have only half the tonnage of the average French ironclad of the line, since only three attributes were necessary: first, a limited power of movement, with a steam speed sufficient for cruising requirements, and canvas adequate for long voyages with cold furnaces; secondly, a crew of respectable size, above all so landing parties could be organized; thirdly, armour invulnerable to the latest guns.[51] All he wanted he found in the *Belliqueuse*, laid down in 1863, displacing only 3,717 tons. The seven of the Alma class that followed in 1865 were only slightly larger, and the three La Galissonières of 1868–9 were the first *cuirassés de station* much to surpass 4,000 tons.

---

[51] Chasseloup-Laubat, 'Note sur l'organisation de la flotte', 43–5. The name he used for the type was the *corvette cuirassée*, which was thereafter often used.

Chasseloup-Laubat believed it was the British who had first developed the type, pointing to the *Research*, *Enterprise*, and *Favorite*. But he was mistaken. They were experiments in the armouring of smaller vessels, rather than colonial ironclads. In Britain, the craft used, or designed, for colonial duties, apart from those for harbour defence, were fully the size of the *Gloire* and her sisters. At first, some of the converted screw-liners were deployed on distant stations, for which their coppered wooden hulls made them suitable. Then, in 1867–8, the four of the Audacious class and the two Swiftsures were specifically laid down for such tasks; but these displaced between 6,000 and nearly 7,000 tons. Admittedly, the Board had originally specified a tonnage of only two-thirds this, but Robinson and the Chief Constructor (E. J. Reed) had successfully argued that what was needed were craft capable of lying in the line-of-battle with the other ironclads.

The implication that there was not a firm division between naval requirements at home and in the wider world, that global naval power implied flexibility of deployment, might lead us to conclude that the Admiralty had not been so dazzled by the coastal-water operations of the Crimea, or the specialization of function made possible by new technology, as to desert traditional 'Blue Water' beliefs. But that would be to go somewhat too far. True, there were hints in the 1860s of such ideas, even in regard to commerce protection. In 1866, as a consequence of the construction by the Federal navy of a class of commerce destroyers, the *Wampanoag* and her sisters, the Admiralty laid down the *Inconstant*, the first of a pair of iron-hulled cruisers of over 5,000 tons displacement.[52] Suddenly, having for long virtually ignored the subject of commerce protection, the Admiralty had at last begun to address it.

The differences and similarities between French and British naval strategy, as well as the ambiguities of the latter, are to be addressed in the next chapter. Present purposes require one to make the obvious point that the contemporary perceptions of warfare were a crucial foundation for the variety of warship types that we have said characterized the 1860s; but what must also be drawn out, and

---

[52] 1870 report on frigates, by Robinson, ADM 1 6177. N. A. M. Rodger, 'The Design of the *Inconstant*', *Mariner's Mirror*, 61 (1975), 9–22. Vessels of the Wampanoag class were not all fast, and all had certain general weaknesses; see E. W. Sloan, *Benjamin Franklin Isherwood, Naval Engineer: The Years as Engineer in Chief, 1861–1869* (Annapolis, Md., 1965), ch. 9.

indeed now emphasized, is that there was a degree of simple confusion in British naval planning that accounts at least in part for the proliferation of types.

At the very time the *Inconstant* was being built, along with the generously proportioned British *cuirassés de station*, work also progressed on a class of monitors to protect colonial harbours, and in 1869–70 four more small monitors were commenced for home defence, along with the larger *Glatton*. One could argue that the Admiralty was following contradictory policies in pursuing both deep-sea and coastal-defence policies. But to prove contradiction, one need go no further than the way that two distinct lines of coastal-defence policy were followed. The four home-defence monitors were considered unfit to go to sea in heavy weather. Thus they were unlike the two earliest British turret-vessels, the *Royal Sovereign* and the *Prince Albert*, dating from 1862, which were fully capable of steaming across the Channel in almost any conditions and attacking French ports. The former represent an ideal of coastal defence where the greatest danger is of grounding on your own shoals; the latter assumed that the proper zone of operations is the enemy coastal waters.

That there was confusion, and not simply a development of ideas between the early 1860s and the end of the decade is strongly suggested by the *Glatton*. In a memorandum of Robinson's of 1864 it was said that a single-turreted monitor was required 'specially designed for the mouths of our rivers, and for the defence of our harbours, which would also be able to prevent any landing on any unprotected beach or harbour of our coast'.[53] The vessel laid down in 1869 had the limited coal supply and low freeboard appropriate to such tasks; but why then did she have virtually the draught of one of the small seagoing battleships? As built, *Glatton*'s purpose is as obscure now as it was to the man responsible for drawing up the design to fit the Board's specifications—E. J. Reed. As he said, 'She was designed strictly upon orders which I received and upon the object of which I was never informed.'[54]

The present and the previous chapters have dwelt on the connection, sometimes an intimate one, between Anglo-French diplomacy and the development of naval *matériel* from 1840. Any conclusion

[53] Report by Robinson on the ironclad fleet, 13 Dec. 1864, ADM 1 5892.
[54] Parkes, *British Battleships*, 171.

has to note that in the last half of the 1860s, that same connection did not exist. Unlike in the previous quarter century, the warships were not designed under the repeated goad of Anglo-French diplomatic friction. Indeed, this period was a relatively quiescent one in cross-Channel relations. This had its effects on naval construction. Innovation continued, as has been said. However, it was realized largely at the prototype level. Had the old rivalry been as active as before, more warship classes would have been laid down in lieu of solitary vessels, and by 1870 the two navies would have had less of the look of fleets of samples.

One consequence of the relative quiescence of the rivalry at this time is that we do not need to study the then changes in naval *matériel* in the same detail as was done for earlier years. The implication is not that the 1860s can be lightly treated in other respects; notably that is the period to be addressed with regard to the reasons for the decline of Anglo-French diplomatic friction, and of the naval rivalry itself. But in terms of the build-up of *matériel* on the two sides, in the context of a continuing rivalry where an Anglo-French war seemed a real possibility, one should appreciate that the culminating date of the developments set in train in 1840 is 1863–4, not the very end of the decade.

The period of just under a quarter of a century had seen some enormous changes, and not just in terms of naval technology. The naval strategic balance had perceptibly shifted. Doubtless, back in 1840 there had been a chance that the French Mediterranean squadron might have defeated its British rival in a pitched battle. But as far as the mobilized strength of the two fleets was concerned, the British were then handsomely in the lead. The later position is summed up in a memorandum of 1863 by the Controller, dealing with the totals of seagoing iron-clads on the two sides. Robinson noticed first that the French had a numerical lead in ironclads. This, he realized, was passing away, but what he saw remaining was the fact that the Ministry of Marine had designed its armoured battleships to act together as a battlefleet, with similar handiness, degree of protection, and speed; a speed, moreover, superior to that of any line-of-battle composed of all the British ironclad battleships, where the faster vessels would have to keep formation with the sluggish Hector and Valiant types. Robinson thought that even by the beginning of 1865, the result of a battle between the two forces would be unpredictable: 'in the first days of

January 1865, compactness and homogeneousness would be on the side of France—individual power on the side of England:—a decided superiority nowhere.'[55]

By the early 1860s, therefore, *la Royale* had enormously improved its relative position since the Syrian crisis, putting itself if not quite on a level with the Royal Navy as far as the entire fleet was concerned, then at least giving it a greater relative power than it had achieved since at least the time before the American Revolutionary War, and perhaps even since Richelieu's day. Given that the Royal Navy, and the British government, had fought hard to prevent this relative accretion of power, one must conclude that it represented a remarkable success for the naval policy-making of France and, by contrast, a failure for that of Britain.

[55] Folder 11 Feb. 1863, ADM 1 5840.

4

The Militarization of Naval Warfare in the Mid-Nineteenth Century: Tactics and Strategy

I

Probably the most obvious point about the ideas current in our period concerning naval tactics is the initial painful slowness with which they changed to meet the fact of steam-power. From the early 1840s onwards, numbers of powerfully engined steamers were in service in the British and French navies, yet they were not generally seen as introducing any radically new tactical element; instead, they were assumed to be simply a valuable means of supplementing existing plans. The height of battle planning in the mid- to late 1840s was steam-towing: in practice evolutions, each sail of the line was escorted by a powerful steamer, and was taken in tow by her before 'battle' commenced.[1] This method gave greater flexibility than had been possible in the age of purely sailing-fleets: the strength and direction of the wind no longer exercised the old degree of tyranny. Nevertheless, the overall likely shape of naval engagements was little altered. Towing was feasible only in good weather conditions, when the water was comparatively smooth. Moreover, the limitations of the steamers involved also had to be considered. Paddle-vessels offered great and vulnerable targets to enemy fire: not only the paddle-boxes, but also a proportion of the machinery had to be above the waterline. It was suggested that one answer was to strap the paddler alongside the liner it was escorting, thus giving protection to at least one flank whilst still enabling the battleship to be manoeuvred by steam. But this savours of a half measure that avoided the thought of building steam-battleships. At

---

[1] See Lord Auckland to Sir William Parker, 22 Mar. 1847, Parker Papers, PAR 157a.

least in retrospect, it is clear that towing had severe drawbacks and, whilst offering some tactical novelties, represented only a passing phase.

A few, a very few officers, had had more radical ideas of how to exploit the paddle-steamer. For instance, back in the 1820s not only General Paixhans but also Captain Sir John Ross had published works that described steam battles involving fleets of simply paddle warships.[2] In the early 1840s there was a junior French naval officer, N.-F. Labrousse (later nicknamed *le précurseur*) who suggested the use of steam paddle 'rams'. He relied on classical examples for inspiration, seeing in naval tactics under oar a guide to tactics under steam, both being largely independent of the wind. He even went so far as to borrow the ancient idea of using light flying-bridges (*corbeaux*, he called them, following the Latin name), over which boarding parties could be passed on to an enemy vessel.[3]

The crucial difficulty with such plans was the limited offensive and defensive power of paddle-vessels. Not until the 1840s did what one might regard as true steam-warships appear—the screws, with their engines, boilers, and shafts lodged beneath the waterline, and carrying full broadside armaments. They constituted the warship type that was to bring a serious rethinking of battle tactics.

Again, however, ideas changed only slowly. It was not as if the naval authorities had realized the enormous superiority that a screw-fleet would possess over sail of the line in a sea battle. As we saw earlier, the first screw-battleships were sanctioned on other grounds. The British blockships were built as mobile coastal batteries; and the *Napoléon* herself was designed rather to avoid battle than to engage in it. Even after these prototypes had shown their paces, no serious study of steam tactics was undertaken. The *Blenheim* trials might have amazed observers, but did not convince the Admiralty that the sail of the line was obsolete. Nor was the Ministry of Marine yet much more perceptive. Only after the successful trials of the *Napoléon* in 1852 did the Ministry come to approve wholeheartedly of the steam line-of-battle. Even then, effort was not put into tactical theorizing. As was said by a tactical commission of

[2] H.-J. Paixhans, *Nouvelle force maritime* (Paris, 1822). John Ross, *A Treatise on Navigation by Steam* (London, 1823).
[3] See the discussion in the *Conseil d'amirauté* of 23 and 30 Dec. 1842, AN BB8 853 (*marine*).

1853, in justification for building first, and then thinking what to do with the results — 'Le mot ne vient qu'après la chose'.[4]

So the tactics were to be articulated only after evolutions under steam could show what was possible, and the evolutions depended on the existence of a screw-battlefleet. By 1854–5 the British and the French each had such a fleet but, thanks to the war with Russia, the times were hardly propitious for trials. Some were undertaken, but these were intended to prepare for engagement should the Russians come out; no attempt was made to mount a series with the proper aim of testing the limits of the feasible. The varied and immediate needs of war made it virtually impossible to address steam tactics properly; in any case, it became quite obvious, in the first half of 1854, that the Tsar did not intend to risk his obsolete battlefleets at sea, thus steam battle tactics seemed of little urgency.

Only with peace was it feasible to turn to the subject, and it was the French navy that was the first to act and to develop a tactical doctrine. In 1856 a tactical commission was set up to discuss the subject, but the most serious initial work was done at sea. Both in 1857 and 1858 the *escadre d'évolutions* practised proposed battle manœuvres under steam with canvas furled, followed by analysis by the officers at sea and back in Paris. The consequence was the issue of new signal books. In contrast to the rapid action of the French, the Royal Navy procrastinated; furthermore, it reversed the order of priority of action, demonstrating what one might describe as a French faith in theory over practice. Signals and evolutions committees met in 1858, and signal books were issued, but steam trials on any scale were not undertaken until 1861, at last satisfying the questions raised three years before.[5]

Though different in approach, the two navies came to many of the same conclusions. The great lesson was that much of what steam appeared to make easy — at least when planned on paper — proved to be very difficult on water, or even quite impossible. It had been thought by some in the mid- to late 1850s that steam would bring a hitherto unknown speed, dexterity, certainty, and precision to naval tactics. Naval battle, it was suggested, would

---

[4] AN GG1 25/6 (*marine*).

[5] For the 1858 committee, see ADM 1 5714. Dossier Capt. P.176 contains several interesting submissions on tactics by officers. A few details of the 1861 trials are given (albeit misdated) in Mrs Frederick Egerton, *Admiral of the Fleet Sir Geoffrey Phipps Hornby, G.C.B.: A Biography* (Edinburgh and London, 1896), 80–2.

take on many of the characteristics of battle on land. One of the most forceful proponents of such ideas was Sir Howard Douglas, whose *Naval Warfare with Steam* appeared in 1858. He was perhaps the most important of the British naval pundits of the time, but the fact that he was a general is all too evident from his book. He wrote at one point:

Well-exercised steam fleets, like well-trained armies in the field, if skilfully commanded, should be kept concentrated in columns, or lines of bearing *en échelon* . . . Modern military science renounces the practice of fighting in parallel order, line against line . . . and it substitutes for that rude and primitive formation, the more skilful and less sanguinary methods . . . [of] turning the enemy's flank by an oblique movement, in attacking him while on the march; or by tactical combinations, bringing a vastly superior force upon the point attacked.

He followed this argument with diagrams of various ideal form-ations, one of which arranged twenty-seven battleships in line abreast or *en échelon*, giving, as the author himself put it, the effect of a line of fortifications, bastions and all, one possessing 'great military strength'.[6]

However, the French and British trials cast strong doubts on the feasibility of such grandiose formations. For one thing, the ships in the trials, steamers though they were, found it difficult to maintain their positions within even comparatively simple formations; and this, of course, was without the fog, shot and shell, and debris of war. It was not only expensive in coals but also a strain on the engines to keep formation precisely.[7] The steamers of the period were delicate hybrids, not dependable cogs in a military machine.

We gain an idea of how troublesome early screw-machinery could be from a letter of 12 May 1859 sent by Jurien de la Gravière to the Minister of Marine. Jurien's squadron had spent an irritating day steaming from one breakdown to the next. First, the battleship *Eylau* had needed replacements for some rubber valves on her air-pumps. That had taken three hours. But scarcely had the squadron

---

[6] Sir Howard Douglas, *Naval Warfare with Steam* (2nd. edn., London, 1860), 108–9, 126.

[7] In one French trial of 1857, when the squadron cruised in a 'V' formation (forming two lines of bearing at an angle of 90°), no ship tried to keep exactly its place relative to the others, but had leave to creep forward or fall back slightly, according to the performance of the engines. Vice-Admiral Tréhouart to the Minis-ter of Marine, 5 Sept. 1857, AN BB4 750 (*marine*), 145.

again got under way when a frigate, the *Impétueuse*, broke down. Her problem was fortunately not serious, and was soon seen to, but then it was the turn of the *Napoléon*. The ship had been troubled previously with inflows of water through the waste-pipe whenever she stopped. Consequently, when the *Eylau* had broken down, the troublesome pipe had been closed. But when the time came to get under way again, it was found that a cotter-pin had snapped, and the discharge remained hermetically sealed. Luckily, the weather was fine, so the vessel was heeled over in the water, and someone went over the side and managed to move the diaphragm. At last the squadron was able to steam away together, doubtless to enthusiastic murmurings against steamers and about how everything had been much better in the age of sail.[8]

The lesson for informed naval officers by the late 1850s was that there were strict limitations on battle tactics, despite steam. At the end of the trials of the *escadre d'évolutions* in 1858, the Commander-in-Chief, Romain Desfossés, said that the major moral to be drawn was the crucial importance of simplicity. No complex formation could be long sustained, he thought, particularly once battle was joined, for either the enemy would break it up himself, or it would simply fall apart, perhaps due to the confusion brought by the vast clouds of smoke produced by the black-powder propellants and charges then in use, perhaps by battle debris in the water fouling screws.[9]

Even one of the formations most favoured by writers on tactics was now shown to be somewhat too complex: this was the line of bearing or line *en échelon*, a formation suggested either for battle or as a transitional stage between the line ahead and the line abreast. After experimenting with screw gunboat evolutions, a British officer, Astley Cooper Key, asserted that such a line could be maintained only in good visibility and with great skill and attention.[10] Furthermore, it was not found to be a formation of great utility. Certainly, it could be swiftly transformed into either the line ahead or abreast, but what was the special value of the latter to a squadron of line-of-battleships? This question leads one to the

[8] Jurien de la Gravière, AN BB4 1802 (*marine*), 67.

[9] Despatch to the Minister of Marine, 21 June 1858, AN BB4 757 (*marine*), fos. 58–61.

[10] A. Cooper-Key to W. F. Martin, 5 Oct. 1858, 14 Mar. 1859, Martin Papers, BM Add. MS 41409, fos. 312–15.

serious objection to 'fancy formations'. Nothing could alter the
fact, given that the screw-warships of the late 1850s had their armament arranged almost entirely in broadside batteries, that the line
ahead was not only the simplest order of battle to maintain, it was
also the primary order of battle. This point was accepted by the
British evolutions committee. It was also accepted in Paris: the
Signal Book of 1861 said 'la ligne de file est la ligne de bataille des
bâtiments dont l'artillerie est rangée de chaque bord'.[11]

The last few paragraphs appear to show that the militarization of
tactics proposed by some writers faded away once lit by the experience of evolutions under steam at sea. But tactical militarization
actually gained strength as time went by. In large part this was
because it was operating at more subtle (or insidious) levels than
has so far been suggested.

One level of military influence was the semantic one. The French
tactical commission of 1856, scarcely the most radical of bodies,
admitted that it had had to borrow some terms from land warfare
simply because the navy did not yet have ones of its own to
describe some of the manœuvres made possible by steam.[12] At least
the commission had the grace to apologize for what it had done,
but some writers were less punctilious, employing military vocabu-
lary unashamedly.

Another route for tactical militarization was the way that by the
mid-1850s, more than ever before since the supremacy of the galley,
it was seen as important to have a body of 'sea soldiers' on board
each warship. One reason was the growing degree to which naval
forces were thought to have a crucial role to play in coastal and
land warfare, implying that warships had to carry powerful
contingents suitable for duties ashore. Sailors alone were not
thought to suffice. They had marvellous qualities of improvization
and spirit; they made an excellent attacking force, a superb 'forlorn
hope'; but they were less effective when it came to holding together
in a retreat. And if men accustomed to strict military discipline
were needed for land operations, they now appeared more than
ever before also to have a part to play in sea battle, thanks to the
introduction of the rifle. In the 1850s smooth-bore muskets were
being replaced by the new weapon, one that had a range of 600

---

[11] Jurien de la Gravière, 'Considérations générales sur la tactique navale: (escadre
d'évolutions, 1868–70)', lithograph, V 38L.11.
[12] AN GG1 19 (*marine*), dossier 2.

yards or more, equal to or even greater than that of the shell-cannon then in service. Thus rifle-fire seemed to have a valuable role to play in ship-to-ship engagements, and at least a proportion of a ship's crew had to be trained as riflemen. It was felt that the task was more appropriate to sea soldiers than to sailors. There was also another duty for such men—at least if sea battle took the form envisaged by Labrousse and some other French naval officers, notably the energetic if somewhat egregious comte Bouët-Willaumez. The latter was the first man to publish a work specifically on steam-battleship tactics, his *Projet de tactique navale pour une flotte de vaisseaux à vapeur*.[13] Bouët eagerly adopted the idea of *corbeaux* for screw steam tactics, foreseeing steam-liners running swiftly alongside their opponents, and swinging the bridges across, so that the boarding parties would be able 's'élancer sabre et pistolets au poing sur le pont ennemi après avoir ravagé de leurs carabines'. Here, too, was a role for sea soldiers.

But who were the men to be? The Royal Navy, of course, had its marines, but there was no French equivalent. The *infanterie de marine*, though in theory supposed to provide troops for service afloat, in practice was limited to garrisoning arsenals and colonies. So, in 1856, a new body was set up, the *fusiliers marins*. A school was organized at Lorient, and some 400 to 500 recruits were trained each year. By 1860 there were over 2,000 *fusiliers*, and a second battalion was added in 1861. There were great hopes for the future, including calculations that the fleet would eventually require 12,000 *fusiliers*—a figure close to the establishment of the Royal Marines —giving 195 sea soldiers to each first-rate battleship, and *pro rata* to the lesser vessels.[14]

Thus, in the 1850s, one saw military infiltration into the language of naval tactics, plus the development of the purely military element in the personnel. But with the following decade, militarization increased even further, thanks to a weakening in belief in the importance of tactical simplicity. This was due above all to new *matériel*, but also to some sea trials that appeared to show that a clockwork-like tactical precision really was possible.

By the middle of the 1860s the main battlefleets of Britain and of France were armoured, and innovation in guns and armour was proceeding at a fast pace. This was of great significance for

[13] Drawn up in 1853, pub. in a restricted, lithographed edn. in 1855, V 36L.10.
[14] Dossier, 'Fusiliers: Bataillons de Lorient . . . 1856–76, AN CC3 1195 (*marine*).

tacticians. Vessels like the *Napoléon* and *Blenheim* were unprotected wooden steamers and, according to one estimate, could have been sunk by three well-directed shell broadsides in as many minutes.[15] With the ironclad, however, the balance swung strongly from the offensive to the defensive. Given the guns of the time, it was difficult to see how a well-designed and strongly built ironclad could be sunk by gunfire that was anything short of a long-sustained onslaught. The gun-makers attempted to address this problem: large smooth-bores were developed, above all in the USA, that had significant armour-piercing qualities, at least at short-range, though in general it was rifled-cannon that were concentrated on, and ever more penetrating weapons were constructed, ones with better range and accuracy than the best smooth-bore guns, though sharing with them the tendency to increase in size with each improvement. Nevertheless, at least during the 1860s, the manufacturers of armour managed to keep pace, and battleships retained a high degree of resistance to shot and shell.

The creation of bigger guns was in itself tactically significant. Thanks to the heaviness of armour-piercing cannon, on top of the demands made by the fitting of the armour itself, the early ironclads could carry batteries of only some forty or fifty guns. By the end of the 1860s the latest battleships could carry only a handful of the latest guns. The 'tyranny of the broadside' disappeared, for naval designers were able to arrange the few pieces of ordnance so artfully in each vessel, perhaps by mounting them in sponsons, that a warship could concentrate a heavy fire on almost any quarter, and especially fore and aft.

In retrospect we may well argue that the designers of the time were wrong; that they overestimated the accuracy of ordnance, and thus ignored the importance of concentrating as much fire as possible, a concentration that could come only through broadside fire. But they were led astray by a factor that encouraged them to favour fore and aft fire. With the gun slighted in its traditional role as 'ship-killer', attention had turned to possible alternatives. Once again, the classical example was taken to be pertinent and, beginning in 1859 with the French *Magenta* and *Solférino*, battleships were commonly equipped with ram bows. The aim of battle, it was said, was now to hide your flank from an enemy; in so doing you would

[15] Sir John Briggs, *Naval Administrations 1827 to 1892: The Experience of 65 Years* (London, 1897), 84.

protect your most vulnerable part, and present your own ram, supplemented by all the forward firepower the designer had managed to accommodate.

Events appeared fully to justify such a belief. With the battles of Hampton Roads in 1862 and Lissa in 1866, the efficacy of the ram, and the relative impotence against armourclads of shot and shell, appeared to be fully proved. At the first, the Confederate ironclad *Virginia* rammed and sank the unarmoured sloop *Cumberland*, shrugging off her victim's heavy fire. At the second the Austrian flagship, the *Ferdinand Max*, rammed and sank the *Re d'Italia*, one of the two largest ironclads in the Italian fleet. Ram enthusiasts ignored the less positive aspects of these sinkings, notably the way that both victims had been stationary, perfect targets, when attacked. It is actually very difficult to ram a moving target at the correct angle for success, and has been more often achieved by accident than intention. Experience later in the century suggested that the best one could normally achieve was a collision at an acute angle that would not penetrate the enemy's hull, the two ships coming away shaken but not sunk. But, in the 1860s at least, few officers seem to have doubted the efficacy of the ram.[16]

Armour-cladding, enhanced fire fore and aft, and ram tactics: all these related developments added new elements to the tactical scene. They encouraged officers to think again about the probable shape of naval battle, and in consequence some progressed to one of two opposite tactical extremes. One can discern both in embryo in the 1850s, but they took their fullest shape only in the succeeding decade.

One of these was a revived military (or precisionist) school. The leading light was a Russian admiral, Gregory Boutakoff. He mounted a long series of trials in the early 1860s that seemed to prove the value of his own brand of clockwork tactics. Only by strict overall control of the fleet, he believed, could the ram be used at its most effective. One suspects strongly that speeds had to be kept very low—under five knots, as against the eight to ten likely in battle—so that the formations could keep their order. Nevertheless, the trials, and the admiral's views, attracted a good deal of attention in the West. Boutakoff appeared at a meeting of the Royal United Services Institute on at least one occasion, and his work on

[16] One interesting exception was Rear-Admiral T.-F. Page. See his article 'Lissa, 20 Juillet', pub. anon. in *Revue des deux mondes*, 66 (15 Nov. 1866), 295–328.

naval tactics, and that of his aide-de-camp, Lieutenant Semechkin, appeared in translation in the leading (and semi-official) French naval journal, the *Revue maritime et coloniale*, where they encouraged some like-minded French officers.[17]

In contrast to the above school there was what one might well call the 'chaos school'. Instead of anticipating that steam would enable the admiral to exercise greater control, the men of this persuasion foresaw more spontaneity and delegation of command, where the important unit was not the fleet or the division but the small squadron or even the individual ship. According to this view, the fog of war, the likelihood of breakdowns, the wide range of options available to the steamers on both sides, and the centrifugal effect of ram tactics on fleet formations meant that no detailed plans formulated by an admiral previous to battle could survive the first contact with the enemy, nor could the admiral hope to exercise any overall control while the engagement lasted. Battle, it was believed, would soon develop into a mêlée, where victory would go to the side with superior morale and *élan*.

Not surprisingly, perhaps, the 'chaos school' was stronger in France than in Britain. One consolation after a defeat, on sea or land, is to believe that while the victorious rival had had a more thorough training or, better yet, superior numbers, one's own side had been the superior in terms of spirit. Thus, although French commentators might have accepted that at Trafalgar the English had shown themselves the better seamen, it was suggested that France would have won had it been a question of fighting man-to-man. This is a common enough sort of nationalist myth, and expresses itself in such stereotypes as *furor gallicus*, or *furor teutonicus*. To much of French opinion of the mid-nineteenth century, it was axiomatic that French soldiers and sailors were more suited than others to the cut and thrust of modern war, being quicker thinking, more lively, and so better able to take immediate advantage of circumstance.

Such thinking informs the work by Bouët-Willaumez mentioned earlier. The fast moving and exciting scenario that he painted of

[17] G. Boutakoff, 'Nouvelles bases de tactique navale pour les navires à vapeur', *Revue maritime et coloniale*, 10 (1863), 741; 14 (1865), 388–96. L. Semechkin, 'Lectures sur la tactique navale et les évolutions', *Revue maritime et coloniale*, 26 (1869), 787–821; 27 (1869), 173–98, 359–75. For an example of Boutakoff's influence on the French, see the work of a *capitaine de frégate*, L. Pagel's *Tactique navale* (Toulon, 1866).

naval battle, he said, was entirely appropriate to the character of the French sailor. In works written in the 1860s, reflecting exercises undertaken when he commanded the *escadre d'évolutions*, one observes that Bouët has adapted his ideas to the new *matériel*, and in so doing made himself the premier spokesman of what we have called the 'chaos school'.[18] Battle, he tells us, will be a mêlée; but this did not mean that all tactical formations would be lost. Bouët thought it wise to train officers and men to fight in formations that could survive in a mêlée. One of his practice exercises was to form the fleet into what were called *pelotons*, each consisting of between two and five vessels trained to support one another in battle, grouping together the better to ram an enemy or to ward off an attack aimed at one of them. Naturally, the admiral could not expect to exercise any strict control over a fleet of fast, independently moving *pelotons*. He could infuse his officers with his own ideas and enthusiasm (the 'Bouët touch', perhaps), but then they had largely to be left to their own devices.

The parallel between Bouët-Willaumez and Nelson necessarily has a sarcastic edge, but is not wholly to be discounted. It reminds us that the ideas of the 'chaos school' did have something in common with those of the great admiral of the days of sail—the realization that a commander-in-chief cannot hope to control all eventualities, and must have confidence in his officers. It is in its making room for the unexpected that the 'chaos school' best showed its appreciation of the realities of war, had its most striking link with the days of sail, and most determinedly resisted the military influence that we have been describing.

We appear to have discovered at least one bastion against tactical militarization. But it was not a very secure one. Consistency was not always seen as a virtue, and some men adopted ideas from the 'chaos school' on one occasion only to abandon them later. Bouët himself was something of a tactical catholic, and when in command of the *escadre d'évolutions* showed himself willing to try some rigid formations.[19] Indeed, here we have touched on a prime characteristic of

---

[18] L.-E. Bouët-Willaumez, *Tactique supplémentaire à l'usage d'une flotte cuirassée* (Toulon, 1865, and a later edn., Paris, 1868). See also the work by one of Bouët's *epigoni*, S. Bourgois, *Méthodes de navigation, d'expériences et d'évolutions pratiquées sur l'escadre de la Méditerranée sous le commandement du vice-amiral Sénateur comte Bouët-Willaumez en 1864–1866* (Paris, 1866).

[19] For instance, the *ordre en carré naval*. See *Revue maritime et coloniale*, 27 (1869), 693–7.

most tactical writers of the 1860s, whatever school one might try to put them in—open-mindedness (though uncertainty might be a better word). The technical developments of the 1850s, and the continuing progress in the following decade, proved very unsettling. A few points remained fixed in the tactical firmament: notably, few doubted the importance of the ram. But how best ought one to deploy a fleet to use the ram? That was a question of great argument and frequent changes of mind. Discussions on tactics in the Royal United Services Institute, for instance, could well end with the participants stressing their doubts, and even speaking at length about their unfitness to say anything.[20] More trials took place, but these could not answer the important questions about the power of the ram, or the extent to which evolutions feasible during peacetime trials would still be so during the stress and uncertainty of battle. Only in the two decades after 1870, with the evidence from a few (admittedly minor) engagements and, perhaps more important, with time to assess the power and the significance of steam, did something of a stable and sensible tactical consensus establish itself.[21]

Although one may not speak of anything so formal as a tactical consensus in the 1860s, it would be true to say that most writers on tactics during that decade tended to occupy some position in the middle ground between the two extreme schools we have identified. This was true especially of British senior officers, to whom extreme positions have often been proof of unsoundness. Yet, given the influences we have been discussing in this section, it was inevitable that even those in the middle should have been deeply imbued with military ideas about naval tactics. Indeed, one factor alone would probably have sufficed to produce this result —the uncertainty evinced by many officers about the precise effect that the coming of steam had had on naval war. Navies, like nature, abhor a vacuum. It was all too natural for ideas, forms, and terms to be borrowed from land warfare, where certainty had not been lost. In 1871 'Jacky' Fisher commented that the basis of the elaborated tactics of the British, French, and Russian navies appeared to be 'the principle which guides the manœuvres of a battery of field artillery'.[22] This has all that one expects from the

[20] *Royal United Services Institute Journal*, 11 (1868), 527–47.
[21] T. K. Ropp, 'The Development of a Modern Navy', doctoral dissertation (Harvard, 1937), 175–80, 199.
[22] R. F. Mackay, *Fisher of Kilverstone* (OUP, 1973), 87.

man's *obiter dicta* — force, exaggeration, and a lack of appreciation of *nuances*, all combined with an undoubted kernel of truth.

II

In regard to naval strategy, militarization was even more striking than in the case of tactics. One notable point is that thanks to this militarization, British and French strategies came to align themselves. With tactics it was different; even before the 1840s the two navies had been very similar. Certainly, in the eighteenth century, the tactics of the two navies had shown great differences, British officers usually attempting to force battle, French studying to avoid it. But the failures of the Napoleonic Wars had been a potent lesson for *la Royale*, and in the decades after 1815 it had shown little less interest in the tactics of how to fight and win battles than had its rival. Towards strategy, however, the two sides retained widely different attitudes right up to the 1840s: only afterwards, under some of the same pressing influences, did they begin to converge.

What one might call the traditional strategic preoccupations of the two navies had shown themselves well during the Napoleonic Wars. Britain, with not only the home islands but also a worldwide empire to protect, and dependent upon maritime commerce for her survival as a nation, had tried to deny to any enemy the use of the sea, and was able to draw on large resources in that effort. France did not have the same degree of colonial involvement or dependence on maritime trade. Moreover, unlike Britain, which kept only relatively weak army detachments at home, France did not have to rely primarily on the fleet to guard the metropolitan country from seaborne invasions: her senior service was the army. Finally, France almost always had the weaker fleet. The two naval ministries, in consequence, had quite different naval priorities. The Admiralty had to accept a broad, even global strategy. The Ministry of Marine concentrated on priorities closer to home. The protection of the important coastal trade was one French priority. Another was co-operation with the army, sometimes supporting the military's efforts to defend the coast, sometimes becoming little more than a superior transport service, taking the army where it wanted to go. Of course, the wars with Britain led to occasional grand naval gestures, such as the despatch of squadrons to strike blows in distant areas, the Americas or the Indian Ocean. Yet, at its most ambitious, French naval policy in the days of sail lacked strategic tenacity, in large part because the resources to support it could not be maintained. What long-sustained, geographically ambitious naval efforts there were almost always took a form that was potent, but not ultimately decisive — the *guerre de course*,[23] the strategy of the weaker naval power.

In the 1840s French naval strategy retained much of its old, limited outlook. The capability of despatching fleets to distant points was retained, but the main naval objectives were close to home. The evidence from discussions and planning within the Ministry of Marine suggests that there were at this time five naval priorities.[24] The navy had the responsibility in wartime to help defend the coast; to protect the colonies; to give the army mobility; to ensure communications between Metropolitan France and the new colony of Algeria; and to be a serious threat to England. The last was very general, and even somewhat nebulous in intention, but in essence it was to bring England to respect France, and to make her cautious in her assertions of maritime supremacy, her encroachments on the 'freedom of the seas'. The threat was to be composed of one or more of the following options: invasion, *guerre de course*, and France acting as the core of a great alliance of lesser maritime states that could overpower *le tyran de la mer*.

Thus baldly stated, French naval priorities seem very ambitious. Yet they should not disguise what in effect was a concentration on affairs close to home. One should note particularly that the wartime protection of the colonies would not have entailed a major maritime effort. The Treaties of Vienna had left France with only a few, scattered possessions overseas; and these depended for their protection largely on their garrisons. Colonial defence figured so largely in the Ministry of Marine's priorities first because the colonies were part of the Minister's portfolio: not until the end of the century did

[23] This can mean a mercantile war waged by state warships as well as by privateers.
[24] See the discussion in the *Conseil d'amirauté* of 8 Nov. 1847 and 29 May 1852, AN BB8 876 (*marine*), 193–9, and BB8 853 (*marine*); also the war plans of 15 July 1848 and June 1850, AN GG1 31 (*marine*). Also pertinent are the debates in the great parliamentary inquiry into the navy, 1849–51, *Enquête parlementaire sur la situation et l'organisation des services de la marine militaire* (2 vols., Paris, 1851), i. 137–84. For a telling example of earlier French strategic planning, see the Dalbarade plan of June 1793, N. Hampson, *La Marine de l'an II: Mobilisation de la flotte de l'océan 1793–1794* (Paris, 1959), 78–93.

they finally gain their own ministry. Secondly, the colonial garrisons were made up from the navy's own soldiers, the *infanterie* and
artillerie de marine. Wartime colonial defence would not necessarily
have entailed the sending abroad of any more purely naval forces
than would have been required in any case for the *guerre de course*.

With regard to one colony the position was rather different. This
was Algeria. Algiers itself was occupied in 1830, and over the next
two decades, sometimes with great difficulty, the rest of the territory was subdued. The defence of this colony was not a burden
for the navy: the large army of occupation was sufficient against
almost any threat. But to the navy did fall the task of ensuring
communications between France and this jewel of her empire.
'Coûte que coûte', said one senior admiral at one of the important
meetings of the *Conseil d'amirauté* in November 1847 that dealt with
the *vaisseau à vapeur*, 'il faut que nous assurer des communications
promptes et que rien ne puisse empêcher avec nos possessions
d'Afrique, si la guerre venait à éclater.'[25] This new responsibility
helped to concentrate the minds of French naval policy-makers on
European waters.

Also influential was the nature of the vessels that were coming in
the 1830s and 1840s to supplement the sailing fleets—the paddle-
steamers. Their mediocre sailing qualities meant they were at their
most effective when steam was raised, but this made them dependent on their coal-bunkers which, with the greedy engines of the
time, could supply enough fuel for only a few hundred nautical
miles. But, for European operations, where the main lines of
operation were relatively short and coal depots plentiful, paddle-
steamers were well adapted. They had limits, but these very
limitations encouraged the tendency in Paris to see naval warfare
primarily in European terms.

That the Admiralty had wider concerns is suggested by the screw
cruisers built in the mid- and late 1840s specifically to counter
the presumed threat of the French steam-navy, where steam was
combined with strategic range. In building one counter to the
French challenge in Europe, the Admiralty had not abandoned the
possibility of extra-European deployment.

But it will be remembered that even at this stage a concession
had been made, for another part of the Admiralty building effort

---

[25] AN BB8 876 (*marine*), 195.

was the *Blenheim* and her three sisters. These proved eventually to be very useful vessels, with a surprisingly wide sphere of operations; but to their designers they had been merely mobile coastal-defence batteries. In other words, they were the first British battleships since medieval times intended for only European operations. Thanks to the French response, they proved to be the harbinger of later Admiralty policy, since that response was to build the first *vaisseau à vapeur*, and later improved sisters. They presented the Admiralty with the choice between imitation, in which case, it seemed, much of the strategic capacity of the fleet would be lost, or leaving the French fleet dominant in European waters.

The intention of the Ministry of Marine in authorizing the *Napoléon* had indeed been to make problems for the English. The vessel might not have been the consequence of a developed vision of the shape of battle, but underlying the project was an undoubted strategic aim. The doubts about her concerned her cost and the technical boldness of the design. The strategic possibilities if she lived up to the promises of the designer were obvious even to many who opposed her being laid down. As Dupuy de Lôme had forcibly argued in the papers he submitted with his plans, *vaisseaux à vapeur* were well suited to French needs. Even if the enemy had a larger battlefleet, as long as it was composed of *vaisseaux mixtes*, the French would be able to break blockades, ensure communications with Algeria, play havoc with the enemy's merchantmen, fight a battle — or not — as they chose, and have suitable escorts for fast troop transports mounting a 'bolt from the blue' on any hostile coastline.[26]

Despite Tupinier's pleading in 1847, a crash programme of fast battleship construction was not undertaken. Instead there was a concentration on *mixtes*, and that unfortunate experiment with the *Montebello*. Only at the end of 1852 was the decision made to undertake a building programme of fast steamers of all rates.

The Admiralty followed hesitantly, taking more courage only after that embarrassment at the Dardanelles when the British *vaisseaux mixtes* remained helplessly by whilst the *Napoléon* towed the French flagship through the straits in brave fashion. From this point, it appears, the Admiralty decided also to build numbers of screw-warships of great power, whatever the disadvantages.

[26] Dupuy de Lôme, *Notice sur les travaux scientifiques de M. Dupuy de Lôme* (Paris, 1866), 16–20.

The British decision did not necessarily mean the desertion of the Empire. For one thing, neither of the rival fleets relied entirely on the new type. There were the *bâtiments mixtes* already built, and their number swelled as the 1850s progressed. After all, the conversion of sailing-vessels to *mixtes* was one way of saving important naval resources from total obsolescence, without the excessive expense entailed in conversion to *bâtiments à vapeur*. Economy thus ensured a continuing supply of vessels suitable for colonial detachment. Admittedly, from 1853–4 onwards *new* construction was usually of the latest fast type, and this gave the two fleets an increasing Eurocentric emphasis. However, one can well argue that this was not necessarily alien to British strategic tradition. Britain's (or England's) main naval rivals had always been European powers, and thus the major part of the Royal Navy had been concentrated in European waters. This did not imply that the colonies were undefended. Once the rival navies were 'bottled up' in Europe, the Admiralty knew that British interests in the rest of the world could be safeguarded with a light scattering of naval forces.[27] Naturally, the battlefleet had to be capable of mounting distant operations, just in case an enemy admiral managed to evade any blockade and lead his squadron overseas, as de Villeneuve had taken the Franco-Spanish fleet in 1805. But the Royal Navy's main tasks were in Europe, and a challenge mounted there had to be met, whatever the terms in which it was posed. Thus, to one way of thinking, the Empire was not abandoned by the Admiralty's decision to build fast warships: rather, its shield was strengthened. Yet, it must be allowed, the fact that the shield was now increasingly composed of vessels specially suitable for European operations, gave officers an added excuse for focusing on these operations, and even encouraged them to forget about the global context entirely.

The narrowing of focus brought by the fast battleship furthered the development of a militarized naval strategy, but it did not begin it. That beginning lay in the introduction of the paddle-steamer. As with tactics, so with strategy, the coming of steam led to comparisons being made between war on land and at sea. We find the Duke of Wellington arguing in 1843 that one ought henceforward to speak not of naval but of maritime warfare, and thus

---

[27] G. S. Graham, *The Politics of Naval Supremacy: Studies in British Maritime Ascendancy* (CUP, 1965), 9, 22–3.

recognize that the old firm division between operations on land and sea no longer held.[28] Also, as with tactics, more was involved than the borrowing of ideas and forms from land warfare. Maritime war, it was foreseen, would make extensive use of soldiers. More than a few detachments of *fusiliers marins* or marines were meant. With steam, combined operations, even those involving large armies, were to have the same speed and certainty as operations on land. As Palmerston said in that famous speech of 1845, steam had made a bridge over the Channel.

With fast screw-warships, the threat of a steam descent on a coast appeared all the greater. The *Napoléon* had shown at the Dardanelles that currents and winds were no longer the barrier to naval operations they once had been. The war that followed gave further cause to believe naval warfare had been changed radically. As is common, the hard-won experience of war was a more powerful influence on strategic thought than years of peacetime theorizing: equally as common, that experience served largely to mislead.

Four main naval lessons were drawn from the Crimean War. First, that amphibious operations able to rely on steam were more sure and speedy than those depending only on sail. Second, that modern, well-built maritime fortresses were very difficult to capture. Third, that even the largest and best designed screw-battleship could be dangerously vulnerable to enemy fire, whilst ironclad-vessels were proof against almost anything that could be thrown against them, and fourth, that steam-flotillas were an important new element in naval warfare. The evidence for the first point, of course, came from the allied expedition to the Crimea, which crossed from the west coast of the Black Sea in a few days, and landed the troops safely at the beach-head. The crossing had been opposed by the majority of the senior British and French army officers involved; 'C'est l'expédition de Sicile', some were heard to mutter.[29] But the final operation confirmed the experience gained in the Civitavecchia operation of 1849.[30] This earlier crossing had in itself attracted admiration, but had not been on anything like the

[28] Evidence before the Parliamentary Select Committee on Shipwrecks, PP (1843) ix. 382. As early as 1824 the Duke had expressed fears of a French steam descent on Sheerness, letter of 18 Aug., in the folder 'Sheerness Defences' dated Aug. 1830, WO 44 122.

[29] Papers of Jurien de la Gravière, entry in private journal, 1 Sept. 1854, AN BB4 1798 *bis* (*marine*).   [30] See p. 53.

same scale as the Crimean one, and had lacked the ingredient that had most worried the allied generals about the latter—the possibility of interception by the large, although obsolete and numerically inferior, Sebastopol fleet. The fact that nearly 60,000 men were able to cross the Black Sea despite an enemy fleet in being was one of the triumphs of the affair, and something particularly to worry British officers thinking ahead to the possible shape of a future Anglo-French war.

Yet if the crossing had been a success, the consequent siege of Sebastopol proved to be bloody and long-drawn-out. It took nearly a year to occupy the city, and even then not all the fortifications were captured. Hence the second wartime lesson: the tenacious resistance possible by modern maritime fortresses even against heavy assaults from land and sea.

Furthermore, the attack on Sebastopol by sea made more clear than before the vulnerability of warships to gunfire. Already in November 1853, when some of their number had been descended on by a much more powerful Russian force, Turkish warships had shown themselves very vulnerable to enemy fire, particularly that from shell-guns. In October 1854 the allied warships themselves came under Russian fire when they added the weight of their broadsides to the attack of the besieging armies on Sebastopol. Despite the relative success of the *Agamemnon* and *Sans Pareil*, the attack reconfirmed the traditional view that warships could not match well-handled land batteries. Their guns were necessarily less accurate and their wooden scantlings were easily damaged. The coming of steam to the battlefleet had not greatly altered the balance of advantage in these regards. Indeed, steam had made warships more vulnerable to enemy fire, even if engines and boilers were fitted below the water. Luckily for the allies, their vessels did not suffer greatly during the bombardment, but the incidents that nearly led to disaster suggested forcefully that it was not only Turkish warships that might blow up in battle.

Admittedly, not all drew such lessons. For instance, at the end of the 1850s Dupuy de Lôme still believed that steam gave even wooden, unarmoured vessels a great advantage in attacking shore defences, and believed that screw-battleships could force their way past any batteries into harbours, and then—unless there was a mobile defence ready to meet them—play havoc with quayside

facilities and unmanned warships.[31] That he was not entirely wrong
is suggested by the experience of the Austrian screw-liner *Kaiser* at
the battle of Lissa in 1866, which was terribly mangled by Italian
guns, but still survived.

Dupuy de Lôme, of course, would have been the first to agree
that ironclads would be even more effective in attack. He had been
a proponent of armour at sea since the 1840s, but had not been
taken seriously; trials with armour had been disappointing. Then
came the war with Russia. The special needs of that war, specifically the problem of how to attack maritime fortresses from the
sea, spurred first the French and then the British to approach with
more intelligence the mounting of trials of armour, and at last it
was discovered that, with a thick wooden backing, wrought iron
some four inches thick could shrug off almost any projectile, even
solid shot. The Ministry of Marine was thus encouraged to think
about armoured ships of the line, and by the end of the decade first
the French and then, inevitably, the British navy had begun to
build large ironclads.

Naturally, the coming of the seagoing ironclad had its own effect
on naval strategy. But so too did another major innovation, the
other one to emerge from the Crimean War. It too owed its initial
development to the needs of coastal warfare; but in this case its
effect on strategic thought was a perverting one.

It was a means of attack developed primarily for the Baltic,
where there was never any real prospect of a large allied army being
sent. Only if Alexander II had stubbornly refused to make peace
after the fall of Sebastopol would the position perhaps have
changed. True, 10,000 troops were sent in 1854 to help take
Bomarsund; otherwise, carrying the war to the enemy depended on
the allied navies. It was realized that even though one could not
capture the main Russian Baltic maritime fortresses, one could at
least bombard them and burn out their centres. For this task, given
the numerous coastal shallows, one needed small vessels armed
with heavy guns or mortars—in short, a flotilla. The thought
was scarcely new in Baltic annals: during the eighteenth century
Swedish and Russian flotillas had often clashed. These cockleshell
fleets had had to depend largely on oars, on muscle power. Their

[31] Meetings of the *Conseil d'amirauté*, 6 Apr. and 12 Nov. 1858, AN BB8 888, 61–
5, 178–92.

range and seaworthiness were poor. But, by the middle of the nineteenth century there was the technology to build screw-flotilla craft.
Freed from dependence on muscle, and surprisingly robust in
heavy seas, the new vessels were capable of being deployed far
from home. For the first time, consequently, Britain and France
were able to maintain coastal-water squadrons in the Baltic. And
in August 1855, with the attack on Sweaborg, the steam-flotilla
demonstrated that it could burn out a fortress's heart. It was a
potent example of what could now be done by sea forces against
land forces, in that old battle of the whale against the elephant, and
at very slight cost to the whale.

It was the lessons of the Crimean War, on top of previous
experience and theorizing, that produced the characteristic British
and French naval strategic beliefs of the late 1850s and 1860s,
militarized not only in the emphasis put on naval operations against
land targets, or the way that the language of land battle was
extended to sea battle, but even to the degree that some pundits
began to argue that warfare on land and sea had largely become
one, and that troops would not only be used extensively in maritime warfare but that naval forces would be invaluable elements in
continental warfare.

The degree to which land and sea warfare were synthesized
changed according to the strategist concerned, and changed even
according to the country; French thinkers tending to show themselves more enthusiastic than British ones. That there should have
been differences was inevitable, and they can be addressed later. At
present it ought to be emphasized that in the years after the
Crimean War the strategic attitudes of the two navies were in
general similar, and to a remarkable, even unprecedented extent.
The Royal Navy and *la Royale* fellow-travelled down the same naval
strategic road. More than ever before, the important element in
policy-making appeared to be defence rather than offence, and both
navies looked fearfully over the Channel in the expectation that the
other side was about to unleash on its recent ally the weapons just
honed against Russia. They each thought their country's coastline
horridly open to attack. The naval arsenals appeared particularly
vulnerable. With his steam transports the enemy could attempt a
coup de main; with his invulnerable ironclads he might steam in
unharmed past the defending batteries and batter the soft heart of
the dockyard; or he might not bother to come so close, but deploy

his flotilla at a safe distance and plaster the arsenal with explosives. Naturally, each side had its particular worry. The British, possessing a relatively small army, feared above all the descent of an enemy army corps. The French, whose screw-flotilla force was far smaller than the vast armada Britain's superior industrial might have enabled her to build up in 1854–6, had most reason to fear steam coastal warfare. But both responded in the same way to the threats. Of course, they tried to improve the rate at which the fleet could be mobilized. However, this raises questions of manning, the building up of stores, and the maintenance of ships in reserve which fall outside the ambit of this chapter. What is pertinent is that the two sides put enormous efforts into building up coastal defences, in order to avoid suffering their own Sebastopols or Sweaborgs.

Traditionally, bricks and mortar coastal defence had been emphasized in France, so naturally it was in this country that the threat of steam naval attack first prompted added preparations on land. In 1841 a mixed commission of artillery, engineers, and naval men was set up under General Lahitte to see what improvements in coastal protection had become necessary. Construction began on the proposed supplementary defences in 1845, and by 1859 some 147 defence works had been completed or restored at the great ports, costing over nine million francs.[32] It is a sign of the naval development of the 1850s that by 1859 even this scheme had come to appear inadequate. Three new commissions were set up, two of which investigated means of raising more gunners to man the coastal batteries. The third, for whose inception the Emperor was directly responsible, was a reconstitution of the 1841 committee, headed by Marshal Niel. It recommended a large extension and improvement of the coastal-battery complex, plus the organization of a corps of 14,000 men to serve the guns in wartime. The new plans were accepted by both service ministries, and in 1859 over twenty million francs were credited to help realize them.[33]

In Britain during the 1840s the emphasis was still on mobility. The main coastal protection proposed by the defence commission of 1844–5 consisted of the steam blockships. Significantly, by the following decade, just as in France, well-developed fixed defences,

---

[32] Measures for coastal defence, 1841–8, AN BB4 1034 (*marine*), dossier 2.

[33] Ibid., dossier 3; and 'Défense des côtes de France (Commission de 1860)', AN DD2 1105 (*marine*).

masonry and concrete, appeared vital. The Crimean War had had
its effect—including in one way not so far mentioned: the demonstration by the vessels of the Blenheim class in that conflict, that they
had a far greater range than originally thought, caused some critics
to say that they were too good for their purpose, and that—if
invasion did come—they might not be deployed where they ought
to be, off the South Coast. The implication was that only im-
moveable defences offered true security. Where mobile defences
were spoken of, there was often a caveat made that the vessels
comprising it should be of very short range, incapable of being
lured away from what was seen as their task. A traditional Admiralty belief, that it might be a better defence to have one's warships
off the enemy coast than off one's own, was now rarely considered:
a purely naval defence seemed suspect.

Proposals in 1857 for new outworks at Malta were another sign
of changed British sensibilities.[34] Furthermore, in the following
year a Royal Commission was set up, including officers of both
services, like the Niel commission, to consider how best to protect
the principal home dockyards from assault. The report, presented
in 1860, proposed the construction around the yards of fortifications on the latest pattern. Even after trimming by the House
of Commons, the cost was to be over £10 million, an enormous
sum for the day, about the same figure as the annual naval budget
and over ten times the special 1859 French fortifications credit.
However, once the scheme was complete, the commissioners
argued, the yards would be safe from purely naval attacks, whether
by ironclad or flotilla. Even if a French army landed, all would not
be lost. Secure behind their new walls, the 'cradles of the navy'
could mobilize reserves and repair damaged ships, so that a naval
force could be built up that would, as always, give Britain victory
in the final battle.[35]

One could discuss many aspects of the report, but the one that
surely must be underlined is its absurd mixture of optimism and
pessimism. On the one hand there were worst-case analyses of the
blackest hue, assumptions that the British battlefleet would not be
ready, or be lured away, or be sunk, and thus the French would be
able to send thousands of troops successfully across the Channel
with all their ancillary equipment. On the other hand, it was argued

[34] Report of May 1857, ADM 1 5682.   [35] PP (1860), xxiii. 431 ff.

that even if the French army did establish itself in Britain, and the French fleet gain mastery of the Channel, all was not necessarily lost for Albion. The country's maritime trade links might have been largely cut, the Home Counties and perhaps London itself ravaged by French troops, the government fled, the capital market in chaos, but—so it was said—recovery was still possible as long as the dockyards were inviolate. One must conclude that, if the commissioners were right about the degree of threat, they were wrong about the adequacy of their solution.

It is not surprising, even in the days when the Royal Navy was the largest in the world, that there should have been some men somewhere in Britain who were capable of such an emphasis on guns behind masonry. Engineer officers were always willing to preach that the only true defences were fixed defences. They are the Boullées of military history. As Napoleon III wrote in 1861 to one of his marshals:

Je suis fâché de le dire, mais l'esprit qui domine le corps du génie est étroit, il voudrait défendre toutes les bicoques, tous les défilés, tous les passages de rivières, toutes les côtes et, de cette manière, on éparpille ses forces; on a partout des murailles sans avoir des soldats pour les défendre et on dépense des sommes immense pour un bien mince résultat.[36]

What is surprising is that the naval officers present on the Royal Commission agreed with the final recommendations. That this marked a striking change from previous days is well shown by a comparison between the 1858–60 inquiry and a mixed commission of 1785. At the latter the naval officers present, who included the formidable Sir John Jervis, laughed out of court a proposal to spend large sums to improve the dockyard fortifications.[37]

Of course, much had changed in terms of naval technology in the intervening three-quarters of a century. Naval officers of our period were very aware that the means of attack had increased, while tending to forget that the means of defence had also benefited. But technological change had an even wider effect on their attitudes, one that we have to appreciate in order to understand the roots of the militarized strategy of the time.

A fundamental point is that technology had given the dockyards a more important role to play in the 1850s than had previously been

---

[36] Letter to Randon of 27 Nov., Randon Papers, 249 A.P. 5, dossier 2.
[37] *Reports* (London, 1785), vii. 70, p. 6. *Accounts and Papers* (London, 1786), x. 144.

the case. Steam-warships were more vulnerable than their purely sailing forebears to accidents, to breakdowns, and—as had been at least suggested at Sebastopol—to gunfire. The coming of the seagoing ironclad did not altogether change this position. Machinery, for instance, remained liable to breakdown. Admittedly, armour addressed one problem — that of shell-fire — but added new ones, at least in the early years: iron-hulled ironclads needed regular scraping of the hull to remove marine growths, and wooden-hulled ones—which could be fitted with the usual copper sheathing— suffered from galvanic action between the copper and the lower strakes of the armour belt. Even if they remained in good order, and here there was little or no advance on what had been the case with unarmoured vessels, the ironclads needed frequent resort to a port for overhauls and resupply, particularly of coal. If in need of serious repair, then a first-class dockyard might be the only resource.

In consequence, the change to steam-warships entailed large expenditure on dockyard facilities. It cost thousands of pounds simply to build up a coal depot, and that was but one expense. Also costly was the construction and maintenance of steam factories to cope with repairs and even, in some cases, to produce engines of their own. Furthermore, since steamers tended to be longer and perhaps more deeply draughted than sailing-vessels of the same rate, building slips and dry docks had to be enlarged, or new ones built to the latest specifications, and channels and basins had to be dredged more deeply.

Dry docks were seen as the most important of all dockyard facilities for the new steam fleets. It was wise to inspect screw steamers below the waterline regularly, notably to look for wear and tear on the screw-gland. Moreover, it was well understood, in Paris as in London, the ability to repair and return ships to sea after battle would depend on the available dock space. That this space had to be large followed from the somewhat apocalyptic picture that both navies had of naval battle. As the Minister of Marine wrote to Napoleon in January 1854 (after Sinope):

Les instruments de destruction sont si nombreux et si formidables que le vainqueur lui même après un combat de quelques heures, peut être exposés à ne pouvoir tenir la mer et à rentrer dans le port pour réparer ses avaries.[38]

---

[38] AN BB8 108 (*marine*), 122 ff.

The introduction of the ironclad made little difference to such expectations. Damage to the hulls from rams, it was believed, would still mean a heavy reliance on dry docks after battle. Not unnaturally, therefore, in the 1860s as in the 1850s both navies put large sums into building and extending docks. Significantly, strategically placed small yards were not neglected. After a battle the state of the fleet, or pursuit by an enemy, might mean shelter and repair had to be sought at the nearest friendly port. Here lay one important reason for the approval by the *Conseil d'amirauté* in 1858 of a new dock for Algiers, even though the great resources of Toulon were but a few hundred miles distant.[39] The expected shape of battle also further encouraged dockyard fortification. After a serious engagement, the fleet would need repairs, and while these were being done (by implication leaving the sea open to the enemy), attackers had to be kept at bay. The danger of attack appeared so great that nature as well as art was called upon by planners. Each navy took an increased interest in those of its dockyards most difficult of access by enemy naval forces—Rochefort and Chatham, connected to the sea by the winding and shoal-infested channels of the Charente and Medway respectively.[40]

It appeared that a network of well-fortified dockyards had become a crucial support to a naval strategy. Fleets were no longer seen as possessing their old flexibility. The radius of operations had shrunk, and the centres of those operations were fortified arsenals. Maritime fortresses were taking up in sea warfare the role occupied on land by land fortresses. In naval strategy as well as tactics the language of land warfare was seen as applicable, and one finds maritime fortresses being built with the intention of flanking possible enemy lines of advance, and rival ones then appearing to outflank the outflankers. As early as the 1840s the Duke of Wellington successfully pressed for fortified harbours of refuge to be commenced in the Channel Islands to cover the great port being built at Cherbourg, and to threaten the line of advance of an invasion fleet issuing from there for the English coast. As he said, 'whoever has possession of the Channel Islands has the key to the English Channel.'[41] In reply, to counter this new Torres Vedras stronghold, the French built

---

[39] AN BB8 888 (*marine*), 132–9.
[40] On Chatham see PP (1861), xiii. 4, 9. For Rochefort, see the report of 3 Apr. 1858, AN DD2 1123 (*marine*).
[41] Conversation with a Mr Walker, Somerset Papers, 1392 M.A.3.

their own works on neighbouring islands.[42] A start had been made by the British even before work began on the Channel Islands, with the harbours of refuge built on the South Coast. These had been intended largely as centres of action for the paddle-steamers of the day, the then battlefleet having the range to act for months free of the shore. It is a sign of how quickly things had changed that by the following decade the battlefleets, of Britain as well as of France, also appeared to be on a leash, intimately linked to their land bases.

The final impression is very reminiscent of that from a previous stage in naval history. We have noted at various points the importance of lessons from classical times to the writers we have been studying. The British and French navies of the mid-nineteenth century did not fully revert to the days of Salamis or Actium, but in reading about their strategic attitudes one is strongly reminded of the symbiosis between warships and fortresses characteristic of galley warfare in the Mediterranean during the sixteenth century.[43]

But, one might well be impelled to ask, surely the picture of naval warfare so far presented was not accepted by all British and French naval officers? Moreover, surely it was not accepted equally by the two navies? History, geography, and culture are worth something, even when confronted by the divine flame of technology: the views of the British and French strategists must have differed to some degree. So, indeed, they did: there were exceptions and differences. For instance, most noticeably in Britain, there was a naval generation gap. Amongst older officers who had served in the Great War, the belief seems largely to have held firm that steam had not altered the old naval truths. Some veterans, at least, would have agreed with Jervis's opinion of coastal fortifications—'of no other use than to calm the fears of old ladies both in and out'.[44] But the younger officers were more likely to believe that steam had altered everything and made merely tiresome the advice of their seniors.

The differences between the beliefs of the younger British and French officers were less striking, more nuanced. Take the case of

[42] Discussion in the *Conseil d'amirauté* of 11 Oct. 1853, AN BB8 883 (*marine*), 254.
[43] J. F. Guilmartin, *Gunpowder and Galleys: Changing Technology and Mediterranean Warfare at Sea in the Sixteenth Century* (CUP, 1974), ch. 3.
[44] P. H. Colomb, *Essays on Naval Defence* (London, 1893), 134. As representatives of the veterans there are Lord Dundonald, Sir Charles Napier (though he was not always consistent), and Sir Maurice Berkeley: Dundonald Papers, GD. 233 62 2a: *Hansard*, Ser. 3, vol. clx. cols. 495–506, 545–6.

flotilla operations. One certainly finds that British officers tended to accept that small screw-vessels would have a crucial part to play in future naval wars. Henry Codrington, son of the victor of Navarino, went so far as to say in 1855 that all naval warfare in future would be littoral in nature.[45] It appears that belief in the power of the steam-flotilla penetrated even to the highest political echelons of Whitehall. Changes in maritime law approved by the British government during the Crimean War, and enshrined in the Declaration of Paris of April 1856, involved the loss of certain long-standing British maritime belligerent rights. Notably, the right to seize enemy goods carried on neutral merchantmen was abandoned, although it had been a potent instrument in Britain's previous wars. In exchange, Whitehall got the agreement of the other signatory powers to the abolition of privateering, a practice that was anathema to the country with the world's largest merchant marine. But the exchange was not a fair one, and Whitehall's agreement to the bargain depended on two considerations. First, the Crimean War had suggested that with steam-warships blockades could be made tighter than in the days of sail. Thus the need to intercept enemy goods on the high seas became less pressing.[46] Secondly, and more pertinent from our point of view, the opinion was gaining ground that with the steam-flotilla there was now a better way than through trade war of bringing naval pressure directly to bear on an enemy.[47]

The flotilla, therefore, was well regarded in Britain, but on the other side of the Channel it was studied more seriously and its potential was most highly rated. Notably, it interested probably the best writer of his day on naval strategy—not Bouët-Willaumez but a friend, junior, and at times aide-de-camp of his—Richild Grivel. His work, it is interesting to note, did not largely reject the lessons gained in the wars between sailing fleets. This, one strongly suspects, was due to the influence of his father, Admiral Jean-Baptiste

[45] Letter to Rear-Admiral Richards, 7 July 1855, Codrington Papers, COD. 109/2.

[46] One would think that this would have given the Admiralty greater confidence in the navy's ability to check the French navy, and thus to defend Britain with maritime means alone. But blockade demanded a large superiority in numbers or efficiency, something the Royal Navy did not have in regard to its chief rival during the 1850s and 1860s.

[47] C. I. Hamilton, 'Anglo-French Seapower and the Declaration of Paris, 1856', *International History Review*, 4 (1982), 166–90.

Grivel (1778–1869). The naval family was one of the ways in which the experience and understanding of naval warfare could overleap even the generation gap brought by steam. Nevertheless, the younger Grivel was a man of his time, as one sees from his interest in the effects on warfare of the new technology, including his particular emphasis on coastal operations.[48]

In comparison with one brother officer, however, Grivel appears somewhat conservative. Though in exile from his country after 1848, the prince de Joinville remained in touch with many of his former colleagues in the French navy, and never lost his interest in naval affairs. In an article of 1859, he presented a paean of praise to the steam navy, from the battleship to the gunboat, arguing that it had changed the whole face of war—including war on land. There was no more powerful or fruitful development, he wrote, 'que le concours prêté aux armées de terre par les flottes à vapeur'. He meant, on the one hand, that seaborne invasion was now far simpler than it had been: combined operations had gained with steam a speed and mathematical precision hitherto unknown. The coasts of Europe, the prince went on, offered 'mille points vulnérables', and even if the opponent had an extensive telegraph network, he could still not rely on an advance warning of attack— 'Autant vaudrait lui demander, quand un orage se forme au ciel, le lieu où doit tomber la foudre'. Nor would his railways be of much use as a defence since, unlike a fleet, they could not throw 15,000 men on to a beach in an hour, or mount a crushing fire that would sweep away all opposition. Then there was the contribution that Joinville believed the steam flotilla could offer once the army was ashore or, indeed, in ordinary land operations. The gunboats would penetrate deeply into enemy territory to support the army's advance, via the rivers—even those guarded by batteries, for 'il est peu de barrières que les navires à vapeur ne puissent aujourd'hui franchir'.[49]

With the benefit of hindsight, much of the Prince's article seems like simple fantasy. But what did contemporaries think? One present-day critic has said that they thought the author was

[48] See his *Attaques et bombardements maritimes* (Paris, 1857), and his series of ten articles, 'De la guerre maritime avant et depuis les nouvelles inventions', *Revue maritime et coloniale*, 24 and 25 (1868), and 26 (1869). On the man himself there is Félix Julien, *Un marin: le contre-amiral Grivel* (Paris, 1883).

[49] 'La Marine à vapeur dans les guerres continentales', *Revue des deux mondes* (Feb. 1859).

dreaming.[50] But this is perhaps harsh. The Prince did not go far beyond what his fellow officers accepted as reality, or at least possibility. After the Crimean War there were conflicts that lent weight to his analysis. Despite a setback in 1859, when an attack was repulsed bloodily, the experience of the Royal Navy in China was that the screw-gunboat had a great part to play in at least some fluvial operations. Then there was the US Civil War. Federal attacks against the Confederate coast, and penetration up Southern rivers, justified much of what the Prince had said—at least where the foe in question was poorly armed and his country vast.[51]

French naval officers had particular cause to be conscious of the various ways that naval forces could co-operate with the military. There was the war in Italy against Austria, 1859–60, when the navy carried enormous quantities of men, horses, and supplies to help feed the war front. Moreover, the navy was inevitably involved in the combined operations of the 1860s that carried French armies to the Lebanon, to Indo-China, and to Mexico. And on the level of war planning, if not of actual operations, the Ministry of Marine showed that it realized at least some of the opportunities for naval intervention in land war that seemed to be offered. For instance, though they were not ready in time to be used, in 1859 some small armoured steam-gunboats were manufactured for use on the rivers of northern Italy. Furthermore, in the war against the German Confederation in 1870–1, there was a plan to descend with an army corps on the German coast, though the enemy advanced so quickly into France that there were never the men available to carry out such an operation.

The Ministry of Marine, it seems probable, had not been influenced by the prince de Joinville: rather, both drew from the same, common stock of ideas. And these were ideas, to reiterate, that were stronger in France than in Britain. French theorists and planners took into account the fact that their country had a large army, and was likely to be drawn into continental wars. From this came the considerable emphasis on the use of troops in naval operations and the attempt to sketch out what the navy could contribute in a major land war. In Britain the same conditions were lacking: planners in Whitehall were forced to distribute with a

[50] André Reussner, 'Joinville et la politique navale', *Neptunia*, 32 (1953), 42–7.
[51] For an interesting example of Joinville helping to plan a combined operation, see R. Reed, *Combined Operations in the Civil War* (Annapolis, Md., 1978), 100–2.

meagre hand contingents of troops for combined operations; there
was a far greater interest than in France in purely naval attacks on
coastlines; and there was no idea at all, as far as can be judged, of
letting screw-flotillas be drawn into fluvial operations in a continental European war.

We have just described a fundamental factor on the French side
that helped differentiate naval strategy there from its fellow over
the Channel. There was a factor on the British side that had a similar differentiating effect. Though they tried hard at times, the
Admiralty could not completely forget the importance of protecting the country's maritime trade and its colonies.

Commerce protection was for long almost completely ignored:
not until, first, the Confederates showed in the US Civil War the
effect that a few marauding cruisers could have on an enemy's
merchant fleet and, secondly, the Federal navy began the construction of the Wampanoag class, did the Admiralty even begin to look
seriously at the subject. The consequence was the Inconstant class
of fast, heavily armed cruisers. Their appearance suggests that the
country's interests made it impossible for the Admiralty ever totally
to lay aside traditional naval policy.

Not that the new cruisers meant the end in Britain of the
militarized strategy. As suggested before, naval strategists of the
period were fully capable of believing two conflicting ideas at one
time. In the long term, however, the conflict could not be borne,
and the needs of commerce protection ultimately helped wean the
Admiralty away from an over-narrow European perspective. Yet,
even more important in this regard, making its influence felt to a
degree even at the time of the dockyard commission, was colonial
protection.

As late as January 1857 we find the First Lord, Sir Charles
Wood, penning the following note to a colonial governor who
wanted a naval force permanently stationed off the coast:

It is impossible to supplement the local defence with a Royal Naval force
that will not quit the coasts. The most effectual defence of a colony may
be by the presence of an armed force at a great distance from it . . . At
the time of Lord Nelson's well-known pursuit of Admiral Villeneuve, the
protection of the coasts of England might have been as effectively secured
by an action in the West Indies as by Sir R. Calder's action in the Bay of
Biscay or the subsequent battle of Trafalgar . . . [besides, in real emer-
gencies] there is no service of any Kind which the Royal Navy is not ready

to render, such has always been the case and will My Lords are confident always be the case with officers of H.M. Navy.[52]

This was a fine, reviving blast of traditional Admiralty opinion. One could well argue that it came directly from the First Naval Lord, Sir Maurice Berkeley, a veteran of the French Wars. However, younger officers were at times capable of similar sentiments. After a splendid naval review at Cherbourg in 1858 had worried her about the advanced state of French naval preparations, Queen Victoria asked some very pointed questions of the Board of Admiralty. Alexander Milne, the Third Naval Lord, was one who replied, sending a sketch naval-war plan which, interestingly enough, suggested a deployment of fleets and measures—notably blockades of Brest and Cherbourg—clearly drawn from the kind of strategy adopted in the French Wars, in which he had not served.[53]

However, Milne's attitudes were more traditional than those of most officers, as far as one can judge. Here, too, one might see the influence of the naval family in action, the younger Milne transmitting the beliefs of his father, the respected Admiral Sir David Milne (1763–1845). By the end of the 1850s, even at the Admiralty, such beliefs were no longer accepted as received wisdom. By December 1859, after Berkeley had gone, one finds the Wood letter being indirectly denied. A circular was sent to the colonies stating:

that it was wholly out of . . . [their Lordships'] power to maintain in every part of the world, such a force as would be able to cope at all times with such squadrons as other nations might concentrate for a special purpose at distant parts of the globe.

William Romaine, Permanent Secretary of the Admiralty, explained the Board's reasoning in a memorandum of May 1860. Any war, he said, would require a quick concentration of RN forces, and consequently colonial ports could be left open and could be plundered or captured by hostile cruisers. Moreover, the naval C.-in-C.'s knowledge that the principal places in his station were free from attack by single enemy cruisers would give him a great freedom in operations.[54]

The circular is reminiscent of the 1860 dockyard commission. The impression that a militarized strategy was being extended to the colonies is in some respects strengthened by a reading of two

---

[52] Comments attached to a report of Sir William Denison, Governor of New South Wales, 14 Aug. 1856, forwarded to the Admiralty on 23 Dec., ADM 1 5678.
[53] Milne Papers, MLN P. B. 3. h.   [54] ADM 1 5642.

other inquiries, one a departmental committee on the expense of military defences in the colonies (reported April 1860), the other a select committee of the Commons on colonial military expenditure (reported July 1861). The evidence given before them confirms the development implied by the contrast between the Wood letter and the 1859 circular. In his evidence the Inspector-General of Fortifications, Sir John Burgoyne, pressed hard for colonial defence works on a large scale. This was only to be expected. But the naval officer evidence was itself distinctly equivocal. Rear-Admiral Erskine said bravely that once naval supremacy was assured, colonial fortifications and garrisons were largely superfluous. However, as W. C. B. Tunstall has pointed out, Erskine seems to have envisaged naval defence in terms of steam-gunboats and batteries acting as a cheap form of fortification.[55]

Yet this does not mean that a militarized strategy had been extended with success to the colonies. The colonial defence inquiries of 1860–1 had a perceptibly different concluding tone from that of the dockyard commission. This was unavoidable. There simply were not the necessary military and naval resources, either in Britain or the colonies, to extend the new strategy to a vast maritime empire. Imperial defence had to rely largely on what Mahan famously called 'those far distant, storm-beaten ships'. Once men began to study colonial defence, and also commerce protection, it gradually became clear that the crucial question was how to use sea communications oneself and to deny them to the enemy. It was no accident that it was in studies of defence beyond Europe that the theoretical framework was laid for the 'Blue Water' school, one that eventually was seen to be relevant to the European theatre itself. The seminal work here was J. C. R. Colomb's *The Protection of our Commerce and Distribution of our Naval Forces Considered*, (published in 1867). This still contained echoes of the militarized school, such as the comment on page 86 that the 'interior economy' and 'general system' of the naval service was gradually assimilating itself to that of the army. Yet it was also the precursor to the later school.[56] The conclusion must be that, thanks to her global

---

[55] PP (1860) xli, PP (1861) xiii. W. C. B. Tunstall, 'Imperial Defence, 1815–1870', in J. Holland Rose, A. P. Newton, and E. A. Benians (eds.), *The Cambridge History of the British Empire*, ii (CUP, 1940), 832, 835–6.

[56] See B. M. Ranft, 'The Naval Defence of British Sea-Borne Trade, 1860–1905', doctoral dissertation (Oxford, 1967), 10, 21–32, 33, 37, 40, 41 ff.

interests, there was a maritime factor in British policy that could not be always ignored, and which eventually asserted itself to vitiate any excessive concentration on land-based defence.

This is not to imply, by extension, that French maritime policy totally lacked a similar maritime factor. France, too, had a merchant marine, although relatively small. France, too, had distant colonies, small in comparison to the British ones, though there was a significant expansion in the 1850s and 1860s. Large territories were seized in Indo-China[57] and, thanks to the building of the Suez Canal, Egypt for a time became a quasi-protectorate. One consequence was the development of a significant colonial force, as best evinced in the construction of the *cuirassés de station*.

However, the French maritime factor did not imply a necessary denial of the militarized strategy. Most French naval strategists accepted that there was no hope of out-building the Royal Navy. The experience of the 1850s and 1860s had been that by innovating first, the French navy could hope at times at least to equal its rival in certain warship categories, but this was clearly not sufficient for a global maritime predominance. What was achievable was regional naval supremacy in those areas vital to national interests—along the French coastline and in the Mediterranean. And there were hopes that a line of influence and local predominance could be built up stretching out from the Mediterranean eastwards via some of the major French colonies. This line was to be based on the same articulation of forces and facilities described earlier, with naval and military elements co-operating intimately, with the accent on comparatively short-range operations, each one reliant on a well-protected and developed shore base. At one end was Suez, with basins and a dock built for merchantmen of the *Messageries impériales* but capable of taking second-class battleships. Further down the Red Sea was the port of Obock, seized in 1862 as part of the development of French influence in the east. Right at the other end of the arc were Tahiti and New Caledonia, most important of the island possessions, and each with their garrisons of *infanterie de marine*. But before them was Saigon, the major French Far Eastern *point d'appui*, with its large garrison, protective batteries and new dock. All in all this was a very modest arc of influence

[57] John F. Cady, *The Roots of French Imperialism in East Asia* (Cornell University Press, 1967), ch. 16.

in comparison with the British Empire, but because of that it was not a nonsense to think of depending on a militarized strategy.[58]

The above discussion suggests that the strategic ideas we have been describing in this chapter, to the degree that they were viable at all, satisfied the aims of French naval policy rather than British. The question is therefore raised, why did the Admiralty adopt such a strategy, at least for Europe? One undoubted part of the answer is that the Royal Navy's strategic planning suffered from the same kind of problems as did the planning of steam tactics and the planning of warship types: indeed, the three were functionally very closely allied. The extent of the failure of British naval-war planning suggests that more was involved than any simple Admiralty failure to cope with the implications of technological change. Some basic failure was involved, a failure whose main symptom was an excessive degree of mere copying. Mimicry, as we shall argue later, is a characteristic of any serious rivalry, but it is striking how far it was one-sided in the example under study. One certainly finds cases where the French navy copied its rival, even after 1848; but the main current was in the opposite direction. The fact that the French navy acted in a particular way was all too often a sufficient incitement for the Royal Navy unthinkingly to follow.

At some stage we shall have to explain why this was so, but that can await the general explanation. The necessary task at present is to complete our description of converging British and French naval strategies—which will mean adding somewhat to whatever mitigation has been made already of any impression of rampant militarization. It must be admitted that there was at least one factor favouring convergence that very largely contradicted the general militarized strategic trend. This grew from the very success of French naval policy, the way it produced a fleet so nearly equal, at points even superior, to the Royal Navy's. Whatever the strategic ideas that lay behind it, the very flexibility of the naval instrument was bound to encourage a wide use of the fleet. Where naval capability existed, political opportunity would take advantage of it, with the consequence that a primarily coastal-shelf force would be

---

[58] Dossier, 'Suez, 1861–3', AN DD2 1097 (*marine*). See pamphlet, sponsored by the Ministry of Marine, by Théophile Bilbaut, *Le canal de Suez et les intérêts internationaux* (Paris, 1870), and the letter of Chasseloup-Laubat to Drouyn de Lhuys (Minister of Foreign Affairs), 10 Dec. 1863, Chasseloup-Laubat Papers, iv. 318–38.

almost insensibly drawn out to take up a global role not unlike the Royal Navy's in nature, if naturally more limited in extent. To put it another way, the more French naval policy was successful, the more it was pushed to a 'Blue Water' perspective. The expedition to Mexico is eloquent in this regard. Convergence, one might well suggest, was due to complementary movements. On the one hand, and surely the more radical of the two, there was the Royal Navy edging towards French maritime traditions by narrowing its strategic focus; on the other, *la Royale* approached closer to being a global naval power not just through a development of a military–naval arc east of Suez, but also because of the great potential for action built into almost all the vessels that went down the slipways during the Second Empire. Naval power could not be restricted to the formulas of a largely alien strategy.

If one agrees with this, then one must agree also that an Anglo-French war in the mid-nineteenth century would have been even more surprising for most of the strategists of the day than wars normally are. Conflict would have made obvious the significant differences between the maritime resources and interests of the two nations, and surely any idea of a common, universal naval strategy would have been exploded. War with France would have jolted the Admiralty into a more traditional strategy, operational experience demonstrating that steam had not changed matters so very greatly. For instance, it would have been seen that *bâtiments à vapeur* were capable of greater endurance than had been thought. After all, they were rigged, and thus not absolutely reliant on their engines for range. Their stowage space was less than that of sailing-vessels, but this was a problem that the British, at least, could have significantly mitigated by requisitioning part of their enormous merchant marine to act as supply ships, and by building up depots at some of the many available colonial ports. The war might even have shown that serious mechanical breakdowns did not always imply recourse to a first-class dockyard; all wars have shown that prodigies can be achieved with modest resources as long as one has energy and ingenuity.

If wartime evidence of the range and durability of the steam fleets would have been one powerful blow against a militarized strategy, another and surely even more powerful one would have come from the coups that were not attempted. We have been studying strategic ideas characterized by a basic fault, the assumption that steam-warships were powerful in attack, but impotent in defence unless stationed directly off the point threatened. War would have brought a valuable correction, if by nothing else than the demonstration that the French services did not dare to attempt a descent in real force on the English coast, not being willing to run the horrible and real risk of having heavily laden troop-ships intercepted by even a weak RN steam-force, a risk that a strong convoy escort could not completely obviate. The French generals had been frightened enough at the prospect of crossing to the Crimea, and in that case the defending fleet had consisted almost entirely of sailing-vessels, where the officers and men lacked the degree of dedication and sheer seamanship that historically has marked so many of the exploits of the Royal Navy.

Finally, war would have given an intellectual stimulation to British naval officers, cleared away the inertia natural to a peacetime service, and encouraged a re-examination of old verities. It was, after all, in response to Queen Victoria's questions that Milne produced his 1858 plan: war posed somewhat greater emergency for the Admiralty even than a royal command, and might well have produced a yet higher degree of salutary atavism.

But what an Anglo-French war did not do, time and other conflicts did. By the 1870s, in France as in Britain, a militarized naval strategy was falling out of favour, and the two sides were beginning to strike out in their individual ways. Several elements were involved. In Britain there was that growing interest in colonial and commerce protection: the 'Blue Water' school was beginning. For what the Wampanoags had helped begin, technology encouraged. Already during the 1860s steam-engines were giving promise of more reliability, and in 1869 the Admiralty sanctioned the construction of the Devastation class, the first seagoing battleships without sails. In the following decade came the general introduction of the compound engine, with its comparatively modest coal consumption. Now possessing better reliability and range, steamers had less reliance than before on dockyards and depots. They could not rival the old sailing-vessels in these respects, but by encouraging the development of new docking facilities in the Empire, Whitehall ensured that they did not have to. All in all, with new ships and new docks, no longer could it appear quite unreasonable to apply to steam naval strategy the general lessons learned during the old wars.

In France the decisive influence was the terrible experience of the war with Germany. The Prussian General Staff showed a remarkable ability to move hugh armies with great celerity by railways, making the kind of descents suggested by Joinville appear limited and irrelevant. However, the main significance of the war to the French government was that henceforward, more than ever before, the army had to be the main priority. After 1871 French naval credits were squeezed, and the French navy accepted a more modest strategic role, again emphasizing that traditional tool of the weaker naval power—the *guerre de course*. In consequence, the temptation for the Royal Navy to copy *la Royale* was greatly reduced.

There is one final aspect of the vitiation of a common, Anglo-French militarized naval strategy. It should not be thought that French or British naval officers were wholly pleased at the military tone of tactics and strategy in the mid-century period. To some, the navy was becoming a very inferior service to the army, almost a mere transport service. In 1859 the prince de Joinville wrote:

Avec l'emploi de la vapeur la militarisation de la guerre navale ira en train et si nous n'avons pas un corps permanent de matelots fusiliers et canonniers à commander nous ne tarderons pas à voir l'artillerie et l'infanterie embarquer. Nous ne serons plus alors qu'un corps de *masters* sans importance comme sans influence.[59]

As in the case of the comment of Fisher quoted at the end of the previous section, the picture was too luridly drawn. But the words of both men suggest an uneasiness that surely helped the British and French services swing away from militarization, and probably with a heartfelt whistle of relief.

[59] 29 Feb. 1859, to Commandant J.-L. Jaurès, Joinville Papers, 300 AP III 110.

5
The Personnel

I

In the days of sail, a simple equation seemed largely to account for the relative standing at sea of the various nations: naval power equals the number of seamen in the population. Landsmen could be sent to sea, and very often were, but it was the men brought up from their youth as seafarers, whether on fishing vessels, merchantmen, or warships, who were thought of as best fit to man the warfleet. In the long series of wars between Britain and France, from the seventeenth century to the beginning of the nineteenth, the French government often had cause to be conscious of the great superiority in size of the British seafaring population over their own. British naval power depended only to a certain extent on the skills of admirals or financial strength: what underpinned it were the 'nurseries of the Royal Navy'—the thriving merchant and fishing fleets.

Once steam-vessels began to appear, however, some men began to wonder whether the old equation remained valid. Once one could depend on steam, it was suggested, one would no longer need crews of men long experienced in the arcana of wind and current. General Paixhans predicated much of his idea of the superiority of small steamers armed with shell-guns on the assumption that naval power now depended, not on the number of seamen, but on the total number of the population. This implied France could be the premier naval state since, when Paixhans wrote, she was still the most populous great power outside Russia. Paixhans, of course, was a general; but it was not just military men who thought as he did. Many French naval officers shared such enticing and patriotic beliefs, including the prince de Joinville, whose 1844 pamphlet echoed what Paixhans had said two decades previously about steam annulling the British superiority in seamen numbers.

The general was as wrong on this point as he was about the abilities of small paddle-steamers. He did not realize, at least when writing *Nouvelle force maritime*, that the steam age was better suited to British resources than to French. Britain had the advantage in coal, iron, and capital. She also had the larger number of what some imaginative observers described as the new seafaring population—naval engineers.[1] However, seamen remained a vital support to British naval power. There was a fundamental objection to any bland dismissal of the superior British maritime population: steam power cannot supplant seamanship even today, and it was all the more true for the transitional sail- and steam-fleets of the mid-nineteenth century. Navies continued to recruit their crews from the maritime community.

Admittedly, changes in technology did have some implications in matters of personnel. Notably, there were effects on the methods of training and recruitment of men for naval duties. Given the increasing complexity of warships and their equipment, even merchant seamen and fishermen could not be expected to be efficient man-of-war men after only a minimum of training. Time had always been necessary to form an efficient warship crew out of the crowd of individuals who made up a complement at the outset of a commission, whatever their previous experience: it took six months to a year before the men could work well together and had a sense of *esprit de corps*. What was different by our period was the greater importance of specialized and often lengthy training. Increasingly, the skills necessary for military seamen differentiated them from their colleagues. What became important to a naval power was to train men for its own use, whether they were to be employed regularly in the warfleet, or to act as a reserve and to spend most of their time in civilian service until mobilized for war.

One significant step was taken in 1830, when the Admiralty set up a school on the sail of the line *Excellent* to train seamen-gunners. The Ministry of Marine followed slightly later, commissioning the *corvette* (later *frégate*) *école d'artillerie* in 1837. But better training, whether in such special schools or as part of a commission in an ordinary seagoing warship raised a problem. The effort was largely wasted if the newly trained men served only a short period before departing for employment in the civilian sector. This was all too

---

[1] Sir Howard Douglas, *On Naval Warfare with Steam* (London, 1858), x–xi.

common in both the British and the French navies of the first half
of the nineteenth century. The recruitment systems of the two
navies were then very different, but they shared at least one characteristic: seamen were allowed to leave government service just
when they were most valuable.

In the Royal Navy, apart from odd cases where magistrates
offered petty offenders the choice between gaol and a term afloat,
recruitment was voluntary after peace came in 1815. Men signed up
to serve in particular ships, which in some circumstances could take
months to gather their crews, for instance when their captains had
the reputation of being martinets. Once recruited, unless death,
desertion, or incapacity intervened, the sailor served for the duration of the commission—three years as a rule—and was free to go
where he wished when the ship paid off. He might decide to sign
on on another warship that was commissioning, but he might
well decide instead to sign on on a merchantman, or even to take
a job ashore. The British peacetime manning system was thus not
only sometimes slow, but there was a great wastage of expertise: a
man might serve the Crown only once, never to return, and all the
time he had spent on the arduous great-gun exercises, or whatever,
would be totally lost; or if he did eventually come back he would
have forgotten most of what he had painfully learned, or would
find that the march of progress had swept away the equipment
he had known. The Admiralty did what it could to lubricate the
system, taking care, where possible, to arrange for a warship to pay
off in a port where there was another vessel that was signing
seamen on, in the hope that, after duly celebrating their new freedom, seamen would take the opportunity of re-entering the service.
On occasion, warships nearing the end of their commissions were
even ordered home to pay off early, so that such a fruitful
juxtaposition could be arranged. Even so, the manning system
clearly needed reordering.

The 1840s saw a great improvement as the Admiralty moved
towards creating professional man-of-war men. By a circular of
September 1846, any well-regarded seamen being paid off could
have their names entered on the books of the flagship in the dockyard concerned; the men were then granted leave of absence for six
weeks, and on their return could sign on whatever warship they
chose that was commissioning. In 1849 the period of leave was
extended to eight weeks, and men were further encouraged to stay

in the Royal Navy by the offer of a retirement pension after twenty-one years' total service, where there was an interval of no more than five years between any two commissions. On this basis grew up the body of what were called continuous servicemen, a process further encouraged in 1853 with an increase in pay and privileges.[2] These men, it was hoped, would make the manning of the fleet less uncertain, and reduce the wastage of trained men. By early 1854 this hope was being realized, since approximately one-third of all seamen in the Royal Navy had signed up under the system.

The French navy was manned very differently: during peace as well as war, it was the *inscription maritime* that found the seamen. This dated from the time of Colbert, and was a system of conscription covering all those adult males who gained their livelihood on the *eaux maritimes*. In exchange for the right to earn a living at sea, and for certain privileges such as freedom from the army conscription and a small pension on retirement, French sailors were obliged to serve the state for up to six years, and for longer in the case of a national emergency. During its long history, the system had been slowly improved, and in 1835 came the important institution of the *levée permanente*, intended as a means of regulating recruitment in time of peace and of forming a good reserve of trained men for war. Each year from 1835 a *levée* of strong sailors who had recently reached the age of twenty was taken into the navy, and usually remained for three years. Some 5,000 sailors were taken each year, and were the chief source of naval manpower during peacetime.

The French approach had some obvious advantages over the British, at least before the coming of continuous service. But it was inferior with regard to quality. It was notorious that the average French man-of-war man was smaller and weaker than his British and US counterparts. Much of this deficiency was due to the relatively poor standard of living in France's maritime provinces, notably Brittany—which provided something like half the country's seamen. We must also remember the relative youth of the men taken by the *levées permanentes*. They could not compare with the mature and seasoned men who mostly manned the Royal Navy. In a survey made in 1862 of the sizes of clothing issued to the *levées permanentes*, it was seen that only some 5 per cent of the men attained 1.75 m., against 25 per cent at 1.69 m., 40 per cent at

[2] Memorandum of 3 Apr. 1853 by Alexander Milne, ADM 1 5622.

1.64 m., and 30 per cent at a mere 1.58 m. The significance of these figures can be seen by the fact that 15 per cent of a crew was supposed to be of the standard proper for gunners, which was taken to be men over 1.70 m.[3] The annual *levées*, consequently, were not an adequate source of gunners.

One answer was to recall older men to the colours. Since sailors were obliged to serve the government for six years, and yet most appear to have served only three on their first call-up, there was an available source of more mature seamen. They could be called up by what were described as *levées extraordinaires*. But the government was reluctant to use these to any great extent, at least in peacetime. A large proportion of seamen married after leaving the *levées permanentes*, becoming the breadwinners of families, and calling them up again always gave rise to general discontent and numerous representations for exemptions.

Another possibility was to draw on *conscrits*, men recruited by the army and turned over to the navy. This source was scarcely touched during the 1840s, very possibly because the navy preferred not to absorb many landsmen when it was avoidable; but the more frequent mobilizations of the following decade made the navy less particular. These *conscrits* could hardly be generally expected to have the practised suppleness, the nerve, and head for heights that made the most valued of all types of hand—the *gabier*, or topman. But at least they were on average a little older than the men of the *levées permanentes*, and thus ought to have been better muscled and better able to work the great guns. In practice, though, they were not always good material. Naturally enough, the army usually passed on the leavings of the *appel*. One naval officer complained that the army sent men shorter than those in any of its special corps—even the light cavalry: only the *sapeurs-pompiers* of Paris were as small.[4] The greater reliance on *conscrits* in the 1850s would not have seriously affected the argument of La Roncière Le Noury in an article published in 1849: he uttered what was a common judgement that the physical force of a sailor in the Royal Navy to one in the French service was of the order of five to four.[5] In order

---

[3] *Préfét maritime*, Brest, to the Minister of Marine, 23 July 1862, folder 'Canonnage et timonerie, "Louis XIV" et "Montebello"', AN CC3 1205 (*marine*).

[4] 'Un officier de vaisseau', *Essai sur l'organisation du personnel de la flotte* (Paris, 1851), 33.

[5] 'La Marine et l'Enquête parlementaire', *Revue des deux mondes*, 4 (1849), 1073.

to compensate, French warships had to carry relatively larger crews.

Physical force was not the only thing lacking: intelligibility must have been another. As Professor Weber has shown so well, patois was predominant outside the Île de France. The French language was spreading, but Brittany in particular was still a bastion of incomprehensibility to most French-speakers during the mid-century.[6] The large number of Bretons who went into the navy must have been a cause of some linguistic trouble to many of their officers, at least at the beginning of a commission before the men called up for the first time had learned sufficient basic French to make them efficient. (It was just as well that a good proportion of the officers also came from Brittany.) Another obstacle to the formation of an efficient crew came from the *conscrits*. Some of them might have been suitable as gunners but, of course, with the odd exception they were not seamen. The *conscrits* generally made good deck-hands, but they were an element somewhat foreign to the men from the *inscription* — the *inscrits* — and must have hindered the development by the crew of a sense of *esprit de corps*.

It was not as if the Ministry of Marine could rely on their professional seamen greatly to promote the cohesion of a crew. There was relatively little continuity of service on the French lower deck; few equivalents to the British continuous servicemen. Some French sailors called up at age 20 decided to continue in government service after their first term had ended, despite the fact that the government paid only half to two-thirds the wage that private shipowners offered. There were also some, seamen and a few landsmen, who joined the navy voluntarily and served for some years. As in the Royal Navy, the most valuable volunteers in *la Royale* were those who had been in the navy since they were boys, perhaps having joined as *mousses* when they were 10 (a lower limit raised to 12 in 1854 and 13 in 1856), becoming *novices* at 16, and graduating as *matelots* at 18 or so. It was from the sailors brought up in the service that the navy preferred to draw its petty and warrant officers, the *premier*, *second*, and *quartier-maîtres* — the *maistrance*. However, the number of *mousses* and *novices* remained comparatively small: in October 1853, for instance, there were

[6] Eugen Weber, *Peasants into Frenchmen: The Modernization of Modern France, 1870–1914* (London, 1977), 82–3.

respectively but 692 and 1,971 of them afloat.[7] All in all, the French navy depended very little on volunteer long-service seamen. Admittedly, the *conscrits* served up to seven years (the period of army enlistment), but by law they could not form more than one-third of any crew. Thus the men of the *levées permanentes* were in the majority, and scarcely had time to be trained before they were returned to the civilian world. Doubtless, they recalled some of their training if they were called up again, but only some. The Ministry of Marine certainly became very conscious during our period that improvement was needed in the manning system.

If in peacetime the British manning system had the advantage in terms of seamen quality and crew homogeneity, an advantage significantly enhanced by continuous service, in wartime the French took the palm. The greatest indictment of British naval policy of the two hundred years after the *inscription maritime* was set up is that the Royal Navy did not develop an equivalent method of rapidly mobilizing naval manpower. There was just the cruel and inefficient press-gang. The continuous service system was no solution for the problem of lack of reserves, and the beginning of the Crimean War proved an embarrassing time for the Admiralty. It was fortunate that fewer seamen were needed to fight against Nicholas I than had been needed against the first Napoleon. One hundred thousand extra seamen and marines were not called for; between 1853 and 1855 naval manpower was increased from 45,000 to only 67,000, but even this effort strained every nerve.

The press-gang was not called upon: that was the *ultima ratio*. Besides, it hardly seemed an appropriate measure in the liberal Britain of the mid-nineteenth century, as is suggested by Cobden's suggestion that if the gangs were sent out again, they would be shot by liberty-loving Englishmen. Instead, the Admiralty was reduced to various methods of recruitment. The ex-naval men serving in the Coastguard and royal dockyards were called upon, yielding 2,500 recruits in 1854. They were experienced but often over-mature, and rarely limber enough to be topmen. Another source of men was the Royal Naval Coast Volunteers, formed in 1853, and composed of part- and full-time fishermen and coastal traders, similar to the rather unsuccessful Sea Fencibles of the Napoleonic Wars. But, by their contracts, these men could be

[7] Return of 19 Jan. 1854 on the maritime population of the previous Oct., AN CC4 63 (*marine*).

required to serve only up to 300 miles from the UK shores, so could hardly be incorporated in a Black Sea or even a Baltic squadron. The corps was not even as large as had been intended: by October 1855 only 4,673 men fit to serve had come forward of the 10,000 hoped for. True, 188 of them were persuaded to sign on for the Baltic fleet, but this was a poor return for the £20,623. 5s. 2½d. that the whole corps had cost the taxpayer by 30 September 1855.[8]

The only other recourse was to the volunteer. The First Lord, Sir James Graham, refused to allow a bounty to be offered to attract men. As was to be seen in 1858, when one was offered, a bounty did not necessarily attract many seamen. But Graham rejected the device rather because of what it showed about the navy than because it was inefficient. In February 1854 he wrote firmly on the subject to Sir Charles Napier, who had urged not only that a bounty be offered but also that the seamen on the Queen's yacht be transferred to the fleet, and that a plea be printed to urge all gentlemen to lay up their yachts for the duration. Graham described the proposals as 'signs of distress which I consider impolitic and unnecessary, and which I cannot sanction'. Yet the distress still showed. The Admiralty had to scour the country for men. Maurice Berkeley, then Second Naval Lord, was especially active in the chase. As one captain confided in a letter in March 1854, Berkeley was at the Downs all one afternoon, 'pretending to be very busy about men—but doing nothing useful. He has filled us up on paper—but in reality we have at least 50 men of the Coast Guard who are worse than useless.' Giving his story added point, one of the men assigned to him died that night![9]

Another officer, Sir John Hay, then Captain of the *Victory*, has left us a tale about Berkeley and the grim manning situation. In his autobiography Hay tells us that he refused for service a somewhat elderly volunteer who —despite his wooden leg—had never been to sea before. Berkeley was allegedly highly indignant at Hay's action, and immediately ordered that the volunteer be accepted on another ship.[10] Hay was quite possibly exaggerating; retired admirals' tales often look more convincing after a good dinner than any wholly true story should. But we do know that many of the wartime

[8] Report of 9 Oct. 1855, ADM 1 5660.
[9] H. B. Martin to T. B. Martin, 25(?) Mar. 1854, Martin Papers, BM Add. MS 41467, fos. 84–5.
[10] Sir John Hay, *Lines from my Log-books* (Edinburgh, 1898), 189.

recruits were inexperienced, and constant exercises were needed
in the newly formed Baltic squadron to bring efficiency out of
near-chaos. Moreover, despite inferior men being accepted, ships'
complements were often below establishment, and Graham and his
successor urged the British Baltic commanders in 1854 and 1855
quietly to take on any Swedish or Norwegian sailors who could be
obtained—albeit with scant success.[11] The end result of all the
activity, of course, was that observers quickly discovered the Royal
Navy was under strain over manning.

It was almost an article of faith with those Britons who had been
most concerned in the 1840s about the threat of the 'steam bridge'
that the French navy could mobilize seamen for war far more
quickly than the Royal Navy could. This belief was what made
invasion look all too possible, since speedy mobilization could give
the French navy a numerical superiority in warships in the Channel
during the first few weeks of war, a superiority that could be
employed in protecting an invasion fleet of transports. It came as
no surprise to many British observers, therefore, that the Ministry
of Marine was not reduced in 1854 to the embarrassed fumblings
for seamen of the Admiralty.

The necessary measures to man the French fleet in a crisis were
clearly marked, and the mechanism to carry them out had long
existed. The *levées* already serving were retained, and were swelled
by the next contingent of 20-year-olds and by *levées extraordinaires*.
To these were added *conscrits* from the Ministry of War—some
6,000 in 1854 and 2,000 the following year. And there were a few
other ways of obtaining men. For instance, there were two state
schools for *mousses*, one at Toulon, the other at Brest. The former
had never been of much use: the boys were lured away by the
attractions of Marseilles, or Paris: they usually left the school as
soon as they could. Brest, however, was more geographically
isolated: its school was more successful and was eagerly drained by
the French Baltic Fleet. Although welcome, such sources were relatively minor: the *inscrits* and *conscrits* were by far the most important
elements in the crews of the warfleet, and they made possible the
increase from some 28,000 sailors afloat in 1853 to 49,000 in 1854
and 54,500 the following year. This was a rather higher order of

---

[11] Graham to Napier, 5 and 11 Apr. 1854, Napier Papers, BM Add. MS 40024,
fos. 114–17, 132–3. Wood to R. S. Dundas, 30 Apr. 1855, Melville Papers, GD.51.
2.1088.2.

increase than that of the Royal Navy over the same period, and it was far more impressive, since Britain had by far the larger number of seamen in the population. Xavier Raymond estimated in the early 1860s that with an *inscription maritime* Britain would have something like 700,000 *inscrits*, whilst France then had only 170,000. Other, less speculative figures, give the same order of difference. In 1853 the merchant ships of the British Empire were manned by 253,896 seamen and boys (although not quite all of these were British, or white). On 1 October of the same year, even including ships' masters and long-distance fishermen, only 51,783 Frenchmen and boys were reported as serving afloat in commerce —very likely an overestimate. Given the available resources, the French Crimean mobilization was very successful.[12]

That the *inscription maritime* proved effective during the Crimean War was due only in part to the excellence of its organization. The success also reflected the fact that French seamen largely accepted that the government had the right to demand their services, and regarded duty in the war navy without an aversion close to revulsion. Here was a crucial difference from the position in Britain. A British seaman could easily pass his whole career without a day's service in the Royal Navy. His opinion of life on a warship was often based on the horrible stories—usually quite true ones, one suspects—of what the navy had been like during the Napoleonic Wars. There was a deep prejudice against serving in the fleet, as is suggested by the slowness with which volunteers came forward in 1854. Better pay and conditions were slowly breaking down this prejudice, but it lasted at least into the 1860s. A French seaman, on the other hand, was almost certain to know from personal experience what warship service was like. He might dislike that service: the discipline was more strict than on merchant vessels, and the pay was lower; moreover, a warship discharged her crew in an arsenal, often far from the men's homes and families, whilst in civilian life a seaman could take employment on a vessel that operated from his home port. But dislike of serving the state was based on experience rather than prejudice, and was therefore the less powerful.

Nevertheless, signs of strain can be found in the *inscription maritime* during the Crimean War. There were groans of protest from

<hr />

[12] Ministry of Marine letters and decisions on the *inscription*, early 1854, AN CC4 465–6 (*marine*) and CC4 63 (*marine*). Raymond art. in Maurice Block, *Dictionnaire général de la politique* (2 vols., Paris, 1864), ii. 269. PP (1859), sess. 1, vi, app. 19.

inscrits who were called to serve for a second time. Naval pay was sufficient for a young bachelor called up at age 20; but married seamen naturally resented being called up in a *levée extraordinaire*, knowing their pay would not keep their families from want. Clearly, the *inscription* could be a great burden. Government grants to families, and private charity, helped ease the sailors' economic concerns in 1854–5, and the mobilization continued. Even so, there was a shortage of men: goodwill was not the true problem; there were simply not enough French seamen. The Black Sea Fleet was soon brought up to strength, but the manning of a squadron for the Baltic had to wait for the return of French merchantmen on distant voyages when war broke out, bringing back more men who could be called up. Four battleships and two frigates were waiting at Brest to complete their crews from March until July 1854. Moreover, Parseval-Deschênes found he could not bring the main part of his fleet to the Baltic until June—some two months later than Napier had managed. Even then, the French force needed time to organize and to train and, as in the case of the British squadron, there were numerous complaints about the lack of first-class seamen.[13] Despite what some British observers had thought, therefore, the *inscription maritime* was scarcely capable of quickly providing almost unlimited numbers of seamen.

As with almost all wars, the one against Russia put the premium on the amount of cannon-fodder rather than on the calibre. The flaws that the war showed in the manning systems were principally those to do with shortfalls in the number of men recruited, not their suitability. If, however, one considers the British and French systems on the basis of their effectiveness in peace as well as war, it becomes obvious that each had its own major defects. The British defect was always in quantity; the French one always in quality. As we shall see, during the years after 1856, albeit with some procrastination and changes of mind, the two navies attempted to mend these faults. In the process they built up manning systems which, though they could never become quite identical, did at least become more alike.

British postwar manning policy showed itself, initially at least, to be even more myopic and maladroit than has generally been

[13] But see Gicquel des Touches, 'Enquête sur la marine marchande: Réponse aux questions posées par la Commission d'enquête parlementaire', *Revue maritime et coloniale*, 29 (1870), 631–2.

the case during British demobilizations after victory. The essential difficulty was that demands from the Treasury for peacetime economies coincided with a general increase in demands for naval demonstrations, the latter demands being due to the need to deal with diplomatic problems that had arisen whilst Whitehall was absorbed by the war, as well as a conscious effort—above all by Palmerston, Prime Minister since 1855—to demonstrate to the world that, whatever had been the embarrassments of the British army in the Crimea, Britain remained a first-rate power.

For the first few months after the treaty with Russia, Palmerston had his way, and additional naval forces were sent to China, West Africa, the Mediterranean, Central America, and the West Indies. Sir Charles Wood became very concerned about where the necessary forces were to come from. In September 1856 the fleet still had about 4,000 men above the vote—which was itself larger by some 5,000 than the pre-war figure. By the following March there were still 8,500 more men than there had been in 1853, and Wood was being squeezed intolerably between the Foreign Office and the Treasury. By April he was insisting that fewer demands be made on the navy, joining those urging economy. Financial reasons appeared paramount: as Wood wrote to R. S. Dundas in January 1857, it was politically impossible to keep the income tax at the then level, and consequently the number of seamen had to be cut. Of course, the Prime Minister was not sympathetic. To Palmerston a nation's armed power depended on its policy, and not vice versa. He commented that Wood spoke of naval force as though it were a fixed quantity, but in reality it had to fluctuate according to diplomatic needs. However, the cabinet supported Wood, and efforts were made to reduce the number of ships in commission.[14]

Despite what Palmerston had implied, neither the reduction nor the increase of ships in commission was a simple matter. One could not easily vary the number of seamen to accord with the mutability of the international world. British naval seamen were no longer casual labourers, hired for the duration of a commission and then loosed again upon the market. An ever higher proportion was formed of continuous servicemen, trained in skills that often had little relevance outside a war navy, expecting to stay in the service

[14] Wood to Dundas, 26 Jan. 1857, Melville Papers, GD.51.2.1088.2. Palmerston to Clarendon, 14 Sept. 1856; Wood to Clarendon, 11 May 1856, Clarendon deposit, C50, fo. 42; C70, fo. 538.

for a number of years and to retire with a pension. Not only was it in their interest to remain in the navy for a long term, but with the higher wages, better food, and less barbaric discipline introduced in the mid-century, many seamen were coming to prefer government to merchant service. Wood certainly found difficulty in reducing numbers. He complained in April 1857 that he could pay-off a ship, but the men would not go!

If I pay off 800 men I don't get rid (may the Marine Deities pardon such an expression as applied to sailors) of 100 and I am nearly 8,500 above the numbers proposed to be voted.

An extreme step was necessary, and in an Admiralty circular of 13 May Wood offered to free continuous servicemen from their liability to serve for a fixed term—if they would leave the navy at once.[15] Wood thus reversed the previous policy of accumulating these valuable men: in doing so he not only reduced the navy by 2,994 good seamen, but also encouraged the notion that the service did not give a secure employment or hold to its promises. There was also another unfortunate effect. The developing crisis in China and the outbreak of the Indian Mutiny meant that two months after the circular the Admiralty was desperately grubbing around the ports for the very men so recently allowed to leave. By July appropriations had to be granted for 2,000 sailors more than had been allowed by the April estimates.

Wood's circular seemed even more unwise in 1858, when the Orsini crisis forced the Admiralty to try quickly to organize a Channel fleet. A bounty of £10 was offered to seamen volunteers; nevertheless, great difficulties were found in manning ships. Sir John Pakington, the First Lord in Derby's second ministry (1858–9), bewailed the continuous servicemen lost by Wood's circular, and the adverse effect that circular had had on sailors' view of the royal service. He said in the Commons in April 1858, 'I cannot too strongly lament the course taken by my right honourable friend opposite last year.' He admitted that there had been great pressure for economy in 1857, but wished

that the right honourable Baronet (Wood) had possessed sufficient firmness and vigour to say that the national interests should not be tampered with, and that the country should not be deprived of the advantages of

[15] Wood to Clarendon, 8 Apr. 1857, Clarendon Deposit, C70, fo. 498. For a copy of the May circular, see the Halifax Papers, BM Add. MS 49560, fo. 73.

an important improvement in out naval administrative system (continuous service).[16]

But if Pakington laid blame on Wood with one hand, with the other he took advantage of what his predecessor had been able to achieve concerning something of far more importance than a few thousand serving seamen—the wartime reserve. Also in April 1858 Pakington grandly promised that, if an emergency arose, no fewer than twenty battleships could be manned and stationed in the Channel. On the *matériel* side the promise was slightly rash. The fact that on the manning side there was something of a solid basis to his promise was due largely to Wood. Pakington intended to get his men from several sources. He probably anticipated that many patriotic volunteers would come forward in case of war. But there were also three rather more certain reserves. The first was marines in barracks on land. By July 1858 there were 6,000 of these, of which 4,000 were considered as a reserve. Unfortunately, though marines were excellent for many purposes, they were not seamen, and can be considered as somewhat analagous to the French *conscrits*. The other two notable reserves did consist of seamen. The one was the Naval Coast Volunteers, in a better state by this time than it had been in 1854. By March 1858 it amounted to 5,754 men: 3,901 of these had been trained in the firing of heavy ordnance and small arms, and another 441 were still in training. Moreover, some naval officers thought highly of the men's quality and reliability. Admittedly, their service was still limited to 300 miles from the British coast, but at least the corps could be drawn on for a Channel squadron.

Finally, there was the Coastguard, and this was the best seaman reserve of all, one that had been only recently regrouped and developed. The main credit for their improvement must go to Wood. In late 1856 he had argued the need to create a better wartime reserve, dismissing not only the men available from the dockyards but even the Coast Volunteers as insufficiently large and reliable. The Coastguard, on the other hand, had recently provided 2,200 men in two years of war, and—so Wood believed—could be even more valuable in future. The corps needed enlarging in any case, he said, since 1,900 miles of British coastline (out of a total of 7,633) remained unprotected against smugglers, and the whole coast of

[16] *Hansard*, Ser. 3, vol. cxlix, col. 889.

Ireland was not patrolled at night. He thought that 2,000 more men, bringing the corps up to a total of 6,700, would be sufficient to give full coverage, and that the increase — and the whole Coastguard organization — could be so managed as to benefit the Royal Navy greatly. First, he wanted extreme care to be taken over recruiting, giving preference to prime ex-navy men. Secondly, the Revenue Department was to hand over control of the Coastguard to the Admiralty. This change would reflect the new military role of the corps, and make it possible to match the Coastguard divisions with the Coast Volunteer ones, so that men from both organizations could be trained in the great-gun exercises at the depot ships in their areas.[17]

Wood's plan was implemented. As he wanted, only the best recruits were taken, which meant that the corps increased slowly, gaining under 1,000 men in the first year. And with the extra men came much more powerful depot ships. In 1857 the Coastguards' sailing depot ships were replaced by the nine blockships. The previous duties of some of the blockships as guardships of the steam-ordinaries were henceforward carried out by screw-liners. From now on the nine Coastguard zones — the North Coast of Ireland, Portland Roads, Leith, Greenock, the Humber, Liverpool, the South Coast of Ireland, Harwich, and Falmouth — each had a slow but still powerfully armed steam-battleship at hand. It was reasonably expected that in time of war these ships could be speedily manned by a mixture of Coast Volunteers and Coastguards, and Pakington relied on them for virtually half the Channel battlefleet he promised in April 1858. Nor was this all the Coastguard could supply. When detailed for the new duties, each of the blockships was accompanied by one of the Crimean gunboats as a tender. These small but potent vessels, aided by the small steamers that since 1852 had been replacing the traditional Coastguard sailing revenue-cruisers, could have had a crucial role in the event of an invasion attempt. Such a steam-flotilla, taking advantage of shallow waters and of an intimate knowledge of local conditions, would have been ideal for interrupting a landing at its most vulnerable stage, when the troop- and horse-transports were disgorging their cargo on to a beach.

Despite the improvements in the Coastguards, the 1858 crisis suggested strongly that they were not of themselves sufficient. It

[17] Wood's memorandum, Broadlands papers, GC.WO.123. 1–9.

remained clear that—short of the press-gang—the Royal Navy did not have a reserve system that would answer in the event of a first-class naval war. The navy in commission—the 'standing navy' as we might call it—was increased in size, and by 1860 (including seamen, boys, and marines) amounted to just over 70,000: but even this figure was only just over half what would be needed in a war with France. A good reserve system remained essential. Fortunately, in 1858 a Royal Commission was set up to inquire into manning the navy: there had been previous similar attempts made to address the manning problem: this time they were to be adequate.

The commissioners (or at least a majority of them: one dissented) agreed on a whole series of changes affecting manning in peace and war. The peacetime changes were essentially improvements to continuous service. Instead of one training-ship for boys, the commissioners wanted five, which were to supply the navy with most of its recruits. Thus not only would the peacetime navy be manned primarily with continuous servicemen, but most of these men would have been raised from boyhood in the naval service. Moreover, the service itself was to be made more attractive, with better rations, a free issue of bedding and mess utensils to men signing up for ten years, and new incentives to what was the core of the crew—the Petty and Warrant Officers. All these proposals were approved, either by Derby's government or by the succeeding Palmerston ministry.

Whilst encouraging the professional man-of-war man, the commission's plan was intended also to change the general attitude in the British maritime population towards the Royal Navy. Service on a warship, it was hoped, would henceforward be seen as very desirable, and the traditional dislike that many merchant seamen still had for the navy would be broken down. The change in attitude was seen as important because the commissioners wanted the navy's wartime reserve to be drawn from the merchant marine, envisaging the establishment of a voluntary Royal Naval Reserve of 20,000 men. This force was to be formed from the best merchant seamen; it was to be regularly trained in those arduous great-gun exercises; and it was to be called upon for service (as against training) only in cases of international crisis. Furthermore, unlike the Coast Volunteers, no geographical limit was specified. Here again, the government approved. The RNR was no instant panacea. Seamen were at first suspicious and reluctant to join. But thanks to the surge of patriotism engendered by the crisis with Washington in 1861–2 (the *Trent* incident), recruitment did become considerable. The corps rose to 16,500 men by 1865 and, though it fell away subsequently, still comprised some 15,000 men during the rest of the decade.

With the establishment and growth of the RNR, the other chief reserves—the Coast Volunteers and Coastguards—went into a decline. Economy cuts trimmed the latter during the late 1860s, and the former was badly affected by the decision to remove the limit on distance of service from the UK. (By 1871 only just over 2,000 men remained on the books.) One new large source of men was the body of continuous servicemen who had left the navy with their pension. There were about 6,000 of these by 1871, and—by an act introduced by Graham in 1853—all naval pensioners were liable to serve during an emergency. Nevertheless, even including the latter, the total reserve by 1871 was only some 26,000 men, a decline of about 4,000 since 1866. And the 1871 figure was only 10,000 above the reserve available in mid-1858, apparently little recompense for all the efforts of a Royal Commission and the organization of the RNR. But the disappointingly small rise in paper numbers disguises a radical real improvement. The reserve at the end of our period consisted mostly of serving or retired deep-sea mariners: one source says nearly 20,000 were AB by mercantile standards. Moreover, all the reserve had been trained in gunnery.[18]

There was one other important improvement by this time. Despite hopes, continuous service did not of itself greatly improve the reputation of the navy amongst the British seafaring population. Continuous service, and the extended boys' training scheme, rather served to draw a clearer divide than before between private and government service afloat. Nevertheless, the 1860s did at least see the clearing away of many of those old horror-stereotypes of life in the Royal Navy, for which it seems that two factors were primarily responsible. The first was the RNR itself, which

---

[18] R. Taylor, 'Manning the Royal Navy: The Reform of the Recruiting System, 1852–1862', *Mariner's Mirror*, 44 (1958), 302–13; 45 (1959), 46–58. The present section owes a great debt to the above, to the excellent volume edited by J. S. Bromley, *The Manning of the Royal Navy: Selected Public Pamphlets, 1693–1873* (Navy Records Society, London, 1976), and to Michael Lewis, *The Navy in Transition, 1814–1864: A Social History* (London, 1965). Also essential were the reports and evidence of the manning inquiries of 1852 and 1858, PP (1852–3), lx. 9–58, and PP (1859), sess. 1, vi.

introduced large numbers of merchant seamen to a taste of modern naval training and service. The second was a decline in the employment of the 'cat-o'-nine-tails'. Continuous servicemen were hardly tame and meek: even with an increasingly professional lower deck, desertion and drunkenness remained surprisingly high, and a series of minor mutinies around 1859–60 demonstrated that discipline could not always be taken for granted. Yet the harsh punishments used previously could now be safely allowed to fall into disuse. Already in the 1850s, spurred by a public dubious of the need for heavy floggings, the Admiralty had encouraged its officers to reduce the use of the 'cat', and the pressure continued into the next decade with a series of naval punishment acts that effectively abolished floggings as a regular punishment. With the end of the lavish use of the 'cat' went perhaps the principal aversion of seamen to the Royal Navy.

However, what did the various changes in the manning system mean for the Royal Navy in comparison with *la Royale*? The answer obviously depends on what improvements that force had been making: the French certainly did not sit with hands folded while the Admiralty busied itself with the creation of an effective reserve. Of course, the French navy already had a good system of war mobilization: the prime manning concern of the Ministry of Marine was to improve the training and readiness of the peacetime force. The aim was greater seaman professionalism.

One consequence was noted in the last chapter—the creation of the *fusiliers marins* in 1856. It was but part of a trend of increasing specialization. Improved ships and weapons made ever more important the differentiation of skills, and this fact was recognized by a fundamental change in the way that the men of the *inscription maritime* were organized.

Since 1824 the navy's sailors had been divided, at least notionally, into *équipages*, and subdivided into *compagnies* each of which contained a certain number of the vital skilled men, gunners, topmen, and so on. A proportion of the total number of *compagnies* was supposed always to be retained on shore, in barracks in the arsenals, so that when it was decided to commission a ship there were men available to act as the core of the new crew. The vessel received the number of *compagnies* proportionate to her size (for instance, six and a half to a first-rate), and the rest of the crew was made up with whatever men were available, probably green *inscrits* only just recruited. The system was good in theory, but did not work well in practice. After the mid-1840s it was found to be too expensive to keep the *compagnies* on shore up to full complement: when they were needed they were hastily made up with an assortment of men from the depots of the *inscription*. Thus came complaints from officers about the thoroughly variable quality of the men sent to them.[19]

A decree of 5 June 1856 abolished the *équipages de ligne*, replacing them by *équipages de la flotte*. More than a change of name was involved. The new *équipages* were organized on a new principle —that of *l'unité individu*. The skilled seaman was henceforward the basic unit, grouped into *compagnies de spécialités* of which there were four types. In the first were gathered the *gabiers*, *timoniers* (helmsmen and signalmen), carpenters, sailmakers, and caulkers; the gunners formed a second; the new *fusiliers marins* a third; and—a novelty, since they had been left out of the old *équipages de ligne* system— the mechanics and stokers a fourth. Far greater control over the composition and quality of a crew was now to be possible.[20]

The necessary concomitants to the *compagnies de spécialités* were training-schools to turn the raw *inscrit* (or *conscrit*) into the skilled man. Gunnery was one of the most crucial skills, and there had long been a training-ship, but it became clear in the 1850s that the supply of trained gunners was inadequate—and not only because of a shortage of sturdy recruits. The Royal Navy entered the decade with two gunnery-training battleships: to the *Excellent* at Portsmouth had been added the *Cambridge* at Devonport. The French navy still had only a *frégate-école*, but expansion was not long delayed. A second-rate battleship became the school, replaced in 1860 by the large if slow *Montebello*. The latter was stationed at Toulon, and in 1863 a second school was set up at Brest on the *Louis XIV*. (Unfortunately, budget cuts soon forced the Minister to close one of the two: the *Montebello* was decommissioned in November 1865, and the *Louis XIV* replaced her at Toulon from 1866.)[21] As with the gunners, so with the other specialists. The *école*

---

[19] Meeting of the *Conseil d'amirauté*, 13 Nov. 1855, AN BB8 885 (*marine*), 209–23.

[20] Pierre Fournier and M. Neveu, *Traité d'administration de la marine* (3 vols., Paris, 1885–1905). P. Jullien, 'L'habillement et le costume des matelots', *Revue maritime*, 185 (May 1935), 605–40.

[21] Chasseloup-Laubat to the comte de Gueydon, 9 July 1865, Chasseloup-Laubat Papers, vii. 75–7.

des fusiliers was set up in 1865. In 1860 a school for *timoniers* followed, at first crammed with the gunners on to the *Montebello* and later the *Louis XIV*. In 1862 came two *écoles des mécaniciens*, one at Brest, the other at Toulon; and four years after that the school for *gabiers* appeared.

Better training was made possible not only for adults but also for young sailors and even boys. Boys from 13 to 16 were already catered for in the two *écoles des mousses*, but in the 1860s two further schools were set up, completing a hierarchy of professional training for the young sailor from the time he left infant school at 7 until he was 18 and could join the navy as a junior seaman. The first of the two, opened by the Empress Eugénie on 15 November 1862, was the *Pupilles de la marine* at Brest. This charity hostel cum school cum nursery of the navy was open to the orphans of maritime families: the boys were to enter at 7, and to remain *pupilles* until they were 13, after which they were supposed to join the nearby *école des mousses*. Once they had reached the age of 16, then they went to the other new institution, the *école flottante des novices*, established in 1863 on the capacious but by now sadly obsolescent *Bretagne*. Boys studied there for two years, until they were 18 and eligible for the navy.[22]

The organization of the *équipages de ligne*, and the great efforts made in training men and boys, had important consequences for the *inscription maritime*. The conservation and full employment of the expensively taught skills implied longer periods of service for the best men. This meant calling on the Ministry of War for more seven-year *conscrits*, or attracting far more volunteers, or requiring longer periods of service from the *levées permanentes* than the usual two or three years. The first possibility was unpalatable to the Ministry of Marine, given the limitations of the *conscrits*. In any case, the Ministry of War would hardly have been eager to call up more men for the good of the other service: it was in bad enough odour in the country with the *appel* at its existing level. Thus the navy was left with only two feasible courses. During the ministry of Chasseloup-Laubat attention turned to ways of increasing the number of volunteers, and the delicate task was undertaken of recasting the *inscription maritime*. It was delicate because by the early 1860s the whole institution was being perturbed from within and

<hr/>

[22] E. Eymin and A. Doneaud, 'Brest: établissements de la marine', *Revue maritime et coloniale*, 17 (1866), 496–8, 502–4.

without, from within by the *inscrits* who resented the increasing demands made on their time by the wars and expeditions of the Second Empire, and from without by the shipowners who resented being deprived of their crews. Chasseloup-Laubat had to find a policy that would quieten the complaints, and at the same time increase seaman professionalism.

Ultimately, perhaps, the task was impossible. French shipowners could not be fully satisfied with anything short of abolition of the *inscription*. They had long complained about the way that the annual *levées* called away their best men at the most inconvenient times.[23] Their complaints grew more vocal with war. The call-ups of the Crimean War found them in fine voice, and one gauge of the manning strain of that war is the groans of the *armateurs* as they found themselves being denuded of seamen: in 1854 only the important Iceland and Newfoundland cod fleets were left largely untouched by the *inscription*.[24] The war against Austria in 1859–60 renewed their complaints, and they reacted with increasing antipathy as during the following years imperial policy brought the country close to war on more than one occasion. What made the *inscription* even more intolerable to them was that the country's economy was prospering, yet—apart from the coastal trade, reserved by law to French vessels—most of France's growing maritime trade was carried by foreign vessels. French merchant shipping did slowly revive, and this was greatly boosted by the precipitate decline of the US mercantile marine during the Civil War, but economic liberalism in the later 1860s brought sharper competition and a renewed climate of complaint.[25]

But the navy had to retain the *inscription*, even in peacetime. An equivalent to the British all-volunteer system would have been too expensive, meaning wage-competition with the private sector. Instead, some way had to be found of getting *inscrits* to serve longer that would pacify not only the *armateurs* but also not unduly annoy the seamen. The latter, indeed, were probably more kept in mind by the Ministry than the former. The *armateurs* had always complained, and one suspects the Ministry was less disturbed by

[23] See e.g. F. Le Pomellec (*armateur* and Mayor of Saint-Brieuc), *Mémoire au Roi sur la nécessité de réformer l'inscription maritime des matelots* (Saint-Brieuc, 1843).
[24] Ministry of Marine letters on the *inscription*, Jan.–Apr. 1854, AN CC4 465–6 (*marine*). Note the letter of 4 Mar. to the Chief of Service at Saint-Servan.
[25] T. Ropp, *The Development of a Modern Navy* (pub. version, Annapolis, Md., 1987), 61–2.

them, important as they doubtless were, than by the fact that in the 1850s and early 1860s there were dangerous signs of unhappiness from the usually resigned mass of the *inscrits*.

French seamen did have to bear a heavy burden. One observer argued that the *inscription*, despite its benefits (including a small retirement pension), pressed more onerously on seamen than the army conscription did on other French men.[26] Perhaps, even probably, he was right: and it is certain that many Frenchmen agreed with him. French sailors themselves appear to have been conscious of some injustice, above all with reference to the *levées extraordinaires*. Both during the Crimean and Austrian wars, seamen's dependants received not just the standard miserable state dole, but also a supplement from private and public charity; but this did not wholly reconcile the maritime community to the *levées* or, indeed, to the regularity with which hostilities occurred. An occasional emergency might have been accepted with good grace, but with the Second Empire wars—and *levées extraordinaires*—followed too quickly on each other. To the seaman, as well as to the *armateur*, a pattern of imperial bellicosity was unfolded: as both might well have agreed, *l'Empire c'est l'épée*. The repeated burdens were unacceptable, and instead of merely complaining (seamen have as good a right to be called *grognards* as any soldiers), more *inscrits* took positive steps to avoid service.

There were two avenues of escape, apart from old age and death. One of them was renunciation of a career in the *eaux maritimes*. If a war did not occur within twelve months of the renunciation, the man was free of the *inscription*. There were two drawbacks. First, of course, the man was henceforward barred from gaining his livelihood on water. This bar made renunciation virtually impossible for many, particularly Bretons, because the harshness of life in their province either made them go abroad to other parts of France in order to live, or forced them to earn their bread at sea. The second drawback was that withdrawal from the *inscription* made one liable to the *appel*, and a young ex-sailor might easily find the national conscription lottery had chosen him for army service. Small consolation that here he could purchase a replacement to serve for him, something that was forbidden to the *inscrit* (until, that is, the decree of 22 October 1863). But in the probable event that he could not find

[26] *Enquête parlementaire sur la situation et l'organisation des services de la marine militaire* (2 vols., Paris, 1851), i. 243–50.

the 500 francs (or even much more) needed for a replacement,[27] there would follow seven years of army service, unless he—as an ex-sailor—was passed on to the Ministry of Marine as a *conscrit* and found himself in the service he had hoped all along to avoid.

The other method of escape from the *inscription* was emigration, perhaps to serve on board foreign vessels. This was illegal. However, it was very difficult to check the leakage of seamen. Already in 1853, according to a report sent to Sir James Graham, there were some 12,000 *inscrits* serving abroad.[28] And it appears that, whether permanent, or temporary (to avoid an approaching mobilization, one of the storms seamen kept a weather eye open for), French seaman emigrants increased significantly in number during the second half of the 1850s. One indicator, the figures for desertions from French commercial vessels, shows a definite peak reached by 1860 (1,017 deserters as against 612 in 1851). The number of men escaping the *inscription* via renunciation also increased over the same period. There was an average of over 200 a quarter in 1857 and 1858, but this rose in 1859, and during the third quarter no fewer than 1,556 seamen foreswore the sea.[29] The cumulative effect of these losses was that the total number of *inscrits* on the state lists, having increased regularly since 1815, showed a definite fall. The total in August 1859 was 202,075, but three years later it was only 190,692.[30]

Manning reform was thus an important matter. One change was made in the dying weeks of Hamelin's ministry, by the decree of 30 September 1860 which announced that *inscrits* who had served six years could be called out again only by an imperial decree— that is, only on very serious national grounds. But the greatest reforms came under Chasseloup-Laubat. He fully realized that the attacks on the *inscription* had to be met and checked. He accepted that it would be prudent to limit the practice of calling *levées extraordinaires*: during his time as Minister he called such *levées*

---

[27] On army replacement, see Bernard Schnapper, *Le Remplacement militaire en France* (Paris, 1968).

[28] Second report on French manning, Mar. 1853, Netherby Papers, box III, 20 c.w.

[29] Reports on renunciations, 9 Apr. and 1 Oct. 1858, 1 Apr. 1859, and 2 Oct. 1860, AN CC4 67–9 (*marine*). For desertions, see the returns in the annual *Ministère de la marine et des colonies: Compte définitif des dépenses* (Imprimerie impériale).

[30] Report of the *directeur du personnel* to the Minister, 21 Aug. 1862, AN CC4 73 (*marine*).

only twice, and found that to get 1,000 men the whole littoral was perturbed and thousands of claims were generated.[31] His reforms were also shaped to produce a more solid and professional *cadre* for ships' crews. He tried to satisfy the various aims by the decree of 25 June 1861 and the more important one of 22 October 1863. These encouraged volunteers and re-engagees with the offer of extra pay (highest of all in the case of men of the *spécialités*, who had anyway always been paid more than ordinary seamen were). Furthermore, members of the *levées permanentes*, though still liable to up to six years service, would get a *prime* after three, and they could not be recalled once they had left the navy by anything short of an imperial decree.[32] Thus better pay was to make the navy more attractive, both volunteers and men from the *levées* were on average to serve longer periods (building up the number of *matelots de choix* in the service at any one time), and the much disliked *levées extraordinaires* were abolished for anything short of a war. There was even an improvement in the reserve system, since *inscrits* released before their full six years were induced by the offer of quarter-pay to accept employment only on the *cabotage*, *bornage*, and *petite pêche*, and thus be available to serve almost immediately in a crisis.

The reforms proved to be quite successful: too successful, in some ways. The navy found it got rather too many volunteers and re-engagees for the health of the budget, and a few alterations were made in 1865. Re-engagement with *prime* then became not a right but something available only to the better sailor; and the quarter-pay reserve was abolished as being too costly. However, the essence of the reforms remained. The needs of the service were satisfied and the temper of the seafaring population was improved. Even the *armateurs* were somewhat happier, though it would be naïve to think that they could be wholly pleased, and by the end of the decade one finds that they had managed to get under way a parliamentary inquiry into the *inscription*. But Chasseloup-Laubat had succeeded: the *inscription* had been softened in its effects sufficiently for it to long survive not only his period in the rue Royale but also the Second Empire itself.

* * *

[31] Chasseloup-Laubat to the *directeur du personnel*, 22 Jan. 1866, Chasseloup-Laubat Papers, viii. 6–14.

[32] *Nouvelles annales de la marine*, 26 (1861), 183–7; 31 (1864), 40–4. Chasseloup-Laubat to Napoleon III, 17 June 1861, Chasseloup-Laubat Papers, ii. 124–35.

What did the post-Crimean changes in the French and British manning systems imply for the relative power and efficiency of the rival navies? One consequence, suggested already, was that the two systems converged. In large part this was due to the way that the two admiralties were reacting to the same factors, primarily the need to encourage greater seaman professionalism. One should note also a certain mimetic effect, something we shall be looking at in Chapter 8. A pertinent example here is the *Pupilles de la marine*, which bore a strong resemblance to the Greenwich Hospital School, set up much earlier.[33]

However, significant differences still remained between the two sides. Take, for instance, the subject of the spirit below deck. The tensions that vibrate to some extent through every human organization, and which in a navy can be transmuted into *esprit de corps* had, in the decade or so after 1856, taken forms below the decks of the two navies that were more distinctive than can be accounted for by national peculiarities of habit, belief, or diet.

Since the *inscription* was passing through a troubled period, we may assume that the temper of the seamen in the French navy was at times ruffled, uncertain. It is probable, for instance that the older *inscrits*, the ones brought back by a *levée extraordinaire* and thus nursing a sense of grievance, would have been less quick than otherwise to adopt the traditional role of the experienced and older men, that of the centre of stability. It is more likely that they were centres of unease, even disruption; something that the French service was in some ways more susceptible to than the rival service, because its seamen were less homogeneous. There was a basic division between the *inscrit* and the *conscrit*; but there were also sub-divisions. Despite the lure of a *prime*, the *inscrits* of at least the decade after 1856 proved reluctant to volunteer to be trained in one of the *spécialités*. The relationship between ordinary *inscrits* and the men who decided to become the new *hommes d'élites* was surely delicate, at least while the *compagnies de spécialités* were seen as an innovation. Nor were the *conscrits* homogeneous. Most *conscrits* were sent to be either *fusiliers marins* or *canonniers*, these making up the majority of both corps; but the similarity between rifleman and gunner was not great. The great-gun exercises were very arduous, far more so than rifle

[33] H. D. T. Turner, *The Royal Hospital School, Greenwich* (London, 1980), 1–28. F. E. Chadwick, *Report on the Training Systems for the Navy and Mercantile Marines in England and France* (Washington, DC, 1880), 59 ff.

practice. *Inter alia*, this helped the relative popularity of the *fusiliers marins*; as, indeed, did the policy of the Ministry of Marine, which obviously tried to foster the development of the new corps by sending it the best available men, a policy which also encouraged the riflemen somewhat to look down on the gunners.

Whatever the various frictions and incipient rivalries within the French service, it was on the lower deck of the British service that tensions were highest, or so at least the evidence suggests. According to the gauge of the number of desertions, the seamen in the Royal Navy around 1860 were distinctly more dissatisfied than their opposite numbers across the Channel were. In 1860 more seamen deserted from the Royal Navy each month than deserted from the French navy during the whole year, a ratio well out of line with the relative establishments of the two forces. Yet, though startling, the figures prove little. The British seaman had far greater opportunities to desert, and greater temptations. The Royal Navy maintained a larger presence around the world than its rival did, offering a wide spectrum of coasts and ports to large numbers of men, including the most alluring gold-rush zones of the nineteenth century. There was also the lure of language; anglophone territories greatly outnumbered francophone ones. The significant comparison for the 1860 British desertion rate is not the contemporary French one, but earlier British figures; and it is telling that the number of deserters in the first nine months of 1860 was twice the total for 1858.[34] The British seaman's morale, one might conclude, slumped quickly at the end of the decade.

An indication that this is truly what happened is the extraordinary series of small mutinies that occurred in 1859–60. Ship after ship fell victim to the troubles, the *Liffey*, the *Caesar*, the *Hero*, the *Neptune*, the *Orion*, the *Forte*, the *James Watt*, the *Calypso*, the *Edgar*, the *Mars*, the *Donegal*, the *Lynx*, the *Princess Royal*, and the great 131-gun *Marlborough*, flagship of the Mediterranean fleet. There were riots in some cases, occasionally including the traditional game of rolling shot on deck to catch unwary officers; and there were even some respectable strikes, like the orderly refusal of the marines of the *Edgar* to do work on deck.[35]

[34] PP (1861), xxxviii. 141.
[35] Report of Captain of Marines of *Edgar*, 11 Apr. 1860, A710, ADM 1 5732. Eugene L. Rasor, *Reform in the Royal Navy: A Social History of the Lower Deck 1850 to 1880* (Hamden, Conn., 1976), ch. 4.

One probable reason for the incidents, and for the slump in morale, was the recruitment during the 1858 crisis of some poor landsmen and second-rate seamen. The new men had a disturbing effect on life below deck, swelling the number of trouble-makers and sea lawyers.[36] But there was a much more deeply seated root of the troubles. A ship is a little state which, like its larger brethren, is most vulnerable to disturbances when conditions are improving, notably the conditions relative to authority and discipline. The changes in punishment decreed by the Admiralty, and the greater pride and expectations of the continuous servicemen, were new elements that co-existed uneasily with many officers' harsh ideals of discipline and their deep suspicions of seamen, attitudes that owed much to the traditions (in the case of the older officers even the memories) of the Napoleonic Wars. It is interesting to note the French navy's better position: for the important developments below deck in that service did not coincide in the 1850s, or even coincide at all. The *inscription*, as we saw, was altered during the 1860s, and the vicious elements in French naval discipline had been removed some time before. Ducking from the main yard (*la petite cale*, a relatively minor but still dangerous form of keel-hauling) appears to have died out after 1836. The last recorded cases of running the gauntlet come from 1847; and flogging itself was abolished by the National Assembly in April 1848.[37]

What, however, does all this imply about the relative efficiency of the seamen in the rival navies? Even if the seamen in one navy have a greater sense of grievance than those of another have, we do not necessarily know who will perform best if and when war comes. As was seen during the Napoleonic Wars, a sense of grievance against one's own officers can be turned into great belligerency against the enemy. Once again the analogy between ship and state holds good: an external enemy draws attention away from internal divisions. Any discussion of the potential war effectiveness of the naval manning systems of Britain and France during the

---

[36] The French manning decree of 22 Oct. 1863 for a time encouraged volunteer landsmen, even from the pavement dregs of the cities, and discipline evidently suffered for a short period, Gicquel des Touches, 'Enquête sur la marine marchande', 617.

[37] Yves le Gallo, *Brest et sa bourgeoisie sous la monarchie de juillet* (2 vols., Paris, 1968), i. 119–20. If keel-hauling was ever practised in the Royal Navy, it had been abandoned before 1797: Edgar K. Thompson 'Note on Keelhauling', *Mariner's Mirror*, 58 (1972), 171.

mid-nineteenth century must rest essentially on questions not of grievance but of number and quality.

In terms of number the French system held the short-term advantage in a crisis, but not as great a one as was often thought in Britain. The total number of *inscrits* is subject to many deductions before one arrives at the number of effective seamen. Taking as a base the total 1854 figure of 160,000, we have to try to deduct the over-aged, the worn-out, and merchant officers, novices, boys, harbour and river pilots, workers and apprentices in the dockyards, men who had in effect given up the sea, and men who had absconded. In the end—and this is a figure attested to by several authorities—we are left with only some 60,000 seamen and non-commissioned officers, including those already serving in the imperial navy. This total would not have been significantly different in the 1840s or 1860s. This total was also not much above what would have been needed in a first-class maritime war. The fleet specified in the ordnance of 22 November 1846 (and hardly different in manpower requirements from the one in existence in the following decades), needed some 59,921 seamen and non-commissioned officers to be fully manned. Thus, even allowing for some second-rate *inscrits*, and some *conscrits* (who by law could form no more than one-third of a crew), it appears that the full mobilization of the French navy would have soaked up the great majority of the country's effective seamen. The later stages of such a mobilization would therefore have been gradual, since the navy would have had to await the necessarily slow return of the up to 20,000 *inscrits* who at any one time could be absent on distant fishing or mercantile expeditions. And some of those men, one should note, would not have returned until the war was over. One source estimated that at least 5,000–6,000 sailors would be captured by the Royal Navy during the opening stages of conflict.[38]

Nevertheless, depending chiefly on men from the *cabotage* and *petite pêche*, the French navy would have been better able to gather men in the first few months of a crisis than the Admiralty would, as is suggested by the experience of the Crimean War. The French Baltic Fleet might have been relatively late in completing its crews, but this was because by May 1854 the French manning effort was already past its peak; earlier recruitment had been very successful.

[38] *Enquête parlementaire sur la marine*, i. 245–9.

In the first four months of the year the Ministry of Marine raised over 15,000 seamen, little below the total number of men attracted by the Admiralty in the whole of the year.

It was this superior initial acceleration that the British most feared about the *inscription maritime*. But how superior was it? Can we agree that in the first few months of a war with Britain the French would have had, to use a modern term, a 'window of opportunity'? The answer is surely that there was a window, but that it was quite small. We may allow three assumptions about a possible Anglo-French war, and make something of a 'worst-case analysis' from the Admiralty's point of view. They are, first, that the British government would not have called out the press-gang; second, that the Ministry of Marine would have equalled its performance of January–April 1854; and third, that British seamen would have been no more likely to volunteer to serve in the Royal Navy than they were in 1854. Even so, it is apparent that in the first few months of war, the French would have recruited only some 10,000 good seamen more than the Admiralty could have achieved. In the context of the 1840s, this lead would have given the French navy a temporary numerical superiority, since in that decade the Royal Navy was maintained at a manning level only a few thousand above that of the rival force. From 1849 onwards, however, both the absolute and relative number of RN sailors was generally higher so by this time the French manning potential could have brought only a temporary *equality* of numbers afloat.

By 1858 even a temporary equality was unlikely, thanks to the Coastguard and the Naval Coast Volunteers. Not that the British manning system was thus satisfactory. The Royal Navy had more widespread responsibilities than *la Royale*. It needed an initial numerical superiority. It needed a reserve of good recruits—men better than the poor landsmen too often accepted in 1854 and 1858. One means of ensuring that the right men were at hand, albeit an expensive one, was further to develop the 'standing navy'. This was done to the extent that by 1860 the Royal Navy maintained some 70,000 boys, sailors, and marines, against a French total of only 48,000. (Economy cuts on both sides gradually reduced the two as the decade wore on, but the ratio remained about the same.) The other means, of course, was further to develop the reserve; and this also was done, through the creation of the RNR.

Thus in number and quality the Royal Navy had significantly improved its position by the 1860s. Admittedly, the French navy had made considerable advances of its own, in regard to longer-term service. Yet the British retained the edge in this respect. By 1858 two-thirds of RN sailors were continuous servicemen, and by 1865 nine-tenths: six years later almost all the seamen were both long-term professionals and graduates of the boys' training-ships. The French navy could not afford such lavishness. The school for *mousses* at Brest was the nursery of the *maistrance*, not of the whole lower deck. Moreover, volunteers formed only a small proportion of a crew: in the active fleet of 1869, of 5,716 *hommes d'élite* (the men of the *spécialités*) no fewer than 3,443 were men of the *levées*. The *inscription* remained essential both in war and peace, and under the budgetary squeeze of the late 1860s the average length of service of the *inscrits* declined. In spring 1870, for example, many sailors were sent home after a mere twenty months' service, and only the active complaints of the commander of the *escadre d'évolutions* enabled him to retain his *inscrits* for three years.[39]

We can now reasonably present a few general conclusions about the probable course of events, in regard to manning, if Britain and France had gone to war with each other between 1840 and 1870. Had war suddenly broken out during the first decade, unless there had been a burst of Francophobic patriotism among merchant seamen, and unless the press-gangs had been successful, the Royal Navy would have been at a numerical disadvantage in seamen for a few months. This would probably not have been decisive. Looking for a moment at the wider context, one should remember that this was a time when the Royal Navy had a technological lead. But even restricting oneself simply to the seaman issue, we can appreciate that the French superiority would not have been large, and anyway would have been subject to a discount because of the greater physical strength of the average British man-of-war man. After 1848, with the increasing margin of the British 'standing navy' over its rival, and the creation of continuous service, the French manning advantage diminished. This trend continued in the 1850s with the Admiralty's development of the Coast Volunteers, and even more so of the Coastguards. By 1858, short of successful *ruses de guerre*,

---

[39] Gicquel des Touches, 'Enquête sur la marine marchande', 617–19.

the French could not easily assume that they could mobilize a superior force in home waters even temporarily. In other waters, admittedly, the position was less certain; but in a few years the potential French advantage was diminished even there. At least after 1862, once the RNR had become a considerable body, the Royal Navy was fairly sure of retaining the numerical as well as qualitative superiority in sailors over the French from the beginning of a war, in all the seas where its ships were stationed. By the 1860s, therefore, the *inscription maritime* no longer discounted the large British superiority in maritime population. At great cost, and after too many years, the Admiralty had finally managed to find an answer to the French system of efficiently managed coercion.

II

At the end of the Crimean War, there was a strong feeling amongst at least some German and Austrian observers that the French navy had become the equal of its old rival. These 'german Noodles', as Palmerston dubbed them, had several arguments to offer.[40] They pointed at the success of the *Napoléon* at the Dardanelles in October 1853, at the equal role taken by the French in the naval war, at the Admiralty's fumblings for seamen, and at the incompetence of some of the British admirals. As it happens, they took an excessively partial view. The exploit of the *Napoléon* was allowed to disguise the fact that the Royal Navy had by far the larger number of screw steamers engaged in the war. Moreover, the 'equal role' of the French navy applied only in the Black Sea, and even there it was more a matter of appearance than reality. Many of the fine battleships that upheld French prestige in that zone were merely sail of the line converted to the ignominious duty of troop-carrying. In terms of effective warships, the Royal Navy kept a definite edge. One must also admit the crucial importance of the great British merchant marine: it contributed the ships that made possible the crossing to the Crimea of the allied army and its reinforcement and supply. And if British seapower was predominant in the Black Sea, it was overwhelming in the Baltic—a war zone largely ignored by continental observers.

[40] Palmerston to Clarendon, 11 Aug. 1856, Clarendon Deposit, C49, fos. 527–8. See also the 'Leipzic article' in Hans Busk, *The Navies of the World: Their Present State and Future Capabilities* (London, 1859).

However, the 'Noodles' were in part right about the short-comings of the British manning system, as we saw in the previous section. Furthermore, they were in part correct when it came to the British admirals involved in the war.

In the near-century between Gambier's failure to support Cochrane adequately at the Aix Roads, and the error by Sir George Tryon that led to the sinking of the Mediterranean fleet flagship *Victoria* (and of Tryon himself), 1854 was the year in which British public opinion was most concerned about the quality of its naval commanders-in-chief. There was reason to believe that both Sir Charles Napier and J. W. D. Dundas, commanding in the two most important war zones, were inadequate. Doubtless too much was expected of them by contemporaries ignorantly hopeful of what unarmoured screw-battleships could achieve against Russian land power, but even with hindsight we can agree that the two had important failings.

Most was expected of Napier: nothing less than St Petersburg in ruins. He knew right from the beginning of the campaign that the public was bound to be disappointed in him. His reaction was to attempt from early in the year to shuffle responsibility on to the Admiralty, and by the end of his command he was directing far heavier fire on the Admiralty than on the Russians. Not that he reserved his bad humours entirely for Whitehall. In previous wars he had shown that he was not always a dependable subordinate: in 1854 he fully demonstrated how difficult a superior he could be. Graham had suspected a lack of tact and, after a few officers had refused the post, managed to persuade the gentlemanly and diplomatic Michael Seymour to become Napier's Captain of the Fleet and act as intermediary between Napier and his juniors. The appointment was no panacea. The admiral became openly contemptuous of his officers, and the relations between him and his captains were not at all those proper to a band of brothers.

Of course, a lack of personal charm alone cannot condemn a leader; but the redeeming features of efficiency and luck have to be all the greater. Napier had neither. He could have returned home to acclaim if the Russian fleet had ventured out to fight; but it did not. He might have caught a Russian squadron if he had penetrated the Gulf of Finland to Sweaborg in April, as he could have done, instead of waiting until May. But it appears that his nerve broke when faced by what were certainly the fearsome dangers posed by ice and fog. The weight of command was too great for him, and there were widespread rumours that he began to drink heavily. With the later arrival of 10,000 French troops he did have the opportunity to take Bomarsund, and during the campaign ashore (he had always been something of a soldier *manqué*), he gained a renewed appetite for action. But, rather than turning this vigour against the Russians by preparing the way for the 1855 season, notably by energetically carrying out surveys of the waters around Sweaborg and Kronstadt, it was the enemy back home that most interested him. All in all, therefore, while one may hardly blame him—as many Englishmen did—for not levelling Russian granite with his wooden ships, there are sufficient reasons for feeling that Napier should not have been appointed.[41]

Dundas was a rather different case. Before going to the Mediterranean in 1852 he had been First Naval Lord for a few years, and as this suggests, was far more of a douce administrator than Napier could ever have been. Dundas could be sensitive about his honour, and suggestions from Graham's predecessor that the Mediterranean fleet under Dundas spent far too much time at anchor would have led to a duel, had not distance and friends intervened. Even so, Dundas swallowed some serious slights during the 1854 campaign. He knew well that his second-in-command, Rear-Admiral Lyons, had Graham's confidence and had been sent out to put fire into the naval war effort; yet he generally managed to keep his temper. Napier dispersed his black moods around the fleet by sending particularly vicious reprimands to his captains: at times he was brusque even with his gentlemanly French opposite number, Vice-Admiral Parseval-Deschênes. One advantage of Dundas was that he, unlike Sir Charles, had a little *côterie* on his flagship with which to share his troubles, notably a relative, Colonel Brereton.

Whilst Dundas did not share Napier's glaring personal faults, it must be admitted that he was not obviously a fighting admiral. Graham had been quite right to think that added fire was needed in the Black Sea. One of the Admiralty's particular complaints about Dundas was that he was painfully slow about organizing a blockade

---

[41] C. I. Hamilton, 'Sir James Graham, the Baltic Campaign and War-Planning at the Admiralty in 1854', *Historical Journal*, 19 (1976), 89–112. For a rather different approach, see A. Lambert, 'Preparing for the Russian War: British Strategic Planning, March 1853–March 1854', *War and Society*, 7/2 (Sept. 1989), 15–39.

of Russia's Black Sea ports. More important than that was his reluctance to throw himself into the project closest to Sir James's heart—the expedition to Sebastopol. Dundas did not have the over-optimistic enthusiasm traditional to British flag officers for throwing an army on to a hostile shore. 'Voyez-vous', one French officer records him saying to Hamelin's second-in-command, Vice-Admiral Bruat, 'these soldiers, they fancy we can go where they please—Go to [the] Crimea!—nonsense!'[42] Many RN officers certainly thought he was not sufficiently daring, and some blamed the influence of Brereton—or 'Auntie' as he was known in the fleet. The historian may at least conclude that though Dundas was a worthy officer, he was also weary and hardly inspiring.

Criticisms of Dundas soon joined those of Napier, though they tended to have greater circulation in Europe. As noted before, continental observers concentrated on the Black Sea theatre, and their poor opinion of Dundas was spread by the tale, emanating from Paris, that the Emperor had told the baron de Bazancourt —writing what was in effect the official French history of the naval war—that he was to deal gently with the English admiral.[43]

An explanation of the poor performance of Dundas and Napier could take several forms. One could stress, for instance, that Dundas was often in poor health: as he admitted in a letter in August 1854 to the Parliamentary Secretary of the Admiralty, Bernal Osborne, he could keep on going only thanks to chloroform and the knife.[44] But the essential factor is that the two admirals were too old. In comparison with the 81-year-old C.-in-C. at Devonport, Sir John Ommanney, they were sprightly, but—at 68 —they were not fit to face the very severe trials of war, particularly in the stormy and dangerous seas in which they commanded.

Age, indeed, is also a key to the relatively poor showing of other British admirals during the Russian war. Take, for example, Sir James Stirling, commanding the China and East Indies Station from January 1854 to February 1856. He was blamed by the Admiralty for not showing sufficient energy in the pursuit of a Russian squadron. It had eluded him by passing through to the

[42] Private Journal of Jurien de la Gravière, entry of 6 Sept., AN BB4 1798 *bis* (*marine*).

[43] César de Bazancourt, *L'expédition de Crimée: La Marine française dans la mer Noire et la Baltique* (2 vols., Paris, 1858).

[44] He suffered from anal *fistulae*. Osborne to Graham, 18 Aug. 1854, Graham Papers.

Gulf of Amur by a passage from the Gulf of Tartary: that is, to use modern nomenclature, the enemy had passed through the straits between the mainland and the island of Sakhalin. Stirling had not known about the straits at the time, and their Lordships were not amused by his belated discovery that Sakhalin was an island, nor by his amazement at how well the Russians had kept the secret. The Board pointed out that the latest Admiralty chart had not been fooled. Even though Stirling had lacked a copy, it was felt that he ought to have pursued the enemy more closely, in which case all would have been made clear to him.[45]

Stirling had shown some good qualities in command, notably in discussions with the Japanese over port and trading rights. But the strain of war and the enervating climate had perhaps proved too much for him. He was a typical example of the British flag officers of the time, uniting the usually incompatible attributes of age and inexperience. He had been born in 1791, and posted captain in 1818. But he was only one of the young officers produced by the Napoleonic Wars. Thanks to the fact that promotion above the rank of captain was almost always by seniority alone, coupled with the absence of any effective means of retiring senior officers plus a strict economy that prevented wholesale advancements, an enormous promotion 'block' was created. Promotion was slow, and employment intermittent. Stirling himself remained unemployed, on naval half-pay, between 1816 and 1849.

David Price was another such. He had had a fine fighting record before 1815, and had been posted captain at the peace. He was employed for only eight years from then until 1853, when he was appointed to the Pacific command. When war broke out, he and his French colleague—Rear-Admiral Febvrier-Despointes—decided that their combined forces could take the town of Petropaulovsk on the Russian Pacific coast. The preparations were made, but the evening before the attack the strain and the responsibility proved too much for the 64-year-old Price, and he shot himself.[46]

As a contrast to the above, we can look at R. S. Dundas. He, at least, was not a sexagenarian, having been appointed to his flag in 1853 at the age of only 51. He had been unduly favoured, since

---

[45] Stirling to the Admiralty, S109 and S141, ADM 1 5657; and 5 and 13 Feb. 1855, ADM 1 5672. Replies of 8 Dec. 1854, and 8–9 Feb. 1855, ADM 2 1704.

[46] Michael Lewis, 'An Eye-Witness at Petropaulovsk', *Mariner's Mirror*, 49 (1963), 265–72.

both his grandfather and his father had been First Lords of the
Admiralty. (Incidentally, he was not related to J. W. D. Dundas.)
Even Dundas, though, thought that his flag had come too late. He
once admitted 'I have had forty years service taken out of me . . .
bear in mind the fevers and illnesses . . . [officers] are liable to in the
course of their protracted services in unhealthy climates. Few
officers are really good for much after 50 or 55 years of age.'[47] It
was suggested in an earlier chapter that Dundas was hesitant and
unduly pessimistic during his command in the Baltic, so what he
said about officers seems to apply well enough to himself. On the
other hand, his age, or his sapped physical powers should not be
blamed entirely for his wartime showing. One gains the impression
that Dundas had never lightly borne the weight of decision-
making, had never been among the sanguine. Moreover, the Baltic
was perhaps the worst of all places for him to show his powers, the
Scandinavian twilight reinforcing a native Celtic melancholy.

The implication that age alone is no sure guide to a flag-officer's
ability is reinforced when one looks at the only British naval
commander-in-chief who came out of the Crimean War with an
enhanced reputation—Sir Edmund Lyons. He was 64 when he
succeeded to the Black Sea command, at the very end of 1854, but
retained his mental energies and the ability to lead. He was not still
physically resilient, and was often exhausted by the strains of
command, but was able to give a decided impetus to the war effort,
and was probably the decisive figure in persuading the allied
generals (some of whom agreed with J. W. D. Dundas in the
matter) to strike at the Crimea. Even if affairs of detail did wear
him down, he was an excellent man to work under. His recept-
iveness to new ideas, his charm, his scrupulous fairness in giving
full credit where it was due, his obvious enthusiasm for the fight,
and what was an undoubted (if self-conscious) physical resemblance
to Nelson, all contributed to inspire both officers and men.

Yet with all due allowances made, we must still have the general feeling that British admirals in active service during the war
were too old to be at their best. It is significant that their opposite numbers in the French service were almost all younger
men. Parseval-Deschênes had been born in 1790 (Napier was
four years older); Bruat (Hamelin's successor in 1855) and

[47] Sir John Briggs, *Naval Administrations 1827 to 1892: The Experience of 65 Years*
(London, 1897), 261–2. Dundas died of sudden heart failure in 1861.

Febvrier-Despointes's dated from 1796 (Lyons and Price had both been born in 1790); Hamelin was nearly three years junior to J. W. D. Dundas; and—youngest of all—there was Fourichon, Febvrier-Despointes's successor, born in 1809 (his British colleague, Rear-Admiral Bruce, appointed after Price's death, was nearly seventeen years older). The one exception was R. S. Dundas, if only just: he had the advantage over Charles Pénaud of almost fourteen months.

Not all the French admirals were beyond reproach. Price's second-in-command, Sir Frederick Nicolson, wrote to one of the Naval Lords, Alexander Milne, rather unkindly and perhaps not entirely ingenuously, that the erratic and changeable behaviour of Febvrier-Despointes had been one of the main causes of the strain on Price.[48] This was not altogether unlikely. Febvrier-Despointes was ailing, and did not long survive Price. Apart from him, however, the French commanding admirals were at least competent, and did not end the war surrounded by suspicion and complaint. Furthermore, amongst them were three leaders of considerable merit, Pénaud, Fourichon, and Bruat (who unfortunately died of cholera in 1855). The British might have had Lyons, but overall the balance was definitely tilted towards the French.

The British inferiority was not the result of consistent bad judgement of men by the Admiralty. As the Board was only too conscious, the number of men who were sufficiently senior to be chosen for the high commands and also passably fit in mind and body was fearfully small. The position had been even worse in the previous decade, in part because officers' political affiliations acted seriously to constrain further an already constricted choice. Notably, governments wanted only political sympathizers as Naval Lords, but suitable men were hard to find. Only in the 1850s did there begin to be continuity of Naval Lords under successive ministries: in 1852 Captain Alexander Milne remained on the Board even though Whig had given way to Tory. By that decade, as well, the men who had entered the navy after 1815 began to reach flag-rank, R. S. Dundas being the first, and the Admiralty once again had a junior admiral under 60. Helped by the deaths of increasing numbers of Napoleonic veterans, the promotion 'block' was easing somewhat. Nevertheless, the Crimean War called for far more able admirals than the navy could offer.

[48] Letter of 18 Sept. 1854, Netherby Papers, box III, bundle 24 c.w.

The French flag list was better able to cope. It was not plagued by a great 'block'. There had been many young officers created by Napoleon I, but the changes in regimes after 1815, with the consequent purges and retirements, had helped keep the officer corps trim. More important, promotion by seniority played a relatively small part in the French service. One left the naval officer school as a second-class *aspirant*, and was always promoted by seniority to the first-class (the lowest rank of the *grand corps*). But after this point selection became increasingly important. One-third of promotions to *enseigne* and *lieutenant de vaisseau*, half of those to *capitaine de frégate*, and all those to *capitaine de vaisseau* and to flag-rank were the result of choice — at least allegedly on grounds of merit.[49]

The Admiralty promoted according to a somewhat reversed system: advancement up to the level of post captain was by choice: only after that did the iron rule of seniority take over. One consequence was that, by the 1840s and 1850s, junior British officers were younger than their French equivalents. On average (the figures date from 1853), a British naval officer became a lieutenant at 23, a commander at 30, and a captain at 36. An average French officer, on the other hand, had to wait until he was 29 to become a *lieutenant de vaisseau*, 41 to become a *capitaine de frégate*, and he was 46 before reaching the rank of *capitaine de vaisseau* (all these ranks being equivalent to the RN ones just mentioned).[50]

But for flag-officers, all was different. M. Le Gallo speaks of a wholesale gerontocracy in senior posts of the French service,[51] but it did not compare with the one in the other navy. Since a naval officer in France could be a rear-admiral in his early 50s, a vice-admiral shortly afterwards, and a full admiral before he was 60, it was possible to set reasonable retirement ages. By the law of 17 July 1841, one that might have been regarded as a massacre of the innocents by some of the more experienced British officers, it was laid down that a rear-admiral had to retire at 65 and a vice-admiral at 68. As it was, there were plenty of complaints from elderly

---

[49] In 1836 the rank of *capitaine de frégate* was suppressed, reappearing only in 1848 when it replaced the rank of *capitaine de corvette*. For the details of the service afloat necessary to qualify for promotion, see A. Deschard, 'Organisation du corps des officiers de vaisseau de la marine française', pt. 2, *Revue maritime et coloniale*, 51 (1876), 637–66.

[50] 'Note sur le cadre des officiers de vaisseau' (*c*.1853), AN BB8 108 (*marine*), 299–301.

[51] Le Gallo, *Brest et sa bourgeoisie*, i. 102, 201–2.

French flag-officers who felt they were being squeezed out in their prime. When it was proposed in 1853 that the retirement ages should be reduced by three years, Admiral Mackau arose in the Senate and quoted with approval what Admiral Duperré had said during the debates on the 1841 law: 'C'est ici qu'il convient de rappeler cet axiome de toutes les marines: vieux amiraux, jeunes capitaines.'

Mackau's speech is interesting, though not always convincing. For instance, how should one react to his idea that the English government always chose the best naval policy, since the Royal Navy was the bulwark of national independence? And he stated that in England, an officer gained his flag near the age at which the new retirement law would close a French officer's career: here, at least, Mackau was obviously wrong, since at the time he spoke British officers were on average promoted to the various flag-ranks some years *after* the proposed retirement ages. Moreover, it is difficult to see quite what virtue attaches to young captains and old admirals. The first part is excellent, but why must admirals be old? As with Charles Dupin, and his praise of the Royal Navy's *bâtiments mixtes*, one feels that Mackau's speech tells us a great deal about how international rivalry can reinforce conservatism. The rival's experience is always of keen interest, but Mackau was drawing on it to reinforce his own prejudices. His formula was not even well designed for its purpose. If one is to agree with one observer of the time, Captain Souville, who left an excellent volume of memoirs, full of vivid descriptions of officers he had liked or looked down upon, then if there was truth in what Mackau said about having old admirals, it applied only to the British service. For Souville, at least, would not have agreed with R. S. Dundas: he wrote that the English 'amiraux septuagénaires' were 'beaux et vigoureux vieillards, souvent plus verts et plus actifs que les nôtres à la cinquantaine'. For in France, Souville said, the officer corps was small; French officers served more time afloat than English ones, and were thus soon exhausted.[52]

However, despite the comments by Mackau and Souville, we must accept that the French system of producing admirals was the better one: the Crimean War allows no other conclusion. There were limits even to vigorous Englishmen. 'Old admirals, young

[52] E. Souville, *Mes souvenirs maritimes (1837–1863)* (Paris, 1914), 399.

captains' was but a pretty phrase: as Ducos dryly commented in the margin of his copy of Mackau's speech, it was not what the English had practised at Copenhagen, Aboukir, and Trafalgar.[53]

Mackau's formula does serve as a link to the comparison of British and French officers below flag-rank. As noted already, British captains and junior officers were, on average, younger than their French opposite numbers. Was British inferiority in the upper naval strata thus balanced by superiority lower down? The Crimean experience certainly demonstrated that the Royal Navy had some excellent captains, including R. B. Watson, H. R. Yelverton, Stephen Lushington (in command of the Naval Brigade in the Crimea), Harry Keppel, Astley Cooper Key, Edmund Lyons (son of Sir Edmund, and killed during the war), Bartholemew Sulivan, and William Peel (son of the great Sir Robert). Nevertheless, by making French and British officers mingle socially and professionally far more than they had done before, and thus giving each side a better understanding of the other, the war convinced many observers that in comparison with his French colleague the British naval officer was on average less generally prepared.[54]

Education was the key. The Royal Navy believed in an early beginning to a naval career; by the start of our period the age of entry for a cadet was between 12 and 14. By this age little in the way of a general education had been laid down. The navy did not make up the lack. Concentration was very much on professional topics. Seamanship was the naval be-all and end-all. (Indeed, here lay the reason for the early entry. Senior officers seem usually to have thought that seamanship could be mastered only through service at sea from an impressionable age.) Of course, officers could try to improve themselves, and read beyond naval topics; even so, the wartime comparison between British and French officers showed that in general education the latter were generally superior. This was not too surprising, given the weight attached in France to officers perfecting their *éducation littéraire*. More surprising is that French officers at this time appear also to have had a better general grounding in professional matters.

This too was to be expected. All British cadets began their naval careers on a regular warship in commission, learning what they could from naval schoolmasters during the hurly-burly of life at

[53] Copy of Senate debate of 13 May 1853 bound in AN BB8 108 (*marine*), 4–16.
[54] Lewis, *The Navy in Transition*, 110.

sea. They could expect only two to three hours a day of teaching, and these were constantly interrupted.[55] The French cadets, on the other hand, had a permanent school. The Restoration regime had set up a naval college at Angoulême to give a solid grounding to cadets. Soon, the distance from the sea was seen as a disadvantage, and in 1827 the boys embarked on the battleship *Orion* stationed at Brest. In 1840 the ship was replaced by the three-decker *Commerce de Paris*, also at Brest. She was renamed the *Borda* in honour of the noted scientist and naval officer. The ship was occasionally replaced, but the name remained until 1913, and during that time the *Borda* produced a stream of able officers. The school's strength lay in the breadth of the courses—literary as well as scientific and naval—and the fact that they took two years. Moreover, the boys were taken later than they would have been for the Royal Navy. The regulation of 24 April 1832 set the age of entrants at 13 up to 16. Thus many of the boys could be expected to have a broader general knowledge than their counterparts in Britain. Admittedly, age was not the only factor involved; there was also the excellent *lycée* system, itself better than what was then available across the Channel, though one must admit that many of the candidates for the *Borda* came from *collèges communaux* near Brest, specifically preparing boys for the entrance examination in the same way that crammers in Britain did for potential cadets over there.[56]

The *Borda* had its troubles. We have already noted that there were disturbances on board in the 1840s, reflecting what were the often hectic conditions at the time in civilian schools for adolescents. The 1848 Revolution temporarily made matters worse. Louis-Napoleon eventually brought discipline to the *Borda* as he did to the *grands boulevards*; nevertheless, some of the consequences of the revolution could not be expunged easily. In July 1848 the Second Republic had authorized a large category of new *Borda* entrants by extending the age of entry up to 18 for those who had served eighteen months on a state ship (shortened to one year in August). In October this provision was extended: service on various types of vessel now counted; and instead of serving for a year one could qualify by a single voyage beyond the Equator. The extension gave rise to a peculiar industry. An *armateur* at Le Havre

---

[55] Sir John Pakington's evidence, PP (1861), V, para. 2302.
[56] Patrick J. Harrigan, *Mobility, Élites, and Education in French Society of the Second Empire* (Wilfred Laurier University Press, Ontario, 1980), 70.

ran voyages to Brazil and back for young men who had failed the *Borda* entrance examination, so that they could try again even once they had reached 18. The more generous entrance requirements had a great effect. Out of the promotions of 1852–4 from cadets to *aspirants de la marine* (a title that had replaced that of *élèves de la marine* in April 1848), no less than half had entered the *Borda* at 17 and 18.[57]

It would be difficult to say whether the influx adversely affected the quality of the French naval officer corps. Certainly, the entrants were not necessarily too old to learn seamanship: Lord Cochrane, one recalls, began his naval career at 18. But it is at least probable that too many weak candidates were scraping through into the navy. At any rate, in 1856 the obvious anomalies of 1848 were swept away. Yet the principle of admitting young adults rather than boys was retained: henceforwards, the age of admittance to the *Borda* was from 14 to 17.

One ought not to ignore certain strong similarities in attitudes in the two countries to naval education. The fact that the French naval school was a floating one in itself signifies the concern of the Ministry of Marine that officers should be introduced early to the sea. And both in Britain and in France it was a delicate matter to suggest that the requirements of general education demanded a raising of the entrance age. Older officers tended to feel personally somewhat slighted. Thus when a commission of the *Conseil d'amirauté* did make the suggestion in 1856 that the minimum age of *Borda* entrance ought to be raised from 13 to 14, so that boys could improve 'leur éducation littéraire' before becoming cadets, it felt necessary to add 'il importait de laisser la porte ouverte à ces quelques natures d'élites dont nous avons dans le corps des officiers quelques heureux et éclatants examples'.[58]

Nevertheless, the differences are significant. These were, to sum them up so far, the age difference between cadet entrance in the two countries, the higher educational standard of the French entrants, and the fact that the *Borda* gave not only an unequalled professional training but also put some emphasis on wider topics. Here, one must conclude, was a basic reason for the superiority of the junior French officers over their British colleagues, just

[57] 'Un ancien officier', *Histoire de l'École navale et des institutions qui l'ont précédée* (Paris, 1889), 203–5.

[58] Meeting of the *Conseil d'amirauté*, 22 Jan. 1856, AN BB8 886 (*marine*), 20.

as relative youth was a reason for the superiority of the senior French officers.

After the Crimean War attempts were made by the Admiralty to improve the quality of the officers under its command. Pakington, when First Lord 1858–9, tried to introduce an element of choice into flag-promotions: two-thirds were to be by seniority and the rest by the choice of a full Board of Admiralty. The short life of the ministry ultimately killed the plan, but Pakington also faced heavy opposition from the First Naval Lord, W. F. Martin. Martin upheld some well-established naval arguments. He disliked the part of the plan that would have forced many officers to retire from the active lists at 70. He saw ejection on to a reserve list as terribly insulting to a man, however old he was. Furthermore, and with reason, given the nature especially of Conservative governments at the end of the 1850s, Martin believed that promotion by choice would be abused for political ends. He also thought that selection would encourage jealousy between officers, undermining *esprit de corps*.[59]

The First Naval Lord's arguments might have been inherited from his father, Sir Thomas Byam Martin, effectively last Comptroller of the Navy Board, but they also appear to have reflected the dominant feeling in the officer corps about promotion. This feeling, when combined with the refusal of governments after 1815 to promote enough men by seniority to have at least some young admirals (an obviously expensive method), produced an impasse which was ultimately responsible for the unfortunate appointments of 1854. What relief Whitehall had felt able to offer had been, in the main, limited and late. In 1847 and 1851 strict limits had been placed on the number of officers on the active lists; and inducements had been offered to some of the older men as long as they would move to the reserve lists. These steps were completed in 1864 when the veteran lieutenants were cleared away. By this year one may say that the old wartime promotion 'block' had finally dissipated, and also that no man who was definitely too old would find himself commanding a fleet.[60] However, it was not art

---

[59] Notes by Martin of Jan. 1859, and Pakington's memorandum, W. F. Martin Papers, BM Add. MS 41409, fos. 292–6, 361–79.

[60] Lewis, *The Navy in Transition*, 116–18, and his *England's Sea Officers: The Story of the Naval Profession* (London, 1939), 128 ff. In 1869 Childers trimmed the active lists further, offering incentives to older officers who would accept retirement.

but nature—the mortality among the Napoleonic veterans—that had taken the chief role in the improvement.

If Whitehall's attempts to solve the promotion problem were hesitant, at least cadet education was tackled seriously after 1856. The Board had before them the example of the captain of the boys' training ship *Illustrious*. He had decided to put his own son—officer material, of course—in with the young ratings, and the boy had quickly shown the benefit of a co-ordinated system of tuition on a school-ship. Beginning in 1857, all naval cadets joined the *Illustrious*—displacing the boy seamen—and when the ship proved too small they were transferred to the three-decker *Britannia*. At first the latter was anchored in Portsmouth harbour, later found a temporary refuge at Portland (February 1862–September 1863), and then came to her final home at Dartmouth where the later shore-based cadet college was built (completed 1905). The establishment of a British equivalent to the *Borda* was very beneficial, and the improvement was felt as early as February 1858, when Alexander Milne suggested that a wider variety of lectures should be given at the Royal Naval College at Portsmouth (itself a valuable institution, offering courses on professional topics to officers wishing to improve their knowledge), since, he said, the cadets now often knew more than their superiors![61]

Unfortunately, the British cadets did not necessarily know more than French cadets. The first entrants to the *Illustrious* and *Britannia* could expect to receive only three months to a year of tuition, depending on their ages. By 1862 the course in effect took fifteen months, but this was still nine months less than on the *Borda*. Furthermore, a large age difference remained. In 1857 the ages of entry for a British cadet were raised to 13 to 15, but the traditionalists succeeded in 1859 in reducing this back to the previous 12 to 14. By the latter year, therefore, the French cadet could easily have an advantage of two to three years. And there was one more plus on the French side. Standards on the *Borda* did not remain static after the war: the Ministry of Marine showed itself no less eager than the Admiralty to improve cadet education.

[61] Folder 24, ADM 1 5698 (pt. 1). See also the report of the Committee on Naval Education, 11 May 1856, ADM 1 5676; the Admiralty circular of 23 Feb. 1857, ADM 1 5686; a letter of Sir Michael Seymour of 22 June 1858, plus comments, A1740, ADM 1 5691; and E. P. Statham, *The Story of the 'Britannia': The Training Ship for Naval Cadets* (London, 1904), 33, 56–8.

Complaints had been made about the inadequate grounding of new *Bordaches*, particularly in the English language—'si utile à l'instruction du marin', as one report put it. A careful eye was therefore kept on the intellectual standards of entry. Moreover, constant efforts were made to improve the syllabus and teaching on the school-ship.[62] Chasseloup-Laubat was particularly keen on improvements, and it was during his ministry—in 1864—that French cadet education was significantly developed with the commissioning of the *Jean Bart* as an *école d'application*. This was a far more sensible way of teaching the *métier* of the seaman than throwing new entrants straight on to a regular seagoing vessel, as in the pre-1857 British system, and it was an advance on the previous French system. A *corvette d'instruction* had long been attached to the *Borda* (a *corvette mixte* from 1857), to introduce the cadets to sea voyages, as part of their two-year course. But from 1864 sea experience took an even more important part in the education of the French officer. The new second-class *aspirant*, fresh from the *Borda*, was no longer sent to an ordinary warship, but instead served on the *Jean Bart* for a long voyage. French cadet education in effect now took three years.[63]

Despite the establishment of the *Britannia*, therefore, valuable as it was, the French navy retained the palm in terms of cadet training, and perhaps did so for the rest of the nineteenth century.[64] If not to the same extent as with the problem of over-age flag-officers, in cadet education the Admiralty still relied a little too much on nature rather than nurture. Nature did at least offer an inevitable if slow solution to the first; but its effects on the training of young officers were less dependable.

It seems very likely that the better standards of French officer training were at least in part responsible for the superior facility at innovation of the French navy, encouraging men to take a wider

[62] *Procès-verbaux* of the *Conseil d'instruction* of the naval school, 8 Dec. 1857, AN CC1 783 (*marine*).

[63] 'Un ancien officier', *Histoire de l'École navale*, 209–13. It appears that the *école d'application* actually began in 1863, though not at first on the *Jean Bart*: Chasseloup-Laubat to the comte de Gueydon, 19 June 1863, Chasseloup-Laubat Papers, v. 148–51.

[64] Theodore Ropp, 'The Development of a Modern Navy: French Naval Policy, 1871–1904', doctoral thesis (Harvard, 1937), 84–5. See also the Luard Committee Report (1886) on the education of executive naval officers, ADM 1 6820A, folder 13 Oct.

view of problems, and enabling them to present their ideas clearly and logically on paper.[65] But some other differences between the two corps have to be made clear before conclusions can be reached.

One ought to lead gently into the description, to avoid the impression that the two corps were alike in nothing. That there should have been some similarity was inevitable, given the common functions of the two, as well as the influence that each had on the other. Notably, certain officer attitudes were very alike, particularly in the conservatism characteristic of many flag-officers—those most likely to take important decisions about *matériel*. Younger officers were usually more in favour of change, but in both navies they tended to come up against the amply decorated *embonpoints* of their seniors.

Another link between the two was an increasing 'gentrification' that occurred after 1815. For one thing, there was the retirement or death of those excellent if at times unpolished professional seamen who had become executive officers during the wars of 1792–1815, the 'tarpaulins' and *officiers bleus*.[66] At the same time, an increasing proportion of officer entrants was drawn from the nobility and gentry. Not only were the entrants better born, they were also— not always a concomitant—better behaved. A revival in religious feeling—Evangelical in Britain and Catholic or Calvinist in France —encouraged higher standards of personal morality and politeness. What became the ideal, at least in Britain, was the 'Christian gentle-man' who, as naval officer, was far removed in habits and modes of behaviour from the average officer of pre-1815. The clash between that rumbustious sloven Sir Charles Napier and his relatively svelte and douce captains in the Baltic in 1854 shows how great the dis-tance could be. Significantly, at least some of those captains found more common ground with their colleagues in the French Baltic squadron than they did with their own commander-in-chief.

However, further study of social origins and religious attitudes begins to lead one away from similarities to differences between the two officer corps. To take the second first: the religious revival

---

[65] In a work on French naval officers, *Royal Republicans: The French Naval Dynasties between the World Wars* (Baton Rouge, La., 1985), 81–2, R. C. Hood passes on the suggestion that an *éducation littéraire* could be an unsound basis for a naval officer. Of course, he was dealing with a later period than ours, and by then, it appears, the professional teaching at *Navale* had relatively declined.

[66] One must take care not to simplify the nature of the *officiers bleus*. See Jacques Aman, *Les Officiers bleus dans la marine française au XVIIIe siècle* (Geneva, 1976).

occurred later in France than in Britain. Whilst the Evangelical revival began in force during the war against Napoleon, the French Catholic upsurge post-dated 1830, and even during the 1840s the *Bordaches* were notoriously heathen.[67]

Nor did 'gentrification' occur in both countries at the same time, or even according to the same pattern. (In the French case it was even subject to reversal!) Michael Lewis, working from a large sample of RN officer entrants of 1815–49, found that nearly 18 per cent of the boys' fathers were peers or baronets, and over 27 per cent were members of the landed gentry.[68] Taken together, these two groups would approximate to what 'noble' meant in France, but contributing a significantly higher proportion of the officer corps, at least with regard to the situation by the mid-century. During the Restoration, one finds a high proportion of French cadets with the noble (or allegedly noble) *particule*, but during the Orleanist regime the French nobility proved more reluctant to enter the army or navy, many remaining faithful to the legitimist line. Surveying the 1853 *Annuaire de la marine*, from admirals down to *aspirants* first-class, one finds that only 16.2 per cent of executive officers boasted a *particule*. Only with the Second Empire, it appears, did the old nobility shed some of their hesitancy, and by the 1870 *Annuaire* 19.7 per cent of officers had noble pretensions.

Of course, the *particule* hardly proved blue blood. It did at least prove noble aspirations, in themselves redolent of the attitudes of the officers. But under the noble veneer we know quite well that the wood was often bourgeois, as one sees well demonstrated by M. Le Gallo in his fine study *Brest et sa bourgeoisie*. But what kind of bourgeois? Certainly, we find many scions of the well-to-do professions, just as Professor Lewis has shown in the British case, but it appears that in France it was more feasible for the less affluent or even commercial bourgeoisie to get a son into the executive naval officer corps. In short, the French navy drew on a larger section of society for its officers than the Royal Navy did, making use of more of the available talent.

One way in which this occurred was through state subsidy of cadets whose parents could not properly support their children. On

---

[67] A. Cabantous, *Le Ciel dans la mer: Christianisme et civilisation maritime (XVᵉ–XIXᵉ siècle)* (Paris, 1990), 338–43.

[68] Lewis, *The Navy in Transition*, 21–32. Ropp, 'The Development of a Modern Navy' (thesis), 93 n.

entry a cadet could be given a *trousseau* worth 500 francs and a half or full bursary (350 or 700 francs *per annum*) covering the tuition fees that—on the *Borda* as on the *Britannia*—had normally to be paid by the parents. On successfully passing the exit examination and becoming a second-class *aspirant*, an ex-*boursier* or *demi-boursier* could find his final obstacle to a naval career smoothed away by the grant of a *mise d'équipement militaire* (worth 570 francs). There was no true British equivalent to these boys. A limited number of places on the *Britannia* was reserved for the sons of officers who had died in the service, and there was a sliding scale of tuition charges for cadets from worthy naval (or military) families according to the ability to pay. But, as N. A. M. Rodger has argued recently, the *Britannia* represented an attempt by the Admiralty to confirm social restrictions on the entry of cadets.[69]

Unfortunately, our *Borda* sample is limited, since evidence appears to have survived only from 1859–60; but it seems that the *boursiers* were numerous, then constituting just over a quarter of the *Bordaches*. Moreover, one sees that the fathers of those subsidized cadets had very varied careers. The professions and state service predominated: the list of fathers includes two *professeurs*, a *commissaire de police*, an *avoué*, a notary, and an ex-notary, a retired infantry captain, another who was deceased, a *chef de bataillon*, and a *censeur des études au lycée impériale*. Of course, many of the fathers were in the navy: they formed about a third of the total. The list includes *capitaines de vaisseau* and *capitaines de frégate*, that is, members of the *grand corps*, but there were also lesser men represented, a naval surgeon, for instance, and a *capitaine d'artillerie de la marine*, and even a retired naval *garde magasin*. All the above groups constituted two-thirds of the whole, and were the ones to which we might expect a state to be generous. However, the final third was a somewhat motley collection. One finds mention of a *propriétaire*, a *commis voyageur*, a *commis de maison de banque*, a *receveur particulier*, a *marbrier*, a *marchand des papiers peints*, and an unemployed Protestant minister. All the men were doubtless worthy, or thought to be so by the Ministry of Marine, yet they are still

[69] Somerset to Gladstone, 23 Oct. 1861, Gladstone Papers, BM Add. MS 44304, fos. 100–3. Board Minute, 3 Jan. 1862, ADM 1 5795. N. A. M. Rodger, 'Officers, Gentlemen and their Education, 1793–1860', in E. Freeman (ed.), *Les Empires en guerre et paix 1793–1860* (Vincennes, 1990), 139–50. Rodger also emphasizes how political criteria constricted admission in his period.

redolent of perhaps shabby circles which in Britain might send a boy into the merchant service, or from which a boy might thankfully escape to sea, but which were not thought of as sources for the country's executive naval officers.[70]

Even without a *bourse*, it was still possible for the less affluent to see their boy become an officer. There were, indeed, several alternatives to becoming a cadet. One of these was to win one of the four places as second-class *aspirant* offered each year to graduates of the *École polytechnique*. Admittedly, given the cost of that school, this route was of little use to those who found the *Borda* too dear. The economical alternative for a young man was to serve afloat in some capacity for at least a year, perhaps on a merchantman or as a volunteer seaman on a warship. He could then hope to be accepted in the navy as a *volontaire de la marine*. Once appointed, he in effect became an *aspirant auxiliaire*—indeed, for a time in 1848 that was the actual rank. Each French warship was allowed to take up to half her regulation number of *aspirants* in the form of such *volontaires*. The rank had been designed for seamen who wished to become deep-sea merchant captains, *capitaines au long cours*, and who thus had to satisfy certain preliminary requirements as to service afloat. By becoming *volontaires* they put in the necessary sea-time, and helped the navy with what was usually a short supply of young officers, without choking the promotion prospects of *aspirants*. But very often the *volontaires* were men who wanted to be naval officers. They knew that after two years as a *volontaire*, a man could be appointed an *aspirant* first-class, the bottom rung in the *grand corps* itself. By 1866, thanks to budgetary restrictions on the size of the active fleet, and the fact that the *Borda* had in recent years increased its numbers, there was not the same shortfall in junior officers, and it appears that no more *volontaires* were allowed to make the leap to full officer status. Before that date, however, this side-ways progression had been well known. It appears also that many took it as a way of getting a second chance, rather than because they were too poor to think of the *Borda*. There were certainly complaints from some who had passed through the *Borda* that boys of their own age, dismissed from the school after a year, later managed to re-enter the mainstream of promotion ahead of them.

There was another cross-over point into the *grand corps* at a

---

[70] 'École navale, 1857–1860', AN CC1 783 (*marine*).

higher level. A man who had qualified as a *capitaine au long cours* could serve in the navy as an *enseigne auxiliaire*: indeed, if he was called up by the *inscription maritime*, that was the rank he held: the *capitaines au long cours* were the navy's principal wartime officer reserve. (In the Royal Navy, of course, the large active lists of officers contained its own reserve.) And *enseignes auxiliaires* could be promoted to full *enseignes de vaisseau*. Thus the *volontaire* who failed to become an *aspirant*, and went off into the merchant marine, might still enter the *grand corps*. No less than one-third of places as *enseignes de vaisseau* were awarded, where possible, to those who had either been *enseignes auxiliaires*—or were members of yet another, non-*Borda*, group that has not yet been mentioned.[71]

The men in this group, far more than would be the case with the two latter ones, came from working-class backgrounds, yet they were still able to enter the *grand corps*. We must now concern ourselves with the *maistrance*, the non-commissioned officers who performed the tasks that in the Royal Navy were undertaken by the Petty and Warrant Officers. They may also be compared to the *Deckoffiziere* of the Prussian navy. The juniors in the *maistrance* were the quarter-masters. Above them were the *officiers-mariniers* proper, comprising the second-masters, the masters, and, at the top, the first-masters. Given the relative youth and inexperience of many of the *inscrits*, the *maistrance* was an essential source of expertise. Each officer concerned himself with one of the particular specialities; there were five divisions at the top, the *premiers maîtres de manœuvre*, *de canonnage*, *de timonerie* (or *les chefs*), the *premiers maîtres mécaniciens*, and the *capitaines d'armes* (the men responsible for keeping discipline below decks and in charge of the *fusiliers marins*). The masters and first-masters on a warship composed what was called the *petit état-major*, but a rise to the *état-major* proper was possible. Especially meritorious first-masters (even including the *capitaines d'armes*, renowned as they often were for a stolidity that approached ignorant inflexibility), were chosen for promotion to the *grand corps*.[72]

[71] A. Deschard, 'Organisation du corps des officiers de vaisseau', *Revue maritime et coloniale*, 51 (1876), 297–334, 637–666. 'Un officier de marine' [H. Chassériaud], 'L'avancement dans la marine', *La Nouvelle Revue*, 16 (1882), 481–516. Decree of 31 Dec. 1856, *Bulletin officiel de la marine*, i (1856), 1323 ff.

[72] Eugène Prugnaud, *Législation et administration de la marine* (Rochefort, 1858), 280 ff. Jean Randier, *'La Royale', l'éperon et la cuirassé: L'Histoire illustrée de la marine nationale française des débuts de la vapeur à la fin de la première guerre mondiale* (Paris, 1972), 162 ff.

It is difficult to be sure about the numbers of men who entered the *grand corps* through each of the routes from the lower deck or the merchant service.[73] But we can consult the *Annuaire de la marine*, and that shows us how many officers were never *aspirants*, the ones who presumably were promoted masters, or ex-*enseignes auxiliaires*. Taking again the years 1853 and 1870, we find that respectively 12.78 per cent and 11.89 per cent of the officers had never been *aspirants*, quite a high proportion. This suggests, by the way, that the balance within the officer corps changed little over the eighteen years in question, but it is interesting to see some developments hidden by the overall figures. Notably, there was a significant increase of promotions of non-*aspirants* to *enseignes de vaisseau* with the expansion of the navy under the Second Empire, especially in the mid-1860s: in 1862 non-*aspirants* constituted only just over 1 per cent of new promotions to that rank; by 1864 this had climbed to 46 per cent, but then began to decline and by 1868 was only 3 per cent.

By contrast, the Royal Navy's executive officer corps was far more homogeneous. After 1864 it was possible, if little more than that, for the chief boatswain, gunner, and carpenter to be promoted to commissioned rank. Yet, if anything, the position of the British executive officer was becoming more clear-cut during this time. From 1857 there was only one ship on which a cadet could qualify. And during the following decade one ancient encumbrance began to be discarded. There had long been a division between the duties of the captain, the fighting man, and the master, the navigator: the origin was the medieval distinction between the knight and the shipman. There were increasing doubts about the wisdom of the division in the nineteenth century, especially after one incident in 1861, when the master of the fast liner *Conqueror* ran her aground on Rum Cay in the Bahamas, with the captain standing by, more or less mute. Ultimately, masters were to be superseded, or rather combined in an enlarged executive branch, though the process was typically British in the way it was drawn out. It was not until the 1880s that the change-over had largely taken place.[74]

We can conclude, therefore, that the French quarterdeck showed a greater variety in terms of both means of access and the social

---

[73] Note, though, that returns in the *Comptes définitifs* for the various years show the following number of *gratifications de premier* given to first-masters promoted to the *grand corps*, 1862: 5, 1863: 4, 1864: 11, 1865: 7, 1867: 8.

[74] Lewis, *England's Sea Officers*, 228–9.

origins of the officer. But we are not going to argue that this was a
source of significant advantage, at least in regard to the generation
and encouragement of new ideas. Instead, it will be suggested that
the true strength of the French officer corps lay in an element
within it that was narrow and exclusive. We should recall what was
mentioned in passing earlier—the conservatism of the older officers
in the two navies or, to put it another way, the oppressive weight
of hierarchy. We ought to look for a mechanism that could overcome this. And there was one —on the French side. It resulted not
from the variety of officer creation, but from the fact that there was
a central officer body that had the real power and influence, and
a very highly developed sense of *esprit de corps*. This body was
formed of those who had graduated through the École polytechnique
and, above all, through the *Borda*.

Here, one might say, was the true *grand corps*, with virtually all
the élitist and snobbish implications that the term had had in the
eighteenth century. It was *aspirants* from the two schools who
reached the high ranks.[75] They not only kept their distance from
the seamen, but also had disdain for those officers who had risen
from the *maistrance* —or so the latter believed. They sought by preference commissions on the lesser warships, where the small number
of officers meant that differences of origin were less painfully felt.[76]

Not, of course, that *hauteur* was limited to officers in the French
service. For instance, in both navies, the executive officers appear
to have had an antipathy for their engineer colleagues, men who
were not only polluting the cleanliness and aesthetic appeal of the
warship, but who were also supposed not to be over-desirable
socially.[77] Then there was the excessive amount of distance which
some British officers attempted to keep between themselves and the
lower deck. RN Napoleonic veterans often had an attitude towards
continuous servicemen little different from the one they had held
towards the products of the press-gangs, and thus continued to
maintain the old brutal discipline. Some far younger officers had

[75] Of the 118 members of the *grand corps* born 1815–55 inclusive, who were
important enough to be included in Étienne Taillemite, *Dictionnaire des marins
français* (Paris, 1982), 108 passed through the *Borda*, and 7 through the École
polytechnique, thus leaving only 3—one of whom was the prince de Joinville!

[76] *Enquête parlementaire sur la marine*, evidence of Vice-Admiral Parseval-
Deschênes, 10–12 Nov. 1851, ii. 687–93.

[77] Geoffrey Penn, *'Up Funnel, Down Screw!': The Story of the Naval Engineer*
(London, 1955).

the same approach: prejudice is no exclusive preserve of the old, and we can believe that the weaker young officer eagerly accepted his seniors' reactionary beliefs simply as a means of demonstrating that he also was truly an officer. A few went quite out of control. What, for example, of Lieutenant Collinson, commanding the *Spy* in 1859? He gave very heavy punishments; his idea of a minimum lashing was the official maximum. And his imagination clearly failed when it came to the serious offences: he was reported for giving one marine a blow with the flat of his sword, and for kicking another in the testicles. Admittedly, he was an exception, and his services were soon dispensed with. He is merely a very bad case of what Sir Francis Baring had described a decade before as 'the old style of authority and somewhat brutal rule . . . the Paradise lost of old officers'.[78]

As was noted earlier, the continuation of such attitudes into the 1850s, when much else was changing, encouraged the series of minor mutinies on RN warships. Yet we must not assume that they were general in the British naval officer corps. The fact that they did encourage friction with the lower deck itself suggests that they were exceptional, no longer accepted as normal by the seamen. We do not have evidence of a uniform and wide gulf of suspicion between officer and man in the Royal Navy. It appears, indeed, that the gulf —not necessarily one of suspicion, but certainly one of distance— was greater in the French service. RN observers of the period themselves accepted that there was greater coolness shown by the officer towards the man in the French service than in their own.

There was good reason for French officers to wish to keep such a distance. Even with an experienced *maistrance*, the greenness of many *inscrits* put a greater burden on the French executive officer than his British colleague had to stand. The former had to intervene more frequently to ensure that his orders were being carried out properly, giving more lengthy instructions. Greater intervention, naturally, meant the greater possibility of over-familiarity with seamen. Hauteur can be seen as an obvious protective device for an officer, given such demands of duty.[79]

[78] Report on the Collinson affair by Rear-Admiral Stephen Lushington, 7 June 1859, ADM 1 5711. Baring to Lord John Russell, 12 Dec. 1849, Russell Papers, PRO 30.22.8c, fos. 47–50.
[79] Eugene Pacini, *La Marine, arsenaux, navires, équipages, navigation, atterages, combats* (Paris, 1844), 98.

Yet there is surely another explanation of hauteur, applicable to
the gulf not just between officer and man but also between officers
of apparently similar substantive rank. The relevant points made so
far are as follows:

1. There was an élite within the French *grand corps*.
2. The officers in this élite almost always got the pick of the
   promotion.
3. Some of the élite came from the *École polytechnique*, but the
   rest came from but one school.
4. That school had courses lasting for at least two years, and the
   standard of education was high.

The consequence was an élite possessing a particularly strong
esprit de corps, which began on the *Borda* (as is suggested, among other
things, by the highly developed school *argot* that Roger Coindreau
has brought to our attention[80]), and continuing on through later
service. Naturally, this élite would have been criss-crossed by other
loyalties: those of family, friendship, patronage, and also geography
(one thinks here of the large proportion of Breton names in the
officer lists), and status (the degree of true nobility in the officer
corps, perhaps from *hobereaux* families, is something it would be
very useful to know more about). Moreover, perhaps during the
mid-century one could discern (though again more research is
needed) that division, to be so clearly developed under the Third
Republic, between officers who usually served in home waters or in
Paris, on the one hand, and their 'forgotten brethren' who spent
most of their service on distant stations.[81] Nevertheless, the *esprit de
corps* of the élite appears to have remained strong during our period;
surely stronger than that of the totality of the Royal Navy's executive officer corps. And it did more than encourage hauteur. It
had some advantages, as well. It was of particular importance in
connection with the ruling system of promotion. W. F. Martin, it
will be remembered, had feared the divisive effects on the upper
ranks of the RN officer corps of promotion by merit. The French
officer élite was apparently cohesive enough to absorb such effects.
Indeed, to an extent the principles of selection by merit and narrow
élitism were mutually reinforcing. And there was another boon to
be gained from a particularly strong *esprit de corps*. Within the élite

[80] *L'École navale et ses traditions: L'argot baille* (Paris, 1957).
[81] Ropp, *The Development of a Modern Navy* (book), 47, 155.

the weight of hierarchy would have been lighter than in somewhat less cohesive bodies, encouraging a livelier sense of competition, but not necessarily weakening the spirit of co-operation, or undermining the sense of authority.

That this was only relative must be emphasized. The élite—and the *grand corps* as a whole—could not entirely escape the conservative and traditionalist influences natural to any profession and perhaps to military and naval officers in particular. Even the best French officers showed what might be called their reactionary side. Edmond Jurien de la Gravière, for instance, was one of those who had doubts about the new fast steam-warships of the early 1850s. To him—and, he said, to most of his colleagues—the *Napoléon*, when she first appeared, with her restricted stowage room, somewhat unsatisfactory manœuvrability under sail, and delicate machinery, had seemed inferior to a sail of the line accompanied by a paddle-steamer to act as tug when needed. In 1868, as C.-in-C. of France's fine ironclad *escadre d'évolutions*, one finds him penning the following piece of nostalgia for the days of sail:

Nous ne sommes plus au temps des anciennes escadres qui se suffisaient si aisément à elles-mêmes. Les secours du port deviennent à chaque instant nécessaires à des vaisseaux dont les affûts mêmes sont devenus des pièces d'horlogerie.[82]

Statements like his could easily be found in the writings of British officers. What had no equivalent in the Royal Navy, however, was the extent to which French naval officers were equipped at the *Borda* to think about the naval problems of the day, to express these ideas on paper, and encouraged to submit their memoranda to those above them by the comparative weakness of hierarchical weight and by the need to accumulate merit in a rigorously competitive system of promotion. One of the great surprises for the researcher who turns from the Admiralty records of the mid-nineteenth century to those of the Ministry of Marine is the way that so many mere *lieutenants de vaisseau* were moved to submit their ideas about the important naval issues of their day. That one occasionally finds the same kind of thing in Britain is beside the point, as is the existence of nostalgia for the past in both navies:

[82] Letter to the Minister of Marine, 29 Apr. 1868, AN BB4 1818 (*marine*), 6–9. See also his art., 'La Marine d'aujourd'hui: première partie, la flotte de la mer Noire', *Revue des deux mondes*, 4 (1871), 303.

what matters is that there was relatively greater intellectual assert-
iveness amongst French officers.[83]

The difference is well summed up by the character and career
of the son of Alexandre Bouët, the Mayor of Lambézellec. He
changed his name in 1844 when adopted by the naval veteran
comte Willaumez. Louis-Edouard, comte Bouët-Willaumez was
perhaps the most forceful French naval officer of his day. He had
his detractors, with what one of them—Ernest Souville—described
as his 'air tapageur, son intempérance de parole, son charlatanism':
he was allegedly 'un Breton non pas bretonnant mais gasconnant'.[84]
But he had a keen eye for coming changes in naval warfare, and
had friends in powerful positions—above all, Chasseloup-Laubat.
To an English officer of the last century, of course, he would have
looked even more insufferable than he did to Souville; he was
hardly a paragon of the English gentleman and officer. For
instance, he was far more overt than Lyons in drawing parallels
between himself and Nelson. Perhaps he was not too far wrong.
Nelson, after all, with his patent vanity, his extreme sensitivity, and
acceptance of the unconventional, was himself hardly a typical
representative of either the RN executive officer or of his nation.
But he, one notes, had come to great prominence during a war,
when the ordinary rules of behaviour could be side-stepped. Bouët-
Willaumez rose during peacetime. Clearly, things were ordered
somewhat differently in France. There might have been much
common ground between British and French naval officers during
our period, but it does seem that the latter tolerated a rather
stronger current of ideas and of individuality (as against mere
personal eccentricity). The French navy's superior skill in innovation must have owed something to this difference. Obviously,
this does not explain everything, however. For example, what went
wrong in France during the 1840s? We still have to look at the
naval engineering corps. And there are still the higher levels of
naval organization in the two countries, including the dockyards,
and, above all, the men and boards that reigned over the rival
forces: it was here that the decisions were made about which ideas
would be accepted and which rejected.

[83] On the weight of hierarchy at least at a later date in the Royal Navy there is a
characteristically forceful article by Sir Herbert Richmond, 'The Service Mind', in
The Nineteenth Century and After, 113 (Jan. 1933), 90–7.
[84] *Mes souvenirs maritimes*, 444.

6

Dockyards and Naval Architects

I

War is the decisive test of military organizations, and the Crimean War showed up well certain deficiencies in the government dockyards in Britain and France.

With respect to the royal dockyards, the war with Russia had demonstrated one fundamental difficulty—that of distribution. Whilst Deptford, Woolwich, Sheerness, Chatham, Portsmouth, Devonport, and Pembroke were admirably suited for a war with France, this was not so when Russia was the enemy. There was a proposal in 1855 that a dockyard should be built on the east coast of Scotland, to serve as a Baltic base should one again prove necessary. But it was turned down on the grounds of cost, and also because sufficient shipwrights could not be recruited to man the existing yards.[1] The policy-makers were surely later confirmed in their view by the fact that, the war with Russia past, France rapidly returned to her honoured place as the most likely enemy.

Given this return to normality, the main Admiralty worry about the yards after the war was their inadequacy in face of the growing demands made by steam. Wartime experience not only suggested there was an urgent need to prepare the yards against attack by steam forces. The strain of mobilizing so many steamers for the war effort, plus the added steam construction brought about by the conflict, also made very clear that great efforts were needed to modernize the country's facilities to cope with the new fleets. Large efforts had been made during the 1840s; most yards had been given their own steam factories, and at Devonport the Keyham docks, basin, and factories had been developed. But by the following decade technology had become even more exigent; new types of

---

[1] Wood to Palmerston, 17 Nov. 1855, Broadlands Papers, GC.WO. 28–65. Reply of 5 Dec., Palmerston Papers, BM Add. MS 48579, fo. 87.

warship appeared before the yards were equipped to deal with them. The most serious problem—that is, the one that took the most money and time to solve—concerned the docks. Each new screw-steamer seemed to be longer than its predecessor, necessitating ever longer docks. Furthermore, their glands around the screw-shafts required regular inspection, so docking had to be more frequent than in the case of sailing- or paddle-vessels. The royal dockyards had thirty-three docks complete or under construction in 1861, but most of them were comparatively small, and work on the construction and repair of screws was impeded. In 1859, for instance, the Surveyor found himself severely constrained in his plans for the conversion of the frigates *Sutlej* at Portsmouth, *Phoebe* at Devonport, and *Phaeton* at Sheerness: they could not be lengthened sufficiently to take larger engines because the only docks available for the work were too short.[2] Even more demanding than wooden screw-vessels were the large iron-hulled ironclads. At the time the *Warrior* was completing for sea in 1861, there were only two docks in all the royal yards that could accommodate her, and even then only at certain states of the tide.[3]

Docks were only part of the problem facing the Admiralty in the late 1850s. It was realized that the yards were also short of sufficient wharfage and deep-water basins, with apparently serious implications for the mobilization of the fleet. Moreover, most of the yards were bedevilled by shoal water.

An exception can be made for Devonport—as Plymouth yard had been renamed in 1853. It enjoyed comparatively deep-water channels, and was well equipped for the fitting out of all classes of warships. Much was owed, here, to the Keyham extension. As the steam navy had grown, so had Keyham. Begun in 1844, designed to cost £400,000, by 1849 the plan had been greatly extended, at triple the cost; and ten years later further improvement was under way. However, the other yards were not so well endowed, either by Nature or the Exchequer. The two small Thames yards, Deptford and Woolwich, suffered particularly from inadequate depth of water. Woolwich had been the first British yard to have a steam factory (1838), but could fit out and repair only vessels of light draught. Deptford, further up river, was useless even for that. Both

---

[2] Walker to Board of Admiralty, 20 May 1858, ADM 1 5698, pt. 1; and 3 Mar. 1859, ADM 1 5799.

[3] PP (1862), xxxiv, Graving Docks, 505–7.

could be used as building yards, though newly completed ships had to be floated down river to be fitted out at one of the deeper-water establishments. Chatham, on the Medway, was in one way well suited to that task, but—at least before the large dredging operations of the 1860s—had no deep channels, and large vessels could not be fitted out. It was a good building yard, but seagoing warships with their machinery on board, or with guns and full coal-bunkers, could not get within four miles of the quays except at high water. Pembroke was the same, both in respect of shoal water and being good only as a building yard.

One yard that had excellent deep-water channels was Sheerness, but it had impediments all of its own. It was built on a lee shore, exposed as was no other royal dockyard to high seas and storms —and also naval bombardment. Bad weather at times cut off all communications between the yard and the ships in harbour. Moreover, for several days during each spring tide the basins could not be opened to allow vessels in or out. Despite the deep water, therefore, the Admiralty had been reluctant to keep this yard up-to-date in terms of steam. A steam factory was built, but the five docks were not made fit to cope with the steam battlefleet: a first-rate screw-battleship could not be docked anywhere in the yard, and two of the docks were not capable of accommodating even sailing-ships of the line.

The remaining yard, Portsmouth, was second only to Devonport (including Keyham) in size and development. In the late 1840s a steam basin had been opened, and by the end of the next decade the steam factory accompanying it had also been completed. Unfortunately, here too shoal water was a curse. Constant dredging made it possible for large warships to pass the bar and enter the dockyard harbour; even so, they could not go in or out if they had all their coals, guns, and stores on board. Warships had to be finally fitted out in the roadstead of Spithead which was a dangerous proceeding if, as the Royal Commission on dockyard defences believed, the means of protection available in the 1850s were insufficient to prevent a determined enemy from penetrating to Spithead.[4]

---

[4] Surveyor's report on the dockyards, 20 May 1858, ADM 1 5698, pt. 1. Letter of W. F. Martin, when Admiral Superintendent at Portsmouth Dockyard, Jan. 1855, W. F. Martin Papers, BM Add. MS 41434, fos. 69–70. For Keyham, see PP (1865), xxxv, pt. 1, 598.

The conclusion of a parliamentary select committee of 1861 was 'that the facilities for fitting out ships of war, rapidly and safely, possessed by other powers, are incomparably superior to those afforded by the naval establishments of this country'.[5] Already, during the late 1850s, expenditure on improvements within the dockyards had climbed notably. The 1859 estimates alone included half a million pounds for the purpose, twice the 1852 figure. The list of new works was impressive, including the lengthening of ten building slips, to give a total of nineteen capable of taking first-rates; and more docks were to be brought up to first-class standards so that nine, instead of four, would be capable of taking any vessel (though this was before the *Warrior* set new standards). Of course, dredging had a high priority. This was the most rapid means of improving dockyard capabilities, as is well illustrated by what became possible at Portsmouth once 5 feet was scraped from the harbour bar, giving 30 feet of water at high spring tides. On 11 July 1861 the yard was able to send the great *Marlborough* from the harbour with all her guns on board. But since 'other powers'—yet another soubriquet for France—had apparently maintained a lead, it was accepted in Whitehall that much more had to be done. Thus, by 1869, Keyham had been extended yet further, and both Chatham and Portsmouth had gained large new basins, docks, and factories.

Admittedly, there had been some contraction as well. By the end of the 1860s the Treasury was clawing back a little of the ground lost during the earlier naval race: funds became tight, plea bargaining by the Admiralty was now the rule. In exchange for more money to keep up the cruiser fleet, it was agreed that Woolwich and Deptford would be closed down in 1869. Yet this loss did not alter the trend towards greater development of the royal yards. It did not even reduce the importance of the Thames and Medway as a centre of naval power. Woolwich and Deptford were small, cramped yards, covering under 90 acres together. Their loss was more than compensated for by the enormous extension of Chatham. In 1860 this yard covered only some 80 acres, with no basin and only four docks. But then the neighbouring St Mary's Island was annexed and drained, adding 335 acres, on which it was decided to build five first-class docks, nearly sixty acres of basins

[5] PP (1861), xiii, 'Report from the Select Committee on Chatham Dockyard Extension', 3.

(over three times the area of Keyham's basin), and various storehouses and manufactures. To enable the largest warships to approach the yard when fully laden, a 600 ft. wide channel was dredged in the Medway, with a mean depth of 27 feet at half tides. The Medway was still a long and winding means of reaching the sea, but steam, it was said, meant that the river presented no real obstacle to navigation. Indeed, distance from the sea then appeared to be a positive asset; the further inland the yard, the easier was defence from naval attack. The extension of Chatham, it is apparent, was a twofold recognition of the arrival of steam naval warfare. The new facilities were approved since they seemed to be a necessary support to an efficient and large steam fleet; and they were given to Chatham in such plenitude largely because of its relative security from the kind of naval attacks on land targets that were an obsession of the naval strategists of the day.[6]

Surveying all the royal yards, it is clear that, at least before the great improvements beginning from the late 1850s, there were some obvious and serious weaknesses. However, was the 1861 select committee correct to believe that 'other powers' had 'incomparably superior' resources? We have to turn to the French yards, and here we are in the strong position of being able to draw on a series of internal reports dating from the late 1850s, drawn up by an authoritative source. That source is M. Reibell, who between 1838 and 1854 was responsible for the work of completing the great mole at Cherbourg, and in 1856 was appointed *inspecteur général des travaux maritimes*, after which he toured around the country's naval arsenals, reporting copiously and knowledgeably.[7]

[6] PP (1861), xiii. 1–26. PP (1864), viii. 72–3. PP (1865), xxv, pt. 1, 597–611. Philip Banbury, *Shipbuilders of the Thames and Medway* (Newton Abbot, 1971), 72–107.

[7] On Cherbourg, Jan. 1858, AN DD2 1120 (*marine*); on Brest, Feb. 1858, DD2 1121 (*marine*); on Lorient and Indret, Oct. 1857, DD2 1122 (*marine*); on Rochefort and La Chaussard, Apr. 1858 and Dec. 1855, DD2 1123 (*marine*). To supplement these early Reibell reports, there is the series of articles in the *Revue maritime et coloniale* on the yards and supporting works: a general one by A. Doneaud, 29 (1870), 74–114; J.-M.-Y. Calvé on Toulon, 15 (1865), 453–90, 801–19; E. Eymin and E. Doneaud on Brest, 17 (1866), 225–61, 477–506; J. Hébert on Lorient, 18 (1866), 5–72, 346–81; M.-E. Bouchet on Rochefort, 19 (1867), 325–57, 633–60; F.-F. de Bon on Cherbourg, 19 (1867), 769–834, and 20 (1867), 89–122; J.-A. Babron and J. Turgan on Indret, 23 (1868), 123–43, and 24 (1868), 494–526; C. Corbier and De Champs on La Chaussard, 25 (1868), 257–92, 709–20; and Lescot on Ruelle, 28 (1870), 477–524, and 29 (1870), 132–65.

His reports, added to what we know otherwise, show that the French navy made serious efforts during the 1850s to adapt the yards to the needs and purposes of a steam navy, at a time when the Royal Navy was generally reluctant to embark on any new, large projects in the yards. Hardly had the Second Empire been established when it took up a proposal long discussed and argued over during Orleanist times, though never undertaken. This concerned a new complex at Castigneau, just to the west of the Toulon yard. During the hectic ministry of Ducos, work commenced there on a new basin, a large steam factory, and three first-class docks—one of them capable of taking a first- and a second-rate at the same time. The whole scheme was completed in 1865, though expansion at Toulon continued, since four years previously work had begun alongside Castigneau on an even larger basin and series of docks at Missiessy, with completion planned for 1870–1. Nor was this the limit of the nurturing of the bases of the French Mediterranean fleet. Approval was given in the 1850s to a modest development of the yard at Algiers. Moreover, facilities at Port Vendres, close to the Spanish border, were improved to render the harbour more suitable as one end of a regular steam-packet service between Algeria and the metropolitan country.

Whilst the needs of the *Levant* fleet were being seen to, those of the *Ponant* fleet were hardly being ignored. Rochefort was given a new long dock, as was Lorient. The latter also had a dock extended and—to reinforce her position of being, with Toulon, one of the two main centres of French warship construction—gained some new building slips. Brest, the chief Atlantic arsenal, saw some large works; the most impressive was an excavation at Salou, just up the river from the arsenal, where many tons of schist were blasted away in the process of creating an enormous double dock. The largest of all the new works, however, were at Cherbourg. Behind the slowly lengthening mole, a set of basins and docks were created on a very large scale by the various regimes after 1815. Napoleon III devoted great sums to the completion of the works, seeing another case where he could bring to a triumphant conclusion a scheme commenced by his uncle. As it happens, the idea of a vast artificial harbour at Cherbourg, sheltering a first-class naval arsenal, had not originated with Napoleon I. The Bourbons had wasted millions of *livres* on a scheme for a Cherbourg breakwater before the

Revolution. But Napoleon I at least put the plans on a sounder footing (albeit himself wasting millions in the process), and his nephew had the pleasure of seeing both the mole and the outer basin finished in their essentials. In August 1858 he personally opened the *arrière-bassin*, which thus became the *bassin Napoléon III*. The occasion was made into a spectacular affirmation of French naval power. The *escadre d'évolutions* broke off its steam trials to come round from the Mediterranean to grace the event, with the flagship *Bretagne* the scene of a grand celebratory banquet.[8] Slightly discordantly, perhaps, the event was used to try to repair the Crimean *entente*. A British squadron crossed the Channel to take part in the opening, bringing two illustrious guests, Queen Victoria and Prince Albert. Victoria, like many of the other Britons present, found the occasion enjoyable but uncomfortably pointed. Remembering the so-recent naval scare, the magnificent fitting-out and docking facilities at Cherbourg appeared very threatening. France now had a first-class dockyard in the Channel, to British observers a finely tooled weapon directed at their country's jugular.

As Reibell was only too aware though, behind the superb façade of power and preparation at Cherbourg, much remained to be done at the other yards. He noted particularly in his reports the way that many of the workshops and factories were still housed in wooden buildings: he remembered too well the expensive conflagration at Toulon in August 1845 to feel over-sanguine about dockyard fire hazards. (Indeed, there was to be an especially destructive fire in the large cooperage works at Brest in 1866.) Moreover, however well-suited yards had been to the needs of sailing fleets, there were often serious difficulties in converting them to a steam navy. Take the example of Brest. The blasting at Salou was but part of the heroic efforts needed to extend the yard. The arsenal had grown up along the steep and rocky banks of the River Penfeld, and to find space for a steam factory the engineers were forced, between 1841 and 1845, to build on top of the Plateau des Capucins—no less than 70 feet above the quays. Communication was made possible by an ingenious system of lifts and inclines, but was still somewhat troublesome.

Admittedly, Brest was somewhat exceptional: most of the other

[8] The menu is shown in AN BB4 758 (*marine*), fo. 132.

French naval arsenals had been built on open, deltaic sites. With its hard rocky perches and turbulent grey skies, Brest contrasted vividly with its great rival, the warmer and more spacious port of Toulon. But all the old-established yards shared certain drawbacks; most notably, as with the British yards, their depth of water was often insufficient for the latest large screw-warships. Dredging was undertaken with great energy in all the French yards during the 1850s, part of the large improvement programme of the time, but this could be only a partial solution. It made much possible, but affected only marginally the basic geography of a port, as is shown in the case of one arsenal the Ministry of Marine felt it had special cause to favour—Rochefort. It was set 26 kilometres up the winding, shoaling Charente, and could not receive or despatch fully laden first-rates in any state of the tide. The larger warships had to be sent to fit out down river. Dredging could alleviate this problem, but there were other difficulties as well. The Charente was not only tortuous, it was also crowded with commercial traffic. Then there was an impediment to extending the yard, the reverse of the one at Brest. There was no mountain of schist in this case, but the yard lay on heavy alluvial mud, which made it expensive to put down foundations. Finally, the port was salubrious for neither man nor ship; termites attacked a good third of the vessels on the stocks, and malaria attacked the people—though new drainage schemes meant that by the mid-century this last problem was not as serious as it had been. In partial compensation, Rochefort—like Chatham, with which it was often compared—was comparatively secure from sea-borne attack, a highly regarded advantage after Sweaborg. There was only one weak defensive point: the arsenal was safe, but the warships it despatched to fit out, did so at the Île d'Aix, a much more exposed position where the English had destroyed several battleships in 1809.

This survey of the British and French naval arsenals, as so often in our comparison of the two navies, seems to suggest lines of similarity rather than of difference. This is only to be expected: the yards had the same essential function, and both navies were facing the same problems in adapting existing organizations to meet technological change. But why, then, should certain Britons, notably the men on the 1861 select committee, have seen a stark difference? One thing that must have influenced them was a variation in the timing of dockyard development. The British yards, though tending to lead in improvements in the 1840s, fell back relatively in the next decade. Only after 1861 was lost ground made up. Two other factors have to be considered. One of them was the assumption by mid-nineteenth-century strategists that the only dockyard facilities worthy of serious consideration were those well-protected from attack. The 1861 committee was very conscious that while the French yards were fortified (even if not always to the latest standards), the British ones had not yet begun to benefit from the Royal Commission on dockyard defences of 1859–60. The second factor was that British opinion tended to judge French yards by the standards of the one closest to the South Coast, opened with such panache in 1858. The similarities between long-established dockyards, whether in France or in Britain, were often overlooked.

Certainly, if one compares the available facilities on the two sides, even at the point most disadvantageous to Britain (around 1860) one is not struck by any significant French superiority. The French yards had rather more building slips and larger basins, but the British ones had more docks (thirty-three complete or under construction in 1861, as against a French total of twenty-six, although the latter tended to be newer and longer). In terms of dockyard stores, the French had a large lead in timber for construction, twice or even three times the British level; this was due to the relatively well-stocked French forests, and the country's closeness to the valuable hard oak supplies of Italy.[9] This abundance was exceptional. One French writer boasted in 1872 of the richness of his country's naval supplies; of the 382 separate types of nail, the 280 types of screw, and the total of 28,000 different categories of goods kept in the dockyard store-rooms.[10] Of course, such variety was common to all large navies. Moreover, in comparison with the British yards, the French ones were relatively poorly stocked in terms of depth, with the exception of timber. The Ministry of Marine had a comparatively shallow purse; an emergency could swiftly drain stocks, and replenishment would be slow. According to Henri Garreau, *commissaire de l'escadre* for the Baltic fleet of 1870,

---

[9] R. G. Albion, *Forests and Sea Power: The Timber Problem of the Royal Navy 1652–1862* (Harvard University Press, 1926), 405–6.

[10] L. Bouchard, 'Le Contrôle des arsenaux de la guerre et de la marine', *Revue des deux mondes*, 97 (Feb. 1872), 678–93.

the navy was still suffering from shortages caused by the Mexican expedition of 1863–7.[11]

One might have more sympathy with the arguments of the 1861 committee had a slightly different point been emphasized: that the royal dockyards compared badly with French ones because the Royal Navy required far higher standards of dockyard facilities than did its rival. Relevant here is the nature of the warships in the two fleets. British screw-liners were of the same general dimensions as French ones of the same rate and horsepower; but the Admiralty ordered more first-rates than did the Ministry of Marine, which meant a larger demand for the few available first-class docks. With the ironclads, there was an even greater divergence between the two fleets. The French ironclads of the 1858–60 programmes were little larger than first-rate screw-liners, but their first British equivalents were enormous in comparison. The *Warrior* and *Black Prince* were well over 100 feet longer than the *Victoria* or *Marlborough*, themselves mighty examples of their type. Admittedly, some British ironclads were on the scale of their French contemporaries, and there was an increasing interest shown in 'tubbier' ironclads from the early 1860s onwards, but the *Warrior* and her sister were scarcely alone in demanding extremely lengthy docks: the *Achilles*, *Minotaur*, *Agincourt*, and *Northumberland*, all laid down in 1861, were even more demanding. Moreover, there was the fact that most British ironclads, whatever their length, had iron hulls, so they required frequent docking which was another strain on the yards' facilities. With its fleet of medium-sized, largely wooden-hulled ironclads, the French navy was far less exacting.

The Royal Navy also needed superior dockyard facilities because it had a larger fleet to mobilize and support in case of a first-class maritime war, and greater, more widespread responsibilities. At least with regard to dockyards outside the British Isles there was an obvious superiority over France. Even after the seizure of a large colony in Indo-China, the French Empire overseas remained comparatively modest, possessing few good ports or naval depots. In contrast, the Royal Navy had the ports of a global empire to depend upon, including a number of imperial establishments. There were small dockyards at Gibraltar, Malta, Halifax, Bermuda, Jamaica, the Cape of Good Hope, Trincomalee, Singapore, and Hong Kong. Victualling yards existed at Malta, Halifax, Jamaica, Ascension, Sierra Leone, the Cape, Sydney, Barbados, Auckland, and Esquimalt. Furthermore, there was a store-ship based at Callão, in Chile. At Malta, Bermuda, Jamaica, the Cape, and Hong Kong there were also naval hospitals.[12]

Obviously, however, the home dockyards were the crucial government naval facilities, and it was hardly unreasonable to suggest that there was a striking inadequacy there—even leaving out of consideration the question of whether or not they were under threat from bombardment or other types of assault, remembering that they had to bear the full weight of war—preparing the entire fleet for sea, supplying and repairing it, and supporting an appropriate construction programme. The dockyard delays during the 1858 scare would confirm this impression. The French naval arsenals, given the smaller size of the French fleet, were not similarly open to criticism; they were more in scale with the force they were supposed to maintain. Admittedly, come the 1860s, the Admiralty set under way some large dockyard extensions, above all at Chatham. Nevertheless, one may conclude that even at the end of our period, and all the more so earlier, the royal dockyards were less capable than the French state yards of bearing the full weight of servicing their country's naval forces.

It might be thought that we have isolated an important difference between the military effectiveness of the two navies, but the picture is incomplete. The 1861 committee may have been right to think that the royal dockyards on their own were inadequate to support British naval pretensions, but there were other supports which the Royal Navy could draw on in time of need. We must not ignore the private sector, vital to the Franco-British naval equation.

We have seen that French and British government yards had much in common. Indeed, some of them were easily 'twinned'. Apart from the obvious Chatham and Rochefort pairing, one could mention Lorient and Pembroke: each had but one dock (for a time); both had troubles with shallow water in the harbour; and both were on Celtic soil. But British and French *private* yards and port facilities were not amenable to such an analogy

[12] A. C. Ewald, *The Complete Guide to the Civil Service* (11th edn., London, 1869).

game. Where, one might ask, were the equivalents in France to the vast improvements being made during our period at London, Liverpool, and the other thriving commercial ports in the UK?

Certainly, there were some significant port developments on the French side. New commercial docks were built at Marseilles. Also, one has to consider St Nazaire at the mouth of the Loire. One basin was begun there in 1845. It became popular (*inter alia* the port was at one end of the packet-boat service with Brazil), and by 1860 consideration was being given to building a second. In the case of both these ports, the Ministry of Marine fully realized the relevance of the improvements to a naval war. Indeed, the navy had an important part in encouraging the new Marseilles dock, and it was seen that St Nazaire in particular could be the centre of bold enterprises against the English. For instance, though soon to become of secondary importance due to the advance of steam, one of the arguments used in favour of the port's first basin was that, because of rocks and prevailing winds, the Royal Navy's warships (sailing-vessels were meant, of course), would not be able to blockade St Nazaire as they had so often blockaded Brest and Lorient.[13] Nor did improvements take place at only these two ports: other French commercial ports also advanced greatly during the mid-century period. Nevertheless, the Ministry of Marine could not hope to benefit as much from the private sector in time of war as the Admiralty could. A state with barely a million net tons of steam- and sail-merchantmen (in 1860) could have nothing like the port infrastructure of an empire that had nearly six million. In addition, the British had more private shipyards, marine engineering works, and a generally more advanced and extensive manufacturing base. This was of obvious importance to the balance of naval power, especially once the decision was taken to convert the war-fleet to steam, and even more so when iron warships were accepted. The first industrial nation had an enormous advantage in a naval rivalry based on steam and iron. Apart from anything else, these naval resources were a vast potential naval reserve that would have compensated for any shortcoming that might have existed in the royal dockyards in the event of a first-class naval war. In the mid-nineteenth century, Britain's naval superiority over France lay ultimately in the depth and breadth of her industrial and commercial economy.

[13] Notes and Plans of 1846 and 1860 on the port, AN DD2 790 (*marine*).

II

The strident mid-nineteenth-century critics of the royal dockyards tended to be good, bourgeois liberals, and they would have found pitifully inadequate the praise of the private sector that ended the last section. It had long been an article of faith with many Whigs, at least since the time of Lord St Vincent's brave but unsuccessful attempt to purge naval corruption, that the royal yards were inefficient and even corrupt.[14] The liberal economists of the nineteenth century added to the prejudice. They judged all government-run industry to be inefficient by its very nature, and the royal dockyards were the largest of all government industries. The Crimean War confirmed this belief. The great administrative confusion in the supply and succour of the British troops in the Crimea proved to many the almost wilful incompetence of government, and its lack of the middle class's self-proclaimed virtues of drive, judgement, and economy. If the Horse Guards at first bore the brunt of suspicion and demands for reform, the Admiralty itself was soon under attack. In the late 1850s and early 1860s, spurred on by the uncertainty and confusion of Admiralty shipbuilding policy and the undeniable success of the French navy, increasing doubts were being voiced not only about the direction of the navy at Whitehall but also about the dockyards.

Naturally enough, Cobden's *The Three Panics* (1862) was in part concerned with 'dockyard profligacy', but the most energetic of the tilters at the yards was a journalist, P. Barry who, in a pamphlet and two books in 1863–4, tirelessly repeated himself about the sins of government industry and the virtues of the British private dockyards. The major reason for French naval success, he argued, was that the Ministry of Marine had not burdened their own establishments with great factories and enormous, expensive stocks of all kinds of naval stores. Rather, he said, it had looked to the country's private yards and engineering works to provide as much of their production as was suited to the naval service—at a lower cost than the navy could produce for itself—also obtaining general naval stores on the free market, largely as and when required. He believed the Admiralty ought to follow this excellent example, even as far as relying on private yards to build and repair the nation's

[14] Roger Morriss, *The Royal Dockyards during the Revolutionary and Napoleonic Wars* (Leicester University Press, 1983), 193–9.

warships. Only trust to the ideas and capacity of private enterprise, he concluded, and Britain's naval supremacy would be assured, and at the lowest possible cost.[15]

There was a great deal that was absurd or ill-considered in Barry's scheme. He ignored the fact that British private ship-builders had shown themselves fully capable of producing shoddy goods. A large number of the gunboats ordered under contract for the wartime construction programme suffered from hasty and mediocre workmanship. The royal yards might have taken longer to complete their share of the programme and spent more money per ton of ship in doing so, but the standard of finish was excellent. In war, as in peace, the quality of dockyard workmanship was high. Moreover, a large number of the contract gunboats suffered from the fundamental handicap of being constructed from inadequately seasoned or even green wood. Here, too, the royal yards were superior, being able to draw on their stocks of seasoned building timber. The private yards, either because they built mostly in iron, or because they were short of capital, did not keep similar reserves. The implication of Barry's writings was that the free market could supply any naval store at will, but this was certainly wrong, at least with regard to good timber. As we saw earlier, British timber requirements in peacetime could only just be met, and war brought a decided shortage. The state yards could spare none of their own stocks, so the private builder had to have recourse to inferior supplies. This well-illustrates something that Barry never seems to have realized. Perhaps some of the dockyard stores were unnecessary, or even obsolete—and reductions were to be made in the economy drive at the end of the 1860s, apparently without serious consequences—but at least some of the 'fat' in the dockyard store-rooms was merely a prudent reserve.

Barry was on somewhat firmer ground when he accused the dockyards of inefficient administration. A fine example dates from just after the Crimean War, with the Admiralty uncertain about the state of work in progress on the battlefleet. At this time the dock-yards were crammed with work. Naturally, efforts were concentrated on the repair, fitting, and maintenance of screw-vessels that had seen extensive service, and on coping with the damage and general

[15] P. Barry, *The Dockyards and the Private Shipyards of the Kingdom* (London, 1863); *Dockyard Economy and Naval Power* (1863); and *The Dockyards, Shipyards and Marine of France* (1864).

wear and tear resulting from demanding wartime operations in hostile seas. Little time was left to inspect, let alone repair, vessels built during the war that had seen little service, or had never been completed; above all, the numerous gunboats of the wartime programme drawn up in reserve at Haslar, at Portsmouth, were largely ignored. Perhaps more critically, however, construction suffered as well as repairs. In 1858 Sir Baldwin Walker cited the examples of the *Royal Frederick* (later *Frederick William*) and the *Lion*. The conversion of these sail of the line to the screw had been authorized in 1856, but two years later only one of them had even begun to be taken in hand.[16] Such slowness in construction would not have mattered so much had Whitehall known the extent to which it was happening. Unfortunately, the lack of sufficient dockyard capacity to deal with repair and construction work was compounded by administrative confusion. Thus it was with a note of genuine surprise that the Admiralty discovered in early 1858 that the British battlefleet (leaving aside the blockships) was hardly larger than the French one.

Part of the confusion was at the Admiralty, thanks primarily to too much attention being devoted in the years after the war to mere problems of demobilization. But it is also true that the information received from the dockyards about the progress of work was at times quite misleading. For instance, there was the bad practice of what was called 'reserving a margin', brought to the attention of the Board in 1858 by the captain of the guardship of the Steam Ordinary at Sheerness. He showed that the master shipwright of the yard had been guilty of making returns about work completed that were, if not absolutely mendacious, then at least somewhat premature. For instance, on 21 May he had said that the work on the *Terrible* was finished, but on that date fifteen shipwrights and five joiners were still engaged on the vessel. The First Naval Lord agreed that the practice was unacceptable, and despite the master shipwright concerned saying that the margin had the sanction of authority—by which he perhaps meant it was a traditional abuse—the Board insisted that in future 'complete' should be held to mean precisely that.[17]

Other improvements were also made. To speed future

[16] Submission to the Board, 27 July 1858, ADM 1 5705.
[17] Halsted to Martin, 25 May and 2 June 1858, and reply of 29 May: W. F. Martin Papers, BM Add. MS 41435, fos. 93–6, 102–3, 108–10.

mobilizations, a greater check was kept on dockyard stores; those that were depleted were filled, and the rate of work on vessels in Ordinary was increased.[18] Nevertheless, fundamental problems remained with British dockyard administration, as was asserted by a parliamentary commission appointed in August 1860 to inquire into dockyard control and management—itself a manifestation of the degree of unease that existed about the yards. The finding was that there was inefficiency, reaching up to the Board of Admiralty itself. It was said that there had long been a lack of unified control of the yards, inadequately defined responsibility, ill-organized subordinate departments, and consequent duplicated effort and waste.[19]

As it happened, the Admiralty was trying to tackle at least some of these problems even before the commission met. At the beginning of 1860 the Surveyor was given greater powers over the yards, together with the new title of Controller of the Navy. Henceforward, this officer was to exercise the single authority that had up to then been absent, and his importance was further enhanced in 1869 with a seat on the Board of Admiralty.

The lines of responsibility leading from the yards to the Board were therefore made clearer, but other administrative deficiencies that the commission had pointed out remained, above all in accounting. One complaint was that no sufficiently full and accurate records were kept in the yards, so that it was difficult to discover just what was produced with the public's money. Commonly, important information was not put down on paper, or it was noted in a confusing way. At times, furthermore, as with the shipwrights' 'margin', there was error in what was written down. The commission discovered particularly serious accounting errors at Woolwich, one of which —and it is difficult to see this as an accident—made it appear that the royal yards could manufacture and build more cheaply than could their private rivals. It was not until the late 1860s that accounting methods were somewhat improved, and even then there was no simple way of discovering what the real cost was of building in the dockyards. As Ashworth has shown, only in the 1880s were there significant improvements in dockyard accounting.[20]

[18] Captain Spencer Robinson to W. F. Martin, 10 Sept. 1858 and 13 Feb. 1860, W. F. Martin Papers, BM Add. MS 41409, fos. 78–9, and 41411, fos. 1–2.
[19] PP (1861), xxvi. 5–13.
[20] W. Ashworth, 'Economic Aspects of Late Victorian Naval Administration', *Economic History Review*, 22 (1969), 491–505.

With regard to the government yards in France, it is interesting to see that, there too, serious doubts were expressed in their efficiency, in the belief that no state enterprise could be wholesome. There seems, indeed, to have been something of a bourgeois liberal international. The attacks reached a crescendo in France during the *Enquête parlementaire* of 1849–51, when the committee members approved the suggestion that the state steam factory at Indret should be closed down, and the navy should rely for its steam-engines exclusively on private enterprise. Perhaps only the sweeping away of the inquiry by Louis-Napoleon's *coup d'état* prevented the proposal being carried out.

In France, too, there was some substance in the attacks. Accounting techniques were hardly more adequate there than in Britain. We have the testimony of Henri Garreau that in the 1870 Baltic fleet the procedures for supplying vessels were complicated and expensive, and that it was impossible to be sure what had been done, or who was responsible.[21] Moreover, general administrative inefficiency was scarcely unknown in the French service either, even if after 1845 it does not appear to have descended again to the level of the corruption discovered in that year at Rochefort.[22]

One further parallel is that the Ministry of Marine was hardly more satisfied with the organization of its yards than the Admiralty was with its own, and regularly tinkered with the structures of control and costing. There was uncertainty in both countries about the best relationship between central and local control, something encouraged by the developing technology of the century. With the telegraph and the railway, the central administration had an increasing ability to supervise what was going on at the periphery, but despite the technology that made it possible, referral to the centre inevitably led to delays and, some argued, took decisions out of the hands of those best equipped to make them. No satisfactory compromise was found; perhaps one was never possible. Instead, dockyard administration oscillated between degrees of centralization and decentralization.

It might well seem that dockyard inefficiency and the attempts at reform were as universal as dry rot, or self-interest, or at least technical innovation, but this does not imply that once again we have

[21] Report to the Minister, Lamy Papers, AN 333 AP 44, dossier 1.

[22] C. Châtelain, 'Le Contrôle de l'administration de la marine', *Revue maritime et coloniale*, 156 (1903), 657–62.

to stress only the similarities between Britain and France. There are dissimilarities that can be brought out between the two countries' dockyards; ones, moreover, that are crucial to a proper understanding of Barry's argument. They concern first the size of the yards, and second the degree to which they depended on goods provided by the private sector. To Barry, of course, the French yards held the palm in both respects, since he presented them as being smaller and less self-sufficient. As we shall see, though, he was not entirely correct.

As far as size is concerned, it does seem to be true that the British yards were the larger, at least in some important respects. The matter of stores has been mentioned already. Moreover, the Royal Navy had more reserve warships to be maintained in the dockyard ordinaries. The French navy might have been close to catching up numerically in terms of the latest warship types by the late 1850s, but the rival had a large accumulation of obsolete and semi-obsolete vessels, the heritage of previous decades of naval superiority, and the royal yards had to preserve them. By 1859, whilst the French navy possessed only fourteen sail of the line and forty sailing-frigates, the comparative British figures were respectively forty-three and fifty-eight. The royal yards also had a relatively heavy maintenance burden in an advanced warship type — the screw-gunboat. The vast and unequalled fleet of British Crimean gunboats was mostly kept in reserve, primarily at Portsmouth, by Haslar naval hospital, where many gunboats were drawn up out of the water, sheltered by a series of sheds. The maintenance of reserve vessels, new and old, naturally required a large work-force. But so too did the needs of construction, and the royal yards built a greater tonnage of new vessels than did the French ones; though in the 1850s this showed itself not so much in ships of the line as in craft of lesser rates, the warships suitable for the myriad policing duties of empire or anti-slavery. It is not surprising to see that the Admiralty employed on average 40 per cent more workmen in government yards than did the Ministry of Marine (ignoring the workers in the steam factories).

This difference in size raises one possible point. If the British yards were so large, given the universally poor accounting techniques of the time, one might say that they had to be less efficient than the French ones. But we cannot be certain, especially remembering that the two yards so far mentioned unfavourably

—Woolwich and Rochefort—were amongst the smallest of all. Even if we were to be for once gracious to Barry, and to allow him this point, there is a far more serious one that most certainly does not favour him, and even seriously undercuts his whole approach. Yes, the British yards were larger, but with the surely vital exception of their steam manufactures. Barry's method of comparison between the two sides, it is not too strong to say, was to ignore in France what did not suit his arguments. Notably, he left aside the large number of men working in the French dockyard steam factories. For instance, he did not find it necessary even to mention the extensive works on the Plateau des Capucins at Brest. (Though perhaps they were too far above the quays for a rational observer to understand that they were part of the yard.) He also left out of the account the large state naval factories that were well beyond the dockyards. Quite properly, as he had not dealt with the ordnance factories on the other side of the Channel, he did not concern himself with the gun works at Ruelle, Nevers, and Saint-Gervais. But he certainly should have mentioned the complex at La Chaussard, originally purchased by the state in the late eighteenth century, which manufactured chains, anchors, and various other pieces of naval ironwork, including large forgings.[23] Moreover though he did note the existence of Indret, he briefly dismissed it in a way that is inexplicable except in terms of ignorance or bad faith. The factories there were large, employing a work-force that in the year 1855–6, the peak wartime construction time in Britain and France, equalled the number of men employed in all the steam factories in all the royal yards. (At the beginning of 1855, indeed, the Indret force was nearly twice the British total.[24])

The French state steam factories, inside and outside the yards, were not only larger than the British ones, in total work-force, but their function was different. True, much of their effort was devoted to repair work. But they also manufactured on a large scale. The British steam factories, on the other hand, did little manufacturing. There was no British equivalent to La Chaussard, for instance: most of the Royal Navy's iron goods came from the private ironmasters. Similarly, almost all the engines fitted in HM warships

---

[23] See the article by Corbier and De Champs, cited in n. 7; and Reibell's reports of 1855, 1857, and 1859, AN DD2 1123 (*marine*).
[24] *Revue maritime et coloniale*, 24 (1868), 511. PP (1859), xiv. 730.

during our period came from private manufacturers.[25] A high proportion of French warships, on the contrary, obtained their engines from the state factories. Take the example of the French screw-battlefleet, which ultimately comprised thirty-eight vessels. Just over half of them had engines built either at Indret or in the dockyard factories, the former providing just over two-thirds of the total. The French navy was thus *less* dependent on private enterprise than its rival was.

The difference was hardly the result of chance. The French navy manufactured so much because it could not rely on French private industry to produce the necessary goods to the sizes, tolerances, quality, and quantity demanded by the naval service. The only immediate alternative was to turn to *British* manufacturers, an obviously unpalatable and even imprudent step, though one that was regularly taken, even to the degree of ordering whole engines: at least three French screw-battleships had engines by Napier. In the long term, however, the Ministry hoped to be able to build up the French private sector, so as to avoid unnecessary heavy capital investment in the yards, and to widen the country's reserve of naval strength. In the 1850s, and all the more so during the great ironclad programme of the following decade, large orders for metal goods of all kinds were placed with home manufacturers; and these orders, very demanding in specifications, were a means of encouraging the private sector to improve its standards and to invest in the latest equipment. The Royal Navy was able to rely on the thriving British metal-manufacturing sector. The French navy saw naval construction, and a carefully gauged programme of orders to private industry, as a possible method of reducing France's industrial inferiority to its great rival.

The conclusion must be that Barry quite misunderstood the matter. There was no facile distinction between, in France, a conscious reliance on the superior excellence and economy of private manufacturers, and, in Britain, a capricious retention of necessarily wasteful state enterprise. It would be slightly more accurate to argue that the reverse was the case, but it would be even better simply to note that the balance between private and public naval manufacturing in each country was a function of the

[25] PP (1859), xv. 543–6. R. A. Buchanan and M. W. Doughty, 'The Choice of Steam Engine Manufacturers by the British Admiralty, 1822–1852', *Mariner's Mirror*, 64 (1978), 327–47.

development of the economy as a whole. That development was but one of the factors to be considered by the naval authorities in their planning. Virtue in naval policy-making was hardly just a matter of adherence to *laissez-faire* economics.

III

So far, our key words in studying the British and French dockyards have been *economy* and *efficiency*, but there are two other very pertinent ones—*ideas* and *innovation*. In respect to these, also, there were many who believed that private enterprise was superior. Barry, naturally, was one. And the famous civil engineer, Sir John Rennie, went so far as to argue that no great invention had ever come from the royal yards.[26]

Certainly, several famous names appear if one looks at the list of general engineers in the private sector in Britain who applied themselves successfully to the problems of naval engineering: the Maudslays, the Napiers, Penn, Fairbairn, and the two Rennies, George and John. Predominantly, they were important in the design of engines. But there are two more men to be added to this list, William Rankine and William Froude who, according to Sir William White, the greatest of the Directors of Naval Construction, were the investigators responsible above all others for the advancement of naval architecture in Britain after 1860.[27] Furthermore, one must note the way that the British private shipyards turned so enthusiastically to iron construction during the 1840s and 1850s. These yards—and, indeed, the extensive private engineering works —were invaluable repositories of skill and development in the working of metals, unequalled throughout the world. No wonder Dupuy de Lôme and his compatriot naval architects were such eager tourists.

In comparison, the royal yards, as described so far, appear far less stimulating places. One recalls in particular the plodding and costly empiricism that characterized the early days of the conversion

---

[26] Sir John Rennie, *Autobiography . . . comprising the History of his Professional Life, together with Reminiscences dating from the Commencement of the Century to the Present Time* (London, 1875), 289–90.

[27] William White, 'The Progress of Shipbuilding in England' (pub. anon.), *Westminster Review* (Jan. 1881), 23.

in the yards of sailing-warships to the screw. Almost certainly one fault was the inadequate training of government shipwrights. Just as (until 1857) the budding executive officer in Britain learned his trade by being thrown as a cadet on to a ship in commission, so the budding naval architect was thrown into the hurly-burly of a dockyard. This emphasis on a practical education is perhaps best demonstrated by the chequered careers of the government schools of naval architecture. One was set up at Portsmouth in 1811, with fine new buildings that had cost some £35,000. It did some valuable work, offering the students a good theoretical and mathematical grounding, and went at least some way towards counteracting the long-established French advantage in warship design. But it was abolished in 1832 by the First Lord, Sir James Graham, who did not think it worth the cost. The successful counter-attack by the scientific man against his practical cousin came only in 1848, when the School of Mathematics and Naval Construction was established, again at Portsmouth. This took young shipwrights from the dockyards, ones who had passed through four years of apprenticeship already and proved themselves suitable for advanced training. But in 1853 Sir James Graham returned to the Admiralty, and since he was a man who believed in consistency as well as strict economy, he abolished the new school.

It is also instructive to look at the man who for fifteen years was the Admiralty's chief naval architect, William Symonds, appointed Surveyor of the Navy in 1832. Under him were experienced shipwrights, notably John Edye, entrusted with the detailed calculations and drawings, but Symonds had the chief responsibility for warship design. Though he was a professional naval officer, he was only an amateur boat-builder, the 'practical man' *par excellence*, who had first established a reputation with a small yacht of his own design, the *Nancy Dawson*, which proved particularly fast under sail. As Surveyor, he gave all his designs, admittedly adapted somewhat from rate to rate, the same kind of peg-top hull section that had proved so suited to his pleasure craft. Like the *Nancy Dawson* they were fast; and there were many tributes to the beauty of their appearance. But they had important shortcomings as well. In certain seas their motion was very uneasy and, thanks to their not having the usual full lines below the water-line, had relatively poor stowage room.[28]

---

[28] D. K. Brown, *Before the Ironclad: Development of Ship Design, Propulsion and Armament in the Royal Navy, 1815–1860* (London, 1990), 38–43.

The last point was obviously unfortunate when conversion to steam was under way, creating added difficulties for the designers trying to squeeze in the engines, boilers, and coals.

The picture we have drawn so far of naval architecture in the Royal Navy seems a damning one, but there were redeeming features—indeed, far more than observers in private industry appear to have realized, or at least admitted. There was a tradition in the yards of respect for scientific standards that, whilst deficient in some ways, at least was well in advance of anything that could have been found in the overwhelming majority of private yards. The 1840s saw this tradition coming to the fore, sweeping away some of the excesses of the rule of thumb. From 1843 schools were set up in the yards which shipwright apprentices were compelled to attend when not otherwise engaged. They varied somewhat in quality. Devonport school was especially well regarded, in part because of its high standard of mathematics' tuition, in part because of the good preparatory schools near the yard which gave a better grounding than was available to candidates for apprenticeship living by any of the other ports. It is significant that of the sixteen shipwrights sent from the yards when a new central architecture school opened in 1864, four came from Devonport—one of whom was the young William White.[29]

Moreover, it was in the dockyards that there began the recovery that was to press Symonds, and much of what he stood for, into retirement. The second school of naval architecture had a brief life, but some dockyard men did graduate with a solid mathematical training, and they—with a few of their more prescient colleagues who had not been to the school—were the ones who led the attack against architectural amateurism. By 1842 a group of senior shipwrights, later called the Chatham Committee, was allowed by the Admiralty to design vessels on its own. This permission was in itself a serious reflection on the authority of the Surveyor, a damaging suggestion that the Admiralty now had some doubts about his principles. Even worse, from Symonds's point of view, was the creation in May 1846 of the Committee of Reference.[30] This short-lived body (it lasted two years at the most), was the nearest equivalent in the Royal Navy to the French *Conseil des travaux*.

[29] Frederic Manning, *The Life of Sir William White* (London, 1923), 9.
[30] Correspondence about the committee of naval architecture, ADM 7 577.

It consisted predominantly of master shipwrights from the yards (eventually including a member of the Chatham Committee): men who were thus in theory subordinate to the Surveyor, yet their committee was appointed to oversee his plans. This anomalous body was perhaps destructive of discipline, and it was certainly annoying to Symonds, who resigned in 1847. He was succeeded by Sir Baldwin Walker, who was himself not a trained naval architect, but in his case it was made clear that he was not to design the ships himself, merely to oversee the work of the architects set under him.

More was needed to establish rigorous standards, above all a new central school of naval architects. In 1848, as we saw, the second school was set up; only to be closed in 1853. As so often, however, fortune smiled on muddlers. The graduates of the first school gradually came to prominence during Symonds's period of office. One of the ablest was Isaac Watts, who eventually became Walker's chief assistant. Eventually, he and his fellow graduates had to retire, and as was confessed by the First Lord at about that time (1861) there was a great want of young, scientifically trained shipwright officers.[31] But at least the few graduates of the second school, including E. J. Reed and Nathaniel Barnaby, were by now mature, thus the navy had some talent to take the burden from the older generation. Willy-nilly, there was a certain continuity.

Clearly, though, the future was unprovided for, and by the early 1860s the pressure for the establishment of another school of naval architecture was becoming impossible to resist. The growing concern about standards of naval design expressed itself in 1860 in the creation of the Institute of Naval Architects, which itself became a lobby for improved educational standards. One of the members, John Scott Russell, was particularly active in this regard. His views were forcibly set out in a paper he delivered to the Institution in 1863. He described the sad fate of the two previous central schools, adding, albeit with a little exaggeration, that since 1853 the only refuge of learning for his profession was the room of ship models in Somerset House. Even this relatively poor storehouse of precedent had been virtually extinguished, he added, since it was now thrust down into a cellar. 'Thus in England', he went on, 'we have at the present moment professional science and

---

[31] PP (1861), v, Report of the Select Committee on the Board of Admiralty, 88.

education expelled from the navy and professional precedents and principles locked up in a cellar of Somerset House.'[32]

Such speeches, plus the acknowledged lack of sufficient trained shipwrights in the navy, plus, it seems possible, the influence of another of the Institute's members, Sir John Pakington, First Lord 1858–9, gave added weight to what was surely the central factor: the example of the French system of teaching naval architecture. In 1861, one finds Graham himself admitting, grudgingly to be sure, that he was not certain, if given the chance again, whether he would still abolish the school of naval architecture.[33] Finally, in 1864, under the sponsorship of the Admiralty and of the Institute of Naval Architects, the third school was set up. It was in South Kensington, and open (at least initially) to pupils from the private sector as well as from the royal dockyards. With this renaissance, naval architecture in Britain began to take a rank in accordance with the importance in the world of the country's merchant marine and the Royal Navy. By 1881 William White felt able to say that the school gave 'the most complete course of training available in any country'.[34]

If the Royal Navy thus asserted itself in terms of global (or, rather, European) standards, one must stress that—whatever the critics had said—it had never been seriously lacking in purely national terms. It is significant that the new school also admitted pupils from the private sector. Apart from the institutions set up before 1864 by the state (in the dockyards or elsewhere) for its employees, there was nowhere in Britain where one could be formally taught the principles of naval architecture. How, then, had private shipbuilders learned their trade during this dark period? The answer is suggested by a speech of the shipbuilder Joseph Samuda, before the Institute of Naval Architects in 1863. In it he delivered himself of the perhaps surprising judgement that Eton gave as good a basis as any for a boy who was going to design ships. He went a little too far for one member of his audience, the Old Etonian Sir John Pakington, who announced afterwards that Eton was the last kind of place for the budding naval architect.[35]

[32] 'On the Education of Naval Architects in England and France', *Trans. of the Institute of Naval Architects*, 4 (1863), 64.

[33] PP (1861), xxvi. 468.

[34] White, 'The Progress of Shipbuilding in England', 20.

[35] *Trans. of the Institute of Naval Architects*, 4 (1863), 176–85.

But, if expressed somewhat extremely, Samuda's reasoning was not exceptional. It seems unlikely that he had been lured by the English feudal idea, supposedly so fatal to the industrial spirit. Furthermore the argument that a classical education, as Eton then offered, would promote a boy's fancy and imagination—desirable qualities in an engineer—probably never occurred to him. He spoke in the common belief that the only place to learn how to become a naval engineer was a factory or shipyard, and that it was thus largely immaterial where a boy went to school or what he learned there. The important stage in his career would come when he left school, dirtied his hands, and picked up some useful practical knowledge.

In so far as this was a common belief of private shipbuilders, it undercuts the fine pleas made about their superiority over the designers in the royal yards. As we saw, one of the main faults in the dockyards was too much crude empiricism. The private yards could not counterbalance this; indeed, they were even more afflicted. There is little basis for agreeing with those who argued that warships had to be designed and built in the private yards. Apart from anything else, their motives were not necessarily pure. Professor Pollard suggests that much of the enthusiasm in Britain during the early 1860s for private enterprise in ship construction was fuelled, perhaps unconsciously he accepts, by the speculative warship-building of the time. He believes it was in the royal yards that the science of naval architecture was most forwarded, not in the private ones, though he allows an exception for what he describes as the 'brilliant individual contribution' of John Scott Russell, the one private naval architect of note.[36] True, there were also the private civil engineers to be considered, above all Rankine and Froude, but it was in the royal yards that their ideas were most vigorously applied and best consolidated.

It appears that, with regard to innovation as to efficiency, the contrast between the British state and private yards is something of a canard, offering no easy explanation for insufficiency in British naval policy-making. With respect to the training and organization

[36] Sidney Pollard, 'The Economic History of British Shipbuilding, 1870–1914', doctoral thesis (London, 1950), 249 ff.; and '*Laissez-faire* and Shipbuilding', *Economic History Review*, 5 (1952–3), 100–1. On Scott Russell, see the biography by G. S. Emmerson, *John Scott Russell: A Great Victorian Engineer and Naval Architect* (London, 1977).

of naval architects, the significant contrast is between the state yards in Britain and France. As was noted earlier, it was the example of the French system of training naval engineers that was the main incentive for the improvements in the British system realized in 1864. Once again, our enquiry forces us to straddle the Channel.

During the eighteenth century it had been a commonplace that French naval architects were superior to British ones. Newly captured French warships were carefully studied, and frequently were models for later British construction. With the nineteenth century, however, British standards began to improve significantly, as is evinced by the Portsmouth school, and also by the work of certain shipwrights, above all Sir Robert Seppings.[37] With Symonds's arrival, this advance slowed. Discussion of naval architecture in Britain became more parochial as quarrels developed over the 'peg-top' system. This introspection was made possible by the relative quiescence of the international naval scene, but once France began to take up again her old role of chief naval rival, it was inevitable that the plans of her engineers, and the means of training those men, should attract greater attention — inevitable, that is, once French engineers had begun clearly to demonstrate that they had important lessons to teach. However, it was not until well into our period that this began to happen. In the 1840s, whilst some British observers were struck by some French designs (inevitably, perhaps, steamers combining heavy armament with a large troop-carrying capacity attracted much attention), it was difficult to avoid noticing that French naval constructors had serious problems to contend with.

Plodding empiricism was hardly absent from the French yards in the early days of the screw-warship. The *Pomone*, one remembers, was first armed in August 1846, but her steering was found to be so faulty that she was promptly returned to the arsenal for further work, not emerging again until May 1848. Other instances of faulty design include the small sailing-warships that proved so fragile in bad weather, and there was the embarrassment that the great *Valmy*, after her launching in 1847, proved to have insufficient stability, and required a *soufflage*. The French navy also had its share

[37] Brown, *Before the Ironclad*, 16–19, 31–4.

of teething troubles in converting sail of the line to the screw, and
the resulting *vaisseaux mixtes* were not much different from those
in the Royal Navy. One has to understand, though, that French
architects faced more difficulties than their British opposite numbers when it came to such work. One factor was the inferiority
of the engines produced by the French navy, at least during the
1840s, in comparison with those from Britain's private engineering
works. The former were in general heavier and bulkier per horsepower, and thus made more demands on the ingenuity of designers
engaged on conversions. The fact that French sailing- and screw-
warships tended to be more heavily rigged than British ones of the
same rate (itself perhaps a function of greater French technical
confidence), was also significant. The margin of stability in which
French engineers worked remained smaller, with all the more need
for precision of calculation. With the various obstacles, the fact that
French conversions were at least not significantly worse than
British ones was in itself praise for the *ingénieurs-maritimes*, but this
was not entirely obvious at the time. Only with successful new
designs from up and coming engineers, above all Dupuy de Lôme,
did the Admiralty begin to become uneasy, and to pay more attention to the way such men were educated.

One of the difficulties facing an Admiralty concerned about any
French advantage in teaching warship constructors was that they
would have had to look not just at one or two schools, but at
a whole system that favoured technical education. The French
secondary schools offered a better grounding than was generally
available over the Channel. Then there were the specialist
institutions. Catering to the needs of private industry were the *écoles
d'arts et métiers*, and the *École centrale des arts et manufactures*: from the
first came mechanical engineers to man the workshops; from the
second came those who directed the others' efforts. The state's
engineers, on the other hand, went by a more select route. Their
central institution was the *École polytechnique*. Entrance requirements
were rigorous, not only a *baccalauréat* but also a stiff competitive
examination. Yet, once accepted, a student could be sure of the best
general technical education then available and, apart from its
unmatched cachet, the school was the only means of entering the
écoles d'application of the various state engineering corps. Successful
graduates wishing to become civil engineers, for instance, went to

the *École des ponts et chaussées*, and prospective army engineers and artillerymen to the *École de l'artillerie et du génie*.[38] Budding naval architects followed a similar path, as we can see from the career of Dupuy de Lôme, who was exceptional in talent but typical in education. He was 19 when he entered the *École polytechnique* in 1835, having passed the entrance examination tenth in his class. There he studied for two years, showing enough promise to win entry to the *École d'application du génie maritime*, then at Lorient (it was transferred to Paris in 1854). There, as an *élève du génie maritime*, he studied for two further years, concentrating as did his fellows on the theoretical and mathematical aspects of his craft for much of the year, but also spending some time in the local dockyard (Lorient was principally a yard of construction), so as not to lose sight of the practical side. (After the school moved to Paris, the summers were reserved for work in the yards.) In 1839 he finally became a *sous-ingénieur*, third-class, and began his climb in the naval hierarchy.[39]

The implication is that, certainly before the foundation of the British 'third school' in 1864, and even after then, the formal aspect of a naval architect's training was more accentuated in France. This raises the question of the balance between practical and theoretical education, which in Britain was on the side of the former, and in France on the latter. The history of ship construction in the nineteenth century shows that to a certain degree skills learned in apprenticeship, through example and demonstration during the building of a hull or engines and boilers, could replace instruction on a more theoretical or scientific level.[40] Similarly, theory can to a degree be a substitute for experience. The balance can go too far in either instance. Before 1864 the British surely depended too greatly on instruction through practice. In France one notes that there were complaints about excess of theory in the education of naval

[38] F. B. Artz, *The Development of Technical Education in France, 1500–1850* (MIT Press, 1966), 265–6. Robert Fox and George Weisz (eds.), *The Organization of Science and Technology in France, 1808–1914* (Cambridge University Press, 1980), notably introduction, pp. 1–28; Terry Shinn, 'From *Corps* to *Profession*: The Emergence and Definition of Industrial Engineering in Modern France', pp. 183–210; and C. R. Day, 'Education for the Industrial World: Technical and Modern Instruction in France under the Third Republic', pp. 127–53.

[39] C. François, 'A la mémoire de Dupuy de Lôme', *Revue maritime*, 211 (July 1937), 1–4.

[40] Paul L. Robertson, 'Technical Education in the British Shipbuilding and Marine Engineering Industries, 1863–1914', *Economic History Review*, 27 (1974), 221–35.

architects. The director of naval construction at Toulon testified before the *Enquête parlementaire* in 1850 that the training at the *École d'application* was insufficiently practical.[41] It seems possible, indeed, that the fumblings of both the British and French yards in the 1840s, when beginning to tackle the screw, demonstrate the inadequacies of too great a reliance on either theory or practice.

Yet one point deserves stressing. It mattered less to the French if their predeliction for theory went too far, than it mattered to the British if they were too firmly wedded to a 'hands on' approach. One recalls the frequent visits made by French engineers to the busy British private workshops and shipyards in the 1840s. It was far easier for a Frenchman to look over to Britain to seek an empirical basis for his theories than for a highly practical but mathematically sub-literate Briton to look in the other direction and be able to find theoretical guidelines for future practice.

The conclusion is that the training of the *ingénieurs-maritimes* and their ability to draw at will on British practical experience put them in an excellent position to formulate and articulate new ideas. But one must add that they were helped in this by the very way in which they were organized. First, they had their own corps. (Only in 1883 was the Royal Corps of Naval Constructors set up in Britain.) Moreover, that corps was small: there were only about a hundred naval engineers of all ranks, excluding the *élèves*. And it was socially homogeneous, drawing almost all its recruits from the *haute bourgeoisie*. (The sheer cost of training was a serious obstacle to the less affluent: the *École polytechnique* cost 1,000 francs a year in tuition fees alone.) Then we must remember the importance of a shared experience of a common education, one where the pupils were fully conscious of how they were set apart by their expertise, by the sheer mystery of their craft—or perhaps one should say science. In brief, the *ingénieurs-maritimes* formed a small, unified, self-conscious *élite* with a highly developed *esprit de corps*. Doubtless, there were disagreements, and probably something of a fracture between the older engineers, wedded to a sailing navy, and the others who made up the rising 'steam generation'; though the one case of fracture we have seen so far was between two engineers of the same generation—Charles Dupin and Tupinier. Nevertheless, it does appear that French naval engineers largely listened

[41] *Enquête parlementaire sur la situation et l'organisation des services de la marine militaire* (2 vols., Paris, 1851), ii. 242.

sympathetically as well as knowledgeably to each other, and the baneful influence of seniority and hierarchy must have been limited. On this we have the testimony of P. Dislère, who joined the corps in 1861. He spoke in a memoir of the 'sentiments d'estime et d'affection qui n'ont cessé de regner entre tous', adding that he could cite numerous examples 'de cette bonne camaraderie fondée sur une estime réciproque des ingénieurs les uns pour les autres'. This good fellowship, he tells us, was able to endure even the two most serious of tests: he meant promotion by selection, and politics.[42]

This is highly reminiscent of what we have seen before. The French advantage in training and organization, enabling naval engineers properly to formulate ideas, and encouraging discussion of those ideas among colleagues, quite possibly gaining acceptance for them, is something we first described (albeit taking a more dilute form), with regard to the *grand corps*. Both in its naval engineers and in its executive officers, consequently, the French navy had a valuable potential base for a bold and innovative policy, a base the Royal Navy did not possess to the same extent. It was only potential, however, because the ultimate decisions about policy had to be made at the highest levels. Success in naval policy crucially depended on the ability of the central naval administration to make the correct choices from those offered to it. Therefore our next step is an obvious one: to compare and contrast the Admiralty and the Ministry of Marine.

[42] P. Dislère, 'Note historique sur le Corps du génie maritime', *Revue maritime*, 16 (1921), 450-1.

7

The Admiralty and the Ministry
of Marine

I

The Ministry of Marine was well housed in the more easterly of a fine matching pair of buildings flanking the rue Royale and fronting the place de la Concorde. These buildings—and, indeed, the whole square, originally called the place Louis XV—had their origins in the eighteenth century. The plans were drawn up by the architect J.-A. Gabriel, and approval came in letters patent dated 1757. The building that concerns us was constructed in 1766, intended as the *Garde meuble de la Couronne*, for which purpose it was conveniently close to the royal palace of the Tuileries. At this time the Ministry of Marine was not in Paris: it had offices at Fontainebleau and Compiègne; but, in common with the other ministries, the centre of administration was at Versailles. In 1789, with the enforced move of the King to Paris, the ministries followed helter-skelter, and—thanks to personal rather than official connections—the Minister of Marine managed to squeeze his department into part of the *Garde meuble*. The position was not ideal. The riots and battles of the revolution swept by just outside the gates: on one occasion some Swiss guards escaped death only by taking refuge inside the Ministry, the janitor later furnishing them with civilian clothes for their escape. Furthermore, by some inevitable irony the place Louis XV became the place de la Révolution where, during the first four months of 1793, the guillotine was established, dealing with a stream of the condemned, including the *ci-devant roi*. Even when the guillotine was moved, at first it was taken no further than the Tuileries gardens. The Terror was not a time when *fonctionnaires* or *employés* in any government department were able to work in decent tranquillity, but workers in the Ministry of Marine must have been more disturbed by events than most.

Of course, there were certain matters to draw their attention away from the daily spectacle of the people's justice, and which remained long after the Terror ended. The naval war with England had to be managed. Then there was the other serious war — that for the *Garde meuble* itself. As the years went by, the navy encroached more and more on the building. By 1792 its presence had been officially recognized. Five years later all the building was allotted to the Ministry, although only in 1806 was full possession taken. By this time all the main departments of the Ministry were at the rue Royale, and over later years most of what remained outside was brought into the fold. The naval archives, for instance, came in from Versailles in 1837. The *Dépôt des cartes* was a clear exception. It had a curious peregrination, finally settling in 1817 upon 13 rue de l'Université. But, by the mid-century, everything else of importance had been centralized. Room after room of the old *Garde meuble* had been partitioned off to cater to the needs of the *bureaux*. The part given over to be the residence of the Minister and to serve as cabinet and reception rooms remained exempt, however. Here the accent was on the grand and the decorative, particularly after the renovation and embellishment of 1842–3, when gilded-relief plaster-work was lavishly applied.

One may see the two sections as complementary. The *bureaux*, beyond — as it were — the green baize door, provided the day-to-day direction of naval affairs. From the Minister's section came the decisions on the most serious matters. It was also where, aided by the rooms' noble proportions and ornamentation, the Ministry consciously attempted to assert French naval prestige, giving splendid receptions and parties intended to impress and overawe. Perhaps the most splendid — and pointed — of such events was the *Soirée allégorique* of 12 February 1866, during the Ministry of Chasseloup-Laubat. It was mounted at great expense, with some 3,000 invited guests, including the pick of the foreign residents in Paris. The high point was a lavish spectacle, a *Cortège des quatre parties du monde*, surely a not too subtle argument in favour of naval power and colonial expansion. The building in the rue Royale, one might well conclude, had — like the British monarchy — a decorative as well as a useful element.[1]

---

[1] H. de Fontaine de Resbecq, 'L'administration centrale de la marine et des colonies', *Revue maritime et coloniale*, 88 (1886), 428–36. Martial de Pradel de Lamase, 'La Marine, rue Royale, de 1789 à 1815', *Revue maritime*, 229 (Jan. 1939),

One cannot honestly say that the decorative element of the British naval administration was pronounced. The construction of the Whitehall Admiralty building (later called the Old Admiralty Building) dates from 1722–5, and the architect was Thomas Ripley, an ex-carpenter whose designs have never had a high reputation. Pope mentions him unflatteringly more than once, dealing a glancing blow in *The Dunciad* (iii. 327), and a more characteristically vicious one in *The Epistle to Burlington* (ll. 17–22). Magnificence, he tells us, is not to be expected from Ripley. The judgement is well confirmed by the Old Admiralty. What one finds to praise either pre- or post-dates Ripley's contribution. It was perhaps from the previous Admiralty building, erected in 1695 (though decaying rapidly), that there came the fine wood carving which now adorns the fireplace in the Boardroom; it was naturally attributed to Grinling Gibbons, though is probably not by him. In 1759–60 came the handsome screen across the courtyard, designed by Robert Adam. Some thirty years later it was decided that the accommodation for the First Lord in the Ripley block was inadequate, thus the elegant and comfortable Admiralty House was built immediately to the south (1786–8).[2] However, even with the later additions, neither in outward proportion nor in inward splendour may the Admiralty of our period be compared with the *hôtel* in the rue Royale.

Is this of great significance? One might argue that, though doubtless unfortunate in having a somewhat paltry centre in Whitehall, the Royal Navy had less need than its rival to rely on outward show. It was secure in the affections of the British people, was not overshadowed by the British army (as the French army certainly overshadowed the navy), and almost always possessed a clear numerical superiority over any other fleet. The Royal Navy did not have to rely on the intangibles of power: it had the reality. The Admiralty building, untrammelled by fripperies, could concentrate on the important task: the efficient management of the navy.

The argument has little merit. It dismisses too easily the fact that—in naval operations as in administration—outward show is

55–69, 230 (Feb. 1939), 201–16; and 'Chasseloup-Laubat reçoit a l'Hôtel de la Marine', *Revue maritime*, 215 (Nov. 1937), 626–45.

[2] Viscount Cilcennin, *Admiralty House, Whitehall* (*Country Life*, London, 1960). Christopher Hussey, *Country Life*, 28 July 1923: 105–6; 17 and 24 Nov. 1923: 684–92, 718–26. Pevsner, as always, is invaluable.

an aspect of power. More important, it overstates the degree to which the Admiralty could administer efficiently. The main difference between the building in the rue Royale and its fellow in Whitehall was that whilst in the former virtually all the organs of central control were gathered together, the latter was simply part of an administration weakened by subdivision.

In the eighteenth century British central naval administration was scattered between several buildings, some widely separated from each other. Apart from the one at Whitehall, there was the Pay Office building at Old Broad Street (near the present Liverpool Street Station); and, to the south, around Tower Hill, was the Navy Office (home of the Navy Board), close by the house of the Victualling Commissioners. In 1780 came what seemed at first like a further scattering when the Navy Board moved to Somerset House, the first of the truly grand buildings in London designed for government use. Actually, the move was a first step in physical concentration. Eventually, the Pay Office followed the Navy Board, as also—by 1830 at the latest—did the Victualling Commissioners. However, for long no further concentration took place. At the beginning of our period, central naval administration was carried on in two separate establishments, half a mile apart. The Whitehall building contained what was called the Secretary's Department, where the higher command functions of the Admiralty were exercised. At Somerset House were gathered the various other departments. Some attempts were made to integrate the work. For instance, under Lord Haddington occasional meetings of the Board were held at Somerset House, a practice that became more regular in the 1850s. Nevertheless, it gradually came to be appreciated that there was great inconvenience from the physical division of the administration. True to the tradition of reforming only when matters became intolerable, it was under the strains of the Crimean War that a bold move was made. For some time the Admiralty had been taking over houses to the west of the Ripley block, and it was here that residences for the Naval Lords—originally in the main building—had become established. In 1855 these lords lost their homes, and with the extra office space thus made available, the Surveyor's Department could be moved from Somerset House. The example was developed further between 1869 and 1873; more houses were taken over in Whitehall, and the remaining naval departments were moved from Somerset House. A centralization equal to that of the Ministry of Marine had been achieved. Unfortunately, the Admiralty's quarters were cramped, and became ever more so with the fleet expansion of the late 1880s and afterwards. In 1894–9 a large new court of buildings was raised, supplemented in 1911 by the Admiralty Arch. Altogether, the extensions were of a somewhat vulgar ostentation, but this was appropriate enough on the verge of a century in which the Royal Navy was to find itself on occasion only too reliant on the 'intangibles' of power and not the 'reality'.

II

The physical division of the British central naval administration during our period, while being an undoubted disadvantage, can hardly explain serious lapses in naval policy-making. Notably, while the division would have added to the 'friction' which is as natural in bureaucracies as in battle, it cannot have greatly impeded the naval high policy-makers, who were anyway concentrated at Whitehall (at least after 1855 when the Surveyor's Department moved). So now we turn from questions of place to other, surely more important ones. The first is the easiest to ask, and the most difficult to answer with precision—the one concerning the number of administrators on the two sides. To begin with the Ministry of Marine, it might appear that all we need do to discover the size of the staff is to look at the figures given in the annual published accounts.[3] In 1851, we are told, there were 196 *fonctionnaires* and *employés* in the Ministry (apart from the Minister himself), 229 in 1852, 227 in 1853, and so on. (The number of porters, messengers, and *gens de service* is given, but will be left aside.)

Such figures, though, need vigorous massaging truly to reflect French central naval administration. First, one must subtract the forty or so workers in the *direction des colonies*; for, with the exception of the years 1858–60, the rue Royale was responsible for French colonial administration during our period. In general, however, we have to add to the numbers shown in the accounts. There were various permanent commissions, committees, and other bodies which, though essential to the central administration, were

[3] *Ministère de la marine et des colonies: Compte définitif des dépenses*, pub. annually, some two years after the date of the *exercice* concerned.

not formally considered part of it. There was the *état-major* of the Minister, plus the *Conseil d'amirauté*, the *Conseil des travaux*, the *Conseil des prises*, the central audit department (*Contrôle central*), the *Dépôt des cartes et plans*, the commission to improve the training on the *Borda*, the central inspectorates for the *Génie maritime*, *Service de santé*, *Travaux maritimes*, *Artillerie* and *Infanterie de marine*, and a few other lesser lights. Attempting not to count the same men more than once (a plurality of committee posts, then as now, was common), the members of these bodies (including the clerks responsible for the minutes and correspondence) have to be included in our totals.

Unfortunately, imponderables spoil the calculation. For instance, one cannot be certain whether some men shown on the books of the dockyard were actually employed in Paris. The practice became well established after 1870 when the Ministry was attempting, by sleight of hand, to prove to a suspicious National Assembly that the navy was run economically. By 1871 some twenty-nine workers in the central administration were paid on the dockyard acccounts.[4] It is quite possible that the same kind of thing occurred during the Second Empire, though for reasons of budgetary convenience rather than through a conscious effort to deceive, and presumably thus on a small scale. There are also other uncertainties. The Minister was empowered to take on temporary clerks during an emergency, and such recruitment was not necessarily made plain in the accounts, the added cost perhaps being hidden away in the budget, probably in the morass of the supplementary budget made necessary by the emergency that had demanded the extra clerks in the first place. As well as the temporary clerks, there were the supernumeraries. These were given no stipend; they were juniors on trial, hoping eventually to be appointed as established clerks. Their number was in theory limited. In the 1840s there were supposed to be no more than twelve in all the *directions* of the Ministry. In 1852 Ducos changed this to a maximum of two per *direction*. It is quite possible that the administration recruited up to the level permitted. It is also possible, of course, that on occasions the limit was surpassed: few things would be less surprising given the fluctuations during our period in the number of *directions*.

There is also a margin of error in estimating the size of the Admiralty staff, despite the avid appetite of the House of Commons

[4] Guy Thuillier, *Bureaucratie et bureaucrates en France au XIXe siècle* (Geneva, 1980), 6 n.

for official returns and blue books on the establishments of government offices. The main problem is unknowable fluctuations in the temporary staff. Numbers could fluctuate sizeably from month to month, due to the practice of taking on large numbers of temporary clerks in an emergency. We know, for instance, that in 1860–1 the departments at Somerset House had up to ninety-seven such clerks at work. The average for the year, though, was only eighty-three, and the low point may well have been in the forties, but we cannot be certain. We are even less certain about temporary writers, paid by the hour, sometimes known as 'law writers' or 'law stationer's clerks'; we occasionally find them employed in the Admiralty, even in the Secretariat itself, although the Chief Clerk himself did not necessarily know that they had been recruited.[5]

Then we come on to problems of comparability. Since we have to compare like with like, we have to omit from (or enter on) the British side types of personnel already excluded from (or included in) the French. Thus porters and messengers, left aside in our assessment of the Ministry of Marine, must also be ignored in the Admiralty's case. Furthermore—a crucial if elementary point—we have to include the naval bureaucrats at Somerset House as well as their fellows at Whitehall, or British central naval administration would appear a model of spartan economy.

Unfortunately, complete comparability is impossible: gross errors can be avoided but, since the two administrations were so different in structure, some lesser ones remain. The most intractable one concerns the *inscription maritime*—something the British infamously did not have, although there was a system of registering seamen (at least the beginning of a war reserve system, though it never developed as intended). In one way, therefore, if we are going to include in our totals the men at the rue Royale in the *bureau de l'inscription maritime*, some of whom were concerned with planning for wartime manning, we ought to include on the other side the sixty or so men in the Register Office of Seamen. But there are objections to doing this. First, though the Register Office was still part of the Admiralty in 1851, it was afterwards transferred to the Board of Trade, administratively a quite distinct department. Secondly, the greater part of the administration of the *inscription* was not in Paris but was scattered around the dockyards and ports: many of the clerks who

---

[5] Chief Clerk's minute of 30 July 1860, ADM 1 5743.

performed analogous tasks to those of the men in the Register Office were not even in the rue Royale. It might be best, therefore, to exclude from consideration both the clerks in the Register Office and those in the *bureau de l'inscription maritime*. But this too is difficult. One cannot simply exclude this *bureau*. It also dealt with various extraneous matters. It is impossible to say what proportion of the work was devoted to the *inscription*. Besides, the administration of the *inscription*, unlike the work of the Register Office, had a crucial peacetime significance: the French navy depended heavily on the *inscrits* in peace as well as in war. One cannot easily divorce this portion of the administration from the normal peacetime one. It tackled work that in Whitehall and Somerset House would have been dealt with by personnel sections. The best solution is to include the *bureau de l'inscription maritime* in our totals, while excluding the Register Office, and to admit that in this respect, as in some others, there is not perfect neatness.

With all apologies made for imprecision, one comes to a peak figure for the French central naval administration in our period (covering all the *fonctionnaires* and *employés*, civilian and military, dealing in Paris with purely naval matters) of between 270 and 280. (This applies to the early 1860s.) The comparable British figure (taken from the returns for 1861) is 460 to 470.[6] Despite the admitted margin of error, two points of importance are clear. The first is that, compared with the naval bureaucracies of today, the administrations under study were tiny. The second point is that the Admiralty was larger than its rival to an extent not adequately explained by the superior size of the Royal Navy. We have to remember here a certain duplication of manpower necessitated by the division between Whitehall and Somerset House. When amalgamation finally came, after 1869, reductions in staffing levels became possible. Another factor is involved as well. The figures suggest what one would in any case gather from the greater average

---

[6] Included on the British side are the Lords, the Secretaries, the departments of the Secretary, the Controller, the Hydrographer, the Storekeeper-General (including the Contract Office), the Accountant-General, the Medical Director-General, the Director of Works (formally made one of the Principal Officers in 1865), the Controller of Victualling and Transport, plus the Harbour Branch, the Coastguard Office, and the office of the DAG, Royal Marines. See PP (1861), xxxviii. 111–16; PP (1862), xxix. 153–4; PP (1872), xxxix. 343–6; PRO T1 6668B, Admiralty proposal of Jan. 1866; and the *Navy List* for the period. On the French side are all the elements named specifically earlier, the central administration plus the various committees, but not the *direction des colonies*.

distances between the central administration and the dockyards in France compared with Britain, and the poorer state of communications. In France the yards had to be given a relatively larger degree of administrative autonomy, and thus the Ministry of Marine could be comparatively slim. As one finds in several other respects, the centralizing power of the French state has been rather greater in reputation than in fact.

To give an idea of how the administrations changed in size over our period, there follow figures of the number of clerks in the Secretary's Department for certain years, and also for *fonctionnaires* and *employés* at the rue Royale according to the annual accounts, but excluding colonial administrators.

Admiralty clerks: *1840* 36; *1850* 39; *1855* 51; *1861* 59;

Rue Royale: *1837* 136; *1848* 174; *1851* 155; *1858* 177.
(The number for 1861 was about the same as for 1858.)

Our attention now turns to the allied topics of the recruitment, composition, and promotion of personnel, and the nature of their work. Concentrating for the time being on the civilian personnel, one finds a clear general similarity between the Admiralty and the Ministry of Marine.

In both countries, inevitably for the time, the social origins of recruits were very largely the same. The various strata of the middle class contributed the overwhelming majority of the clerks. (Moreover, and this is also to be found in both countries, certain families developed a tradition of sending sons into the naval administration, as happened with the naval officer corps, and one finds certain names recurring in the lists of clerks.) Admittedly, some social differences, or at least nuances, would have been found between the two administrations resulting from differences in the British and French roads to appointment. The main way of becoming a clerk at the rue Royale was to serve two years as a supernumerary, in the hope of a permanent position. Clearly, this favoured the rather better-off families who could afford to maintain their sons during their apprenticeship. This was somewhat balanced by the fact that the period without pay could be reduced, perhaps even severely. Guy de Maupassant, for instance, served only a few months before being advanced to a salaried post. Moreover, though the French system encouraged recruits from relatively affluent families, there was also a means of entry for the relatively poor.

A boy could start as a paid *écrivain* in one of the dockyards, then after at least three years service he might be able to gain a transfer to Paris — though evidence of the numbers of such transfers appears to be lacking.

The intellectual requirements of entry also had much in common in the two countries. They were low — at least at the beginning of our period. Applicants had to pass qualifying examinations, but these seem to have been largely formalities. Change did come, albeit with a certain amount of slippage between the two countries. In France during the mid-1840s came increasing suggestions that the *concours* should become a serious hurdle to entrance to the civil service. In 1848, with the revolution, there were great hopes of building up a service based on ability rather than patronage or class. They took principal expression in the *École d'administration*, set up at this time to train the functionaries of the future. There was also an added enthusiasm for a strict *concours*. However, with the growing conservatism of the Second Republic, and the fall of egalitarianism into disfavour, the principle of merit naturally suffered. This is shown best by the disbandment of the *École d'administration* in 1849.[7] Enthusiasm for the *concours* weakened too, above all with the coming of the Second Empire. The latter brought an increased authoritarian element into government at all levels, something of a *Führerprinzip*, enhancing the power of each minister, and encouraging him to dislike and disregard regulations that threatened his ability to appoint just as he wished. Not that the level of the *concours* quite fell back to that of a mere formality. Apart from the obvious importance of weeding out the blatantly incompetent recruits, there was the argument that other countries were strengthening their civil services, and that France could not afford to fall far behind. There were German examples. Yet more telling, there was an example even from the home of the amateur — Britain.[8]

The famous Northcote-Trevelyan report of 1853 had advocated competitive entrance examinations for the civil service — *concours* in the full sense of the word. Full implementation came only after two decades, but a modified scheme was instituted in 1855; not one of open competition between all candidates, but of limited

[7] Vincent Wright, 'L'École nationale d'administration de 1848–1849: un échec révélateur', *Revue historique*, 255 (1976), 21–42.
[8] Thuillier, *Bureaucratie et bureaucrates*, 334–62.

competition, between selected men. The system was not foolproof. Men of little ability were able to pass through—in some cases simply because the examination results were disregarded. It appears that in the late 1850s the Admiralty appointed some men who had failed in the competition, a path that was not closed until 1859 by legislation that made a civil servant's pension contingent on his having a certificate of successful examination. Nevertheless, whatever the loopholes, it appears that limited competition did improve standards. As evidence there is the large number of complaints made after 1855 by patrons whose *protégés* had been rejected by the examiners. Specific to the Admiralty, there is the testimony of R. M. Bromley, appointed Accountant-General of the Navy in 1854. In 1860 he felt able to say, apropos of the clerks in his department who had entered since the new regulations (about half his staff), that they had shown themselves to be better and harder workers than their predecessors.[9]

If in regard to recruitment by merit the British civil service tended to be slightly ahead of the French, when it came to promotion the similarity was closer, with each side progressing at more or less the same pace. The principle of seniority was initially virtually as powerful in Paris as it was in London, but in both cases there was a change of emphasis towards promotion by selection (and thus, theoretically, by merit) before 1870: the change, though, was slight and subject to partial reversal.

In the French case, the Second Empire brought greater ministerial initiative in promotion, as in recruitment. This encouraged the merit principle, though disgruntled senior *employés* spoke rather of favouritism. Unfortunately, as the Empire became more established the zeal for reform abated, and the seniority principle regained some lost ground. In 1863 it was seriously proposed that *chefs de bureau* in the rue Royale should be advanced only on grounds of seniority.[10] Such a bold stroke against the Minister's power of choice had little chance of success, but demonstrated that even under the authoritarian Empire promotion by merit was not universally applauded.

If Britain did not have the Second Empire, at least it had the Northcote–Trevelyan report, which recommended the merit

---

[9] PP (1860), ix. 256–7. Maurice Wright, *Treasury Control of the Civil Service, 1854–1874* (OUP, 1969), 65, 67, 71, 74.

[10] Thuillier, *Bureaucratie et bureaucrates*, 375 n.

principle in promotion. Though not implemented in full until after 1870, the suggestion did have some influence before then, encouraging those within government who distrusted the seniority rule. In the Admiralty, merit was openly lauded by a few during the 1850s, above all by R. M. Bromley, who was still only 40 when appointed Accountant-General, and who seems to have seen himself as living proof of the value of promotion according to ability. He stated in evidence given before an inquiry in 1855 that since his appointment he had promoted men in his department by seniority only twice, and had been mistaken each time. The way to improve administration, he went on, was to recognize merit; adding that he even encouraged his junior clerks to suggest improvements! But Bromley was exceptional at his level. The other Admiralty departmental heads, and the senior clerks, were far less radical. One story became popular, very possibly a canard spread by the reactionaries, that in departments where merit ruled, clerks hid memoranda from each other the better to keep ahead and make a good impression. There was certainly also the traditional bureaucratic response to unwelcome innovations: accept the new form, but retain the old content. At the same inquiry before which Bromley testified, Bernal Osborne, then First Secretary, responded in just this way; and what he said also well-reflects a common opinion in both the British and French naval administrations during our period. Staff appointments, he argued, should not go to the senior as a matter of course. All well and good; but he promptly undercut this by what he said next: 'although it has frequently happened that the senior was the best man, by the testimony of Mr Dyer and Mr Pennell, and the heads of the department whom I consulted.'[11]

When we come to study the nature of the work of the naval bureaucracies, we find that it was well suited to the kind of organizations we have been describing. Office hours, for instance, were scarcely unreasonable, ten to five being normal. In Paris during the Directory and again during the Restoration, attempts had been made to enforce attendance at the Ministry of Marine from nine to four, but these had not been very successful. Many of

[11] Testimony from the joint Admiralty–Treasury inquiry into the Secretary's Department, named after Thomas Phinn, Second Secretary, pp. 147–63, 127–32, ADM 1 5660. Dyer was the Chief Clerk, and Pennell a first-class clerk and Dyer's eventual successor.

the *employés* lived too far from the city centre to be able to reach their offices by nine with ease. Besides, the usual hours of business in Paris were ten to five, and it was sensible to follow the same pattern. This the Ministry had certainly done by the beginning of our period. Not that this necessarily meant all the staff was now able to arrive on time. Maupassant describes in *L'Héritage* the promptness of the Ministry staff on one particular morning, passing like a fleet under the great entrance gate, but, the author tells us, this was very exceptional, for the New Year was approaching, 'époque de zèle et d'avancements'. In London, too, it seems likely that the civil servants were not always prompt. Attendance registers in the Admiralty were not scrupulously kept or inspected. The chiefs would be able to see at a glance who was missing from their desks, but these men normally arrived only at eleven o'clock, and it would not be surprising to learn that some of their juniors managed to slip in only just in time to avoid being seen to be late.

Of course, not all were lackadaisical. Some men arrived before they had to, like the ambitious young Lesable in Maupassant's story. Then there were the few who were responsible for the essential preliminary work of the day, and had to be in early. One example is John Briggs. He eventually retired as Chief Clerk, with a knighthood, but for many years he had been Reader to Their Lordships, responsible for arriving at 8.30 each morning to arrange the correspondence for the daily meeting of the Board (the Lords themselves being generally at their desks by 10 a.m.).[12] Nevertheless, to the modern eye, the general atmosphere in the naval administrations in Paris and London was both leisurely and genteel. Exceptions to this generalization are to be found not primarily between Paris and London, but rather between the two parts of the Admiralty. At Somerset House the clerks commonly left at four, but this was reflected in their lower salaries as compared with the Secretary's Branch. Naturally, therefore, Whitehall was the more desirable for the aspirant naval clerk, and—at least after 1855—the examination for a position there was more severe than for one at Somerset House. One consequence was that the tone in the latter was less consciously gentlemanly than in Whitehall, as one gathers from the smug comment of one of the witnesses before the 1855 inquiry: 'there will not be found', it was said, 'in any of the offices

[12] Ibid. 2–3, 17, 22.

of Government, a more gentleman-like, well-conducted, intelligent, and willing class of men than the present clerks of the [Whitehall] Admiralty.'[13]

However genteel, the clerks at Whitehall engaged in work of a nature hardly differing from that of their colleagues at Somerset House — or, indeed, from what the men at the rue Royale faced. The usual occupation of most was the drudgery of longhand copying: only right at the end of our period did it seem feasible to introduce a degree of mechanical copying. But this does not explain why so many administrators spent a large proportion of 'their careers — sometimes the whole of them — as drudges to the pen. We have to realize that there was no firm distinction between the duties of a recruit clearly destined by his abilities to a position of high responsibility and another who was not likely ever to be more than a copy clerk. New clerks had to devote themselves to purely mechanical tasks before being allowed to progress to the intellectually more demanding responsibility of drafting documents. This apprenticeship commonly took a long time: for instance, in the Secret and Political Branch at Whitehall, all clerks spent their first ten to fifteen years in copy work, though this was perhaps exceptional.[14] The effects of years of almost unthinking penmanship on a man's hopes, enthusiasm, and intellect, hardly needs emphasis. Did Bartleby exist only in fiction?

Such had long been the general pattern throughout government in London and Paris, but by the mid-nineteenth century there were reformers eager to improve matters. Inevitably, Trevelyan and Northcote were among them. Their report advocated a firm division being made in all the government offices between those undertaking intellectual work and those whose duties were merely mechanical.[15] In France, there were similar proposals or attempts to divide the clerks into two classes, the *rédacteurs* and the more lowly *expéditionnaires*. In the Ministry of War there was at least a partial division as early as the 1830s, but, as in Britain, there was opposition, much of it from senior clerks who had risen under the old system. The Ministry of War returned to its *corps unique* of clerks in 1850.[16] In some British offices, a division was achieved after 1854, but one sometimes finds that both sides were treated largely the

[13] Ibid. 87.   [14] Ibid. 55.
[15] M. Wright, *Treasury Control of the Civil Service*, 110–15.
[16] Thuillier, *Bureaucratie et bureaucrates*, 316–33.

same in terms of promotion and work. Not until after 1870, with the pace being set in Britain, did a division of work truly become established in the two capitals. Indeed, one could argue that only during the First World War, with female typing-pools, did governments have workers available who, by sex as well as training, were not likely to be thought of as anything other than mere mechanicals.

The two naval administrations inevitably shared in the trend to the specialization of clerkly functions. A thorough division of work began from 1869 in the Admiralty, somewhat later in the Ministry of Marine, but at least a hesitant beginning had been made before then in both. In 1866 the Admiralty introduced a class of 'writers', regularizing and developing the previous occasional recourse to law stationer's clerks. The newcomers actually did work very little different from that done by the junior clerks, but represented an important move towards specialization. In the Ministry of Marine, on the other hand, the *corps unique* of civilian bureaucrats at the rue Royale remained undivided during the Empire; but military bureaucrats were divided, beginning in 1863. We have to understand that much of the work of administering the French navy was carried on by a military corps, the *Commissariat de la marine*, consisting — at its widest interpretation—both of officers (the true *officiers de plume*), and of what were called the *employés du commissariat*, the latter consisting of two grades, the *commis de marine* and the lower *écrivains*. Men from the corps could be found afloat, serving on all but the smaller warships, performing duties that in the rival service were the responsibility of the paymasters (as the pursers were rechristened during the mid-century), their clerks, and the captain's secretaries. Moreover, men of the *corps* would be found in shore establishments abroad, in the various ports of the *arrondissements maritimes* (where they were mostly concerned with drawing up the lists of *inscrits*), in the dockyards, and in the rue Royale itself. Before 1863, following the common pattern, a recruit had to spend years of mechanical drudgery as an *écrivain* and *commis de marine* before he could aspire to the intellectual duties natural to the *officier de plume*. Then came the decree of 7 October. Henceforward, the more capable men began not as copyists but as cadet-officers, *élèves-commissaires*. A new, separate, and subordinate corps was created to deal with the less exacting duties, largely recruited (and this is eloquent of the degree of imagination and flexibility required) among *sous-officiers* of the navy and *infanterie de marine*.[17]

In touching on the *Commissariat* we have moved at last to a serious point of dissimilarity between the two naval administrations. The Royal Navy had no equivalent body. What that corps did in the French navy was performed in the rival force by a combination of civilians, ratings, and officers. Among the latter, of course, were those important non-executive (or civil) officers, the paymasters, who might seem to be a comparatively close analogue to the *officiers de plume*. But they were only poor cousins, lacking any well-developed hierarchy (even after reforms in 1855).[18] The *Commissariat*, on the other hand, had an impressive hierarchy, with several grades from *commissaire-général*, first-class, down to *aide-commissaire*, plus — at least up to 1863 — two grades of apprenticeship. Secondly, the officer ranks were fully assimilated with those of the other officer corps, including the executive officers. Every *officier de plume* knew with precision his place with regard to his immediate colleagues and to the other officers in the navy. We are dealing, in short, with a military corps of administration, something alien to the British tradition of government.

The military element given to the Ministry of Marine by the *Commissariat* was reinforced by the presence not only of members of the *grand corps*, but also by other officers, like the *commissaires*, who in Britain would not have had any similarly developed military hierarchy of their own. These were the *officiers de santé*, whose relationship to the RN surgeons was about the same as that between the *commissaires* and the paymasters. Then there were the men who in Britain would have been mere civilians: the *ingénieurs-maritimes* and the *ingénieurs des ponts et chaussées* (two officers from this corps were lent from the Ministry of Agriculture to work at the rue Royale); plus those from the corps that were in effect specialist off-shoots of the *Commissariat*, bureaucrats all, the *officiers de l'inspection des services administratifs* (the *contrôleurs* or auditors), the *personnel administratif des directions de travaux* (accountants),

[17] A. Deschard, 'Notice sur l'organisation du corps du commissariat de la marine française depuis l'origine jusqu'à nos jours', *Revue maritime et coloniale*, 60 (1879), 303–12, 314–15, 318–26. For the reasoning behind the 1863 reform, see the letters of 3 Feb. 1862 and 8 Sept. 1863 by Chasseloup-Laubat, Chasseloup-Laubat Papers, iii. 35–9; iv. 239–45.

[18] Michael Lewis, *The Navy in Transition 1814–1864: A Social History* (London, 1965), 143–5.

and the *agents comptables de matières* (book-keepers).[19] Even the least military-sounding of these corps—like the *Commissariat* or the *grand corps* itself, not only had its own hierarchy of ranks, but those ranks were assimilated to those in the other corps. Thus, despite enormous differences in function, the men from all the various corps formed one great, integrated, military hierarchy.

The effect of this hierarchy on the atmosphere and working of the Ministry of Marine was obviously in part a function of its integration. But its size was also important, and research shows that it was large. Again taking 1861, we find that there were twenty-five officers from the *grand corps* alone in the central administration, including all its peripheral committees and commissions. Then there were the men from the various other corps, above all the *commissaires*. The *Annuaire de la marine et des colonies* shows that forty-five of the latter were serving in Paris in the year in question. Unfortunately, we cannot be certain how many of these were working in the *direction des colonies*, which was excluded from our earlier count. The figures are once again somewhat speculative, therefore, but it does appear that a large proportion of the Paris naval administration—some 40–45 per cent—was military. Admittedly, this element was concentrated in certain parts of the administration. The peripheral committees, for instance, were almost entirely composed of officers. And the *Dépôt des cartes et plans* was a home for several *ingénieurs-hydrographes*—another corps that had no British equivalent: RN surveyors were executive officers. Similarly, one finds several *ingénieurs-maritimes* in the *direction du matériel*. In most of the *bureaux*, on the other hand, the military element would have been less obvious than our average figure suggests. Nevertheless, even there it would have been far stronger than would have been found in the Admiralty, apart from on the Board itself. In 1861 there were only thirteen executive officers in the Admiralty, including Somerset House. There were even fewer civil officers, comprising four masters, an engineer, and a brace both of paymasters and medical men. We have also to note two Royal Marines officers and, acting as a conservator in the Harbour Branch, a captain in the Royal Engineers. Thus the military element in the Admiralty was not only more weakly structured than it was in the Ministry of

[19] For the duties of the two latter corps, see Maurice Block, *Dictionnaire de l'administration française* (Paris, 1856), 1098–9.

Marine, it was far smaller in proportion to the administration as a whole — only a quarter of the French equivalent.

The difference is interesting in itself, but does not lead us very far in our search for the cause of the superiority of French naval policy-making. Why, after all, should a *commis de marine* be a better worker, or a *commissaire* be more far-sighted, than a civilian *employé* or *fonctionnaire*? All are bounded by the four walls of the office, by the dull even stupefying routine of administration, by the need to stop paper accumulating on the desk. Indeed, one could argue that the presence of a large and elaborately structured military element in an administration could have a depressing effect upon work. The weight of hierarchy in a military organization is surely almost always heavier than in a civilian one, helping to snuff out originality in a junior. Moreover, the morale and enthusiasm of the civilian workers in a mixed organization could be adversely affected if the military element is unduly favoured — and, as far as we can now judge, they were affected in this way in the Ministry of Marine. At least some of the executive officers tended to forget that they had some civilians to deal with, and behaved in the rue Royale as though they were still on the quarterdeck. The civilians naturally resented such authoritarian behaviour. In particular they resented it when it came from non-executive officers aping the manners of the *grand corps*. There was a definite friction between the civilian *employés* and the officers of the *Commissariat*. The latter — the *ferblantiers* (tinsmiths), as they were called from the silver braid on their uniforms — could be very peremptory in manner. The clerk at the Ministry of Marine who is the central character in Maupassant's *Au printemps* at one point states that he and his colleagues are treated as *gabiers* by the *officiers plumitifs*. Moreover, and surely the most embittering factor of all, the *commissaires* got the pick of the promotion in the *bureaux*. Civilians hardly ever rose higher than the position of *sous-directeur*, and few enough got that far.[20]

There is another obstacle to any attempt to link French naval-policy success with the strength of the military element at the rue Royale. It was only from the late 1840s that French naval shipbuilding policy became truly adventurous. Yet the military administrators were already present in force well before that time, dating back, as with so much else in French government, to Colbert. Part

[20] Thuillier, *Bureaucratie et bureaucrates*, 8 n.

of the military element at the rue Royale, we shall argue, did contribute to the successes of the 1850s and 1860s, but in a way that will be understood only after we have looked at the administrative structures of the naval ministries in London and Paris.

III

Although during our period the Admiralty was bifurcated physically, in terms of its administrative structure it was largely compact and rational in shape, forming a pyramid. Along the broad base were various departments, responsible for the day-to-day central civil administration of the navy. The most important of these were the five Principal Offices, which had been created in 1832 to take over the work of two abolished administrative committees—the Victualling Board and the Navy Board. Each of the five was headed by a Principal Officer: the Surveyor of the Navy, the Accountant-General, the Storekeeper-General, the Comptroller of Victualling and Transport Services, and lastly the Physician of the Navy or Medical Director-General. As the years went by, and naval specialization—and responsibilities—had increased, other offices developed at essentially the same level. In the 1860s, for instance, one saw the creation of independent departments for naval education, ordnance, and contracts. However, both the old Principal Offices and the new departments were similar in one respect. The men who headed them were each responsible to an authority further up the pyramid, one of the members of the Board of Admiralty. Each member of the Board— with the exception of the First Lord himself—was a 'Superintending Lord' of one or more of the departments below.

There was also a department at Whitehall intermediate between the Board at the apex of the pyramid and the civil offices at the base. This was variously known as the Naval Department, or the Central Office, or simply the Secretariat, or—most usually—the Secretary's Department. After changes made in 1869 as part of the Childers's reforms (to be dealt with later), it became clear that the secretary being talked of was the Second, or Permanent Secretary, the principal permanent official of the Admiralty, rather than his Parliamentary colleague, the First Secretary, who changed with the government. Before that year there was some doubt as to which of the two was the effective head of the Whitehall naval bureaucracy; though in the few decades before 1869 the tenure and thus experience of the Second Secretary tended to give him dominance in day-to-day matters. Although there was a degree of ambiguity, it does not appear to have significantly impeded administration, relations between the two Secretaries generally being amicable; and there was certainly no doubt as to the importance of the Secretariat. All the correspondence between the Admiralty and other departments of state passed through it. So too did all the important purely professional business. For instance, all the despatches between the Board and naval officers took this route.

There was also a very large amount of correspondence between the Secretariat and the Principal Offices at Somerset House. One reason for this was that the Lords were generally to be found at Whitehall, where the Board usually met. Each Principal Officer could refer problems personally to the Superintending Lord when the man was at Somerset House, either for the occasional Board meeting that took place there, usually once a week, or during one of his regular, often daily, visits. But when he was at Whitehall, papers requiring decisions had to be referred to him there, and then they would be processed by the Secretariat.

Another reason for the frequent scurrying of Admiralty messengers up and down Charing Cross was that many matters involving not just the serious but also the minor had to be referred to the Secretariat anyway: some Principal Officers complained that they should have more powers to deal with minor questions themselves, and that Whitehall tried to grasp at too much detail.[21] In the latter regard, some change came in 1869, but even after that the Secretary's Department retained a pivotal position, remaining what has been called 'the central depository of official knowledge'.[22] The fact of its being such a 'depository' in itself gave the Department a greater role than is always implied by the word 'secretariat'; above all because of the way that the personnel of the Board changed almost entirely each time there was a change of government. Thus, this central permanent bureaucracy gave a degree of continuity

[21] C. I. Hamilton (ed.), 'Selections from the Phinn Committee of Inquiry, 1855', paras. 1614, 1821, in N. A. M. Rodger (ed.), *The Naval Miscellany*, v (Navy Records Society, London, 1984).
[22] Sir Oswyn Murray, 'The Admiralty', *Mariner's Mirror*, 24 (1938), 329–52, 458–78.

and official memory otherwise lacking: one that was all the more important because of the role that precedent rather than formal regulation plays in British administrative practice. Personal memory, ingrained bureaucratic practice, and the possession of the main naval record office, were all crucial here in underpinning the authority of the Secretary's Department.

One alternative name—the Naval Department—suggests another reason for its importance, the concern not just with civil but also with military administration. The width of responsibility of the Secretariat becomes obvious when we look at the separate branches that made up the whole. First there was the Military, Secret and Political Branch, devoted to the drafting of despatches on the distribution and employment of the fleet, and on all questions concerning the political and diplomatic consequences of naval action. This was the most important branch of all; recognized for much of our period by an extra stipend granted to the clerk who headed it, conceding a stature second only to that of the Chief Clerk of the whole department. Its importance was shown also by the way that on the outbreak of the Crimean War, it had to be divided into two separate branches, though they were reamalgamated in 1857.

There were also the following branches (state as in 1861):

Civil (or Establishment)
Steam, Packet and Transport
Commission
Warrant
Pension and Pay
Manning and Miscellaneous (or Naval)
Legal

Finally there was the Reader's Branch, plus the Secretariat Record Office.

Perhaps the most mysterious is the Reader's Branch. This helped open some of the despatches, read the important ones to the Board, and made précis and various returns for the Board or for Parliament. Otherwise, the branch names are at least guides to the work tackled; but they are hardly sure ones, and certainly not constant. Responsibilities were naturally affected when branches were divided or amalgamated. We have also to note that business was periodically reallocated between branches even when their number and names remained the same.

All the bureaucratic shuffling was an implicit recognition of the fact that the duties of the Secretariat were vast and not always susceptible to neat categorization. That, ultimately, prevents one from fully describing the Secretariat's work, since one would be describing the functions of naval administration as a whole. However, the important truth about it is contained in the statement by one First Sea Lord at the end of the nineteenth century: the Permanent Secretary, he said, 'is the mouthpiece of the Board, and his Department the machinery by which a great deal of its varied work is carried on'.[23] The comment about the Permanent Secretary really applies only after 1869, but the other comment is certainly valid for our period. The Secretariat, in short, was the primary bureaucratic instrument of the Board, and even the Principal Offices were effectively subordinate to it. Still it was only an instrument, albeit capable, as is any bureaucracy, of taking on some life of its own and helping to shape decisions.

Before proceeding to the Board itself, one ought to single out one of the Principal Officers—the Surveyor (or Controller after 1860). As chief adviser to their Lordships on warship design, the Surveyor's position was bound to be a powerful one in times of technological change, as long, that is, as the Board trusted his advice, which had not been the case in the latter days of Symonds. But Baldwin Walker, and his successor Spencer Robinson, were trusted, and came to have great influence; helped greatly by the removal of their office to Whitehall, close to the Board's ear, in 1855. The Surveyor was something of an anomaly in the Admiralty, falsifying the pyramid image, or at least suggesting a potential for authority to shift within the structure, as he moved closer and closer to being in effect one of the Lords. In 1859, for example, he was given extended powers to correspond directly with the dockyards. He was still subordinate to a Superintending Lord, who generally seems to have been the First Naval Lord, but had more independence than any of his fellow Principal Officers. In 1869 his position was to be recognized by ascension to the Board as Third Naval Lord and Controller, a position lost only temporarily between 1872 and 1882.

Nothing about the Surveyor leads one to question the power

[23] Sir R. Vesey Hamilton, *Naval Administration: The Constitution, Character, and Functions of the Board of Admiralty and of the Civil Departments it Directs* (London, 1896), 56, 60.

of the Board, but the power of one other man does lead to that question. For the very top of the Admiralty structure was not the Board, it was an individual. In theory, according, that is, to the Admiralty patent, decisions within the Board belonged to the majority rather than to one man. The First Lord himself was thus supposedly only *primus inter pares*, but practice did not follow theory.

Admittedly, a good deal depended on individual personalities. Strong personalities can be relied on in any country, in any system, to create a gap between the theory and practice of administration. What was unusual in the case of the Admiralty was that the theory itself was contradictory. On the one hand there was the patent. On the other was the principle behind the reorganization of 1832: individual responsibility.

From 1832, just as the heads of the civil departments were each responsible for the efficient running of his office to a specific Lord, so too it was accepted that each Superintending Lord was responsible to the First Lord for that department. The same principle applied in the Secretary's Department, although there were certain complications. First, there was the doubt about which Secretary had precedence. Secondly, individual Board members were responsible for work carried on within the Secretariat branches that corresponded with work done in the civil departments for which they were responsible. There were occasional suggestions that Lords should be made responsible for specific branches, but this step was not taken: one branch head, therefore, might have to deal with several Lords. Nevertheless, even in the Secretariat one could attach responsibility for decisions to individuals, just as could be done in the other departments. Ultimately the First Lord was responsible for the whole administration.

Given the British constitution, this would have been inevitable, even had individual responsibility not been the watchword of naval administration after 1832. The Minister was responsible to the Cabinet and to Parliament for the efficient running of the navy as a whole.[24] In other words, cutting through the quasi-fiction of Board decision-making were strong vertical threads that united in the person of the First Lord, and continued on up to the very fountain-

---

[24] The occasional existence of a military committee of the cabinet does not seriously affect this description. See M. S. Partridge, *Military Planning for the Defense of the United Kingdom 1814–1870* (New York, 1989), 62 ff.

head of the State. Admittedly, his position might in effect be turned by a particularly dominant colleague on the Board, but at least his position was intrinsically a very strong one.

There was one other factor that strengthened the First Lord's position, one also that we have to appreciate in order to understand properly the 1832 reforms and the ability of the Admiralty to act effectively in the highest questions of naval administration. It emerges in a memorandum written in 1841 by Lord Minto, on his retirement as First Lord:

The labour at present required from the Lords to enable them to conduct the business satisfactorily is very greatly beyond the degree of exertion to be generally found or expected, but without which no efficient direction or controul can be exercised over the subordinate departments . . .[25]

What he was talking about here were the Superintending Lords, the First Lord lacking similar detailed supervisory duties. The pressure on the former only increased after 1841 as *matériel* changed, numbers increased, and the amount of correspondence grew enormously, all resulting in more complaints about the burdens of administration. Partial exceptions might be made here for the Civil Lord and the First Secretary, politicians both, since their administrative burdens were less predictable than were those of their colleagues. Changes in the political temperature meant they paid greater or lesser attention to naval policy, according as affairs in the Commons waned or waxed. The nature of the First Secretary's duties was also affected by whatever agreement he had come to with the Second Secretary as to the apportioning of work within the Whitehall Admiralty. Thus, he or the Civil Lord might find himself seriously harried at certain times, but at others have spare energies for general naval questions. It is at least interesting that Sidney Herbert (First Secretary 1841–5), and H. T. Lowry Corry (Civil Lord 1841–5 and Herbert's successor) appear to have been significant proponents of the screw-programme of the mid-1840s; and when Corry reappeared as First Secretary between 1858 and 1859, he sponsored the first British iron-hulled battleships.[26]

[25] Sept. 1841, ADM 3 265.
[26] D. K. Brown, *A Century of Naval Construction: The History of the Royal Corps of Naval Constructors, 1883–1983* (London, 1983), 31–2, 36; *Before the Ironclad: Development of Ship Design, Propulsion and Armament in the Royal Navy, 1815–60* (London, 1990), ch. 10.

It was the First Lord, though, who had the best chance to contemplate the broader aspects of naval policy. The other Lords were usually engaged in minutiae: he alone was relatively certain of having at least some room for manœuvre, some spare capacity. One sees this clearly during the Crimean War. Even before then, Board meetings had often been little more than occasions for the First Lord to hear the reports of his colleagues on the workings of their departments. The war brought yet greater administrative burdens, and the Superintending Lords had to spend ever more time at Somerset House, or on urgent tours of inspection in the ports, leaving the First Lord at Whitehall. Board meetings now became perfunctory or were just missed, and Graham no longer took professional advice in the usual way. Admittedly, the illness of the First Naval Lord early in the war was a special circumstance here; but it is significant that the First Lord felt capable of regularly circumventing the machinery of the Board, and taking many important policy decisions himself. He lent heavily on the advice of the Surveyor, often seeing him daily, but this itself was subversive of Board discipline, as was Graham's practice of sending out orders carrying the full authority of the Lords Commissioners of the Admiralty, which ought to have had the approval of at least two of them, when they had been drawn up simply by himself and his private secretary.

Graham's successors did not have to deal with the same degree of emergency. Furthermore, the fast growing complexity of warship types from the late 1850s onwards perhaps encouraged the layman to show hesitancy in formulating at least some aspects of naval policy. Thus, the Duke of Somerset, himself a strong character, was willing to let the Board function as a Board, at least as far as it could. Yet even at this point the First Lord hardly fades into the background: one has only to read some of Somerset's minutes, almost always forceful and cogently argued. Graham's successors could only have agreed with the opinion he gave in 1861 before an inquiry, an opinion that is a reasonable summary of Admiralty practice during the mid-nineteenth century.

. . . the First Lord of the Admiralty, in the last resort, is responsible for everything in all the departments . . . the Board of Admiralty can only work by the First Lord exercising power to such an extent as really to render the Board subordinate to his will. In short, I regard the First Lord as Minister of Marine, technically he is not so, but virtually the system can never work unless he really be so.[27]

In France the central naval administration was largely different from the one we have been describing. There was no question in this case of anything contradictory to the regulations that underpinned it; moreover, the practice followed the regulations. One author, himself a *contrôleur général de la marine*, who has compared the British and French naval ministries, described thus the peculiarity of French administration.

Notre esprit français exige des définitions serrées et une codification rationnelle. Nombreux ont été, aux diverses époques, nos règlements organiques; ils ont toujours constitué, non pas un embarras mais un soutien pour les chefs énergiques a l'intelligence clair; seuls, les brouillons, épris d'une autorité qu'ils sont incapables d'exercer, les ont tenus pour barrières en travers de la route sur laquelle ils titubaient, au lieu de les regarder comme des jalons permettent de suivre son chemin sans hésitation.[28]

Clearly, we have here an administrative philosophy quite different from that over the Channel. As Archbishop Temple once wrote, the English 'are suspicious of system . . . the French desire a tabulated schedule of action to be taken in all foreseen contingencies; the English tend rather to deal with the situation confronting them and afterwards discover on what principles they have done so, and what precedent for future action they have established.'[29] In Britain, when practice diverged from regulation, the fact might be ignored — or perhaps never noticed in the first place. In France, by contrast, a change in practice implied that all pertinent regulations would be looked at, and redrawn to meet both the new contingencies and those that might be reasonably expected to arise in the future. In essence, British regulations were either redundant or descriptive: French ones were prescriptive.

[27] PP (1861), xxvi. 465. This opinion was fully in accord with the contemporary parliamentary attitude towards boards — and also with what J. S. Mill had written in *Considerations on Representative Government* (London, 1860): see F. M. G. Willson, 'Ministries and Boards: Some Aspects of Administrative Development since 1832', *Public Administration*, 33 (1955), 43–58.

[28] H. Boyer, 'Les Rouages de l'amirauté britannique', *Revue maritime*, 194 (Feb. 1936), 169.

[29] William Temple, *The Ethics of Penal Action* (The Clark Hall Lecture for 1934, Rochester), 14–15.

What did this philosophical difference mean for naval policy-making in the two countries? Were not the French system's self-proclaimed virtues of order, logic, clarity, and intelligence necessarily an advantage? It is difficult to give a precise answer. There is no single ideal model of administration. Two systems can differ radically, and yet each—in the hands of those accustomed to it—can perform well. Moreover, the 'French virtues' are not necessarily wholly beneficial in their effects. Frequent changes of regulations disturb the even tenor of administration, and one suspects that on occasion more attention is given to the drafting of new, internally consistent rules than looking at what is being administered. Perhaps even intelligence itself is not always an unalloyed advantage. We can sympathize with Trevelyan and Northcote's dislike of the stupid and indolent, but also see that the intelligent and indolent—not an uncommon type, a good fictional example being the mischievous clerk Bixiou in Balzac's *Les Employés*—have their own destructive influence on administration. Even more dangerous is the energetic administrator whose intelligence and enthusiasm are not balanced by common sense or an adequate knowledge of the organization he directs. Camille Pelletan might be cited here: his forcefulness and *idées fixes* made him the most disastrous Minister of Marine of modern times.[30]

This is perhaps special pleading. In general the 'French virtues' *were* virtues, but they were hardly wholly French or wholly lacking on the British side. However, it was surely important that they were spoken of far more than in Britain. The French attachment to their system of administration was conscious, and it seems reasonable to argue that this proved of some gain. As we have seen clearly when speaking of seamen reserves and the education and promotion of officers, there are significant advantages to be obtained from a system consciously geared to the highest needs of an institution rather than to practices hallowed by time. Given that we are dealing with large, hierarchical organizations with long histories, there was never any danger that the voice of experience would be too weak: quite the reverse. It was therefore valuable for the French navy that the very principles underlying the administration encouraged policy-makers to look forwards, to anticipate, and perhaps even to ignore the past.

---

[30] He held the office from 1902–5; P. G. Halpern, *The Mediterranean Naval Situation 1908–1914* (Harvard University Press, 1971), 51–2.

This was of particular importance given the usual numerical inferiority of the French navy. The leading navy can usually afford to wait for challenges to which it has to respond rather than itself making the running. This was the Royal Navy's general policy, and was perfectly rational—as long as it included an intelligent appreciation of possible future challenges. Unfortunately, complacency was quite possible. The future is bound to offer a lesser stimulus to the superior navy than it does to the lesser one. For the latter, there is the encouragement of perhaps being able to overturn the adverse *status quo* at some later time. And having less to lose, the inferior can be less wary about innovation. Admittedly, optimism is not an automatic consequence of inferiority: despair and inertia are possible. But at least one may say that inferiority sometimes spurs greater activity, prompting a reliance on intelligence when brute force is lacking. That is obvious enough: what we can add is that in the French case, this possibility was enhanced by the very philosophy of administration.

Of course, the attempt to plan ahead is not necessarily successful. The French long-term construction plan of 1846 was hidebound. At this time the *brouillons*, or bunglers, at the Admiralty performed far better. To explain how the Ministry of Marine finally began to achieve its aims, we have to penetrate further into its structure during the 1840s and 1850s.

We have likened the Admiralty to a pyramid. The Ministry of Marine was more reminiscent of a solar system, the Minister—Apollo-like—in the centre, with a large number of lesser bodies moving about him in their orbits.

Largest of the circling bodies was the central administration *strictu sensu*, the *bureaux* at the rue Royale. Or perhaps we should see it as a small planetary system in its own right. The clerks were divided up between the *bureaux*, and the *bureaux* were gathered into *directions* under their own heads, each dealing with a particular area of the administration. During 1843–8, when the Minister had heavy parliamentary duties, a department of an assistant-minister (the *sous-secrétaire d'état*) was set up to assume some of the ministerial load by co-ordinating the work of the *directions*. But for the rest of our period the *directeurs* were responsible directly to the Minister for the efficient running of their departments.

Beyond the central bureaucracy of the *directions* there were the various independent committees, and these also have to be considered. The most important of all were the *Conseil d'amirauté*, whose work touched on all aspects of naval policy, and the *Conseil des travaux* which, as the name implies, was concerned with questions of port development and naval *matériel*. All the committees, one must stress, like the central administration proper, were merely advisory; all dependent on the authority of the *ministre-soleil*.

The French structure was more passive than the British one. The Minister was the mainspring of action, presenting specific dependent bodies with proposals on which comment was required, or calling for proposals to be made on certain problems. In the pyramid, on the other hand, there were clear, regularly used lines of communication, leading up rather than down and well suited to the passage upwards of information and advice, for processing. The difference was not absolute. Naturally, much arrived on the Minister's desk that he had not solicited. And in Britain the Board, or perhaps simply the First Lord, often acted as the galvanizing agent, calling for reactions from the administration to certain proposals. Nevertheless, there was a difference of emphasis. The point is that in France the pattern of channels was not as well articulated or as established as in Britain. Moreover, the channels that existed were fully opened only by the ministerial will. This had the important effect that the various dependent bodies tended to act as stores for ideas, waiting —not always consciously—for the time when they could present their case on a particular issue. It is also important that the separate administrative units in such a system naturally had a more developed sense of rivalry than was usual in the case of the Admiralty. The attitude of one committee to a certain policy might well be significantly different from that of another committee, as we have already seen with the response to the *vaisseau à vapeur* of the *Conseil d'amirauté* and the *Conseil des travaux*; and where such differences occurred, the inter-committee friction made a hard-fought argument more likely.

Thus the very structure of the Ministry of Marine made it more likely that brave new ideas would be retained and nurtured in some element of the administration; more likely than in the Admiralty, where freer communications implied the passing along of proposals up and up to the highest level, there quite possibly to be rejected and purged from the system. The French structure could benefit the new in another way. It might be that the Minister favoured a certain policy, but found insufficient support from those around him. The system was flexible enough for him to get bureaucratic self-interest on his side by creating a new committee or even a *bureau* to cater to that policy. In 1863, for instance, in order to encourage the development of better rifled-cannon, an independent ordnance committee was brought into being within the system. There is an even better example in the US navy, which after 1842 had an administrative structure similar to that of *la Royale*. As well as the various *bureaux*, by the first year of the Civil War there were also several advisory committees, and a few of them had duties involving naval construction and design. Unfortunately, from the point of view of the Secretary of the Navy, none wholly approved the *Monitor* concept. All he had to do, however, was to create a separate *Monitor bureau*, and this carried on the fight for the new type.[31] The French structure, to conclude, was better suited than the British to the encouragement of the new.

There is a crucial caveat. The system depended on some good or even inspired administrators. Above all, it depended on the quality of the Minister. He was the only link between all the various elements of the administration. His authority was indispensable for any important measure. Moreover, he could not act effectively on his own. In a letter to Chasseloup-Laubat, Bouët-Willaumez also likened the naval administration to a *mécanique céleste*, or a Jove with his satellites. The reality, the Minister replied, was not that simple, since one man cannot do everything, and everyone in the administration had to play his part.[32] In brief, the Minister needed not just talent, but also proper support. Looking just within the naval administration for the moment, and forgetting about outside political forces, one may argue he was able to create this support, using his plenitude of power by adopting essentially two means. The first has been touched on already: he could adapt the structure to his own requirements—or, indeed, to the talents of his underlings. Second, he could put his chosen men within the existing structure.

One can observe the employment of the second means in 1852, as Ducos attempted to bring new life into what had become a somewhat conservative *Conseil d'amirauté*. In 1848 the revolutionary regime had opened it to younger officers but, as political reaction

---

[31] C. O. Paullin, 'A Half Century of Naval Administration in America, 1861–1911', *US Naval Institute Proceedings*, 38 (1912), 1319–25.

[32] Minister's letter of 18 July 1864, Chasseloup-Laubat Papers, vol. vi.

took hold of the government, *convenances hiérarchiques* led to a re-emphasis on seniority as a requirement for membership. Ducos, whose bump of reverence for senior officers was not pronounced, reversed the trend. As he wrote:

Il y a parmi nos capitaines de vaisseau des hommes jeunes, impatients du progrès, représantants des idées nouvelles dont l'expérience est déjà faite et dont l'initiative peut-être précieuse.[33]

Ducos, and his successors, acted similarly with regard to the other committees, and to the *bureaux*. They had the great strength of being able to draw on men educated to standards not easily available in Britain. Just as there was the *Borda* for young naval officers, so for engineers there was the *École d'application*. Unfortunately, the *École d'administration* did not long survive its founding in 1848, soon falling victim to conservative bureaucrats and jealous academics, so one source of well-educated civilian administrators became unavailable. But there was still the *École polytechnique*, without equal on the other side of the Channel, as with the *Borda* or *École d'application*.

From such sources the Minister could reasonably hope to find the coadjutors he needed. And with his extensive power, untrammelled by even any fiction of board decision-making, a power that was largely increased with the 1851 *coup d'état* which emasculated parliament and encouraged departmental autocracy, the Minister had a greater power of appointment than that available to, say, the First Lord in Britain. Admittedly, those chosen were always few in number: in some years none at all would appear. The average intellectual tone of the bureaucracy, for instance, would not have been greatly influenced, nor the general run of promotion. Nevertheless, the talents of these few, and the active patronage of the Minister, meant that a useful spirit of freshness and enthusiasm could be brought to the naval administration.

The practice was one that applied, by and large, to all the French government. Vincent Wright has said:

Pour atteindre le haut de l'échelle administrative française au milieu du dix-neuvième siècle il fallait généralement avoir non seulement du talent, de l'obstination et du tact, mais aussi bénéficier d'une protection de nature personnelle ou politique — ou les deux. Pour certains directeurs, cette

---

[33] Ministerial note, AN BB8 108 (*marine*), 279.

protection était essentielle, pour d'autre elle était fortement souhaitable. A la différence de l'Angleterre, l'État français était, de loin, le plus grand employeur de jeunes gens intélligents, et à l'opposé de la Prusse il n'y avait pas de règles bien définies pour le recrutement et l'avancement dans la fonction publique. Chaque ministère et chaque corps avaient leurs propres règlements officieux. Dans la jungle administrative qui en résultait, un système de protection—ou de 'patronage'—était inévitable.[34]

However, there were some limits in the case of the navy. The obvious point is that the talented men required tended to be officers of one kind or another; so, when moving men around, rank had to be respected to some degree, as well as acknowledged professional expertise. It would have been foolish for the Minister to use his power of promotion in quite unprecedented ways: that would have led to too much envy. It was perhaps no accident, therefore, that the patronage of the able was sometimes combined with changes to the organizational structure, which quite subverted the hierarchies that might have opposed the new men. Certainly, the patronage of the able was most effective when it had an appropriate organizational basis. One thinks here of the *direction du matériel*, created in 1852 by Ducos, which in January 1857 found its *genius loci* with the promotion of Dupuy de Lôme to *directeur*.

Above all, though, one thinks of another new section, created in 1852 and expressly designed to support and extend the authority of the Minister. It became the single most important administrative organ of the Ministry. Furthermore, it was the one to which the Minister appears to have attracted the very best men he could find, and where their talents achieved their highest expression.

The essence of the change was that the ministerial cabinet, previously simply a small secretarial office, equivalent to the private office of the First Lord of the Admiralty, was extended greatly in size and significance. The cabinet absorbed both the *état-major* of the Minister, and a *bureau* hitherto included in the *direction du personnel* and responsible for the disposition of the fleet. After 1852, as well as being the avenue through which the Minister transmitted his decisions and received reports, the cabinet also had concentrated within it (subject to the final decision of the Minister, of course) responsibility for the highest military functions of the navy.

[34] Vincent Wright, 'Les Directeurs et secrétaires généraux des administrations centrales sous le Second Empire', in F. de Baecque *et al.*, *Les Directeurs de ministère en France (XIXᵉ-première moitié du XXᵉ siècles)* (Geneva, 1976), 48.

It acted, moreover, as the final board of review on the most vital questions of administration and policy. The new cabinet was all the more suited for its functions since it brought high authority (the Minister) intimately together with expertise (the men he chose as his closest professional advisers). True, under the previous dispensation, the Minister had been able to draw on the advice of his *état-major*, but now the *état-major* was directly involved in administration, though without being weighed down with pettifogging detail. The *chef d'état-major* was the director of the cabinet, and thus occupied a pivotal position, something only enhanced by the reform of December 1860 which created a *direction des mouvements de la flotte et opérations militaires*. This body was but a development of part of the cabinet, and was also headed by the *chef d'état-major*, making him into a vice-minister; though this possibly aroused Chasseloup-Laubat's jealousy, and he eventually amended the new system. By the end of his ministry (and the example was followed by Rigault de Genouilly, his successor), the posts of *directeur des mouvements* and *chef du cabinet* were held by different men.

Two points arise concerning the development of the cabinet. The first has already been mentioned: the chief ministerial *protégés* were officers—naval engineers in the *direction du matériel*, and, in the post-1852 cabinet, members of the *grand corps*. It is when we think of the *créatures* of the Minister (going back to a fine word of the time of Richelieu), or of his *instruments* (taking Pepys's equivalent), in connection with certain central administrative organs, that we find the military element at the rue Royale acting with real effectiveness.

The second point about the cabinet is to do with what made it so influential. Naturally, the talent of the members was important. And it was obviously crucial that they were able to draw on the ideas that arose from below, ideas encouraged by the excellent education and *esprit de corps* of the naval engineers, and of officers of the *grand corps*. Furthermore, one must allow for the closeness of the cabinet to the Minister, and the opportunity this gave for proffering advice at the centre of power. But the crux of the matter is that the cabinet was an extension of the Minister's authority, amplifying not only his powers to think and decide, but also his ability to act. It is difficult not to give some credit to this body when attempting to explain the speedy organization in France of trials of steam after 1856, or the approval of new types of *matériel* in the late 1850s and early 1860s. True, even after 1860 the cabinet remained a small body, amounting to not much more than a dozen members, including the clerks. But this was sufficient, given the small size of the total central naval administration. Certainly, in certain regards the small bureaucracies of the nineteenth century could act like the swollen ones of today, but here, at least, there was a difference: in the mid-nineteenth century, although a single man—however great his authority—might well be ineffective, a few like-minded men together could energize a whole administration.

Perhaps in no other way than in regard to the ministerial cabinet does the French system stand out from the British, which had no such organizational underpinning of executive authority. There was the First Lord's private office; but this was strictly secretarial in nature, at least during our period. There was also the Board; but it was too overburdened itself to act as a true planning body, and too jealous of possible institutional threats to its own authority to allow any other body to do so. Occasional committees might be organized to investigate specific subjects, such as signals, or stores, or whatever, but these were dissolved as soon as they had reported. Even a body like the Committee of Reference, although subordinate to the Board, posed an implicit challenge in terms of expertise, and herein lay at least one reason for its failure to survive. The Board (or at least the First Lord) found a similar and even greater fault in a suggestion in 1859 by Lord Clarence Paget, the First Secretary, that a Committee of Inventions be organized. He proposed that it be organized 'on the principle of the *Conseil d'Amirauté*', itself an interesting example of the way that French examples were being studied in Britain. But the plan had absolutely no chance of being adopted, essentially because Paget proposed giving the Board an independent authority. The Duke of Somerset commented tersely that it would be better to reconstitute the Navy Board than to create such a dangerous body.[35]

The lesson we are drawing from the French naval cabinet is strongly supported by the terrible example of the Childers's Admiralty reforms of 1869. In certain regards they were salutary, above all in the way they divided administration on functional lines,

[35] ADM 1 5717, folder, 10 Aug. 1859.

distinguishing between personnel, *matériel*, and finance. Moreover, Childers was responsible for physically concentrating the London offices, certainly long overdue. Departmental heads were given slightly more authority than previously, satisfying some complaints. Also, mechanical copying was encouraged, cutting down on staff. At the heart of the reforms, though, was a change that went quite against the French example and which maimed Admiralty decision-making until further change came in 1872.

Oddly enough, French practices did influence the reforms; or, rather, a misunderstanding of those practices. Some observers at the end of the 1860s believed that the comparative success of the French navy had been due to the omnipotence of the Minister of Marine. London too, it was argued, needed such a figure. Hence Childers brought in sweeping administrative changes that in effect destroyed the Board, turning the Naval Lords (anyway reduced in number) into merely the administrative heads of the various de-partments, leaving the First Lord alone with the power to collate, co-ordinate, and decide. The effect was disastrous. Childers took more and more of the responsibility, and decided on professional issues with even less professional advice than Graham had taken. One of these issues concerned the new battleship HMS *Captain*, which Childers decided to commission, ignoring the doubts expressed about her stability by the Controller, Sir Spencer Robinson, and the Chief Constructor, E. J. Reed. When she cap-sized, and despite his pretensions to supreme authority, the First Lord put the blame on to Robinson and Reed. Even before the disaster, Childers was a sick man, worn out mentally and physically by ferocious hard work; one of the penalties of his supremacy. The death of a son, who went down with the *Captain*, proved the last straw, and eventually Childers had to resign, and his successor Goschen largely restored the Board in 1872: the experiment of a British Minister of Marine had ended.[36]

It had been misconceived from the very beginning. As Graham had said, the First Lord had all the authority he needed. Moreover, the old system had had some virtues. Indeed, it had improved somewhat during the 1860s: the coming of Robinson and Reed had brought a new vision, a new energy—though also, it must be said,

[36] N. A. M. Rodger, *The Admiralty* (Lavenham, 1979), 108–12.

a new acerbity—to the Controller's Department and thus to the quality of the advice upon which the Board could draw in deciding about warship designs.

Furthermore, the pre-Childers Board—whatever its flaws—had at least on occasion acted as an effective maker of high policy. Typically, it took a crisis to concentrate their Lordships' minds, to drag them away from the fascinating minutiae; above all the sudden realization that the French were ahead. Then the Board became willing to approve sweeping measures. It was at such a stage that any radicals in the administration—whether originating from outside the Admiralty, like Corry, or from within—could successfully take advantage of a desperate mood to press their own solutions. Mentioning Corry, though, leads one on to the inescapable political context of Board decision-making during crises. War scares meant supplementary credits, which meant approaching the cabinet, the Treasury, and Parliament; the credits would be approved, but gave the opportunity to Ministers, to MPs, to the political Lords (and to their radical advisers within the navy), to urge steps that in other circumstances the conservatives on the Board would have been able to counter. Sometimes the results were questionable —as with the iron-frigates of the 1840s. More often they were good—as with the first floating-batteries or the iron hull of the *Warrior*. Board crisis management, in short, was not necessarily a sufficient test of the quality of decision-makers on the Board alone.

One must admit that the pre-1869 pattern was hardly ideal. Ultimately, the Royal Navy owed its supremacy not so much to good planning as to, first, a political will at Westminster—which scarcely ever faltered—that the British had to have the premier navy; and, second, to unmatched financial and industrial resources. These made possible the large and sudden expenditures during crises: unfortunately, the occasional largesse could be a substitute for intelligence and anticipation. Waste was almost inevitable. It was bitterly complained about in the 1860s, above all over the excessive construction of screw ships of the line; the kind of waste that Childers had hoped to end through his Admiralty reforms, since economy had been in his mind at least as much as efficiency. But he only made matters worse. He moved in quite the wrong direction. Instead of developing the Admiralty brain, he lobotomized what there was. Goschen undid the immediate damage, but a basic institutional deficiency remained; one that was to be finally addressed only in the First World War with the development of an effective naval staff.

Over the last few chapters we have identified some of the factors that underpinned the success of French naval policy in the 1850s and 1860s, concluding with the crucial institutional advantage of the post-1852 ministerial cabinet. But the picture remains incomplete, and even false in that it exaggerates the inherent strength of the French position. There is always a role for historical accident, chance, personality, or for influences that might be benign at one stage only to turn contrary the next. So it was for the French navy.

There was a fundamental difficulty with the Ministry of Marine: a dependence on the right men being chosen for the main posts. This became all the more so after the cabinet reforms of 1852, when it became crucial to have an able and energetic *chef d'état-major*. Here the French navy was nearly always fortunate—at least whilst the Second Empire endured. One thinks first of Captain Charner, the boldest of the members of the *Enquête parlementaire*, and *chef d'état-major* to Ducos during the decisive period December 1851– August 1853. Second, one must mention Captain La Roncière Le Noury, who was virtually a co-minister with Chasseloup-Laubat, and a forceful and effective one.

If the chief subordinates had to be able, so too did their chiefs. A great deal depended on the Minister: first on his ability to choose suitable subordinates; but also on the personal energy and resourcefulness he brought to his role as the true centre of the naval administration. Here, too, the French navy was fortunate during the Second Empire. Certainly, to pick the outstanding examples, Ducos and Chasseloup-Laubat had the necessary virtues, both in finding excellent men to serve them, and in playing an active part in the encouragement of new *matériel* and the development of naval policy.

However, we have to look further than the Ministry. Outside influences were of significance, and were at times even overriding. One should recall the prince de Joinville (who was, of course, a naval officer, but whose prerogative had quite another source), pouncing on Guizot when the latter was temporarily appointed Minister of Marine, in order to get the first *vaisseau à vapeur* approved. In this case the attempt failed, or at least its success was delayed. It does suggest, however, that the French system, with all power given to the Minister, was a marvellous one for lobbyists.

Convince the Minister and the argument was (virtually) won. Thus the Minister might be inept, but he could still be successful if he listened to the right prompter.

For the Second Empire period there is one 'outside influence' that has to be stressed above all others: the Emperor. If the subordinates in the Ministry of Marine were able, some credit must go to the Minister who chose them. If the Minister himself was able, some credit must go to the man who chose him. Credit is due also because Napoleon, having chosen his man, gave him continuing support. Hamelin and his two successors each had five years in office; and had Ducos not died prematurely he, very likely, would have been treated similarly. Thus French Ministers of Marine under the Empire were able to learn from experience, their authority could be firmly established, and continuity of policy encouraged. This was in striking contrast to the position in Britain, at least during the 1850s, when governments proved relatively fragile. Admittedly, unlike in the previous decade, by this time it was regular practice for one or more of the Naval Lords on the outgoing Board to be appointed to the new one. This gave some continuity, but a change of government still essentially meant a change of Board, with all the disturbance that entailed for naval administration whilst old policies were reviewed and the new men learned to work together. The dislocation was especially severe during the politically troubled years 1858–9, when changes at the Admiralty delayed the approval of the first British seagoing ironclads.[37]

The Emperor did more than encourage continuity of policy-making. He was himself an active 'lobbyist'. The precise extent of his involvement in naval policy-making is uncertain, due to the destruction of so many documents during the Commune, but we know that he took a particular interest in questions of *matériel*, above all in artillery, where he had a genuine expertise. His intervention was perhaps greatest in regard to the obverse side to improvements in naval gunnery: the armouring of warships. In the mid-1850s and afterwards, at first spurred by what he saw as the special needs of the war against Russia, Napoleon encouraged trials of armour-plate and promoted ironclad schemes. Almost certainly, we cannot understand the major French naval innovation of the

[37] J. P. Baxter, *The Introduction of the Ironclad Warship* (Harvard University Press, 1933), 152–3.

end of the 1850s without accepting the importance of the Emperor. Hamelin, the Minister of Marine during this period, was a worthy officer, but his evidence before the *Enquête parlementaire* suggests that he was not one of the most prescient of men. Quite possibly some boldness was contributed by Rear-Admiral Guillois, Charner's successor and inherited from Ducos (who is not likely to have appointed a conservative). Charner himself remained of importance: he headed the *Conseil des travaux* in the late 1850s. But the Emperor appears to have acted as the prime catalyst at this time, even taking the part of a superior Minister of Marine by sending his own proposals for action, and also prompting the appointment in January 1857 as *directeur du matériel* of a man whose ability to look ahead was undoubted—Dupuy de Lôme.[38]

In the following decade the Emperor's touch would have been much less frequent. Other demands on his attention were increasing, his health and energy were declining, and his Ministers of Marine were certainly capable and well supported by their advisers. But even now Napoleon had to be considered: his support remained essential for the same central reason as in the earlier years. The naval building programmes, the development of the arsenals, the swing away from dependence on the *levées permanentes*, and the ambitious enlargement of the overseas empire were extremely expensive. The ironclad fleet was particularly costly: between 1857 and 1860 the vote for construction and provisioning increased by over a half. Furthermore, while it doubtless spurred growth in certain sectors of the economy, the new fleet made heavy demands on scarce industrial and scientific resources. The scope and success of French imperial naval policy cannot be explained simply in terms of decision-making within the rue Royale. The right decisions had to be made there (subject to occasional intervention from the Tuileries), but they could not be carried out without the government allocating the necessary resources—which brings us back to Napoleon; essentially an autocrat up to the early 1860s, and with still very wide powers until the declaration of the Liberal Empire in 1869.

Ultimately, the foundation of French naval power proved to be fragile, dependent on a vision that in 1870 lost much of its credibility. The Emperor had thought that France could be the leading

[38] Ibid., ch. 6.

military power and also, in some senses, rival England in maritime and colonial terms. It is probable, furthermore, that he shared in the belief that a properly planned fleet could seriously bolster purely military strength. 1870 was a cruel shock.

One of the elements of that shock is of particular relevance to our administrative concerns. The French navy showed in war at sea against Germany that it had not properly anticipated and planned for the operations that would be necessary. The administration that we have been praising might have been relatively good at planning programmes of *matériel*, or even thinking about the possible future shape of battle, but was not geared for the meticulous advance accumulation of intelligence and careful staff work necessary to employ that *matériel* to its best advantage in a campaign. However, this was a general failing in war administrations at the time. The Admiralty certainly shared it. Famously, thinking again of the 1870 campaigns, so did the French Ministry of War.

That leads us to the greatest shock of the war with Germany —the collapse of the French army, one that made the navy shine by comparison. But the fates were unkind: it was the army that benefited. The war convinced the general French public that its army was the only guarantee of national security. Despite its poor showing against Von Moltke's forces, precisely because of that showing, the conclusion was drawn that resources had to be concentrated on land forces. The poor navy, and even more so colonies, seemed now to be something of a luxury. There was thus a reversion to the attitude prevailing in 1815. One observes here a rhythm of interest in naval affairs, a growth and then a decline as continental realities reassert themselves, that has long imposed itself on French history.

During the period of maritime disillusion that followed 1870, the French navy found it difficult to obtain sufficient credits. Moreover, with the advent of the Third Republic, it was France rather than Britain that had unstable government and a rapid turnover of naval ministers. Under these conditions the Ministry of Marine showed its weaknesses. Without consistent support from the government or the Chamber, with often inferior men chosen to be Ministers (and doubly damned because of their short tenure of office), the celestial form of naval administration was at its most vulnerable. The Ministry still showed an ability to surprise by taking important initiatives in steel construction, in ordnance, in

armour-plate, and in boilers. But by and large it was the Admiralty
that was now in the stronger position. There was never any question in Britain as to which was the senior service, never any doubt
in Parliament that the Royal Navy had to remain the strongest in
the world (albeit there were disagreements as to the precise degree
of necessary superiority). Also, someprevious French advantages
were being whittled away with improvements in the *Britannia*, the
setting-up of the naval architecture school at South Kensington,
and the creation in 1883 of a special corps for Royal Navy constructors (specifically modelled on the French example[39]). Finally,
whatever the faults of the Admiralty as an administration, however
uninspired it could be, it could still continue to work adequately
even when it was unfortunate enough to have second-rate men on
the Board. The well-established channels and habits that could stul-
tify did at least ensure a kind of continuity. The French system, on
the other hand, demanded first-rate men for it to work properly.
During the 1850s and 1860s it had them, and also had a degree
of support and encouragement from the government—that is,
the Emperor—exceptional in French history. In these decades,
virtually everything favoured the French navy. It is in these terms
that one must see its ability at this time seriously to rival and even
surpass its old enemy.

[39] Brown, *A Century of Naval Construction*, 56–9.

8

The Nature of the Rivalry
and its Conclusion

I

The most striking feature of the naval rivalry between Britain and France in the mid-nineteenth century was its degree of exclusivity. Each side came to see itself as having only one real opponent—the other. In a pamphlet published in 1844, one French naval officer wrote, 'La force et la puissance d'une marine n'étant que relative, il faut un point de comparaison. Ce point, il n'y en a qu'un: c'est la marine anglaise.'[1] What he wrote applied also in reverse. One could argue that the gaze of the Admiralty was somewhat less narrowly fixed than that of the Ministry of Marine. In 1849 Palmerston commented thus on a suggestion by the French Foreign Minister that the two governments should agree to a common reduction of naval force:

the amount of our Naval establishment is governed by so many and such various considerations connected with our commercial and political interests in every part of the world, that it can never be possible for the British government to fix the amount of that establishment with reference to the amount of Naval Force maintained by any one particular power.[2]

The French navy, of course, also had some distractions from the rivalry with the Royal Navy. But British commercial and imperial interests did tend to be more widespread than French ones, and the London government was thus somewhat less prone to gauge its naval force purely by the standard of the one over the Channel. Nevertheless, in the mid-nineteenth century the French navy was at least the prime factor in naval calculations in Whitehall. Palmerston

[1] Clément de La Roncière Le Noury, *Considérations sur les marines à voiles et à vapeur de France et d'Angleterre* (Paris, 1844), 5.
[2] Despatch to the Marquis of Normanby, ambassador in Paris, 25 Jan. 1849, PRO FO.27.834.

admitted this later in his despatch, saying that even before the recent proposal Her Majesty's Government, believing in the good faith of the French administration (more likely observing that the 1848 revolution and financial slump had enforced large economies in the French naval budget), had considerably reduced the number of men in the Crown's armed forces.

It appears that the navies of Britain and France were woven into a bipolar relationship of a particular concentration and simplicity, involving a rivalry—and a concomitant naval race—that can be well described as self-sustaining. The task of the second half of this chapter is to describe how this relationship was ultimately broken in the 1860s. But a preliminary aim is to describe the relationship more fully. We shall try to demonstrate that what we are concerned with was the first modern great power arms rivalry.

One factor of partial validity has been noted already—the strong bipolarity of the rivalry. Such intensity is a frequent characteristic of the modern arms rivalry, notably the post-1945 one between the USA and the USSR. Of course, there are respectable historical antecedents here, above all rivalries involving religion. But there are other characteristics of the modern rivalry that in themselves define it and that also are to be found for the first time in a developed state in the Anglo-French naval rivalry of the mid-nineteenth century. There are five of them. The fundamental one is that the powers involved have the financial, industrial, scientific, and bureaucratic resources to sustain an arms race over a long period of time. This was not the case in the sixteenth or seventeenth centuries, for instance, when arms races were almost always brought to an end by financial or administrative exhaustion, with a consequent slackening of rivalry. Indeed, only by the mid-nineteenth century, and then for only a very few states—Britain and France above all—was there the necessary depth and flexibility of resources and administrative machinery. This is an admittedly banal point, and can safely be taken for granted henceforward while we concentrate on the other four characteristics. The first of these is a high level of technological advance, when virtually every stage in an arms race involves the introduction of significant improvements in armaments. Secondly, a great amount of information is available about the armed forces of the rivals. Thirdly, a large section of the population of each engaged country is interested, even deeply involved, in the progress of the rivalry. Finally, there is a basic similarity between the two sides. Function accounts for much of this. But much is due also to mimicry, the tendency to copy what the other is doing, and natural to a rivalry. There are two types of similarity. The first is conscious, the product, notably, of the unimaginative imitation of innovations in *matériel* by the other side, of which we have given some examples previously. Then there is unrecognized similarity: this is the more important for our purposes, since it is crucial in explaining the vigour of the rivalry.

With regard to technology, one could argue that all arms races involve at least some degree of innovation. What differentiated the race that concerns us from its forebears was, first, the fact that policy-makers came to accept innovation as a vital part of that race, seeing success in terms not so much in having more *matériel* as having the latest and most advanced. Inextricable from this understanding was a hitherto unequalled rate of technological advance and innovation. For the first time in human history, an arms race could be not only a race to build up *matériel*, but also a race to innovate.

Not that innovation was seen from the beginning as an effective policy. Here, at least, we have a difference from later arms races.[3] The Royal Navy had its own attitude to innovation, best displayed by the rather over-quoted remark of a First Lord in the 1820s that it was not up to the premier navy to render its own fleet obsolete through innovating: far better, he said, to wait for others to move, and then overtake them. However sensible, this suggests a fundamental conservatism in the Admiralty; but if so, it was one to be found also in the Ministry of Marine. Both administrations were accustomed to a relative stability in warship design, with at best incremental improvements. Only gradually was it seen that technology offered the means of creating warships greatly superior to their immediate predecessors; only gradually, therefore, was the enormous potential of innovation recognized.

The concomitant was an enhanced interest in the most recent news about the activities of a rival. Here is our second characteristic of modern arms rivalries—a great flow of information between the rivals. One effective means by which information passed was the enquiring visitor, the dockyard tourist, who was to be met with frequently in the mid-century period, crossing between Britain and

---

[3] Perhaps even more of a difference from present arms races in that today innovation is often regarded as a good in itself.

France. The traffic was hardly unprecedented in kind, but our period was exceptional in the number of visitors and in the bias towards technical information rather than details of readiness for sea. Innovation, rather than war-readiness, had become the prime concern.

Some of the visitors were no more than spies. Eugène Sweny, for instance, working in the Surveyor's Department as writer and calculator, was sent a few times during the late 1850s to discover what progress had been made in French yards, government and private. He was a good observer, apparently well versed in how to gain information from dockyard workers, and he discovered much about the latest French technical improvements. Notably, in 1859 he was able to supply plans of the first French ironclad-battleship, the *Gloire*, about which the Ministry of Marine was still somewhat secretive.[4] The *Gloire* was also the object of another suspicious character—though calling him a spy suggests a degree of duplicity he did not always possess. This was Lord Clarence Paget, Parliamentary Secretary of the Admiralty 1859–66. Wearing civilian clothes, he brushed past officials at Toulon to clamber on board the as yet unfinished battleship, and began measuring the height of her battery with his umbrella. Perhaps all that saved him from an arrest that would have had embarrassing consequences was the English tourist's reputation for eccentric inquisitiveness.[5]

As far as one can judge, however, the majority of dockyard visitors were not spies. Most were simple tourists, often attracted by the spectacle of a launching, or the formal opening of a new basin. But there were others whose intent was little different from that of Sweny or Paget, and although the hosts realized full well what these visitors' purpose was, a welcome was still extended. For

[4] Report of 19 Dec. 1859, with covering letter to the Surveyor of 20 Dec., Somerset Papers, 1392.M.A. 3. At least on his tour of French installations in late 1858, Sweny was accompanied by Joseph Large, Assistant Surveyor, giving a semi-official atmosphere; letter to the Surveyor of 21 Jan. 1859, S353, ADM 87 70. Moreover, permission had been gained from the Ministry of Marine, through the Paris embassy, for the men to visit French installations; Board to Surveyor, 27 Sept. 1858, W2369, ADM 87 3. Sweny's visits in 1859, to Essen in Germany as well as to France, were rather different, lacking governmental sanction for visits to state establishments, and involving eavesdropping, aliases, spying into forbidden areas with a telescope, and waiting outside factory and yard gates to pick up talkative workmen.

[5] Sir Arthur Otway, *Autobiography and Journals of Lord Clarence Paget* (London, 1896), 195 ff.

instance, the high-ranking foreign naval officer was almost always able to get permission to tour the yards. The reception was usually excellent: few, if any, facilities were closed to him. The escorting officer might have been told to hurry past certain sensitive areas; on the other hand, the dockyard officers were often only too willing to impress an important guest with details of the latest improvements in equipment and technique. Social rank could be as much of a passport as naval. The highly born, even if there were no naval connections, could also expect a guided tour. To take the extreme example, the sovereigns of Britain and France were sure of a warm welcome in each other's dockyards. Yet such regal visits were not always innocuous from the intelligence point of view. On their visit to Cherbourg in 1858 Queen Victoria and Prince Albert were so struck by the scale of French naval preparations that they added their own pressure to the forces already prompting greater British defence efforts.

Yet neither naval nor social rank was crucial for the spread of information. Another 'open sesame' was the contemporary respect for science. Scientific knowledge was widely held to be an international property, and serious attempts by navies to keep developments secret were uncommon. As in the case of the Russian navy at this time, a 'security blanket' was more likely to be an attempt to hide backwardness rather than innovation. The importance of scientific enquiry is illustrated by a comment of late 1861 made by Chasseloup-Laubat. Spencer Robinson, Controller of the Navy, had requested authorization to visit the French naval arsenals. The Minister said that if the purpose of 'Lord Robinson' was to see whether France's assertions about her naval preparedness were correct, then permission should be denied. But if, as had been claimed by previous Admiralty visitors, the intent was to examine the latest progress of science, there could be no opposition, and Robinson would receive every facility.[6]

Of course, visits to dockyards were not the only way of finding out about a rival navy. By the 1860s the British embassy in Paris and its opposite number in London each had a naval attaché as a permanent member of staff. His prime purpose was to gather naval information and to send it home. The long-serving attaché in London, Captain Pigeard, was particularly well placed to gather

[6] Letter to La Roncière Le Noury, 4 Sept. 1861, Chasseloup-Laubat Papers, ii. 241–5, AN.

news. He had a double entrée into society, one due to his position, the other to his well-born English wife.

There were also other avenues through which one navy learned about the other. The tried and trusted method remained of careful observation by a seaman of the rival navy's vessels at sea or in harbour. An experienced man could tell a great deal from the look of the ship, the speed of exercises aloft, the facility of manœuvre. Increasingly important, though, was another method, not only of gathering information but also disseminating it: the printed word. More than ever before, by the mid-nineteenth century there was a plethora of printed material in France and Britain that dealt with naval or military matters, giving copious details of the state of the fleets and of plans for the future. Naturally, a thorough knowledge would have depended on knowing both the relevant languages. Here lay one of the reasons for the efforts made in both navies to teach the officer to read and speak the rival's tongue. Many officers were thus able to keep up with new publications in both the important naval languages of the time. Others were reluctant linguists, yet even the most stubborn monoglot had at least some access to foreign works, thanks to translations. Notorious pamphlets such as the prince de Joinville's in 1844 were quickly translated into English. Larger works were also tackled: for instance, an English version of the official *Tactique navale* of 1857 appeared in 1859, and Sir Howard Douglas's *Naval Gunnery* appeared in French in 1853, followed nine years later by a translation of his work on steam tactics. Professional journals were particularly important in that they sometimes published translations of foreign articles, or at least summarized or reviewed the more ponderous volumes. The purpose behind their action was made explicit at least in the case of the *Annales maritimes*, edited by Louis Bajot, an energetic publicist. He set out in one issue the advice of the prince de Joinville, urging Bajot to print translations of foreign writings on naval affairs, so that French officers could add to their knowledge of the naval art and of other navies, especially the Royal Navy.[7]

Then as now, the fact that the rival knew a great deal about the other was not necessarily an aid to understanding. Very often the reverse was true. One reason for this was that much of the data was

[7] *Annales maritimes*, 79 (1849), pt. 2, pp. 5–6. On the editor see Martial de Pradel de Lamase, 'Marine et littérature: notre "ancêtre" Louis-Marie Bajot', *Revue maritime*, 200 (Aug. 1936), 180–95.

in statistical form. According to at least one author—Richard Cobden—such data was easily manipulable.[8] He implied that the government could play with figures to give a false impression of British naval weakness, thus leading to panic and to the House of Commons granting unnecessarily large naval credits. As he pointed out, talk in the late 1850s of a 'frigate gap' was based on a misunderstanding of the reality behind the figures—such as those baldly presented by an official report of 6 January 1859 on the British and French navies.[9] The report had included in its table of steam-frigates some nineteen French and nine British paddle-vessels, giving the French navy a lead of thirty-four over the RN total of twenty-six. However, the paddlers were much inferior to the screw-frigates they were counted with, and were not as powerful as the screw-corvettes—a separate category—in which the British had a comfortable lead.

This is scarcely the only example from the period where misleading statistics were presented. Rarely was there an intention to deceive, as far as one can judge. Other factors intervened to ensure that a false impression was drawn.

One of these factors was the engagement of a large section of the public, another of the characteristics of modern arms rivalries. Certainly, thanks to poverty, illiteracy, and poor communications, very many adults—doubtless the majority in a still predominantly rural France—had no interest at all in naval matters during the mid-nineteenth century, but an increasing percentage of the British and French were becoming politically conscious, and naval matters were an important part of national and international politics. The greatest contribution brought by the nineteenth century to political affairs in each of the two countries was the creation of a large, literate, and politically significant public, predominantly middle class and urban in nature, and strongly nationalist and volatile in opinion. This volatile public brought an erratic and largely uncontrollable element to Anglo-French relations, and on two occasions —the crises of 1843–4 over Tahiti and 1858 over the Orsini *attentat* —brought the two countries close to the point of war. Such a public was only too glad, it appears, to have its prejudices or fears confirmed by superficial statistics, and did not put too much effort into penetrating further.

---

[8] R. Cobden, *The Three Panics* (London, 1862).   [9] PP (1859), xiv. 703–44.

Admittedly, the truth was not always easy to reach. We have to understand more fully the significance of our point about the high level of technological advance in the naval rivalry after 1840. This brought an ever-increasing degree of complexity to naval affairs, a complexity that is probably the most important of the characteristics of the Anglo-French armed rivalry, and is the most telling point of similarity between that rivalry and later ones. It was this complexity that meant even professional knowledge and hard work were not always sufficiently penetrating analytical tools. It was a matter of difficulty to decide the true balance of naval force between Britain and France. High amongst the things that bedevilled comparisons was the coming of steam. *Inter alia*, account had to be taken of the age of the machinery in each warship, both because of the speed with which some parts deteriorated (boilers were particularly prone to wear out quickly), and because with the speed of innovation even the age difference of a single year could make the machinery of one warship far superior to that of another.

Of course, it had not been simple even in the days of sail to assess relative fighting values; but the coming of steam added many new complications without removing any of the old. Steam, and the various other innovations, thus increased the possibility of honest disagreement. For instance, in the comparisons he made in the late 1850s between the British and French battlefleets, Sir Baldwin Walker usually omitted from the count the nine slowest and weakest British screw-battleships (the *blockships*). He knew that they had never been able to steam as well as the average screw, and the machinery of even the five most recent ones was already worn out by the time he wrote. On the other hand, there was a case for including them. They formed a large, powerfully armed force, useful at least in home waters, and though slow, capable of matching the slowest French screw-battleship—the *Montebello*—and thus also the squadron with which she steamed. Certainly, the Ministry of Marine usually included the nine in their assessments of the British battlefleet, and thus took somewhat amiss (inevitably thinking in terms of hypocrisy) the British pundits who acted otherwise, especially those encouraging added construction on the basis of the supposed relative weakness of the British fleet.

In this case the British pundits were right to believe that the British fleet was too weak, though they were wrong in offering the insufficiency of screw-battleships as the reason. By May 1858 the three seagoing ironclads of the Gloire class had been laid down, and the Royal Navy had as yet no reply. These vessels rendered the British battlefleet semi-obsolete, though the Admiralty did not at first realize this, through underrating the resisting power of the latest type of armour. Their initial reaction to the *Gloire* was not that the Royal Navy needed its own ironclads, but rather that more *un*armoured battleships on the old pattern had to be laid down. This is a fine example of how innovation can confuse even the experts. It shows also that the experts do not always err on the side of overestimating a rival's innovations, though doubtless *over-* rather than *under*estimation is the more common pattern.

It is interesting to note also that British expert opinion about the Gloires was capable of sudden change. They might have been somewhat disdained at first, but then came some successful sea trials, and British naval opinion quickly accepted the new type. In the mid-nineteenth century, as today, one side's estimate of the military capabilities of the other could change very swiftly. This is contrary to what has been suggested by some military writers during the past few years, who have argued that an opponent's capability remains largely constant, whilst his policy can change overnight: the implication is that one's defence efforts ought to be predicated on the other side's actual forces, not his apparent intentions. However, policy in fact tends to remain rather more constant than perceptions of capability, which twist and turn according to the results of trials, occasionally of wars, and the guesstimates of scientists, military men, and politicians.[10]

It is not even as though a Power can precisely judge its own military capabilities, let alone those of a rival. We have had already a fine example of this, in 1857–8, when the royal dockyards were so crammed with work, largely repair, that the Admiralty was not sure about the progress made with steam-battleship construction.

Of course, one might stress the way that it was the poor accounting techniques of the time that led to such uncertainty. Surely today, the argument continues, a similar degree of error is not possible. Thus here one has a dissimilarity between the modern era and the mid-nineteenth century. On similar lines, one could emphasize the far greater complexity of today's weapons, or a speed of

[10] For a discussion of comparatively recent errors in estimates of Soviet military power, see the article by G. Jukes in P. Towle (ed.), *Estimating Foreign Military Power* (London, 1982), 88–108.

innovation that quite puts in the shade the rate attained in the 1850s and 1860s. These points might be accepted (though the first appears somewhat optimistic!); but there still remain important lines of continuity between the Anglo-French naval rivalry of the mid-nineteenth century and much later rivalries.

Ultimately one has to bring the analysis to the level of the policy-makers: what they thought and how they responded. There have certainly been many changes since the 1840s and 1850s, but as long as arms rivalries have had the kind of modern characteristics that we defined earlier, then the policy-makers have had essentially the same kind of problems, and have tried to meet them largely in the same kind of way. The important point about innovation, for example, is not how it compares in speed with today's hectic stand-ard, but how fast it was in the eyes of the policy-makers at the time. Before the mid-nineteenth century, as we have suggested, the rate was very slow, and the admiralties were accustomed to slow incremental change in warship design. One could merely improve the details of the main warship types, it was thought: radical alterations were contemplated only after 1840. By present stand-ards, innovation after 1840 was still slow, but it was extremely fast as far as the experts of the time were concerned, and at least as bewildering and confusing as the present-day gallop can be to observers.

The same thing applies to one of the consequences of the tech-nical complexity of the mid-nineteenth century—the data that flowed between the two rivals. It was much less than the flow of information concerning the military affairs of the present Super-powers, but was still far greater than had been the case in pre-1840 rivalries. Victorian naval administrators were certainly conscious that they had far more information to deal with than their pre-decessors had had, as one sees from the frequent complaints about the increased correspondence passing through their offices.[11]

Thus, though better off than their modern counterparts in abso-lute terms, mid-nineteenth-century policy-makers—in France as in Britain—still found themselves under unprecedented pressures, and unprepared by previous experience to deal with decision-making more than ever complicated by fulsomely documented technical considerations. It is not surprising that one finds in this period

---

[11] See the Phinn Committee of Inquiry into the Office of the Secretary to the Admiralty, Oct.–Nov. 1855, PRO, ADM 1 5660.

more or less the same kind of automatic, blind decision-making that Professor Steinbruner has argued is to be found in today's inflated defence bureaucracies, where the administrators—overwhelmed by the data—often come to decisions not after considering the available facts and arguments, but by trying to find those that fit their simple a priori judgements.[12]

Where, though, did those judgements come from? Here, too, we find a link between then and now. A common cause of a particular policy being chosen is/was the assumption that the rival power was hostile and aggressive, only awaiting the opportunity to pounce. This assumption certainly underlay the post-1840 Anglo-French diplomatic and naval disagreements, and was fundamental to the rivalry.

The main reason for the assumption was its solid basis in fact: a whole history of Anglo-French conflict and war. But there were other, less rational factors. Unrecognized political and cultural dissimilarities were a potent source of misunderstanding. Confusion was inevitable when observers from the one country attempted to interpret the institutions and modes of behaviour of the rival in terms of their own experience. Take the case of the Orsini crisis. After the assassination attempt, the British government decided to bring a bill before Parliament to check the activities of future murderous exiles, but the Commons, in a fit of super jingoism, threw the bill out. It was at this point that French opinion grew most furious with Britain; something, surely, that would not have happened to such a degree had many Frenchmen not seen the Commons as little better than their own *Corps législatif* (then a mere puppet of the executive). To them the rejection of the bill seemed to be an intentional insult to France by the British government.

Many other examples can be found of a failure in the two countries to understand how differently matters were arranged over the Channel—and with a similar sharpening effect on the rivalry. Thinking of purely naval affairs, one can cite the attempts made to compare the budgets of the Royal Navy and *la Royale*. Too often these failed to take into account the great differences in the patterns of expenditure. French observers tended to ignore the fact that much of the British budget was taken up with half-pay to the large number of ageing officers left largely unemployed after 1815, and

[12] John D. Steinbruner, *The Cybernetic Theory of Decision: New Dimensions of Political Analysis* (Princeton University Press, 1974).

by what were—in comparison with French rates—high wages to seamen. And Britons often forgot that the Ministry of Marine had France's colonies under its authority (bar Algeria), and so its budget had to pay for the *troupes de marine* who made up colonial garrisons, and for other overseas administrative costs. Then there were some more subtle differences in expenditure: in France labour tended to be cheap and manufactured goods such as engines and boilers dear. In Britain the reverse was true. Such variations, since often unrecognized, could bedevil attempts to make comparisons, falsely encouraging fears that increases in the rival's budget meant dangerous increases in his fleet in commission.

Yet differences did not have to be unrecognized in order to encourage suspicion and rivalry: even obvious ones could develop antagonism, support the assumption of the other side's hostility. During the Crimean War, for instance, when British and French naval officers often came together to co-operate, the French— thanks largely to the *Borda*, it seems probable—tended in meetings to show to better advantage, to the chagrin of the other side.

Obvious cultural differences could have the same effect—such as the greater British tolerance for the eccentric. In 1845 Captain Charner of the *Syrène* touched twice at the Cape of Good Hope, calling both times on the Governor and Commander-in-Chief, Sir Peregrine Maitland, and—since he was not received—leaving his card. However, Maitland did not act in the customary manner and offer his services or even respond in any positive way, despite Charner remaining in port for ten days on one occasion. The captain was told that Maitland was somewhat odd. He was a *puritain exalté*, reluctant to make visits. But he was also willing to allow foreign vessels to dig guano on the colony's coasts as cheaply as English ones, saying that all men were brothers and had an equal right to benefit from the gifts of Providence. This somewhat mollified Charner, but he was still annoyed enough to report the affair to the Minister of Marine, who was not at all amused by Maitland's behaviour, and asked the Foreign Minister to complain to Whitehall.[13]

Differences—recognized or unrecognized—could thus feed antagonism; but so too could at least one type of similarity.

[13] The Minister of Marine to the Minister of Foreign Affairs, 11 Mar. 1845, AN BB2 289 (*marine*), fos. 20–1. This was the same Charner who served on the *Enquête parlementaire sur la marine*.

Unrecognized similarities strike one as being a profound cause of international tension. Here we have come to the last in our list of characteristics of the modern arms rivalry.

Previously we have been stressing differences between the two officer corps. Not all have been mentioned. For example, the frequent experience of defeat during the Napoleonic Wars meant that Anglophobia was stronger among French naval officers for long after 1815 than Francophobia was on the other side. But ultimately, in terms of the officers' behaviour and beliefs, it is similarities that strike the observer. It is surely significant that the popular images in the two countries of the naval officer were very largely the same, imbued with the identical virtues of simple honesty, good nature, and a certain bluntness of manner. Apart from his ancient family, there is little to distinguish the amiral comte de Kergarouët in Balzac's *Le Bal à Sceaux* and *La Bourse*, from Admiral Croft in *Persuasion*. The coincidence doubtless in part reflects merely a shared stereotype of the naval officer. But a stereotype necessarily has a certain basis in fact. Moreover, both Balzac and Austen were acute observers of their societies. The latter in particular had good personal evidence for speaking at the end of her novel of '[the naval profession] which is, if possible, more distinguished in its domestic virtues than in its national importance'.

Naturally, the officer on the quarterdeck would have had had virtues—and vices—not always apparent to shore-bound novelists. But here too these would have been the same, or very largely the same, whether the officer was British or French. Perhaps the most serious lines of division running through the two officer corps were not national, but rather generational. French 'Young Turks' dismissed the *Conseil d'amirauté* as a gaggle of old women with little less force than young British officers dismissed the Admiralty. The younger men in both navies at times could show far more sympathy for their fellows in the rival force than for their own seniors. We have the example of Lord Clarence Paget, who as a captain in the Baltic squadron in 1854 found he had much more in common with his French colleagues than he had with his superannuated commander-in-chief.[14]

In other ways, too, the behaviour of the officers on the two sides suggests that ultimately one should stress similarities rather than

[14] Otway, *Lord Clarence Paget*, 105 ff.

differences. Whether he was British or French, in battle the trained and experienced officer was as likely to display great coolness under fire or, where necessary, magnificent rashness. The generous praise frequently given by the men in one force, when observing the other in action, very often suggests not just admiration for individual acts of bravery but also, tellingly, a common perception of what the demeanour and the duty of the officer ought to be.

However, if similarities were quite obvious in the case of officers in action, this was not the case with regard to the senior officers and administrators in the two admiralties. Here, the similarities existed, but were commonly unrecognized. As is shown by research in naval archives in Britain and France, although surprising to the novice (albeit perfectly obvious in retrospect), both admiralties saw themselves as essentially on the defensive, interested in the shield rather than the sword, and saw the other as aggressive, interpreting all that side's preparations as aggressive in nature.

There is perhaps little that is intrinsically modern in the latter attitude. But the strength of feeling behind that attitude when we meet it in the mid-nineteenth century surely is, and we might well wonder where it originated. One source is the fact that officers and naval policy-makers were creatures of their time, and were influenced by the volatile and nationalist public that arose so powerfully in that century. In respect to this public, too, one finds unrecognized similarities between Britain and France. Here we enter—necessarily briefly—the fascinating subject of the collective images held by nations of other nations. It seems that, like individuals, nations unconsciously try to purge their undesirable traits by projecting them on to others, anyway seen as antagonistic. The consequence is that one nation's image of a rival is largely the inverse of that first nation's self-image.[15]

This is not to imply that the naval officers and policy-makers did not make their own particular contribution to this kind of misunderstanding. The men were reinforced in their belief that the other side was aggressive by a certain development—one that also came only in the nineteenth century. This was the professionalization of the civil service and the officer corps. Though there were nuances in the progress it made, as between Britain and France, here was something that worked powerfully to render the two sides

[15] François Crouzet, 'Problèmes de la communication franco-britannique aux XIXe et XXe siècles', *Revue historique*, 254 (1975), 105–34.

more alike — and alike so strongly in no respect more than the attitude to the rival. The men in the two admiralties, above all the
officers, became ever more conscious of their function, and that
function was to safeguard their country from its possible enemies.
They would have found, as a present-day senior naval officer has
done,[16] the words of a character of Montherlant appropriate, 'If
you are telling me all that to put my mind at rest, I should tell you
that men of my calling were not intended to have our minds at rest.'
Of all these enemies, the one most feared was the one that could do
the most damage. At least until the early 1860s when a significant
change occurred, the British and French in the mid-century saw
only one contender for that position: the other. In the minds of the
national guardians, a 'worst-case analysis' was a natural reaction,
virtually a duty, including the assumption that the other side was
hostile and aggressive. Thus the naval function and, indeed, the
whole essential but so often unrecognized similarity of the two
sides, developed and confirmed a misunderstanding about intentions,
a misunderstanding that was basic to the rivalry, and which helped
transform the other characteristics of the rivalry into further fuel
for antagonism and conflict.

II

Given the way that Anglo-French naval rivalry took on a tre-
mendous inertial force, apparently insusceptible to reason, how
did it ever come to an end? It is useful first to ask why the
rivalry never erupted into open warfare: the inherited enmity from
actual war would have prevented passions from cooling when they
did.

Clearly, various factors were involved. One ought to note
the adroitness and good sense of at least most of the leading
diplomatists and statesmen. Then there was the crucial fact that
there was no point of disagreement between the two sides that
ultimately could not be adjusted. They might have argued

---

[16] Admiral of the Fleet Sir Peter Hill-Norton, *No Soft Options: The Politico-
Military Realities of NATO* (London, 1978), 158. For naval professionalization,
see Michael Lewis, *The Navy in Transition 1814–1864: A Social History* (London,
1965).

over many things, but both governments took a broadly similar approach to international problems. Both had liberal outlooks, with sympathy for the cause of nationalism (within reason, of course), and these views often brought them together in opposition to the three reactionary continental powers. Britain and France had more to gain from co-operation than from continued opposition.

Naturally, their naval rivalry often distracted their attention away from the continental affairs over which there was some essential agreement, to others potentially more divisive. Yet a safety factor remained, one inextricably linked with the nature of maritime affairs.

The crucial point is that naval diplomacy is disciplined, largely under control. The naval tool is uniquely flexible. The size of a naval force, and its employment, can be shaped to the policy need. Warships may be sent only to show the flag in distant minor ports, but they can also play a whole gamut of roles, up to threatening the employment of force, or actually employing it, in the rough and tumble of great power politics. The policy-makers have a fair degree of certainty that they can gauge what the response of other governments will be to each particular use of naval force. Land forces, in comparison, are clumsy and dangerous adjuncts to diplomacy. The movement of armies to the frontiers—a direct threat as this often is to the independence of neighbours—can easily have unforeseen effects on international politics. Supporting diplomatic *démarches* by military invasion is even more dangerous. Far more than sending one's warships to make a demonstration off the coast of another power, or even in one of his ports, occupation of his territory by troops pledges the prestige both of the nation that sent them and the nation invaded, thus impeding a settlement. One added complication is that, as such disputes drag on, the invasion force tends to grow, impelled first by the natural aim of the commander to secure his position, and secondly by the prospect that with more soldiers some grand *coups* can be mounted to force the other side to a settlement. Not surprisingly, a supposedly temporary incursion can easily turn into permanent occupation. Naval intervention is not prone to such uncontrolled escalation. Chasseloup-Laubat well-expressed the matter in a letter to one naval officer. Unlike intervention with troops, he wrote, '*l'action maritime*, quelque soit le plus ou moins de succès, n'entraîne guère après elle que les conséquences que le Gouvernement peut vouloir en faire sortir'.[17]

The adaptability of naval power to diplomatic needs had great importance to the question of peace and war. Though Britain and France often deployed their warships to support opposing policies, in general the two governments were able to keep control of developments. Occasionally matters did get out of hand, but this was usually because naval officers far from home had to rely a great deal on their own judgement and sometimes dangerously exceeded their instructions: the difficulties over Tahiti in 1843–4 for instance, originated in the excessive freedom of action taken by the French admiral half a world away from his political masters.

It can be argued that the logic of naval diplomacy was the main reason for there not being an Anglo-French war after 1840. Each government was usually able to make it clear that it did not wish to take any disagreement to extremes. As has been said, the two powers had many common interests, and much common benefit could come from compromise. Through naval diplomacy the desire for compromise could be signalled, valuably supplementing other means. Amidst a great deal that shows them as simple servants of the naval rivalry, in this one important area we must accept that the British and French governments were in control of events, the main constraint being public opinion. It appears that naval rivalry was to an extent susceptible to the conscious will.

However, the fact that some lines of communication and understanding existed does not in itself explain how the rivalry ever came to weaken, although one might see co-operation as a powerful agent of change. For much of the mid-century, to one or other degree of formality, the British and French did co-operate at the naval, military, and diplomatic levels. Was it through this means that the rivalry declined?

Already in the 1830s and 1840s there was some co-operation, with the two navies combining their forces to put diplomatic pressure on various princelings. But co-operation did not necessarily mean warmth, as one sees from two examples described by the prince de Joinville. The first comes from an early stage of the crisis between Mehemet Ali and the Sultan, when Whitehall believed the peril to

---

[17] Letter to Rear-Admiral Roze, Commander-in-Chief Chinese waters, 8 Sept. 1866, Chasseloup-Laubat Papers, viii. 94. For a survey of naval diplomacy, past and present, see K. Booth, *Navies and Foreign Policy* (London, 1977).

Constantinople from the Russians was still greater than that from the Egyptian army. British and French warships gathered at Besika Bay outside the Dardanelles, to help dissuade the Russians from hostile action. Physically the two squadrons were close; but in sentiment they were very distant. The two admirals scarcely ever saw one another. There were hardly any of the usual expressions of friendship between allied forces. No dinners were arranged for the officers of the other squadron. No officers visited their foreign colleagues—apart from Sir Charles Napier calling on his old antagonists from the Napoleonic Wars, and Napier had a well-deserved reputation for eccentricity. Most telling of all was the coolness between the British and French cadets. They had a great deal in common, and were at an age when one is most talkative, friendly, and unsuspicious. Yet, going to the same place to get water, and working only a few steps apart, they remained cold and silent. Both sides were somewhat relieved when Whitehall decided to oppose Mehemet Ali, the French *protégé*, and open antagonism replaced surly co-operation.

The Prince's other example comes from 1848, when the squadrons under Sir William Parker and Charles Baudin came together in face of a Sicilian revolt. This time the most perfect courtesy reigned—both governments insisting on this in despatches to their commanders-in-chief. There were dinners and visits, and the surviving letters from French officers to Augustus Phillimore, Parker's flag-lieutenant, are at least one sign that a common profession and task could bridge the divisions brought by history and nationality.[18] Yet even on this occasion, trust was scarcely perfect. As was understood by both squadrons, each had been despatched not so much to co-operate with the other as to counter it. As Joinville said of the two, 'elles s'aimaient au point de ne pouvoir se quitter'. When one admiral sent a detachment to a certain point, his colleague sent an equal one. When Parker himself left with his squadron, Baudin went too, and vice versa. From the outside the two acted in concert, 'en réalité les mouvements que l'on faisait ensemble n'avaient pour but que de s'observer et se contrecarrer réciproquement'.[19]

[18] Letters from French officers, 1848–9, Phillimore Papers, National Maritime Museum, London, uncatalogued.
[19] Prince de Joinville, introduced by V. de Mars, 'L'escadre de la Méditerranée', *Revue des deux mondes*, 3 (1852), 446, 473.

Admittedly, by the following decade the pattern was rather different. The two powers became more accustomed to working together—particularly when they both took up arms against a powerful common enemy, Russia. One detects during the 1850s a developing sense of common purpose, feelings of friendship, and even gratitude. Nevertheless, there were certain prejudices too deeply laid to be easily removed. Probably the most famous example—albeit involving a soldier—was the occasional habit of Lord Raglan, in command of the British Crimean army, of saying 'the French' when he meant the Russians.[20] Examples of conscious prejudice are also to be found. For instance, in a letter of May 1853 we find Sir James Graham, First Lord of the Admiralty, arguing it was all to the good that the Royal Navy could expect no aid from the French in the Baltic operations, since the French were treacherous. At least, he went on, one could trust the word of Nicholas I![21] Even once war had broken out, Graham showed that while he came to doubt the Russian Emperor, he never entirely reversed his opinion about his country's ally.

Prejudices, one could well argue, were even aggravated by alliances. For instance, sumptuous dinners aboard allied ships did not always encourage greater understanding and tolerance. The impression gained from the correspondence of one French naval officer, Clément de la Roncière Le Noury, is that the more he met the English, the more he loathed them. He survived dinners given by English officers by saying 'Oaoh' as often as possible. This made him pleasant to his hosts, he believed—as he said, 'Oaoh' means a great deal in England—and also relieved his frustration through undetected parody. At least La Roncière Le Noury was intelligent enough to rise above his dislike to appreciate the advantages of an alliance.[22] One suspects that many British and French officers reacted somewhat differently: propinquity could not only fortify prejudice but also encourage enmity.

[20] A letter to Vice-Admiral Sir George Seymour from his son Francis, in the Crimea, and dated simply 'Sunday night', says Raglan acknowledged calling the enemy 'the French' more than once in a council of war, when excited. Seymour of Ragley Papers, CR.114A.526.8.

[21] Graham to Lord Clarendon, 30 May 1853, Clarendon Deposit, C3, fos. 48–51.

[22] Joseph L'Hôpital and Louis de Saint-Blancard (eds.), *Correspondance intime de l'amiral de La Roncière Le Noury avec sa femme et sa fille (1855–1871)* (2 vols., Paris, 1928–9), i. 217, 225; ii. 26–31.

Alliance does more than aggravate the prejudices of those little prone to sympathy for the other power. It adds a powerful element of competition all of its own; one that pervades the relationship between allies, with consequences that outlive the alliance. For alliance fosters some bitter forms of contention and friction. Allied powers are forced into close contact at various levels, from that of the armed forces in the field or at sea up to that of the statesmen and crowned heads. Unfortunately, as with officers dining together, propinquity can be more chilling than distance. Contrast the position of the naval squadrons of two powers supporting a common policy with that of two squadrons supporting different *démarches*. In the second case, it might appear, the sense of rivalry would be the greater: the two forces anchored close together in a port of the victim power, each attempting to face down the rival. But a study of nineteenth-century diplomacy shows that, wisely, governments tried to avoid such confrontations. A small incident might always escalate out of control: the kind of spark that had brought about the battle of Navarino in 1827. The common pattern was for the opposing squadrons to alternate. As soon as, say, the French squadron had left the coast of some Bey whose behaviour was causing a dispute between Paris and London, an RN force would be sent to visit the same area. The rival forces would not necessarily see each other often. But co-operating squadrons were frequently together, the better to demonstrate to foreign diplomatists the unity of their governments. Constantly in each other's sight, the two sides would naturally develop an even sharper form of the competitiveness that exists between the various ships of a single squadron, seeing which could perform more smartly the myriad public manœuvres and exercises inevitable on masted warships. The point can be further developed by quoting part of a letter of Admiral Parker to Lord Minto in 1849, commenting on relations between his and Baudin's squadrons:

tho' desirous of maintaining the most friendly and courteous intercourse with them [the French]—Your Lordship will remember that I had always an [*illegible*] dislike to be beaten with saplings of our own growth. They have already imbibed too much of our training & habits; & tho' now taking the initiative in some new experiments, are too sagacious not to copy still whatever of our system can tend to their efficiency. One day's general exercise of our Ships at Quarters when at Naples induced them to follow our plan of putting the Rammers regularly *into* the Guns instead of

shewing them on the top only; as they previously practised. I fear I was
too narrow minded to proceed afterwards with our usual routine of other
exercises in their presence.[23]

Competition could not be absent on other levels of alliance, each
ally striving not to be outdone by the other. It is, perhaps, more a
matter of national pride to match or surpass the efforts of an ally
than those of an enemy. Furthermore, few things are more humiliating for a power than to have to rely on the generosity of an ally.
Gratitude can have corrosive effects on relations, and fuel later
conflict. The post-1857 French programme to build transport-
vessels, which renewed British fears of the 'steam bridge', was in
large part a consequence of the difficulty found during the Crimean
War of chartering sufficient ships to carry the Imperial Army to the
Black Sea, and the need to rely on vessels hired —with the ally's
kind forbearance—from Britain's merchant marine.

Another pertinent point is that the language of friendship is
potentially more cutting than the one of enmity. The rudeness of
the enemy can be easily discounted or ignored; but the comments
of the candid ally are shrugged off with difficulty, especially when
phrased in that teasing form possible only to friends or colleagues,
jocular in form but vitriolic at heart. There is the example of Vice-
Admiral La Susse, in command of the *escadre des évolutions* when
Britain and France were coming together before the Crimean War.
After his vessels had shown themselves particularly adept at some
exercises aloft, he came on board the British flagship and greeted
his colleague with a sprightly comment to the effect 'Ah, mon cher
Dundas! On peut donner des leçons, hein!' Could anything have
been better calculated to nettle the British admiral? La Susse was
doubtless spurred by memories of the poor state of seamanship of
many French crews during his youth, before 1815, when the British
blockade locked so many warships up in harbour. He thus had
something to prove in his comment, but he could quite possibly
have said the same had the two nations always been perfectly friendly. After all, even perfect friendship, between nations as between
individuals, has its darker side. One should remember the maxim
of La Rochefoucauld: 'Dans l'adversité de nos meilleurs amis,
nous trouvons toujours quelque chose qui ne nous déplaît pas.'[24]

[23] 10 Nov. 1849, Minto Papers, 12068, fos. 172–5.
[24] No. 18 of the *Maximes supprimées*, Garnier edn., ed. Jacques Truchet (Paris,
1967), 139.

It appears that the mere fact of alliance—at least the types of co-operation and alliance so far touched on—does not of itself significantly alter relations between states. Yet, of course, what we have to account for is such a significant alteration. By the late 1860s, for whatever reasons, Britain and France were paying relatively little attention to each other—a great change from the situation at the beginning of the decade. The period 1860–1 had been one of particular diplomatic friction, and was also the time when the ironclad-building race was at its most hectic. But from that nadir, albeit with occasional setbacks, relations between the two powers became perceptibly less strained and full of suspicion as the decade progressed, and accompanying this improvement was a decline in naval rivalry. There was, in short, a significant change of attitudes.

An explanation ought at least to mention the Cobden–Chevalier treaty of 1860, which reduced trade barriers between Britain and France, though one has to admit its effects were not great in political terms, nor all to the good in regard to popular opinion. French industrialists felt threatened by the fall in import duties on British manufactures, and Anglophobic reactions were not unknown.

The factors we have to emphasize are of the same type that encouraged the rivalry in the first place: naval and political. To begin with the latter, we have to note that in the 1860s there was an increasing concern in Britain and France with internal affairs, diverting energies that might otherwise have been devoted to foreign policy. This must not let us ignore certain important shifts and complications in the international world, which fragmented or diverted the attention that was still directed outward, thus undermining the old single-minded Anglo-French antagonism.

On the internal front, Britain suffered for the first time in some years from a spate of extremist political violence, caused by the Fenians late in the 1860s. In that respect France was more tranquil during this decade than she had been in the previous one: the closest equivalent to the Orsini incident was an assassination attempt on Alexander II during his visit to the 1867 Paris Exhibition, made by a Pole outraged at the bloody repression of Poland. An attempt on a visiting sovereign was clearly less threatening to order in France than an attempt on Napoleon himself, though admittedly French foreign relations with Russia were hardly improved.

One crucial internal concern was common to Britain and to France. In both countries the 1860s was a time of movement towards the greater participation of the people in politics and government. In France, the Liberal Empire was coming into being as more authority was granted to the Senate and the *Corps législatif.* Not only did internal politics affect foreign policy indirectly by attracting more of the popular limelight to itself, but it had a more direct effect, too. Through the *senatus-consultum* of 31 December 1861, the *Corps législatif* was given some power to control military and naval expenditure, thus helping to restrict adventurism on the part of the service ministries.[25] The far greater political concessions made by the Emperor at the end of the decade, when the executive was made responsible to the Chamber, had even more serious implications. The new government, lacking the authoritarian simplicities of the old—though economic setbacks contributed— found it impossible to meet quickly new manpower and equipment demands being made by the army. As one can now appreciate, only speedy and expensive action could have produced a force fit to encounter the Prussian army. In this case, therefore, the path to democracy led on to the military débâcle of 1870.[26]

In Britain electoral reform was an issue of growing importance during the 1860s at parliamentary and popular levels, becoming politically all-absorbing in 1866–8 as the Second Reform Act was painfully stitched together. The Irish Church Bill and Land Act had the same importance in 1869–70, attracting all the more passion and interest thanks to the Fenian outrages. R. Millman makes the interesting observation that foreign-policy issues were not so much ignored by the Commons at this time as treated as matters of consensus. The parties, it appears, were split on electoral reform and Ireland, but at least agreement over these crucial affairs was found in certain cross-bench groupings. Their solidity was so important that foreign-policy disagreements could not be allowed to imperil it, hence the consensus. This was not arrived at simply by some kind of unconscious process. Nor was consensus limited to Parliament. It was realized at least by some observers at the time that foreign affairs were being 'crowded out'. We find Lord

<hr/>

[25] Casimir Périer, 'La Réforme financière', *Revue des deux mondes,* 37 (Feb. 1862), 948–75.
[26] Michael Howard, *The Franco-Prussian War: The German Invasion of France 1870–1871* (London, 1961), 29–39.

Lyons—Cowley's successor in Paris—writing in June 1869 that the British people 'were too full of the Irish Church Bill to think of foreign politics'.[27] Thus it was that both sides of the House felt that Britain ought not to become involved on the Continent if it possibly could be avoided: quite a change from the attitude in the previous twenty years. Thus one finds a surprising degree of continuity between the policies of Lord Stanley (Foreign Secretary 1866–8) and those of his successor (and predecessor) Lord Clarendon, despite their different party allegiances, the enormous contrast in their characters, and the fact that the former tended to favour Prussia whilst the latter preferred France.

Therefore foreign affairs did not retain their previous fascination for the British and French; yet even if they had, the 1860s still would have seen the joint national attention being drawn away from the old rivalry. This was a particularly unsettled time for Europe. By the beginning of the decade, some of the old bonds that had united the Great Powers no longer existed, and the majority of those powers did not any longer support the *status quo*. Notably, the *entente* between Vienna and St Petersburg had not survived Austria's equivocal behaviour during the Crimean War. Moreover, the Tsar's ministers were seeking means to overturn the noxious clause in the 1856 peace treaty that forbade a Russian Black Sea fleet. Prussia, too, looked for change. Under Bismarck the Berlin government was thinking how best to achieve domination in Germany. One instrument was an arrangement with Russia. Another was the Prussian army—being built into the best in Europe in the early 1860s. A third was growing German nationalism —the factor that perhaps most truly threatened the European balance. The old international structure was weakening at the very time when the forces of change and disruption were becoming ever more powerful.

Even before agitation began about Parliamentary reform, Britain was moving into a more isolationist stance in response to the international world. The heritage of the Crimean War predisposed the country to behave in that way. In the early 1860s the continuing debility and corruption of the Turkish Empire encouraged the attitude in the newspaper-reading public that the costly war to save Turkey from the Russians had been nothing other than a waste,

[27] R. Millman, *British Foreign Policy and the Coming of the Franco-Prussian War* (OUP, 1965), 133 n., 223.

tending only to increase French prestige, and that similar interventions had to be avoided in future. Many politicians drew the same lesson. Thus one finds when the Poles revolted against their overlords in 1863, though there was much sympathy with their plight, British policy-makers refused to consider the use of force, above all since intervention would have been possible only in conjunction with France, and it was anticipated that as before only France would benefit. Lord Cowley feared that France would draw Britain into war again, as he believed she had done in 1853–4. But this time Lord Palmerston was in firm control, and he had no intention—as he saw it—of giving British support to French ambitions. The cabinet rejected even Napoleon's idea of invoking a Congress to consider the Polish problem and the other major questions of the day.[28]

This double blow to the Emperor's hopes insulted him deeply, and marked an end—in Europe at least—to the Anglo-French entente. This was unfortunate for the British government, since it led to a humiliation over the duchies of Schleswig and Holstein in 1864. Palmerston and Lord John Russell (then Foreign Secretary) were led by earlier and more expansive habits in British foreign policy-making to threaten the use of force against Austria and Prussia, in an attempt to make them withdraw their armies from the duchies. But it was a bluff. Napoleon, still piqued, refused his support on any terms the British could accept, and the British were not sufficiently powerful to act without that support. Naval power alone could have no serious influence, and only some 20,000 soldiers were available for an expeditionary force. It was inevitable that the bluff would be called, though perhaps the inevitability came from the fact that Whitehall faced that arch-realist, Bismarck, who did the calling with the cruel comment that if the British army arrived he would have the police arrest it. The slap in the face had to be accepted, and certainly weakened British prestige, but it also had the important effect of greatly strengthening the existing isolationist trend: from now on, non-intervention was the watchword in London.

Changes of personnel reinforced the development. There was death, retirement, and succession in the Liberal Party; Palmerston dying in 1865, to be succeeded by Russell (thus opening the way

---

[28] W. E. Mosse, *The European Powers and the German Question* (CUP, 1958), 114, 126 ff., 141.

for Clarendon to return to the Foreign Office), Russell himself retiring in 1866. In that same year the Tories took charge of the government for the first time since 1859, entailing the appointment by Lord Derby of his son, Lord Stanley, as Foreign Secretary. Stanley ('Young Morose' as Disraeli unkindly but accurately dubbed him) not only believed firmly in the principle of non-intervention, but—and here certainly was a difference from Clarendon's policy-making—made it clear to the continental powers that he would practise that principle, naturally weakening the respect and concern of other powers for Britain.

Given the various changes in Europe that we have been describing, and the British response to them, the cross-Channel rivalry was bound to diminish, if only because non-intervention meant less concern in London over French continental diplomacy. But changes on the Continent meant there was anyway less reason than before to fear France. The same rising power that had humiliated Britain over Schleswig-Holstein posed even greater problems for France. The rise of Prussia must be considered when explaining why two issues—over the mooted purchase of Luxemburg by France in 1867, and the Belgian railways question of 1869—did not become the heated Anglo-French diplomatic quarrels they would have been a mere decade before. First, it was realized in Whitehall that the French attempts to expand to the north and east were not intended as challenges to British interests but were rather aimed at countering the enormous territorial gains made by Prussia after her war with Austria in 1866. Secondly, Whitehall and British public opinion saw that Berlin could be relied on to check such French aggrandisement. As Stanley said in 1866, 'France has a new rival, and in her antagonism to the united Germany which is evidently destined to be, will be found our security and repose.'[29]

The French government, naturally, was even more conscious than the British of the implications of the rise of Prussia. Policy-makers in Paris had never been as free as those in London to concentrate on maritime affairs or on naval rivalry. There had always been the long land frontier to look to, and the need to maintain a continental-sized army. French opportunity lay there, above all in the possibility to extend the French frontier to the Rhine

---

[29] M. R. D. Foot, 'Great Britain and Luxemburg 1867', *English Historical Review*, 67 (1952), 356. G. A. Craig, 'Great Britain and the Belgian Railways Dispute of 1869', *American Historical Review*, 50 (1944–5), 738–61.

mouth. But threat could lie there also, as was seen in the 1859 war against Austria, when Prussia began to mobilize in favour of her German brother, a gesture sufficient to push Napoleon III to seek an armistice with Vienna. Admittedly, such a threat to France across the Rhine was exceptional in the 1840s and 1850s: by and large France had little serious reason to expect attack by land during these decades, hence the ability to look so much to maritime affairs and to spend so much on the navy. Above all, Germany posed no serious challenge at this time, since Prussia and Austria were antagonistic, and balanced each other: only French aggress-iveness—as in 1859—could unite the two. With the 1860s this comfortable equilibrium was upset.

Napoleon had precipitated this through supporting Piedmont in 1859. The consequence by the end of 1860 was the creation of a united Italy—much to Napoleon's regret, since he had wanted only a confederal arrangement. Rather, Italy was not quite united: French troops remained in Rome to safeguard the patrimony of St Peter, and Venetia yet remained in Austrian hands. The former spelt various kinds of political trouble for the Paris government. But the latter was more important because it meant Italy was likely to be an enemy of Austria if war came within Germany, thus increasing Prussia's chances of permanently altering the power balance with Austria in her own favour.

Ultimately, though, the rise of Italy was far less important than the changing pattern of political, economic, and military power within Germany. Not only was Prussia becoming far stronger than Austria but, from 1862, with Bismarck as Prime Minister, Prussian policy was being directed by the most able diplomat of the time. The consequences were seen in 1866: Prussia's Italian ally was badly defeated, though playing a useful part through drawing important Austrian forces to the south. In the north, on the other hand, the Austrian army—and those of Austria's German allies —were overwhelmed by the forces led so ably by the great Von Moltke. Had Napoleon promptly intervened militarily, then France could well have gained territory, but the Emperor knew that opinion in his country was against war. Moreover, much of his army was dispersed around the globe, not just in Rome but in Mexico, Cochin China, and Algeria (where there had been a large-scale revolt between spring 1864 and summer 1865). It also appears that Napoleon himself was ailing, and had lost his sense of timing.[30] Consequently, France did not intervene. Prussia was able to digest her gains, forming Germany into the Northern and Southern Confederations, the first directly under Berlin's control, the second allied militarily to the first, and France gained no compensations whatever. Napoleon's later attempts to gain a quid pro quo, above all the proposed Luxemburg purchase, were blocked by Bismarck, thus merely adding further painful diplomatic rebuffs.

France could not adopt the British response to such rebuffs and turn to isolation. The Rhine was not the Channel; the country was a piece of the Continent, unavoidably involved in European mankind. It was not only the government of France that looked towards Germany in the mid- to late 1860s, fearful, and at the same time eager to regain the prestige lost through Prussian diplomatic and military success; French public opinion was also closely engaged, and newspapers that once had fulminated about English insults to France were now constantly sensitive about Prussian slights.[31] Unfortunately, this did not lead to widespread public support for the government's proposals to increase the size and armament of the army. Fundamental here was the feeling that if war came France could rely again on the *levée en masse*. The scene was thus set for Bismarck to lure France into a war which the essentially unreformed imperial army and a mass of untrained levies were simply incapable of winning.

The political factors we have been describing may be seen as crucial to the slackening of Anglo-French rivalry, even fundamental. We have noted that on most occasions when the naval antagonism between the two countries peaked, the stimulus can be found in diplomatic friction and the celerity with which opinion on both sides of the Channel became engaged in a confrontation.

But one must accept that the rivalry was hardly shaped only by international politics and governmental and popular responses to it. Allowance has to be made for naval circumstances, naval developments; in short, by what one may describe as naval factors. These were commonly not purely naval, one must admit; there was

---

[30] L. M. Case, *French Opinion on War and Diplomacy during the Second Empire* (Pennsylvania University Press, 1954), chs. 8 and 9.

[31] Millman, *British Foreign Policy and the Coming of the Franco-Prussian War*, 183–4.

usually some political colouring. This was inevitable, if for no other reason than that in times of tension naval matters quickly translated into political ones. Nevertheless, we can discern factors that were very largely naval in nature; they affected the rivalry that concerns us, and so have to be considered.

There is an uncharacteristic tone in one despatch written by Palmerston in September 1865. He wrote to Cowley that 'all old sentiments of rivalship and antagonism as between Englishmen and Frenchmen are on our part extinguished'.[32] He returned closer to form ten days later in a letter to Russell, 'As to France, we know how restless and aggressive she is, and how ready to break loose for Belgium, for the Rhine, for anything she would be likely to get without too great an exertion.'[33] However, the two letters are not entirely at odds. Even the second letter does not suggest that France is ready to unleash herself on the South Coast of England or on British shipping; that, perhaps, would be 'too great an exertion'. The first is far from Francophobia, and even the second does not see France as a looming naval threat. Where, one wonders, is 'steam bridge' Palmerston?

A similar kind of discontinuity is to be found later in the decade when, for once, the prospect of serious disagreement with France did arise. This was in 1869 over an attempt by the Paris government to force the take-over of a Belgian railway by a French company. Ten years before, a threat to the independence of Belgium would have led to British fury, and to a first-class naval scare. This time neither Whitehall nor public opinion was roused (though Lord Clarendon, whilst believing there would not be general support for war, did put pressure on the newspapers to avoid encouraging belligerency); and there was certainly not a naval scare.[34] That there was greater assurance about the naval balance can be seen in late 1867–early 1868, when the cabinet investigated it. Naturally enough, the Admiralty pressed for more shipbuilding and greater readiness, and this found some echoes within the cabinet. But one also notes a strong reluctance by some ministers—including the Prime Minister himself—to sanction larger

---

[32] 3 Sept.: F. A. Wellesley, *The Paris Embassy during the Second Empire* (London, 1928), 286–7.

[33] K. Bourne, *The Foreign Policy of Victorian England 1830–1902* (OUP, 1970), 382.

[34] Craig, 'Great Britain and the Belgian Railways Dispute', 753.

naval estimates. The Chancellor of the Exchequer, Disraeli, also
made the point that previous Admiralty worries about foreign
naval development had proven to be ill-founded, and he spoke of
the 'usual exaggeration & false colouring, wh. always accompanies
these estimates'.[35] Ultimately, only three more ironclads were
approved, not the squadrons of earlier days.

Our examples suggest a weakening or even a break in the
previous virtually automatic connection—at the governmental and
popular levels—between British thoughts of French aggression,
a naval scare, and naval preparation. There is some evidence for
a similar break in France, similar to the extent that one finds
indications of lessened tensions over naval affairs even before
the important diplomatic movements of the second half of the
1860s. The implication is that our naval factors not only worked
alongside the political Anglo-French *détente* of the later 1860s
but also helped lay a basis for that *détente*. But what were these
factors?

The first dates from as early as 1856, the Declaration of Paris
issued by the diplomatists gathered to settle the Crimean War.
Historically, there had been serious differences between the great
naval powers over maritime law. The French, for instance, had
accepted the principle of 'enemy ships, enemy goods', meaning that
all the goods on a merchantman seized by an enemy belligerent
were forfeit, even if the goods belonged to a neutral owner. The
British, on the contrary, denied this principle. They also denied
another principle accepted in France; that of 'free ships, free
goods', whereby warships would allow neutral vessels to pass
unhindered in wartime even if they were carrying goods owned by
enemy nationals, as long as those goods were not contraband of
war. Britain and France not only disagreed with each other over
these principles but also with the majority of other maritime
nations, which tended to favour the most generous possible attitude toward neutral rights, and thus denied 'enemy ships, enemy
goods' but welcomed 'free ships, free goods'. The outbreak of the
Crimean War and the resulting need of the western allies to reach a
common practice between themselves—one that would also satisfy
neutral opinion—led the two governments to issue a temporary
regulation that acceded to neutral wishes, and for various reasons

[35] Millman, *British Foreign Policy and the Coming of the Franco-Prussian War*, 149–
52.

this was made permanent by the Declaration of 1856.[36] Not all differences over maritime law were thus removed between Paris and London. In the late 1850s, for instance, there was renewed friction over the 'right of search' because of forced inspections by the Royal Navy of merchant vessels (some of them French) suspected to be slavers. But at least by this time there was greater Anglo-French conformity than there had been previously in such questions, which did reduce the room for quarrels, and this was of some importance in the following decade when the two powers found themselves in the rather odd position of being neutral during a maritime war, that is the one waged between the Federals and Confederates.

The Declaration of Paris also had a more positive contribution to make to the reduction of rivalry, at least on the French side. In one way, admittedly, that Declaration obstructed naval policy in France, causing some resentment at least in the Ministry of Marine, and inevitably reflecting badly on the *entente* and on England. It had long been hoped in Paris that even if *la Royale* was not on its own equal to the Royal Navy, then it still could act as the core of a maritime alliance formed by nations offended by the old tyrant of the seas, an alliance that might well gain maritime ascendancy.[37] But with Britain's acceptance of 'free ships, free goods' one saw the end of the major disagreement between her and the neutral maritime nations. During the eighteenth century that disagreement had been a prime cause of the creation of two powerful neutral blocs aimed at limiting Britain's naval pretensions (the Armed Neutralities of 1780 and 1800). The Declaration was seen in the rue Royale as making such widespread Anglophobia significantly less likely in future, but by no means all seemed lost. French policy-makers still looked to create at least limited anti-English alliances at sea. In the 1860s, for instance, Napoleon III discussed with Bismarck how the Prussian and French navies might co-operate should England again become a maritime bully.[38] Moreover, the Declaration could

[36] C. I. Hamilton, 'Anglo-French Seapower and the Declaration of Paris, 1856', *International History Review*, 4/2 (May 1982), 166–90. See also the wide and interesting study by Bernard Semmel, *Liberalism and Naval Strategy: Ideology, Interest, and Sea Power during the Pax Britannica* (London, 1986).

[37] *Enquête parlementaire sur la situation et l'organisation des services de la marine militaire* (2 vols., Paris, 1851), i. 137–71.

[38] See, for instance, P. Bernstein, 'Napoleon III and Bismarck: The Biarritz–Paris Talks of 1865', in N. N. Barker and M. L. Brown (eds.), *Diplomacy in the Age of Nationalism: Essays in Honor of Lynn Marshall Case* (The Hague, 1971), 138.

be seen as a positive good. England had accepted restrictions on the way she could interfere with neutral traders, and so the Declaration appeared a genuine step towards the 'freedom of the seas': one of the aims of French naval policy articulated by the *Enquête parlementaire* in 1849–51.[39]

The Anglo-French agreement over international maritime law was also an example of what could be achieved through compromise and co-operation between two equal powers. Here, surely, was something even more likely to satisfy French *amour propre* than any move towards the 'freedom of the seas'—itself a somewhat elastic concept. Britain's acceptance of a common maritime practice could be seen as a clear success for French policy-making. True, France had had to make some concessions, and the Ministry of Marine had certainly been very reluctant to give up 'enemy ships, enemy goods'. But Britain had also made concessions, which suggested how much she valued her alliance with France. From the French point of view, the important thing was that the two powers had met as equals to discuss naval matters. The English had not come as tyrants. Implicitly, they had shown respect for French naval pretensions and the French navy. The relevance of this is clear if one recalls how, after the Syrian crisis, many French writers had bemoaned the lack of English respect for France, and argued that only by increasing the amount of her naval force—the one thing the English were supposed to respect—could the position be improved.

This notion of respect—and of the balance of force—has to be looked at in the context of the 1860s, and from both sides of the Channel. The first point to note is that by about 1864 both sides were coming to accept that the balance of naval power being achieved was largely acceptable. By then the Royal Navy had just about gained a numerical superiority in ironclads, and could look forward to this slowly increasing. Some—notably in the Admiralty wished that the superiority could be much greater. We have seen, however, that opinion in political circles was not very sympathetic. Perhaps after some years when the Royal Navy had had no clear lead—or even an inferiority—in certain warship types, even a narrow superiority seemed an achievement.

---

[39] *Enquête parlementaire sur la marine militaire*, i. 137. For the differences between the appearance and the reality see Hamilton, 'Anglo-French Seapower and the Declaration of Paris'.

The attitude in France, perhaps oddly, was scarcely less amiable. There had been a stage, around 1860, when some naval officers had hoped that France might take a permanent lead in warship construction. In only a short time, though, British financial and industrial resources were making themselves felt in the race, and it became clear that such hopes were nugatory. But, from the French point of view, a great deal had been achieved. In the 1840s there had been some cause to think that the British had insufficient respect not only for France but for the fighting qualities as well as the size of *la Royale*. By the early 1860s, on the other hand, the British had good reason to see the rival force as a fighting fleet not much different from their own. Certainly, informed opinion realized that the Royal Navy would remain the larger, but the French navy had run it too close a race, given it too many shocks, to allow for any degree of contempt. By this time the two navies regarded each other as near equals—a precious balm to French susceptibilities, soothing memories of a more cavalier British attitude and dulling the sense of rivalry.[40]

Perhaps something of the same thing occurred in respect to the military balance. British fears of France since the 1840s had been predicated in large part on the power of the French army. Given the much smaller size of the British army, and the way relatively little of it was deployed in the home islands, the dangers were obvious if France managed to land an invasion force. The British army's embarrassments in the Crimea did little to improve its reputation. Hence came the particular concern at the end of the 1850s, when the French seemed close to gaining a naval numerical superiority, so apparently making sea-borne invasion entirely practical. Change soon came. Naturally, the scare brought increases in the Royal Navy. Furthermore, a great programme of fortress-building was undertaken to protect the home dockyards from landward attack, and a large volunteer army was successfully organized. Thus not only did British and French naval forces converge in strength, if never quite meeting; so too did the military ones. It was in Britain as well as in France that feelings of substantial inferiority were removed. The self-confidence of both sides was enhanced.

This obviously in itself reduced feelings of rivalry, but it was most important in that it made it possible for another factor

[40] See Chasseloup-Laubat to La Roncière Le Noury, 4 Sept. 1861, Chasseloup-Laubat Papers, ii. 245–6.

to take effect. Alliance, as we have seen, can be a divisive force, but this is less likely to be the case where the parties are able to co-operate on a broadly equal level, without any striking con-sciousness of inferiority. It is even less likely when the parties are joined against a power that poses a potent threat to crucial national interests of both. France and Britain were brought together in such an alliance—albeit informal—in the early 1860s. The occasion was the US Civil War of 1861–5. Here we return to an essentially political factor, though one distinct from those mentioned earlier. The Atlantic Ocean insulated Amer-ican and European diplomacy, to the extent that London and Paris could co-operate over American affairs at the very time when they were becoming estranged in Europe over Poland and Denmark. Moreover, there was a strong and inescapable maritime element in British and French involvement in the Americas, with consequences for naval relations between the two powers.

The Civil War came after decades when Whitehall had been worried about US power. The prime concerns had been first, the prospect of a US invasion of Canada; and second, the spread of US influence southwards to Central America, where there were hopes of a trans-isthmian canal (of undoubted importance to the first maritime nation); and then to South America proper (part of the informal British Empire of economic dominance). Also, US belliger-ence and aggressiveness were taken for granted by many British policy-makers, and there had been fears that any British involve-ment in a war with a powerful European naval power would be seen by the Americans as an opportunity to despoil their English-speaking cousins.

Initially, the rebellion of the Confederacy offered a chance that a powerful potential rival might be about to fragment, and there were suggestions that the British should encourage this by openly intervening on the Southern side to ensure a dis-United States. Intervention nearly came about in 1862 when a Federal cruiser stopped a British merchantman and arrested two Confederate envoys, Mason and Slidell, but the matter was smoothed over. Gradually, as the Federals advanced against the South in 1863–4, Whitehall became less concerned about intervention than the possibility of a victorious North taking revenge—a revenge for which Washington had sufficient cause, given British help to the

Confederates by the construction of privateers and allowing blockade-runners to operate from Bermuda.[41]

The French government came to have similar fears of US reaction. France was not as bound to the New World as Britain was through Canada and economic interests, but in the early 1860s she bound herself. Napoleon III's foreign policy was still characterized by aggressiveness. Moreover, the naval programme was yielding large-scale results in the shape of transport-vessels and battleships, giving the capability to intervene powerfully overseas. Policy and capability encouraged each other. Thus Napoleon and his ministers took a great interest in the progress of the US Civil War, and were more attracted by the opportunities offered by intervention on the Southern side than was Palmerston's Cabinet. Indeed, it was principally hesitancy in London that prevented a joint move.

The French had a purpose other than seeking the prestige of successful action. The concessions that a grateful South would offer were one attraction. More important, there were the opportunities that would open up further south if US power was broken and the Monroe Doctrine rendered ineffective. Mexico was the principal target. In 1861 the Juarez government refused to honour its foreign debts, thus bringing France, Spain, and Britain to despatch military and naval forces. The latter two powers soon accepted a compromise and withdrew, but Napoleon took advantage of the US Civil War to act more boldly. He decided to make Mexico a monarchy, believing that to be the strongest form of government for a Latin nation. Not only would this give Mexico the discipline to repay her debts, he believed, but it would also give him the chance to offer the throne of Montezuma to a Habsburg scion—something which, he hoped, might persuade Vienna to give up Venetia to Piedmont, thus furthering his aim of reaching a solution in Italy.

Napoleon sent large forces to implement what was his most visionary, most unfortunate of schemes. From the point of view of military and naval operations in Mexico all went well enough. In all other respects there was only failure. France had to keep 30,000 good troops across the Atlantic just when the German situation was becoming critical. Then there was the unfortunate fact that in 1864–5 the Federals were strangling the Confederacy, and making

[41] K. Bourne, *Britain and the Balance of Power in North America 1815–1908* (London, 1967), chs. 6–8.

it clear that their next step might well be to throw the French out of Mexico.[42]

Given the common fears at this time in London and Paris of Federal designs, it was natural that the two powers were drawn together over policy in North America. The Federals had a formidable war machine at their disposal by now. Quite apart from the huge army, plentifully supplied with artillery, there was a vast navy, possessing by the end of 1864 half as many steamers again as the Royal Navy, and twice as many ironclads. Doubtless many of the vessels were good only for coastal operations, but they were potent in American waters, and—with the commerce destroyers of the Wampanoag class, laid down in 1863—there was an instrument of intervention further afield. The reunited USA had the means to attack on land in Canada and Mexico, to defend her coasts against naval reprisals, and to attack British and French maritime commerce.

The British and French governments had been drawn together by common interest in the US Civil War since its very outbreak. Even though a joint intervention was never agreed on, a largely common diplomatic position was concerted, which in itself helped improve Anglo-French relations. But these relations became intimate only under a common threat during a few critical months before and after the capitulation of the last Confederate armies in March and April 1865. It was now that the chances of Washington expanding the war seemed greatest, and it was now that the British and French prepared themselves to fight. In June, for instance, the Admiralty approved a new plan for defensive works at Esquimalt.[43] Concurrently, the two governments put up a great show of togetherness, unprecedented in peacetime and, so it appears, unprecedented in its sincerity. In July and August there was a series of exchange visits between naval squadrons. On 17 July the large French ironclad *Magenta* and a smaller escort were present at Plymouth for an agricultural fête. The courtesy was returned when a British squadron arrived at Cherbourg for *quinze août*, carrying the First Lord of the Admiralty himself, spending five days there with

[42] N. N. Barker, 'France, Austria, and the Mexican Venture, 1861–4', *French Historical Studies*, 3 (1963–4), 224–45. L. M. Case, *Édouard Thouvenel et la diplomatie du Second Empire* (Paris, 1976), ch. 13.

[43] Barry M. Gough, *The Royal Navy and the Northwest Coast of North America, 1810–1914: A Study of British Maritime Ascendancy* (University of British Columbia Press, 1971), 209.

part of the force proceeding to Brest for yet more festivities. At the end of the month the French ironclad squadron, under Bouët-Willaumez, went to Portsmouth for five days, taking Chasseloup-Laubat to reciprocate the recent Channel crossing of his esteemed English colleague. The message to the US government was plain. As the Minister of Marine said of England—though it applied equally well to his own country—'elle ne serait pas fâchée de montrer qu'elle a une grande dame pour amie—Dans le monde cela fait toujours bon effet.'[44]

Relations were not absolutely cordial. For one thing, the estrangement continued in European affairs. Moreover, remembering what was said earlier about rivalry in alliance, absolute cordiality would have been impossible. It was now, for instance, impelled by his experience of Anglo-French wining and dining, that La Roncière wrote sarcastically of the English love of 'Oaoh'. But there was a degree of rapprochement and co-operation with little or no precedent in Anglo-French relations, as one concludes from the warm welcome paid by newspapers on both sides of the Channel to the reciprocal naval visits; and as one might also judge by Palmerston's phrase in September about the extinguishing of rivalry and antagonism—at least a partial recantation by an old campaigner. One draws the same conclusion from a letter of the First Naval Lord, Sir Frederick Grey, just after the visit to Brest: 'I believe it has really so far made our officers and men more friendly, and there is a real desire on both sides to be on good terms.'[45] The implication that there was a popular depth to the *entente* is surely correct. The reports in the *Hampshire Telegraph* and the *Portsmouth Times and Naval Gazette* for 2 September show that the citizens of Portsmouth—surely those who would have been the most hardened naval Francophobes—gave a most enthusiastic welcome to the French visitors. Most telling of all, perhaps, was the mutual friendliness of the sailors on both sides. One source is William Allingham, an uneven poet but an acute observer, who was in Portsmouth on 1 September 1865, and saw warmth between those who all too often in the past had regarded

[44] Chasseloup-Laubat to Bouët-Willaumez, 28 June and 8 July 1865, Chasseloup-Laubat Papers, vii. 66–9, 72–5. Letter of La Roncière Le Noury of 31 Aug., L'Hôpital and Saint-Blancard, *Correspondance intime de l'amiral de La Roncière Le Noury*, ii. 26–31.

[45] Letter to the third Earl Grey, 27 Aug. 1865, Grey Papers.

national differences as an entirely sufficient excuse for suspicion, argument, and hectic brawls in the streets. He wrote in his diary of 'crowds, taverns, French and English sailors drunk together, some arm-in-arm, mutually friendly and unintelligible'. The closest he found to hostility was the patronizing reply of one old boatman to the comment, 'They look pretty much like English sailors'—'Ah! They tries to come as near us as they can!'[46] The *Portsmouth Times* for 2 September confirms Allingham's picture. Significantly, the paper's reporter said that, as far as he knew, there were no disturbances between the British and French sailors ashore.

The American emergency did not last long, the serious common threat was fading even before the drunken scenes in Portsmouth. By 7 August half the Federal army had been demobilized and the navy in commission was down to only one-sixth of the Civil War level. The prospect of war did not recede totally. The claims for damage caused by British-built Confederate privateers caused transatlantic turbulence until the end of the decade, when Whitehall agreed to pay compensation. And, despite demobilization, Washington was able—and willing—to intervene in Mexico, with force if necessary. Under threat, Napoleon eventually agreed to withdraw his army back across the Atlantic. Nevertheless, even by the end of 1865 there was not the same degree of common danger London and Paris had felt there to be back in the summer. In December the Foreign Secretary quickly repelled a French suggestion of an agreement for mutual assistance to discourage any US attack.[47] The two sides thus began once again to draw apart, but they did not again become bitter naval rivals.

The main reason for this was surely the new internal and external preoccupations mentioned earlier. However, we have also to consider a change in the very naval context that had led to the narrowly focused rivalry of the two decades after 1840, narrow in terms of the participants and narrow in geographical concentration. Even without all the other developments we have been considering, this change alone would have been enough to alter the old pattern significantly.

[46] H. Allingham and D. Radford (eds.), *William Allingham: A Diary* (London, 1985), 121.
[47] Bourne, *Britain and the Balance of Power in North America*, 290, 301. John Niven, *Gideon Welles, Lincoln's Secretary of the Navy* (New York, 1973), 506 f.

Its essence was the enlargement and—in certain respects—greater complexity of the naval world during the 1860s. The most obvious element here was the entry of more important (or at least apparently important) players of the naval game. Notably, the balance of forces in the vital area of the Mediterranean became much more complicated. One indication of change from the old simple Anglo-French polarity in that sea came in 1863 when naval pressure was put on the Bey of Tunis. Not only the usual British and French squadrons appeared before La Goleta, but also one representing the lately formed Kingdom of Italy. The Italian fleet rapidly became a powerful one, including a strong ironclad element. That its personnel left something to be desired was shown in 1866 at the Battle of Lissa, but that battle was the proud moment for another newcomer to enter the list of significant Mediterranean naval powers: Austria. Of course, that power was hardly a newcomer to the list of states, but its naval expansion had been spurred by the introduction of the ironclad. The ironclad achieved in the 1860s what the *Dreadnought* did in the early twentieth century, giving a salutary shock to some secondary navies, encouraging internal reforms and new construction. The Spanish navy was another that responded bravely to the ironclad, and by 1870 had seven seagoing examples built or building. Even Turkey built up an ironclad squadron: fed by Western loans, the Turks had fourteen armoured vessels built or building by 1870. Only four or five were fit to lie in a line-of-battle, but this was still a respectable force, albeit on paper only. Proof at least of British reaction to these developments came in 1872 when the naval attaché in Paris was turned into a 'naval rover', whose task was to report on the progress of all European fleets.[48]

One finds at least the beginnings of the same phenomenon beyond European waters as well. New—or more significant—naval powers were in process of creation in the wider world. We have noted already the burgeoning in the early 1860s of the Federal (or US) navy. Furthermore, a few lesser powers began to buy ironclads, albeit only small ones. Some vessels originally intended for the Federals or Confederates found their way into other hands. Japan, for instance, purchased two vessels built for the South (1867 and 1869); and in 1868 Peru obtained two monitors from

[48] Goschen to Lord Granville, received 21 June 1872, Granville Papers, PRO.30. 29.54, fo. 226.

Washington's large war-surplus fleet. In later times, the development of powerful extra-European navies, above all those of the USA and Japan, were to end the ability of Britain and France to play an imposing global naval role cheaply by sending overseas largely light or obsolescent warships. Even in the 1860s something of the future was apparent. London and Paris found that they had to deploy ironclads on distant stations—*cuirassés de station*. And then there was the fear—above all in Britain—of commerce destroyers. One must admit that the attention given at the Admiralty to strategic issues remained inadequate, since there was still no proper naval war-planning organization, a situation that persisted well beyond the end of the decade.[49] Nevertheless, the Wampanoag class caused at least some elements in Britain to think less about the balance of the battlefleets in European waters and more about how one might best guard the country's imperial and commercial maritime routes strung around the earth.[50]

Much was changing, generally involving the weakening of the old cross-Channel rivalry, the old concentration of London upon Paris and vice versa. There was a growing strategic extension, one that resulted from more than the simple fact that more and more serious naval protagonists were emerging, both within Europe and beyond.

The Suez Canal can hardly be ignored in this context. In one way, of course, its existence developed the Mediterranean interests of Britain and France. The new waterway was of great importance to the merchantmen, troopships, and warships of both powers. After 1875 (when the British government purchased the Khedive's shares), Britain and France had the predominant financial stake in the canal's profitable working. It had to be protected. This was to lead to an extended Mediterranean presence, above all for Britain, since with her great merchant marine and her enormous empire east of Suez it was she who benefited most from Lessep's masterpiece. Hence the acquisition of Cyprus in 1878, and the occupation of Egypt itself a little later (however reluctantly at first). But the canal was obviously not merely a desirable object in itself: it was a

---

[49] N. A. M. Rodger, 'The Design of the *Inconstant*', *Mariner's Mirror*, 61/1 (1975), 9–22; 'The Dark Ages of the Admiralty', pt. i, *Mariner's Mirror*, 61/4 (1975), 330–44; pt. ii, 62/1 (1976), 33–46; pt. iii, 62/2 (1976), 121–8.

[50] J. Colomb, *The Protection of our Commerce & the Distribution of our War Forces Considered* (London, 1867).

route. It had transformed the Mediterranean from a cul de sac into a maritime passage. That sea had become more integrated into the global maritime nexus.

However, a more fundamental broadening of the strategic perspective, and a greater degree of integration (albeit in another sense) came to the naval world through improved technology. We saw in Chapter 2 how the coming of steam emphasized the home stations. With all the tactical advantages it brought, steam-power initially restricted strategic possibilities, presenting the two main naval powers with enhanced abilities to attack and defend, but within the boundaries imposed by limited bunkers, high coal consumption, and unreliable engines. This was true of the paddle-steamers; and it remained true — albeit to a lesser degree — for the *mixtes*, for the *bâtiments à vapeur*, and even for the first ironclads. With adequate logistic provision, and an adequate spread of canvas, these vessels could have a global role, but their full potential could be realized only in European waters, where they were close to good supply and repair centres, and operating over distances that could be covered under steam-power alone. They appeared most menacing of all in the narrow confines of the Channel, closely supported by networks of fortified arsenals, and railway and telegraph lines. One saw, even in Britain, the construction of major warships specifically designed to operate in home waters. Thus there was the beginning of a pattern whereby foreign stations were composed not so much of older or even obsolete vessels (common enough in previous times), but rather of ones that, whether they were new or old, tended to have somewhat different capabilities from those stationed at home.

This pattern never became absolute. For one thing, naval architects sometimes built better than they knew, and warships intended for restricted functions were found quite capable of taking more challenging roles. One finds the blockships serving in the Baltic, and Dupuy de Lôme's ironclads crossing the Atlantic. On other occasions, to be fair, naval architects and senior officers knew perfectly well what they wanted — excellent sea-keeping capabilities —and tried to get them when possible. This was above all true of the Admiralty, who were naturally more concerned than the Ministry of Marine with the requirements of operating for long periods in the Atlantic. Hence the size of some of the first British ironclads. But their size meant iron hulls, and that in turn forbade deployment on distant stations, whatever their other good qualities. This changed in the mid-1860s. An effective if somewhat clumsy means of sheathing iron-hulled vessels was developed. Moreover in 1864 the House of Commons agreed to give soft loans to support the construction of docks in the Empire.[51]

Improved technology furthered the process. In the 1860s one saw engines of greater coal economy and reliability, and in 1869 the Admiralty felt able to order the first mast-less seagoing battleship —the *Devastation*—and her specifications included the requirement of being able to cross the Atlantic under steam without needing to refuel. In the following decade even greater efficiency was attained with the widespread introduction of the compound steam-engine. The development of steam-power in the mid-nineteenth century therefore had markedly different consequences for Anglo-French naval relations as time progressed. Initially, it tended to restrict strategic options, and—at its most extreme—left the two rivals staring fearfully at each other across a few miles of water: a situation that was both tense and dangerous. Ultimately, though, steam restored almost all the strategic flexibility it had stolen. This in itself hardly diffused the rivalry, but it did at least give the necessary context for the forces of disengagement and *détente* discussed earlier in this chapter to act more effectively.

III

Just as in the 1840s the budgets of the two navies had chased each other up and up, so in the 1860s they chased each other down, at least after the construction 'bulge' of the early years of the decade was over. The two finance ministries took advantage of the decline in tension over naval affairs to press for reductions in construction, in deployment, and in readiness. They were aided by the support given by the parliaments to these ministries in their efforts at controlling the details of naval expenditure. The French *senatus-consultum* of 1861 has been noted already. On the British side the Annual Committee of Public Accounts after 1861 consistently supported Treasury authority over estimates, expenditure, and accounts.[52] The Committee was part of a long-term increase of

---

[51] PP (1865), i. 171–6.
[52] Accountant-General to Secretary of the Admiraltyy 12 June 1888, Hartington Commission, PRO HO.73.355.3.

Treasury power over the administration as a whole, and it is interesting to note that there was very little change in emphasis during the 1860s in the attitude of the Treasury towards naval expenditure, despite changes of government. The two leading Chancellors were those great opponents Disraeli and Gladstone; but they were in nothing else so alike as in their desire—and ability—to reduce the service votes, perhaps the most notable example of the British 'consensus' over foreign affairs remarked on before.[53]

Between 1861 and 1869 the French naval budget fell from 230 million francs to just over 180 million, and the British from over £12.5 million to just over £10 million. For various reasons, largely the simple cost of improved technology, the expenditure never fell back to the pre-rivalry levels. (The 1840 figures for both navies were not much above half those just quoted for 1869.) One characteristic of all arms rivalries seems to be that, after the thunder has abated, normal service expenditure stabilizes at a new, previously unattained level. Despite the rise between 1840 and 1869, we may still say that the financial indicator does not contradict the idea that Anglo-French naval rivalry had finally quietened down to about where it had been before the Syrian crisis.

Circumstances were never propitious for a renewal of that rivalry, at least not with the same degree of ardour and exclusivity. The world was changing too much for such a repetition, especially with the rise of German power, which ultimately threatened the safety of Britain as well as of France. It seems a suitable conclusion, however, to admit that the rivalry of 1840–70, and above all the very effectiveness of French naval planning, had their own contribution to make to enfeebling later Anglo-French naval quarrels.

The naval race with Britain had led to some notable French successes, but the predominant response to the navy in France for some time after 1870 was one of disappointment. Ropp suggests that the French public might have been as indignant with its navy after the war with the German Confederation as Italians had been with their defeated navy after Lissa, had it not been for the great part played by seamen, naval troops, and ordnance on land, above all in the defence of Paris. During the war, the navy was quite unable to exploit its enormous superiority over the Prussian navy,

[53] C. J. Bartlett, 'The Mid-Victorian Reappraisal of Naval Policy', in K. Bourne and D. C. Watt (eds.), *Studies in International History* (London, 1967), 189–208.

but it contributed 55,300 officers and men, 1,032 guns, 29,300 rifles and a great quantity of other equipment to trying to stave off defeat on land.

If not humiliated, *la Royale* at least suffered in its prestige after the war. In 1872, for the first time ever, none of the graduates of the *École polytechnique* took up either of the positions open to them as *aspirants*.[54] The graduates showed themselves to be prudent guardians of their careers. With the post-war cuts in the naval budget, there was a serious decline in new construction and in the number of vessels kept in commission. This severely restricted prospects of employment and promotion for the numerous officers created during the growth years of the Second Empire. Thus, as in the Royal Navy after 1815, there was a promotion block, which both discouraged new applicants for the *grand corps*, and depressed the spirits of those who had already joined. Since it tended to be those officers on the home stations (closer to the source of patronage), who got what promotion there was, as against the 'pariahs' who served overseas, there was now a serious cause of division and argument in the officer corps.[55]

The promotion block, and added friction between officers were only two of the inheritances from the Empire that tended to weaken the fleet of the Third Republic. The other was the great ironclad fleet of Dupuy de Lôme, in terms of the ships themselves and of the lesson that many drew of what happened when one tried to rival the Royal Navy on its own terms. The ships themselves had a bad influence, in that they represented an enormous capital outlay, far superior to that belonging to any of the other maritime countries—with the one obvious exception—and off which the post-war National Assembly believed the French navy could live whilst the country recovered from the war and built up its main defence: the army. In the circumstances, the policy was inevitable and justified, but had unfortunate consequences for the navy. First, it meant relying on an ageing, increasingly obsolescent fleet. Furthermore, given the concentration on capital-ship construction in the early 1860s, it meant that most of the battlefleet would wear out at the same time. Nor was this crisis very far off: almost all the vessels had been built with wooden hulls, and events showed that

[54] Ropp, 'The Development of a Modern Navy: French Naval Policy, 1871–1904', thesis (Harvard, 1937), 42–3, 90.

[55] Ibid., ch. 10.

they had a short life in comparison with iron-hulled types. The latter stayed seaworthy for decades, but already by the end of the Empire a couple of the earliest French wooden ironclads were showing signs of senility, though admittedly this was due to the use in construction of insufficiently seasoned wood. (Even the French had difficulty in obtaining adequate supplies of good building timber.) Few of their sister ships remained as effective warships after 1880. This meant that at some stage the Chamber would be faced, in an unpleasantly insistent way, with demands for much expanded naval credits.

The inherited battlefleet also brought with it a lesson that had its own unfortunate effect. Even before 1870, the more optimistic French naval hopes raised by the naval programme had been disappointed. As Richild Grivel wrote in an article in 1869, the dangerous panegyrics of a certain school had made some Frenchmen dream of naval superiority. They had been far too hopeful—'l'un des traits les plus accusés de nôtre légèreté gauloise'. A belief that naval mastery could be gained, he concluded, would lead only to a painful awakening.[56] Indeed, already by 1869, with the Royal Navy having attained a significant ironclad superiority, that reawakening had come.

Certainly, during the following decade, there was no serious question of challenging the supremacy of the Royal Navy. As one sees from secret meetings of the *Conseil d'amirauté* in 1879 to discuss strategy, the naval high command did not think then in terms of war with England. The meetings set out aims in case of naval war that are not unfamiliar. The navy was to defend the country's ports and coastlines, and to ensure communications with Algeria: moreover, the fleet was to dispute with all enemies the control of the sea close to France. But there was a firm exception made here for England. The most likely naval opponents were thought to be Italy and Germany, and they were the ones (separate or combined) that the French fleet had to be able to counter in all circumstances. There was no thought of disputing control of the European seas with the Royal Navy. Indeed, war with England was seen as very unlikely: her role was expected to be either neutral or even allied

---

[56] 'De la guerre maritime avant et depuis les nouvelles inventions', pt. 10, *Revue maritime et coloniale*, 26 (1869), 686–8. For an example of extravagant hopes, though from an officer of some mental instability, see E.-C. Lullier, *Mission politique et maritime de la France au XIXe siècle* (Paris, 1865).

if France became engaged in war. But—if by chance, it was said—France did have to fight her, then the prime concern of *la Royale* would be to attack enemy commerce and to protect French colonies. Obviously, there had been a return to the kind of policy aims current before the great imperial building programme.[57]

In the end, therefore, those building programmes had come largely to naught. Despite the financial sacrifices, and whatever the initial construction leads over the rival, economic, industrial, and strategic realities had finally reasserted themselves, leaving British naval supremacy essentially unaffected. The battleships of Dupuy de Lôme and Napoleon III of course remained—as long as their wooden hulls survived—but they were in one way a continual reminder of the disappointment of great hopes.

That sense of disappointment is to be met in many naval observers of the Third Republic, officers as well as politicians, amounting at times to deep frustration. During the late 1870s and 1880s it fostered the excesses of the *Nouvelle École*. Young, energetic officers, stultifying at the same rank for long years, with continually before them the apparent example of wastefulness brought by favouritism to battleships, turned with eagerness to the prospect of a fleet that included large numbers of small *autonomes* (torpedo craft). These would at one stroke increase greatly the number of independent commands, and also—so it came to be thought—be a potent means of waging a naval war even against England, by striking both at her unwieldy battleships and her merchant marine. The *guerre de course* had long been the instrument of the weaker fleet, and one that had never won a war; but with the new torpedo boats, and with Britain's ever-increasing dependence on maritime trade for foodstuffs as well as profit, such a policy was seen by the *Nouvelle École* as a truly decisive weapon. Naturally, French politicians also found this prospect attractive, particularly since they believed (wrongly) that building a fleet of *autonomes* would be cheaper than replacing the old squadrons of battleships.[58]

With hindsight, we may now agree that the *Nouvelle École* was largely in error. Its followers in the Ministry of Marine and the National Assembly, by denigrating battleship construction,

[57] AN BB8 853 (*marine*), sessions of 4 July, 6 and 16 Aug. 1879.
[58] Ropp, 'The Development of a Modern Navy', ch. 9. Henri Le Masson, 'La Politique navale française de 1870 à 1914', in his *Propos maritimes* (Paris, 1970), 181–239.

seriously weakened the French fleet during a period when the battleship still remained a crucial element in maritime warfare. In so far as the *Nouvelle École* was the consequence of the naval policy of the Second Empire, it seems we may conclude that at the very time when *la Royale* came closest to challenging the Royal Navy most effectively, on the latter's own ground, and thus (however much one might argue that the final gap between the two could never be closed) came nearest success in its most brilliant form, the price to be paid was that of helping to undermine French naval policy for over twenty years afterwards.

Appendix of Tables

TABLE 1: First Lords of the Admiralty and Ministers of Marine,
1840–1870, with dates of first appointment

First Lords

19 Sept. 35	Gilbert Elliot, 2nd Earl of Minto
8 Sept. 41	Thomas Hamilton, 9th Earl of Haddington
13 Jan. 46	Edward Law, Earl of Ellenborough
13 July 46	George Eden, Earl of Auckland
18 Jan. 49	Sir Francis Baring
2 Mar. 52	Algernon Percy, 4th Duke of Northumberland
5 Jan. 53	Sir James Graham
8 Mar. 55	Sir Charles Wood
8 Mar. 58	Sir John Pakington
28 June 59	E. A. Seymour, 12th Duke of Somerset
13 July 66	Sir John Pakington
8 Mar. 67	Hon. H. T. Lowry Corry
18 Dec. 68	H. C. E. Childers

Ministers of Marine

12 May 39	L'amiral baron Duperré (V.-G.)
1 Mar. 40	L'amiral baron Roussin (A.-R.)
29 Oct. 40	L'amiral baron Duperré (V.-G.)
7 Feb. 43	L'amiral baron Roussin (A.-R.)
24 July 43	L'amiral baron de Mackau (A.-R.-A.)
9 May 47	F.-P.-G. Guizot (temporary)
21 May 47	N.-A. Lannes, duc de Montebello
24 Feb. 48	D.-F. Arago (provisional)
11 May 48	L'amiral comte Casy (J.-G.)
29 June 48	Jules Bastide
17 July 48	Le capitaine de vaisseau Verninac de Saint-Maur (R.-J.-B.)
20 Dec. 48	Le comte Destutt de Tracy (A.-C.-V.)
31 Oct. 49	L'amiral Romain Desfossés (J.)
9 Jan. 51	T.-J.-E. Ducos
24 Jan. 51	Le général Vaillant (J.-B.-F.)
10 Apr. 51	J.-N.-S.-P. Chasseloup-Laubat
26 Oct. 51	H.-N.-H. Fortoul
3 Dec. 51	T.-J.-E. Ducos
19 Apr. 55	L'amiral Hamelin (F.-A.)
24 Nov. 60	J.-N.-S.-P. Chasseloup-Laubat (in Dec. 1863 succeeded his brother as le marquis de Chasseloup-Laubat)
21 Jan. 67	L'amiral Rigault de Genouilly (C.)

Sources: J. C. Sainty, *Admiralty Officials 1660–1870* (London, 1975); *Annuaire de la marine*.

TABLE 2: Annual Launchings/Undockings of Screw-Ships of the Line

Date Launched	UK			France		
	Name of ship	Converted from sail of the line	No. of guns	Name of ship	Converted from sail of the line	No. of guns
1847						
25 Oct.	*Blenheim*	C	60			
1848						
28 Sept.	*Ajax*	C	60			
1849						
28 July	*Hogue*	C	60			
1850						
16 May				*NAPOLÉON*		90
1851						
16 Jan.				*Charlemagne*	C	80
18 Mar.	*San Pareil*		70			
1852						
22 May	*Agamemnon*		91			
19 Aug.	*Edinburgh*	C	60			
14 Sept.	*Duke of Wellington*	C	131			
15 Sept.				*Jean Bart*	C	76
?				*Austerlitz*	C	86
				Montebello	C	114

TABLE 2 (cont.)

Date Launched	UK			France		
	Name of ship	Converted from sail of the line	No. of guns	Name of ship	Converted from sail of the line	No. of guns
1853						
23 Mar.	St Jean d'Acre		101			
23 Apr.	James Watt		91			
22 June	Royal George	C	120			
23 June	Princess Royal	C	91			
21 July	Cressy	C	80			
8 Aug.	Caesar	C	91			
31 Oct.				Tourville	C	80
1 Dec.	Majestic	C	80	Fleurus	C	90
2 Dec.				Prince Jérome	C	82
				Duquesne	C	80
1854						
26 Jan.	Algiers	C	91			
30 Jan.	Nile	C	91			
31 Jan.	Hannibal	C	91			
13 May	Royal Albert	C	121	Ulm	C	90
12 June				Wagram	C	90

Date	Ship		Guns	Ship		Guns
12 July	Exmouth	C	91			
26 July	Orion	C	91	Navarin	C	90
6 Nov.				Souverain	C	114
Nov.						
1855						
2 Feb.	Russell	C	60			
3 Feb.	Pembroke	C	60			
5 Feb.	Hastings	C	60			
8 Feb.	Cornwallis	C	60			
17 Feb.	Hawke	C	60	BRETAGNE	C	130
20 Mar.	CONQUEROR[1]	C	101	ARCOLE	C	90
2 May	Brunswick	C	80			
1 June	Colossus	C	80			
14 June	Marlborough	C	131			
31 July	Victor Emanuel		91			
27 Sept.						
4 Oct.				ALGÉSIRAS	C	90
25 Oct.				REDOUTABLE	C	90
12 Nov.	Centurion	C	80			
23 Nov.	Mars	C	80			
1856						
15 May				EYLAU	C	90
15 Sept.				IMPÉRIAL	C	90
?				Tilsitt	C	80
1857						
27 Mar.				ALEXANDRE	C	90
				Donauwerth	C	80

Table 2 (cont.)

Date Launched	UK			France		
	Name of ship	Converted from sail of the line	No. of guns	Name of ship	Converted from sail of the line	No. of guns
28 Mar.	*RENOWN*		91			
25 Apr.	Royal Sovereign[2]	C	131			
31 Oct.	*Meeanee*	C	80			
30 Nov.	*Goliath*	C	80			
Nov.				*St Louis*	C	80
?				*Breslaw*	C	80
?				*Duguay-Trouin*	C	82
?				*Louis XIV*	C	114
1858						
1 Jan.	*Aboukir*	C	91			
15 Apr.	*Hero*		91			
13 May	*London*	C	91			
7 Aug.				*VILLE DE NANTES*		90
26 Aug.	*Windsor Castle*	C	102			
23 Sept.	*DONEGAL*		101			
23 Oct.	*Edgar*		91			
2 Dec.				*Fontenoy*	C	80

Date	Ship		Guns	Ship		Guns
?				*Tage*	C	82
?				*Ville de Paris*	C	114
1859						
7 Mar.	*Neptune*	C	90			
19 Mar.	*St George*	C	90			
21 Mar.	*Trafalgar*	C	90			
5 Apr.	*Queen*	C	86			
16 Apr.	*REVENGE*		91			
4 May	*Hood*	C	91			
17 May	*Lion*	C	80			
27 Oct.	*Irresistible*	C	80			
12 Nov.	*VICTORIA*	C	121			
	Waterloo		90			
13 Dec.	*DUNCAN*	C	101			
?				*Turenne*	C	82
?				*Duguesclin*[3]	C	80
1860						
11 Jan.	*Rodney*	C	91			
25 Jan.	*Prince of Wales*	C	131			
7 Feb.	*Nelson*	C	91			
9 Feb.	*Royal William*	C	90			
7 Mar.	*HOWE*		121			
15 Mar.				*MASSÉNA*	C	90
24 Mar.	*Frederick William*	C	86			
21 May				*VILLE DE BORDEAUX*		90

TABLE 2 (cont.)

Date Launched	UK			France		
	Name of ship	Converted from sail of the line	No. of guns	Name of ship	Converted from sail of the line	No. of guns
4 July				CASTIGLIONE	C	90
21 July	ATLAS		91			
16 Aug.	GIBRALTAR		101			
15 Sept.	ANJON		91			
?				Bayard	C	80
1861						
26 Feb.				VILLE DE LYONS	C	90
27 Mar.	DEFIANCE		91			
21 May	Albion	C	91			
25 May	Bombay[4]	C	81			
27 May	Prince Regent	C	86			
13 July	Collingwood	C	80			

[1] Lost on 12 Dec. 1861
[2] Completed as ironclad
[3] Lost in Dec. 1859
[4] Lost in 1864
Note: Capitalization of the name of the ship means the vessel was a *Vaisseau à vapeur*.

TABLE 3: Cumulative Lists of British and French First-Class
Ironclad Construction, 1858–70

Year	UK		France	
	Name of ship	Completion date	Name of ship	Completion date
1860			*Gloire*	Aug.
1861	*WARRIOR*	24 Oct.		
1862			*Magenta*	2 Jan.
			COURONNE	2 Feb.
	DEFENCE	12 Feb.		
			Invincible	7 Mar.
			Normandie	13 May
			Solférino	25 Aug.
	BLACK PRINCE	12 Sept.		
	RESISTANCE	5 Oct.		
1863	*Royal Oak*	28 May		
1864	*Prince Consort*	6 Feb.		
	HECTOR	22 Feb.		
	ACHILLES	26 Nov.		
1865			*Provence*	1 Feb.
			Savoie	25 Mar.
			Flandre	April
	Caledonia	6 July	*HÉROINE*	July
			Magnanime	1 Nov.
1866	*BELLEROPHON*	11 Apr.		
			Guyenne	15 Apr.
	Ocean	6 Sept.		
	Lord Clyde	15 Sept.		
	Zealous	4 Oct.		

Appendix of Tables

TABLE 3 (*cont.*)

Year	UK		France	
	Name of ship	Completion date	Name of ship	Completion date
1867			*Valeureuse*	Feb.
	Royal Alfred	23 Mar.		
			Gauloise	12 Apr.
			Revanche	1 May
	MINOTAUR	1 June		
	Lord Warden	30 Aug.		
			Surveillante	21 Oct.
1868	VALIANT	15 Sept.		
	NORTHUMBER-			
	LAND	8 Oct.		
	HERCULES	21 Nov.		
	AGINCOURT	19 Dec.		
1869	MONARCH	5 Aug.		
1870	*Repulse*	31 Jan.		
	CAPTAIN	Jan. (sank		
		7 Sept.)	*Océan*	21 July
			Marengo	1 July for trials

Notes: Capitalization of the name of the ship means the vessel had an iron hull rather than wood.

On first reference the day and month of completion is given, unless otherwise specified.

Occasionally completion followed some months after the date of first seagoing trials: over a year in the case of the *Provence*. Note that the trials of the *Defence* began in Dec. 1861, giving the British a tiny temporary lead in ironclad construction but she was not completed until the following Feb. (See Ballard, *Black Battlefleet*, 240.)

TABLE 4: Cumulative Lists of British and French Second-Class and Colonial Ironclads

Year	UK		France	
	Name of ship	Completion date	Name of ship	Completion date
1864	*Research*	6 Apr.		
	Enterprise	3 June		
1865	*SCORPION*	10 Oct.		
	WIVERN	10 Oct.		
1866	*Pallas*	6 Mar.		
	Favorite	17 Mar.		
			Belliqueuse	30 Oct.
1867			*Armide*	5 Dec.
1868			*Jeanne d'Arc*	9 Mar.
			Thétis	1 May
	PENELOPE	27 June		
1869			*Atalante*	1 Apr.
			Reine Blanche	15 Apr.
			Montcalm	16 June
			Alma	?
1870	*AUDACIOUS*	10 Sept.		
	VANGUARD	28 Sept.		
	INVINCIBLE	1 Oct.		

Notes: The use of capitals for the name of a ship means the vessel had an iron hull rather than wood.

TABLE 5: Cumulative Lists of British and French Coastal Defence Ironclads

Year	UK		France	
	Name of ship	Completion date	Name of ship	Completion date
1864	*Royal Sovereign*	20 Aug.		
1865				
1866	*PRINCE ALBERT*	23 Feb.	*Taureau*	Early in year
1867			*Rochambeau*	Purchased from USA Arrived in France late in year
1868			*ONONDAGA*	Purchased from USA Arrived in France on 2 July
			Cerbère	20 Sept.
1869				
1870	*CERBERUS*	Sept.		
	ABYSSINIA	Oct.		
	MAGDALA	Nov.		

Note: The use of capitals for the name of a ship means the vessel had an iron hull rather than wood.

Select Bibliography

ABBREVIATIONS

AN	Archives Nationales
BM	British Museum
NLS	National Library of Scotland
NMM	National Maritime Museum
PP	Parliamentary Papers
PRO	Public Record Office
SRO	Scottish Record Office

MANUSCRIPT SOURCES

1. *Official Records*

Almost all the Admiralty record series are to be found at the Public Record Office, Kew. All have an ADM prefix. The most important is the ADM 1 series of Admiralty in-letters. Although for the 1840s this is very slim, the victim of vicious 'weeding', for the following decade it begins to expand, and the files come usually to contain not only Board and secretarial minutes and memoranda, but also draft out-letters. Certain official series, above all some dockyard correspondence and ship plans, are at the National Maritime Museum, Greenwich, but these have not been drawn on for the present volume, either because of lack of importance or lack of permission to view.

Kew is also the repository for the files of other government departments relevant to this study, above all the Foreign Office (FO), War Office (WO), and the Treasury (T).

In France most of the official central naval records are divided between the Archives Nationales, and the *Service historique de la marine* at Vincennes. (The less important collection of relevant papers at Fontainebleau was still being put into order when I was researching, so was unavailable.) It should be noted that certain documentary series have been split between the AN and Vincennes. Commonly this was done on the basis of date: later records tend to be at Vincennes. Date is not the criterion in the case of the crucial BB8 series, which includes two series of minutes, those of meetings of the *Conseil d'amirauté* and also those of the *Conseil des travaux*.

The first series is to be found at the AN, the other at Vincennes. To avoid confusion, references to official French naval papers are prefixed either with 'AN' or 'V'.

The records of other relevant French government departments are at the AN but there is the exception of the Foreign Ministry papers which are at the Quai d'Orsay; the repository is always mentioned in references to these papers.

2. *Private Papers*

This list shows the private papers that were consulted, and the archives where they are kept. Where a collection is divided between two archives, the identifying prefixes used in references are shown.

Baudin, Charles, AN.
Broadlands Papers, *see* Palmerston.
Chasseloup-Laubat. J.-N., marquis de, AN.
Childers, H. C. E., Royal Commonwealth Society.
Clarendon, G. W. F. Villiers, 4th Earl of, Bodleian.
Cockburn, Sir George, Papers of 1844–7 on microfilm in the Seeley Library, Cambridge. Full collection in the Library of Congress, Washington. Only the former were used in this study.
Codrington, Henry, NMM.
Dawkins, Richard, NMM.
Ducos, Théodore, AN
Dundas, J. W. D., NMM.
Dundas, Richard Saunders, in Melville collection at SRO.
Ellenborough, Edward Law, 1st Earl of, PRO.
Fremantle, Charles Howe, Buckingham County Archives.
Gladstone, W. E., BM.
Graham, Sir James, the originals are now in the Carlisle Record Office. Most of the papers were microfilmed, and there is a copy in Cambridge University Library. These are referred to in the notes as the 'Graham Papers': 'Netherby Papers' refers to an original document not microfilmed.
Granville, G. G. Leveson-Gower, 2nd Earl of, PRO.
Gravière, E. Jurien de la, AN.
Grey, Charles and Sir Henry George, 2nd and 3rd Earls, Durham University Department of Palaeography and Diplomatic.
Guizot, François, AN.
Halifax, Sir Charles Wood, 1st Viscount, BM.
Honnorat, Charles, AN.
Hornby, Sir Geoffrey Phipps, NMM.
Joinville, F.-F.-P. d'Orléans, prince de, *see* Maison de France Papers.
Keppel, Sir Henry, NMM.

Lamy, Étienne (including Henri Garreau) AN.

La Roncière le Noury, Clément de, AN.

Mackau, A.-R.-A., baron de, AN.

Maison de France Papers, AN.

Martin, Sir Thomas Byam, and his two sons Henry Byam and William Fanshawe, BM.

Melville, Henry Dundas, and Robert Saunders Dundas, 1st and 2nd Viscounts: if GD prefix, SRO; if Numerical prefix, NLS.

Meynell, Francis, NMM.

Milne, Sir Alexander, NMM.

Milne, Sir David, SNL.

Minto, Gilbert Elliot, 2nd Earl: if ELL prefix, NMM; if numerical prefix, NLS.

Napier, Sir Charles: if Add. MS prefix, BM; if PRO prefix, PRO.

Netherby Papers, see Graham.

Page, T.-F., AN.

Pakington, Sir John, Worcestershire Record Office.

Palmerston, Henry John Temple, 3rd Viscount: if Broadlands Papers prefix, University of Southampton; if Palmerston Papers prefix, BM.

Panmure, Fox Maule, 2nd Baron, SRO.

Pâris, F.-E., AN.

Parker, Sir William, NMM.

Peel, Sir Robert, BM.

Pénaud, Charles, Service historique de la marine, Vincennes.

Phillimore, Augustus, NMM.

Randon, J.-L.-C.-A., AN.

Russell, Lord John, PRO.

Seymour, Sir George (Seymour of Ragley Papers), Warwickshire County Record Office.

Somerset, E. A. Seymour, 12th Duke of (Seymour of Berry Pomeroy Papers), Devon Record Office.

Stewart, Sir A. W. Houston, NMM.

Thouvenel, Édouard: if prefixed 255 AP, AN; otherwise, Quai d'Orsay.

Walewski, A.-C., comte, Quai d'Orsay.

Walker, Sir Baldwin Wake, Library of the University of Cape Town. A small but important part of the collection has been photocopied, and is stored in the NMM. Only this part is cited in the present work.

PRIMARY PRINTED MATERIAL

1. *Parliamentary Papers*

British Parliamentary Papers, or Blue Books, have been invaluable for this work. References to the individual numbers will be found in the notes.

Similar French sources for the period under study are comparatively slight, though one must mention the *Enquête parlementaire sur la situation et l'organisation des services de la marine militaire* ... (2 vols., Paris, 1851). Parliamentary debates are to be found in *Hansard*, the *Annales du parlement français*, the *Archives parlementaires de 1787 à 1860*, and the *Journal des débats*.

2. Official Periodicals

The British *Navy List* and the French *Annuaire de la marine* were essential sources of naval information, as were the *Annales maritimes et coloniales*, the *Bulletin officiel de la marine*, and the *Ministère de la marine et des colonies: Compte définitif des dépenses*.

3. Contemporary, or Near-Contemporary Handbooks and Guides

Blanchard, C.-F., *Répertoire général des lois, décrets, ordonnances, règlements et instructions sur la marine* (3 vols., Paris, 1849–59).

Block, Maurice, *Dictionnaire général de la politique* (2 vols., Paris, 1864).

Chadwick, F. E., *Report on the Training Systems for the Navy and Mercantile Marines in England and France* (Washington, DC, 1880).

Clarigny, M. Cucheval, *Les Budgets de la guerre et de la marine en France et en Angleterre* (Paris, 1860).

Dicey, A. V., and Goddard, J. L., *Admiralty: The Admiralty Statutes* (London, 1886).

Fournier, Pierre, and Neveu, M., *Traité d'administration de la marine* (3 vols., Paris, 1885–1905).

Ministère de la marine et des colonies, *Lois, décrets, règlements et décisions sur l'inscription maritime, les écoles de la marine, les pêches, la navigation commerciale, l'organisation des services de la flotte, et le régime colonial: janvier 1861 à janvier 1867* (2 vols., Paris, 1867).

—— *Règlement général sur l'administration des quartiers, sous-quartiers, et syndicats maritimes; l'inscription maritime; le recrutement de la flotte; la police de la navigation; les pêches maritimes* (Paris, 1867).

O'Byrne, W. R., *A Naval Biographical Dictionary* ... (London, 1849 and 1861).

Parkinson, J. C., *'Under Government': An Official Key to The Civil Service of the Crown, and Guide for Candidates Seeking Appointments* (2nd. edn., London, 1859).

Prugnaud, Eugène, *Législation et administration de la marine* ... (3 vols., Rochefort, 1858).

Tréfeu, Étienne, *Nos marins. Vice-amiraux, contre-amiraux, officiers généraux des troupes de la marine et des corps entretenus* (Paris, 1888).

4. Newspapers

Hampshire Telegraph
Le Journal des Débats

Le Moniteur
Morning Post
Portsmouth Times
La Presse
The Times
L'Univers

5. *Editions of Documents*

Bonner-Smith, D. (ed.), *Russian War, 1855: Baltic, Official Correspondence* (Navy Records Society, London, 1944).
—— and Dewar, A. C. (eds.), *Russian War, 1854: Baltic and Black Sea, Official Correspondence* (Navy Records Society, London, 1943).
Bourne, K. (ed.), *The Foreign Policy of Victorian England 1830–1902* (Oxford University Press, 1970).
Bromley, J. S. (ed.), *The Manning of the Royal Navy: Selected Public Pamphlets, 1693–1873* (Navy Records Society, London, 1976).
Dewar, A. C. (ed.), *Russian War, 1855: Black Sea, Official Correspondence* (Navy Records Society, London 1945).
Guedalla, Philip (ed.), *The Palmerston Papers: Palmerston and Gladstone . . .* (London, 1928).
Hôpital, Joseph L', and Saint-Blancard, Louis de (eds.), *Correspondance intime de l'amiral de La Roncière Le Noury avec sa femme et sa fille (1855–1871)* (2 vols., Paris, 1928–9).
Raindre, G. (ed.), *Les Papiers inédits du comte Walewski, Revue de France,* 1925: I, 74–104, 485–511; II, 39–56; III, 281–305; IV, 82–96, 311–26.
Rodger, N. A. M. (ed.), *The Naval Miscellany,* v (Navy Records Society, London, 1984).
Thouvenel, L. (ed.), *Le Secret de l'empereur: Correspondance confidentielle et inédite échangée entre M. THOUVENEL, le duc de Gramont et le général comte de Flahaut, 1860–1863* (2 vols., Paris, 1889).

1. *Books*

Albion, R. G., *Forests and Sea Power: The Timber Problem of the Royal Navy 1652–1862* (Harvard University Press, Cambridge, Mass., 1926).
Anderson, O., *A Liberal State at War: English Politics and Economics during the Crimean War* (London, 1967).
Antoine, M., *et al. Origines et histoire des cabinets des ministres en France* (Geneva, 1975).
Baecque, F. de, *et al. Les Directeurs de ministère en France (XIXᵉ-première moitié du XXᵉ siècles)* (Geneva, 1976).

Ballard, G. A., *The Black Battlefleet: A Study of the Capital Ship in Transition*, ed. and abbr. G. A. Osbon and N. A. M. Rodger (London, 1980).

Barker, N. N., and Brown, M. L. (eds.), *Diplomacy in the Age of Nationalism: Essays in Honor of Lynn Marshall Case* (The Hague, 1971).

Bartlett, C. J., *Great Britain and Sea Power 1815–1853* (Oxford University Press, 1963).

Baxter, J. P., *The Introduction of the Ironclad Warship* (Harvard University Press, Cambridge, Mass., 1933).

Bourne, K., *Britain and the Balance of Power in North America 1815–1908* (London, 1967).

—— *Palmerston: The Early Years, 1784–1841* (London, 1982).

Briggs, Sir John, *Naval Administrations 1827 to 1892: The Experience of 65 Years* (London, 1897).

Brodie, Bernard, *Sea Power in the Machine Age* (Princeton University Press, 1941).

Brown, D. K., *Before the Ironclad: Development of Ship Design, Propulsion and Armament in the Royal Navy 1815–60* (London, 1990).

—— *A Century of Naval Construction: The History of the Royal Corps of Naval Constructors, 1883–1983* (London, 1983).

Bullen, Roger, *Palmerston, Guizot and the Collapse of the Entente Cordiale* (London, 1974).

Cabantous, A., *Le Ciel dans la mer: Christianisme et civilisation maritime (XVᵉ-XIXᵉ siècles)* (Paris, 1990).

Cady, J. F., *The Roots of French Imperialism in East Asia* (Cornell University Press, Ithaca, NY, 1967).

Case, Lynn M., *French Opinion on War and Diplomacy during the Second Empire* (University of Pennsylvania Press, 1954).

—— *Édouard Thouvenel et la diplomatie du Second Empire* (Paris, 1976).

Church, Clive H., *Revolution and Red Tape: The French Ministerial Bureaucracy 1770–1850* (Oxford University Press, 1981).

Coindreau, Roger, *L'École navale et ses traditions: L'Argot baille* (Paris, 1957).

Contamine, Henri, *Diplomatie et diplomats sous la Restauration* (Paris, 1970).

Corbett, Sir Julian, *Some Principles of Maritime Strategy* (London, 1911).

Courtemanche, Regis A., *No Need of Glory: The British Navy in American Waters, 1860–1864* (Annapolis, 1977).

Curtiss, John Shelton, *The Russian Army under Nicholas I, 1825–1855* (Duke University Press, Durham, NC, 1965).

Duchêne, Albert, *Un ministre trop oublié: Chasseloup-Laubat* (Paris, 1932).

Dunmore, John, *French Explorers in the Pacific*, ii. *The Nineteenth Century* (Oxford University Press, 1969).

Dupont, A., *Les Arsenaux de la Marine de 1689 à 1910* (Paris, 1910).

Fox, Robert, and Weisz, George, *The Organization of Science and Technology in France 1808–1914* (Cambridge University Press, 1980).

Freeman, E. (ed.), *Les Empires en guerre et paix 1793–1860* (Vincennes, 1990).

Friendly, Alfred, *Beaufort of the Admiralty: The Life of Sir Francis Beaufort, 1774–1857* (London, 1977).

Gardiner, R., Chesneau, R., and Kolesnik, E. M., *Conway's All the World's Fighting Ships 1860–1905* (London, 1979).

Gash, Norman, *Sir Robert Peel* (London, 1972).

Gooch, Brison D., *The New Bonapartist Generals in the Crimean War: Distrust and Decision-Making in the Anglo-French Alliance* (The Hague, 1959).

Gough, Barry M., *The Royal Navy and the Northwest Coast of North America, 1810–1914: A Study of British Maritime Ascendancy* (University of British Columbia Press, 1971).

Graham, G. S., *The Politics of Naval Supremacy: Studies in British Maritime Ascendancy* (Cambridge University Press, 1965).

—— *Great Britain in the Indian Ocean, 1810–1850* (Oxford University Press, 1967).

—— *The China Station: War and Diplomacy, 1830–1860* (Oxford University Press, 1978).

Greenhill, B., and Giffard, A., *The British Assault on Finland 1854–1855: A Forgotten Naval War* (London, 1988).

Guillon, Jacques, *François d'Orléans, prince de Joinville 1818–1900* (Paris, 1990).

Hampson, Norman, *La Marine de l'an II: Mobilisation de la flotte de l'océan 1793–1794* (Paris, 1959).

Harcourt, Comte Bernard d', *Les Quatres Ministères de M. Drouyn de Lhuys* (Paris, 1882).

Harrigan, Patrick J., *Mobility, Élites, and Education in French Society of the Second Empire* (Wilfred Laurier University Press, Ontario, 1980).

Hogg, Ian V., *Coast Defences of England and Wales, 1856–1956* (Newton Abbot, 1974).

Hood, R. C., *Royal Republicans: The French Naval Dynasties between the World Wars* (Baton Rouge, La., 1985).

Hoskins, H. L., *British Routes to India* (London, 1928).

Howard, Michael, *The Franco-Prussian War: The German Invasion of France, 1870–1871* (London, 1961).

Isser, Natalie, *The Second Empire and the Press: A Study of Government Inspired Brochures on French Foreign Policy in their Propaganda Milieu* (The Hague, 1974).

Jenkins, E. H., *A History of the French Navy: From its Beginnings to the Present Day* (London, 1973).

Jouan, René, *Histoire de la marine française* (Paris, 1950).

Kennedy, Paul M., *The Rise and Fall of British Naval Mastery* (London, 1976).

Lambert, Andrew, *Battleships in Transition: The Creation of the Steam Battle-fleet, 1815–60* (London, 1984).
—— *Warrior: Restoring the World's First Ironclad* (London, 1988).
—— *The Crimean War: British Grand Strategy, 1853–56* (Manchester University Press, 1990).
Le Gallo, Yves, *Brest et sa bourgeoisie sous la monarchie de juillet* (2 vols., Paris, 1968).
Le Masson, Henri, *Propos maritimes* (Paris, 1970).
Lewis, Michael, *A Social History of the Navy 1793–1815* (London, 1960).
—— *The Navy in Transition 1814–1864: A Social History* (London, 1965).
Lloyd, Christopher, *Mr Barrow of the Admiralty: A Life of Sir John Barrow 1764–1848* (London, 1970).
Mackay, R. F., *Fisher of Kilverstone* (Oxford University Press, 1973).
Manning, Frederic, *The Life of Sir William White* . . . (London, 1923).
Millman, R., *British Foreign Policy and the Coming of the Franco-Prussian War* (Oxford University Press, 1965).
Mollat, Michel (ed.), *Les Origines de la navigation à vapeur* (Paris, 1970).
Morrell, W. P., *Britain in the Pacific Islands* (Oxford University Press, 1960).
Mosse, W. E., *The European Powers and the German Question* (Cambridge University Press, 1958).
Oncken, H., *Napoleon III and the Rhine* (New York, 1928).
Parkes, Oscar, *British Battleships, 'Warrior' 1860 to 'Vanguard' 1950: A History of Design, Construction and Armament* (London, 1970).
Partridge, M. S., *Military Planning for the Defense of the United Kingdom 1814–1870* (New York, 1989).
Penn, Geoffrey, *Up Funnel, Down Screw: The Story of the Naval Engineer* (London, 1955).
Pottinger, E. Ann, *Napoleon III and the German Crisis, 1865–1870* (The Hague, 1966).
Preston, A., and Major, John, *'Send a Gunboat': A Study of the Gunboat and its Role in British Policy, 1854–1904* (London, 1967).
Randier, Jean, *'La Royale', l'éperon et la cuirasse: L'Histoire illustrée de la marine nationale française des débuts de la vapeur à la fin de la première guerre mondiale* (Paris, 1972).
Ranft, Bryan (ed.), *Technical Change and British Naval Policy, 1860–1939* (London, 1977).
Rasor, Eugene L., *Reform in the Royal Navy: A Social History of the Lower Deck, 1850 to 1880* (Hamden, Conn., 1976).
Rodger, N. A. M., *The Admiralty* (Lavenham, 1979).
Sainty, J. C., *Admiralty Officials, 1660–1870* (London, 1975).
Salinis, A. de, *Marins et missionaires: Conquête de la Nouvelle-Calédonie, 1843–1853* (Paris, 1978).
Sandler, Stanley, *The Emergence of the Modern Capital Ship* (University of Delaware Press, 1979).

Schurman, D. M., *The Education of a Navy: The Development of British Naval Strategic Thought, 1867–1914* (London, 1965).

Seaton, Albert, *The Crimean War: A Russian Chronicle* (London, 1977).

Service historique de la marine and Institut d'histoire des conflits contemporains, *Marine et technique au XIXᵉ siècle: Actes du Colloque International* (Paris, 1989).

Shannon, Richard, *Gladstone, 1809–1865* (London, 1982).

Smith, E. C., *A Short History of Naval and Marine Engineering* (Cambridge University Press, 1938).

Statham, E. P., *The Story of the 'Britannia': The Training Ship for Naval Cadets . . .* (London, 1904).

Strachan, Hew, *European Armies and the Conduct of War* (London, 1983).

—— *Wellington's Legacy: The Reform of the British Army, 1830–1854* (Manchester University Press, 1984).

—— *From Waterloo to Balaklava: Tactics, Technology, and the British Army* (Cambridge University Press, 1985).

Sutherland, Gillian (ed.), *Studies in the Growth of Nineteenth Century Government* (London, 1972).

Taboulet, Georges, *La Geste française en Indochine* (2 vols., Paris, 1955–6).

Taillemite, Étienne, *Dictionnaire des marins français* (Paris, 1982).

Thuillier, Guy, *Bureaucratie et bureaucrats en France au XIXᵉ siècle* (Geneva, 1980).

Tramond, Joannès, *Manuel d'histoire maritime de la France* (Paris, 1916).

—— and Reussner, André, *Éléments d'histoire maritime et coloniale contemporaine (1815–1914)* (Paris, 1947).

Turner, H. D. T., *The Royal Hospital School, Greenwich* (London, 1980).

Ward, J. T., *Sir James Graham* (London, 1967).

Wright, Maurice, *Treasury Control of the Civil Service, 1854–1874* (Oxford University Press, 1969).

2. *Articles and Chapters*

Anderson, Olive, 'Economic Warfare in the Crimean War', *Economic History Review*, 14 (1961), 34–47.

Ashworth, William, 'Economic Aspects of Late Victorian Naval Administration', *Economic History Review*, 22 (1969), 491–505.

Bach, John, 'The Royal Navy in the Pacific Islands', *Journal of Pacific History*, 3 (1968), 3–20.

Barker, N. N., 'Austria, France, and the Venetian Question, 1861–66', *Journal of Modern History*, 36 (1964), 145–54.

Bartlett, C. J., 'The Mid-Victorian Reappraisal of Naval Policy', in K. Bourne and D. C. Watt (eds.), *Studies in International History: Essays Presented to W. Norton Medlicott* (London, 1967).

Bourne, Kenneth, 'British Preparations for War with the North, 1861–1862', *English Historical Review*, 76 (1961), 600–32.

Boyer, H., 'Les Rouages de l'amirauté britannique', *Revue maritime*, 194 (1936), 168–80.

Buchanan, R. A., and Doughty, M. W., 'The Choice of Steam Engine Manufacturers by the British Admiralty, 1822–1852', *Mariner's Mirror*, 64 (1978), 327–47.

Charasse, Pierre, 'Les Phéniciens, Mogador, et le prince de Joinville', *Revue maritime* (Oct. 1974), 409–18.

Corbes, H., 'En parcourant les Mémoires d'un administrateur de la marine au siècle dernier (Alfred Guichon de Grandpont, 1807–1900)', *Annales de Bretagne et des Pays de l'ouest (Anjou, Maine, Touraine)*, 81 (1974), 167–208.

Craig, G. A., 'Great Britain and the Belgian Railways Dispute of 1869', *American Historical Review*, 50 (1944–5), 738–61.

Crouzet, François, 'Recherches sur la production d'armements en France, 1815–1913', in *Conjoncture économique, structures sociales: Hommage à Ernest Labrousse* (Paris, 1964).

—— 'Problèmes de la communication franco-britannique au XIXᵉ et XXᵉ siècles', *Revue historique*, 254 (1975), 105–34.

Dislère, P., 'Note historique sur le Corps du génie maritime', *Revue maritime*, 16 (April 1921), 432–64.

Dubreuil, J.-P., 'Contribution à l'histoire des transports au XIXᵉ siècle; La Vapeur dans la marine de guerre: Toulon, 1830–1860', *Recherches régionales*, 10 (1970), 35–45.

—— 'Les Liaisons maritimes entre Toulon et l'Algérie (1833–1853)', *Bulletin de la Société des amis de vieux Toulon*, 96 (1974), 97–118.

Émerit, Marcel, 'La Crise syrienne et l'expansion économique française en 1860', *Revue historique*, 207 (1952), 211–32.

Foot, M. R. D., 'Great Britain and Luxemburg 1867', *English Historical Review*, 67 (1952), 352–79.

François, C., 'A la mémoire de Dupuy de Lôme', *Revue maritime*, 211 (July 1937), 1–32.

Graham, G. S., 'The Transition from Paddle-Wheel to Screw Propeller', *Mariner's Mirror*, 44 (1958), 35–48.

Guihéneuc, Olivier, 'Les Origines du premier cuirassé de haute mer à vapeur: Le Plan de Dupuy de Lôme en 1845', *Revue maritime*, 100 (1928), 459–82.

Guiral, P., 'L'Affaire des soufres de Sicilie autour de 1840', in *Mélanges Pierre Renouvin: Études d'histoire des relations internationales* (Paris, 1966).

Hamilton, C. I., 'Sir James Graham, the Baltic Campaign, and War-Planning at the Admiralty in 1854', *Historical Journal*, 19 (1976), 89–112.

—— 'Anglo-French Seapower and the Declaration of Paris, 1856', *International History Review*, 4 (1982), 166–90.

—— 'The Diplomatic and Naval Effects of the prince de Joinville's *Note sur l'état des forces navales de la France* of 1844', *Historical Journal*, 32 (1989), 675–87.

Jennings, Lawrence C., 'France, Great Britain, and the Repression of the Slave Trade, 1841–1845', *French Historical Studies*, 10 (1977), 101–25.

Jones, Stephen, 'Blood Red Roses: The Supply of Merchant Seamen in the Nineteenth Century', *Mariner's Mirror*, 58 (1972), 429–42.

Jullien, P., 'L'Habillement et le costume des matelots', *Revue maritime*, 185 (1935), 605–40.

—— 'Le Personnel mécanicien de la marine militaire: Officiers et équipages', *Revue maritime*, 234 (1939), 769–99.

Laing, E. A. M., 'The Introduction of Paddle Frigates into the Royal Navy', *Mariner's Mirror*, 66 (1980), 331–43.

Lambert, Andrew, 'Captain Sir William Symonds and the Ship of the Line: 1832–1847', *Mariner's Mirror*, 73 (1987), 167–79.

—— 'Preparing for the Russian War: British Strategic Planning, March 1853–March 1854', *War and Society*, 7 (1989), 15–39.

Lewis, Michael, 'An Eye-Witness at Petropaulovsk . . .', *Mariner's Mirror*, 49 (1963), 265–72.

Meirat, Jean, 'Caracteristiques et carrière de la frégate *La Pomone* de 1845', *Revue maritime* (Nov. 1974), 647–50.

Murray, Sir Oswyn, 'The Admiralty', *Mariner's Mirror*, 24 (1938), 329–52, 458–78.

Osbon, G. A., 'The First of the Ironclads', *Mariner's Mirror*, 50 (1964), 189–98.

Partridge, M. S., 'The Russell Cabinet and National Defence, 1846–1852', *History*, 72 (1987), 231–50.

Pingaud, Albert, 'La Politique extérieure du Second Empire', *Revue historique*, 156 (1927), 41–68.

Pintner, Walter M., 'Inflation in Russia during the Crimean War Period', *American Slavic and East European Review*, 18 (1959), 81–7.

Pollard, Sidney, '*Laissez-Faire* and Shipbuilding', *Economic History Review*, 5 (1952–3), 98–115.

Pool, Bernard, 'Navy Contracts after 1832', *Mariner's Mirror*, 54 (1968), 209–26.

Pradel de Lamase, Martial de, 'Marine et littérature: Nôtre "ancêtre" Louis-Marie Bajot', *Revue maritime*, 200 (1936), 180–95.

—— 'Chasseloup-Laubat reçoit à l'Hôtel de la Marine', *Revue maritime*, 215 (1937), 626–45.

—— 'La Marine, rue Royale, de 1789 à 1815', *Revue maritime*, 229 (1939), 55–69; 230 (1939), 201–16.

Reussner, André, 'Les Sources du naufrage de la *Méduse*: Traditions et vérités', *Académie de marine: Communications et mémoires*, 15 (1936), 33–49.

—— 'Joinville et la politique navale', *Neptunia*, 32 (1953), 42–7.

Robertson, Paul L., 'Technical Education in the British Shipbuilding and Marine Engineering Industries, 1863–1914', *Economic History Review*, 27 (1974), 221–35.

Rodger, N. A. M., 'The Dark Ages of the Admiralty, 1869–1885', *Mariner's Mirror*, 61 (1975), 331–44; 62 (1976), 33–46, 121–28.

—— 'The Design of the *Inconstant*', *Mariner's Mirror*, 61 (1975), 9–22.

—— 'British Naval Thought and Naval Policy, 1820–1890: Strategic Thought in an Era of Technological Change', in Craig L. Symonds (ed.), *New Aspects of Naval History* (Annapolis, 1981).

Sandler, Stanley, '"In Deference to Public Opinion": The Loss of HMS *Captain*', *Mariner's Mirror*, 59 (1973), 57–68.

Strachan, Hew, 'Soldiers, Strategy and Sebastopol', *Historical Journal*, 21 (1978), 303–25.

—— 'The Early Victorian Army and the Nineteenth Century Revolution in Government', *English Historical Review*, 95 (1980), 782–809.

—— 'The British Way in Warfare Revisited', *Historical Journal*, 26 (1983), 447–61.

Taylor, R., 'Manning the Royal Navy: The Reform of the Recruiting System', *Mariner's Mirror*, 44 (1958), 302–13; 45 (1959), 46–58.

Testu de Balincourt, M.-C.-M.-R., 'Les Débuts du cuirassé-ancêtre *La Dévastation* à Kinburn', *Académie de marine: Communications et mémoires*, 9 (1930), 291–333.

—— and Le Conte, P., 'La Marine française d'hier: V. Navires à roues', *Revue maritime*, 154 (1932), 472–512; 157 (1933), 12–52.

—— —— 'La Marine française d'hier: VI. Vaisseaux mixtes', *Revue maritime*, 15 (1933), 345–62; 160 (1933), 483–509.

—— and Vincent-Bréchignac, P., 'La Marine française d'hier: Les cuirassés: I. Batteries flottantes', *Revue maritime*, 125 (1930), 577–95.

—— —— 'La Marine française d'hier: Les cuirassés: II. Frégates cuirassées', *Revue maritime*, 135 (1931), 289–317; 138 (1931), 775–91.

—— —— 'La Marine française d'hier: Les cuirassés: III. Corvettes cuirassées', *Revue maritime*, 143 (1931), 615–31.

—— —— 'La Marine française d'hier: Les cuirassés: IV. Gardes-côtes', *Revue maritime*, 143 (1931), 631–46.

—— —— 'La Marine française d'hier: Les cuirassés: 'La Fin de *Richelieu*', *Revue maritime*, 150 (1932), 759–61.

Thuillier, Guy, and Tulard, Jean, 'L'Histoire de l'administration du dix-neuvième siècle depuis dix ans: Bilan et perspectives', *Revue historique*, 258 (1977), 441–55.

Tunstall, W. C. B., 'Imperial Defence, 1815–1870', in J. Holland Rose, A. P. Newton, and E. A. Benians (eds.), *The Cambridge History of the British Empire*, ii (Cambridge University Press, 1940).

Vidalenc, Georges, 'Le Rôle joué au point de vue maritime par l'Algérie dans la vie de la France avant et après la conquête', *Académie de marine: Communications et mémoires*, 10 (1931), 275–360.

Wallin, F. W., 'French Naval Conversion and the Second Empire's Intervention in Industry', in F. J. Cox *et al.*, *Studies in Modern European History in Honor of F. C. Palm* (New York, 1956).

Williams, Charles S., and Merli, Frank J., 'The *Normandie* Shows the Way: Report of a Voyage from Cherbourg to Vera Cruz, 4 September 1862', *Mariner's Mirror*, 54 (1968), 153–62.

Willson, F. M. G., 'Ministries and Boards: Some Aspects of Administrative Development since 1832', *Public Administration*, 33 (1955), 43–58.

3. *Theses*

Macmillan, D. F., 'The Development of British Naval Gunnery, 1815–53' (doctoral thesis, London, 1967).

Petty, W. M., 'The Introduction of the Screw-Propeller into the Navy, 1830–60' (M.Phil. thesis, London, 1969).

Pitt, M. R., 'Great Britain and Belligerent Maritime Rights from the Declaration of Paris, 1856, to the Declaration of London, 1909' (doctoral thesis, London, 1964).

Pollard, Sidney, 'The Economic History of British Shipbuilding, 1870–1914' (doctoral thesis, London, 1950).

Ranft, B. M., 'The Naval Defence of British Sea-Borne Trade, 1860–1905' (doctoral thesis, Oxford, 1967).

Ropp, T. K., 'The Development of a Modern Navy: French Naval Policy 1871–1904' (doctoral thesis, Harvard, 1937).

Schurman, D. M., 'Imperial Defence, 1868–1887: A Study in the Decisive Impulses behind the Change from "Colonial" to "Imperial" Defence' (doctoral thesis, Cambridge, 1955).

Swain, J. E., 'The Struggle for the Control of the Mediterranean prior to 1848' (doctoral thesis, Pennsylvania, 1933).

Violette, Aurele J., 'Russian Naval Reform, 1855–70' (doctoral thesis, Ohio State, 1971).

Wallin, F. W., 'The French Navy during the Second Empire: A Study of the Effects of Technological Development on French Governmental Policy' (doctoral thesis, Berkeley, Calif., 1953).

Index